Sounds and their patterns in Indic languages

Volume 1: Sound Patterns

Pramod Pandey

FOUNDATION® BOOKS

Bengaluru • Chennai • Delhi • Hyderabad • Kolkata • Mumbai • Pune • Thiruvananthapuram

FOUNDATION®
BOOKS

Foundation Books is an imprint of Cambridge University Press India Pvt. Ltd.

Cambridge House, 4381/4 Ansari Road, Daryaganj, New Delhi 110 002

www.cambridgeindia.org

First published 2014

Printed in India at Bhavish Graphics, Chennai.

ISBN 978-93-82993-92-6 Paperback

Mātā me Nirmalā Devī pitā devo Maheśwarah
Bāndhawāh Nirmalā bhaktāśca swadeśo bhuwanatrayam

Contents

Acknowledgements

The present work has been completed in three phases. In the first phase it was carried out as a major research project funded by the University Grants Commission, New Delhi for the period 1998–2001. In the next phase, it was taken up for improvement and refinement, with short-term fellowships from the Department of Linguistics, Max-Planck Institute of Evolutionary Anthropology, Leipzig and the Rockefeller Foundation at the Bellagio Research and Seminar Centre, Bellagio in the year 2003. It was then further extended with slow incremental work until September 2009, with financial help from the Capacity Build up funds of Jawaharlal Nehru University, and Sabbatical leave for the year 2009–10. In the course of the twelve years since I embarked on this work, I received help from many institutions and individuals, including the following:

The University Grants Commission vide F-5-215/97 (HRP) dated 8 November 1997.

Department of Linguistics, Max Planck Institute of Evolutionary Anthropology, Leipzig, and its Director, Professor Bernard Comrie, for a two-month visiting fellowship as Guest Scientist, April 15-June 14, 2003.

Rockefeller Foundation for a one month fellowship at the Bellagio Research and Seminar Centre, Bellagio, June 18-July 17, 2003.

I wish to thank the Office of the Registrar General, Map Division, Ministry of Home Affairs, Government of India, for permission to reproduce linguistic maps from the *Language Atlas of India 1991*.

I must also acknowledge with gratitude the inspiration I have derived from the scholars whose work inspired me to take up this study and who may or may not be aware about their contribution here: Ashok Kelkar (my teacher), Bruce Hayes, John McCarthy, and late Nick Clements. I was hoping to show this work in its completed form to Nick, but he left too soon.

Ramakant Agnihotri and Bharati Modi encouraged me at the earliest stage to start working on it. Purushottam G Patel (PG) has been a constant support and source of inspiration.

The following persons helped me with the preparation of the materials at different stages-Shashi Batra, Ajay Sarvaiya, both at the Department of Linguistics, The M. S. University of Baroda, Vadodara, and Tulsi Majhi, at the Centre for Linguistics, Jawaharlal Nehru University. Amrendra Singh and Hemanga Dutta took up chunks of materials for typing with care. M. Mahesh took up the task of organizing the material in the final stages and devoted much of his time to it. Sudhanshu Shekhar generously offered to chip in. I am thankful to them for their sincere help.

My colleagues Anvita Abbi, Vaishna Narang, Ayesha Kidwai, Yankee Modi and Hari Madhab Ray, my students Amrita Basu, Philipzo Mangkang, Lienzang Zeite, T. Meiraba and Wichamdinbo, and my colleagues from the office Surendra Singh Rawat and Naveen S. Gusain and my Project Assistant Yogender Gautam have helped me in one way or another in the completion of this work. I am thankful to them.

My colleagues outside New Delhi have been ready to come forward with materials and clarifications of queries whenever I approached them. I should mention here especially Rajesh Khatiwada (CNRS, Paris 3), Anish Koshy (EFLU, Hyderabad), Shailendra Mohan (Deccan College, Pune), Panchanan Mohanty (University of Hyderabad), K. S. Nagaraja (Deccan College, Pune), Natanasabapathy (Annamali University, Annamalinagar), and S. R. Sharma (Deccan College, Pune).

Since the submission of the manuscript to CUP India for publication, it has received very useful comments and suggestions for improvement. For those that have influenced it and led to significant revisions in it I am grateful to Andrea Calabrese and Caroline Féry as well as the two anonymous referees. I am also grateful to P. M. Kulkarni for having found time to look at the tables and give useful suggestions. I am indebted to Anirban Dey, editor at CUP India, who has gone through the manuscript with a fine-tooth comb and brought it to its final shape.

My family – wife Kiran, son Gaurav, and daughter Aditi – have tolerated with my never-ending extension of deadlines set by them in getting the book out of their way, and have been of great help. Kiran, like an ideal wife, has been with it all these years; Gaurav, like a good son, has kept a safe distance from it; Aditi, like a loving daughter, was available when I needed her – with the final computation of the data, keeping late hours for several months.

My parents always took interest in my pursuits. I dedicate this book to the memory of my late father, Sudhakar Pandey, who introduced me to phonetics and to IPA.

Pramod Pandey

Prefatory

The book originated with an idea in the mid 90's of a general source book on the phonologies of the languages of India, where it is possible to find brief sketches of the languages, with an exhaustive bibliography. This would serve the purpose of a reference guide for researching on Indic languages. The idea gradually proved useful since the time it was conceived with a rise in interest in endangered languages. Besides, the phonological segment had come to attract fresh theoretical interest owing to Optimality Theory. The choice of not only the segmental phonemes but also other units and their distribution at the word phonological level in the present work was certainly influenced by the developments in OT.

A grant from the UGC, New Delhi helped me to prepare a preliminary draft of about half of the present sketches and a general bibliography. The fellowship from Max Planck Institute of Evolutionary Anthropology, Leipzig gave me the facilities to refine the descriptions and to work on them from the point of view of phonological typology. Interest in the typological issues relating to Indic languages can be found in the discussion of all the topics.

A Rockefeller Foundation fellowship at the Bellagio Research and Seminar Centre, Bellagio, Italy (18 June – 16 July 2003) provided a very congenial atmosphere and luxury to think on the contents of the book and to grow ambitious in compiling a more inclusive volume.

The grant of Sabbatical leave by Jawaharlal Nehru University for a year (2009–2010) finally helped me to prepare the volume in its present form.

The descriptions of the Indic languages, on which the sketches in this volume are based, are of varied quality. Most of them are refereed publications. But some, especially theses submitted to universities, are not. We have chosen to take them into account on the grounds that they are from trained linguists. Besides, including them in a general handbook such as this has the advantage of adding to the variety of sound patterns. In most cases, as far as possible, care has been taken to verify the data for their correctness. In those cases where the facts on verification were found to be different from the source, the verified facts are presented.

In a work of this nature, based on publications of varied qualities, errors are expected, in spite of our best efforts. We hope that another edition will have less of them.

16 October 2013

Pramod Pandey

Chapter 1

Introduction to sound patterns in Indic languages

1.0 Introduction

The development of phonological theory in the past 75 years has centred around the question of determining different types of phonological regularities. And many issues concerning phonological regularities have sought to investigate into phonological inventories and patterning of the inventories, whether they relate to the composition of phonological segments in terms of distinctive features (e.g. Jakobson, Fant & Halle 1952, Chomsky & Halle 1968, Clements 1985) or the surface manifestation of segments in terms of permissible or prohibitive constraints (e.g. McCarthy & Prince 1985). The title of the present volume echoes many titles, beginning with Sapir's 1925 paper, "Sound patterns in language".

Interest in phonological inventories within phonological theory has been seen to grow in two directions: one, a hierarchy of phonological units above the segment- the syllable, the foot, the phonological word, the phonological phrase and the intonational phrase- culminating in the theory of Prosodic Phonology (e.g. Selkirk 1980, 1984, Hayes 1989, Nespor & Vogel 2007), and two, fields other than phonological theory, especially, computational linguistics (e.g. Gibbon et al. 1997), linguistic evolution (e.g. De Böer 2001), language geography (e.g. Clements & Rialland 2005) and cognitive science (e.g Jusczyk 1986).

The present book addresses the concern for phonological units in various fields in the form of a reference book based on the existing work on the languages of India using the International Phonetic Alphabet, by being limited to the word (see e.g. Hall & Kleinhenz 1999, Dixon & Aikhenvald 2002), and, for the most part, to published work.

The book is organized into two volumes. Volume II, subtitled *Phonological sketches*, contains word phonological sketches of the Indic languages classified into seven main groups, namely, Austro-Asiatic, Dravidian, Indo-

Aryan, Tibeto-Burman, Tai-Kadai, Andamanese, and Contact Varieties, and an additional eighth group, Historical Varieties. The sketches of the languages include the following topics: consonant and vowel phonemes, phonotactic constraints on consonant and vowel phonemes, consonant and vowel allophones, positional environments of vowel and consonant allophones, canonical syllable structures, constraints on clusters, and tonemes and their allotones. The main citations on which the sketches are based are included in the References section at the end of the volume for convenience of reference within the volume. The references are also present in the general bibliography at the end of the first volume, but they are dispersed there for individual languages and language groups.

Volume I, subtitled *Sound patterns*, contains introductory material on the languages and the generalizations on their word-phonological properties, presented in five chapters. The present chapter is an overall introduction to the volume, setting out its goals and explaining the choice of the contents and methods of analysis and description. Chapter 2 presents the sociolinguistic background of Indic languages and their grouping. Chapter 3 deals with generalizations about the phonemic and allophonic inventories of consonants in terms of the frequency of their occurrence in the languages as well as their distribution in them. Chapter 4 follows the preceding chapter for the pattern of presentation of vowels. Chapter 5 deals with units above the segment, including syllables and lexical tone. Volume I contains an exhaustive bibliography in three parts: a) theoretical references used in the discussions on the general phonetic and phonological properties of the Indic languages in the chapters in Part I, b) studies on all or some of the languages of each of the eight language groups, and c) phonetic and phonological studies on the specific languages.

1.1 Earlier Studies and Sources of SPIL

There have been two major projects of phonological inventories. One, the Stanford Project on Language Universals leading to the database "Stanford Phonology Archive" (SPA) and the publication of Greenberg (ed.), *Universals of Language* (UL) (1978) in four volumes. Two, the 'Phonological Segment Inventory Database" (UPSID), University of California, Los Angeles, leading to the publication of Maddieson (ed.), *Patterns of Sounds* (PS) (1984). Both SPA-UL and UPSID-PS contain phonological data on world languages and are concerned with research on language universals.

SPA-UL presents a set of 13 papers on different aspects of phonological structure that can be grouped into three broad types- i) single features or processes or sets of them, e.g., palatalization, stops, fricatives, etc. ii) successive occurrence of phonological units, e.g. consonant clusters, vowel harmony, tone, and iii) sound-grammar/semantics relationship, e.g. word-demarcation, sound symbolism and intonation. The studies use both synchronic and diachronic dimensions for explanation, and have been a general reference for studies on those topics. UPSID-PS deals only with the inventories of vowel and consonant segment phonemes of languages from a total of eleven language families. The number of languages has grown as the UPSID has been revised, from 317 (on which PS was based) to 451 (Maddieson and Precoda 1989), and further to 566 (Maddieson 2001). Although the main concern in UPSID-PS is phonetic, and it has been found to suffer from some inadequacies, it has come to be used widely for substance-based phonological studies (see e.g. Clements 2005).

The present book has drawn inspiration from both the project-studies, but differs from them in scope. Unlike SPA-UL, but like, UPSID-SP, it limits itself to the synchronic phonological data at the word level. As a consequence, the third area in the SPA-UL is naturally excluded. Even so, it is possible to extract information on phonology-morphology relation, as shown by the discussion in section 5.5. Unlike both the studies, it is limited to the languages of a region, India, and aims at providing a substantial basis for phonological typology of the Indic languages, and for a view of the areal phonology of the region. Only secondarily, it hopes to present data for supplementing inferences on phonological universals.

This book is also clearly different in scope from three other publications in this area. One of them is Kaye (1997), *Phonologies of Africa and Asia*, which contains somewhat detailed accounts of the phonological systems of two continents, with illustrative examples of phonological processes. The present book offers, in comparison, less detailed, skeletal descriptions within a fixed format, and is restricted to India. The other publication is Namkung (1998), *Phonological Inventories of Tibeto-Burman Languages*, which contains the phonemic inventories of one of the largest linguistic families. The present study, restricted to India as a region, casts its net wider for the types of inventories of sound units within the word level. The third publication is Ramaswamy (1999), *Common linguistic features in Indian languages: Phonetics,* which includes vowel and consonant phonemes of 100 Indian languages with introductory chapters on the properties of sound structure of these languages.

1.2 The Phonological Sketches

1.2.1 The phonological sketches and the sources

A total of 148 phonological sketches of Indic languages are presented here. The list of the Indic languages forms a subset of about 200 languages originally drawn at the start of the project entitled, Phonological Database of Indian Languages (PDIL) on the basis of lists from a) Government of India Census records of 1991, b) published literature, and (c) research studies submitted in academic institutions. This number mismatched with anthropological lists, which include a much larger number. Singh and Manoharan (1993), for example, have around 350 languages identified. The discrepancy between linguistic and anthropological enumerations of Indic languages, in all likelihood, is owing to the fact that anthropological lists often include the different names of a language in terms of the communities using them, and do not maintain a strict difference between a sub-variety and the main variety. This is not to say that anthropologists are entirely inconsiderate of linguistic systems; the language-dialect boundary, as is often recognized, is often porous. Multiple sketches of single 'languages' in the present volume have been included almost by way of a vindication of the point, apart from the benefit of having a larger set of inventory systems.

With the exception of about a dozen languages, most Indic languages that have been linguistically investigated are included here. The bibliography, however, is close to being exhaustive for individual publications on the languages.

As the studies, especially published in India, are of uneven quality, an effort has been made to present the sketches in a uniform format, using the International Phonetic Alphabet (IPA), after critically comparing the various descriptions. The correct use of the IPA symbols for the sketches has been considered to be crucially important because of the need to increase consistency and accuracy in the phonological sketches.

The book tries to present an overview of the work carried out on the languages of India. Consequently, the language families cannot in all cases be represented according to their size in terms of the number of languages in them. This is the reason why over one hundred pages are given for a language family like Indo-Aryan, while only five pages are given for Tai-Kadai. The actual number of languages in the Tai-Kadai group is much larger, as can be found in the list in Chapter 2. The languages are classified into the following seven language groups: (i) Austro-Asiatic, (ii) Dravidian, (iii) Indo-Aryan, (iv) Tibeto-Burman, (v) Tai-Kadai, (vi) Andamanese and

(vii) Contact Varieties. The seventh group includes well-recognized contact varieties, such as Naga Pidgin and Bishnupuria, as well as a second language variety such as Hindi English, as an instantiation of Indian English. I have fought hard against the temptation to include some other varieties from the main groups into this group, as a large number of Indic languages have features that owe to language contact, on the grounds that the term would lose its sense as a class of language groups.

In addition to the seven groups, five historical varieties belonging to the language groups (ii) and (iii) have been put together in an independent group of (viii) Historical Varieties. The descriptions of these historical varieties are based on written records and extensive documentation. These could not be mixed with reconstructions proposed for other language groups, such as Munda (1970) and Bhattacharya (1975) for Comparative Munda, Sun (1993) for Comparative Tani, and Matisoff (2003) for Comparative Tibeto-Burman.

1.2.2 Selection of language varieties and phonetic details

I faced occasional difficulties in selecting the languages. One common difficulty had to do with similarities of the phonological systems amongst neighboring languages, as, for example, some of the Himalayan languages described in Sharma (1989), and Rajasthani varieties of Bagri, Mewati and Shekhawati described by Gusain (2000, 2003a, 2003b, respectively). The Himalayan and the Rajasthani varieties are so similar to one another in structure within their subgroups that we had to decide to keep one and leave out the others. Quite obviously, the book would have been larger had we included them.

Another difficulty we faced in selecting the languages was of the opposite sort from the one described just above. Some of the varieties are conventionally treated as dialects, but are so different from the major language that they have had to be counted as independent systems; for example, Bhojpuri and Magahi, which are treated here as sister languages of Hindi, rather than its dialects. The latter have also been so treated in important publications, e.g. Cardona and Jain (2001).

We faced a third type of situation where a controversy exists with regard to a language belonging to more than one linguistic group, for example, Gadaba, as described in Bhattacharya (1957), Bhaskararao (1980), and Gaud (1980). The descriptions in the former two are presented here as belonging to the Dravidian group, while in the last as belonging to the Austro-Asiatic group.

The presentation of the sketches has as far as possible been based on the most reliable description. Wherever more than one study has been found to be necessary for reference, more often than not, the decision to include them has had to do with supplementing facts. Controversial issues have been avoided, by being noted in footnotes.

The sketches often differ in details of phonetic symbols from the original source. This is found mainly when the phonetic description of a sound in the source description warrants an IPA symbol that is different from the symbol used in it. Sometimes, the segments in the source description were so marked that they had to be checked for authenticity, with either the author or a speaker of the language variety described or both. In a few cases, neither the symbol nor the phonetic description was found to be correct. In such cases, both the symbol and the phonetic description had to be altered from the source description. The divergences from the sources are so many, especially on account of the pervasive use of non-IPA symbols that we decided not to mention them in the sketches. It is expected that readers will verify the facts for themselves. However, it is pertinent to mention that the differences between the inventories in the present sketches from the corresponding inventories in the source descriptions can be classified as involving three types of changes for segmental sounds, namely, the symbols, the Manner label, and the Place label. These are illustrated below.

a. An example of the use of a different symbol from the source is in the sketch of Darma. Krishan (2001) uses /c/ for a 'voiceless palatal affricate', replaced here by /ʧ/. Other IPA symbols that replace commonly used symbols in the source descriptions are, for example, /j/ for 'y', /ŋ/ for 'ng' or N, /pʰ bʱ/ for aspirated stops ph bh, etc.

b. An example of a different manner and place of articulation label from the source is in the sketch of Tarao (Singh 2002), where there both plosives and affricates are described in the palatal place. On checking with the author and a speaker it has been found that there are no palatal plosives in the language; instead there are alveolar and palatal affricates. The inventory here has thus been modified accordingly.

For the prosodic phenomenon of lexical tone, found in about 35 languages in all, we have followed the Autosegmental-Metrical mode (Goldsmith 1989), used in prosodic models (e.g. Ladd 2008[1996]) and popularized by ToBI (Beckman et al.), for its convenient use for both register and contour tones in terms of H, L, and M for register tones and their combinations, e.g. LH for Rising tone. These labels are at considerable variance with the labels used in the source descriptions; care has been taken to translate the labels faithfully into the A-M terminology.

1.2.3 Analytical issues

There sometimes arose the need for a reanalysis of the data as described in the source descriptions. For example, Ramaswamy's (1982) description of Brokskat presents half-long vowels as allophones of short vowels word-finally. However, since long vowels never occur word-finally in the language, length is assumed to be neutralized word-finally. Half-long vowels, thus, cannot be considered as allophones of short vowels exclusively.

Some other topics related to the analysis of the data had to be critically considered for the sketches. These are discussed below.

a. Diphthongs versus a sequence of two vowels. Maddieson (1980) discusses the difficulty in distinguishing the two. We have tried to find evidence in analyzing vowel sequences as sequences or as diphthongs. These are briefly discussed below.

   Another sort of evidence comes from hiatus- induced processes, as for example, found in Garo. Garo permits vowel sequences lexically but prohibits them on the surface, where they have a glottal stop inserted between them, e.g. [mai] < /mai/ 'what?, but [pi?a] < /pia/ 'break'. In the former word, the vowels are a diphthong, but in the latter, a sequence. Languages differ with regard to whether they permit vowel sequences (see for example, Casali 1996 and Calabrese 2005 for detailed discussions). The difficulty in distinguishing diphthongs and vowel sequences in languages is mainly found in those cases in which hiatus or a vowel sequence is permitted. In languages in which vowel sequences are not permitted at all, it is easy to identify all sequences of vowels as diphthongs. In languages in which vowel sequences are not permitted within morphemes, but permitted across morphemes, all morpheme-internal sequences must be treated as diphthongs. Across morphemes, the constraint requiring hiatus may be resolved by various processes like V-Deletion, C-Insertion, Fusion, and Desyllabification (leading to Diphthongization). The identification of these processes is analytically useful in distinguishing between vowels and diphthongs, as in the case of Garo. It is for this reason that details about vowel sequences in the languages have been noted in the sketches.

   The other sort of evidence comes from the prosodic phenomena of stress and tone. Let us consider stress first. Koren, a T-B language of the Kuki-Chin subgroup, has word-final stress, as described in this book, and shown below.

(1/1) i.	[mei ˈwa:n]	'ashes'	[tʰiŋ ˈlɘi]	'dirty'
	[tʰiŋ ˈkor]	'bark (of a tree)'	[ɘreŋ ˈkʰuo]	'all'
	[arˈ mul]	'feather'	[ɘˈ ci:]	'fear'
	[ɘˈ kel]	'dig $_{\text{(Verb)}}$'	[ɘˈ cei]	'dig $_{\text{(Verb)}}$'
ii.	[ɘri ˈek]	'fat, grease'	[tʰasi ˈet]	'dull'

It is found that in the case of a diphthong versus vowel sequence situation, the stress sometimes falls on the final syllable including both the vowel positions, as in (1/1i), and sometimes on the second vowel. We conclude that in the former case, the vowels are diphthongs, and in the latter case, the vowels are sequences. Considering the significance of word-stress in the phonological analysis of languages, exemplified in the case of segmental analysis of diphthongs versus vowel sequences, the absence of details about word-stress in the sketches is a serious gap.

To turn to tone, in a language with every vowel being a tone bearing unit, the diphthongs in them have a single tone, while a sequence of two vowels has two tones. The distinction is attested in Bodo.

In a tonal language with the tone bearing unit being a lexical morpheme, we have found two clear cues for analysis. One is morphological: in some of the languages, especially the Kuki- Chin languages, morphemes are monosyllabic. With the tone falling on every lexical morpheme, if there is a sequence of vowels, then the two vowels have tone on them. This situation is not distinguishable from that for Bodo. If, however, only the lexical morpheme has tone, then on the surface it is not possible to distinguish a diphthong from a vowel sequence. However, the phonetic realizations of the tones may be different. Zo, as noted in its description here, has been found to distinguish vowel sequences from diphthongs in that way: in the case of a diphthong, the tone ends with the second vowel position, but in the case of a sequence of two vowels, the tone ends on the first vowel position.

b. Consonant clusters versus single consonant phonemes. The issue is relevant in the following cases:

C+ h sequences and aspirated consonants. The criteria used in most cases here is that of a syllable division between or before them. For instance, in Magar, Subba (1972) uses the criterion for the examples as shown below:

(1/2) a.	[ɟu-mʱa]	'fly $_{\text{(Verb)}}$'	[ka-lʱa]	'climbed'
b.	[dul-ɦa]	'bridegroom'	[laŋ-ɦa]	'village'

Note that there is a related issue of a distinction between a consonant sequence and a consonant cluster, which some linguists maintain, while others don't. The Edinburgh school of phonetics, led by David Abercrombie (e.g. 1967), maintain the distinction, with followings, for example, Reddy and Reddy (1986). We have not adhered to this distinction and have treated sequences of consonants as clusters.

c. Minimal Pairs. The notion of contrast is of critical significance in phonological analysis, especially employed in minimal pairs to establish two phonetically similar sounds as phonemes. It has also been found to play a significant role in phonological theory. In the theory of Lexical Phonology (Kiparsky 1982, Mohanan 1986), rule applications are distinguished to be lexical or postlexical on the basis of whether they involve contrastive features: rules involving non-contrastive features must apply in the postlexical module. Underspecification theory is divided into Radical Underspecification (Archangeli 1988) and Contrastive Underspecification (e.g. Clements 1988, Steriade 1995) on the grounds mainly of priority given to maximal economy or lexical contrast.

Many languages are found to have surface sounds that are treated non-identically with other surface sounds, but there are no minimal pairs in the language to establish them as phonemes. There are stray cases noted in languages that can be attributed to borrowings on account of language contact, as, for example, voiced aspirated plosives and nasal vowels in the Himalayan languages of the T-B group or the A-A languages, which are in contact with Indo-Aryan languages. Minimal pairs are difficult to find for these sounds in the languages. For many of the languages with lexicons of limited sizes, non-varying surface segments occur in the native vocabulary that cannot be found to occur in minimal pairs. Examples of such languages are found in the A-N group, e.g. G-Andamanese, Jarawa and Onge, and in the A-A group, e.g. Juang. Thus, Kumar (2010) chooses to establish phonemes in Jarawa without any minimal pairs, by taking into account only their distributional regularities, as for the bilabial voiceless and voiced plosives [p], [b] and the voiceless fricative [ɸ]:

(1/3) *Cons*	*Initially*		*Finally*
p	paʈʰo	'arrow'	a:p 'jac
ɸ			aɸle 'bind$_{[v]}$'
b	boĩya	'small'	le:b 'road/path'

In situations of free variation, Kumar uses statistical criteria. For some of the forms with a predominant [b] in the initial position, it freely varies with [p] in about 10% of the words. The underlying phoneme for those lexical items is assumed to be /b/. Languages like Jarawa, Onge and Juang, in which phonemes have to be established without any explicit use of minimal pairs, present an interesting case with regard to the cognitive significance of the notion of 'contrast', and require an investigation of the notion.

1.2.4 Theoretical and descriptive issues

The presentation of the sketches is guided by the theoretical and descriptive assumptions discussed below.

a. I adopt here the classical categorical and modular view of the representation of sounds and their patterning, with the notion of contrast at its basis (see, e.g. Avery, Dresher & Rice 2008 and Clements 2009 for recent discussions on the central role of contrast in phonological theory), and at least two levels of representation in the grammar: the phonemic level and the allophonic level. The phonemic level is categorical and the allophonic level includes gradient representation.

   This does not in any way deny the significance of the probabilistic continuous view of the representation of sounds underlying the work in current approaches to phonology and phonetics, such as the exemplar theory propounded in Pierrehumbert et al. (2000) and Pierrehumbert (2001, 2002). Our view is only a level more abstract than the latter, and thus more schematic. It is however expected to provide data for questions that pertain to the more abstract level, with which linguistic descriptions have dealt for a long time for lack of instrumental and technological support.

b. The phonological descriptors for the sketches and the generalizations based on them are presented below.

(1/4) Domain: Word

Levels: Phonological and phonetic
Sound units:

Segmental:	Phonemes: Vowels, Consonants Allophones: Vowels, Consonants
Supra-segmental:	Syllables: Onset, Nucleus, Coda; canonical syllable structures.

Stress Feet
Phonological Word

PROCESSES:
Allophonic processes: modification types (aspiration, glottalization, etc.)
Stress Placement
Tones

PHONOTACTICS:
Occurrence of sound units within larger descriptors
Co-occurrence restrictions: Consonant Clusters, Geminate Consonants
Vowel Sequences

The phonological word has occupied considerable interest since the beginning of phonology, so much so that it is customary to divide phonological discussions into the phonology of the word-level and the phonology of the level above the word. However, like many of our assumptions regarding our knowledge of sounds being examined and revised, our assumptions about the word, too, are in the need of close inquiry. The data from the Indic languages, too, suggest the need to turn serious attention to the possible typology of word types: those, for example, requiring minimal prosodic weight, such as Malayalam, or requiring a distinction between the Root and the Word, such as Galo-Lare and Zo, etc.

In the presentation of the word phonologies of the Indic languages here, there is focus on phonotactic restrictions on the following: singleton consonants and vowels in the beginning, middle and end of words, consonant clusters, geminate consonants and vowel sequences, and restrictions on the occurrence of consonant clusters. The data on these aspects of phonotactic restrictions are expected to provide relevant answers to questions of markedness, of positions of phonological contrasts[1], positions favouring strengthening and lenition processes, and phonological universals on output forms.

Allophonic data on consonants and vowels have been presented keeping in view their relevance to two areas: one, input-output relationship, which is of current interest in OT, especially from the point of view of factorial typology (see e.g. Kager 1999), and two, phonological evolution. In spite of being aware about the relevance

[1] Parker (2001), for instance, points out a special case of the South American language Chamicuro, in which maximal contrasts are available in the coda position, instead of the onset position, as is usually the case.

of allophonic alternation in several other areas, I have chosen to be conservative in including them. The lists of allophones in the sketches have only novel allophones in the languages, assuming the presence of 'basic' or 'elsewhere' allophones. Two related topics in consonantal and vocalic allophones have been excluded for the reason that they are predictable. These are contextual nasalization of vowels and the assimilation of an alveolar or dental nasal consonant to a following stop, giving rise to homorganic nasals and stop clusters. Only those cases of nasalization and nasal assimilation have been included that are marked. In the case of nasalization, such an instance is found in Mundari (A-A), where nasalization spreads bi-directionally in relation to a retroflex nasal consonant, but unidirectionally in relation to other nasal consonants. In the case of nasal assimilation, such an instance has been noted for a nasal consonant other than alveolar or dental assimilating to a following stop or vowel, as in the case of Apatani (T-B) and Bhumij (A-A), in which a velar consonant assimilates to a labial and a palatal stop or high front vowel respectively and surfaces as a labial and a palatal nasal.

In the areas above the segment, three topics are selected, namely, canonical syllable structure, consonant clusters and tones. Generalizations regarding these are discussed in Chapter 5. There is also a section on phonological cues for grammatical structure towards the end of the chapter. A serious lacuna in the sketches is the absence of details on word-stress, for the obvious reason that most phonological descriptions of Indic languages do not include information on the phenomenon.[2] Exclusion of details of word stress has in the case of tonal languages adverse effects on the descriptions of tones as well, especially concerning the relation between stress and tone (see Schiering & van der Hulst 2009:69).

c. Finally, some details regarding the charts and tables used in the book. Based on the phonological sketches, tables for various aspects of the word phonology of the languages have been prepared. They pertain in the main to Chapters 3–5. Most of them have been included within the chapters, while a few of them, because of their referential utility and size, have been put at the end of the chapters. These include the lists of the consonant and vowel phonemes (along with the languages in which they occur and their language groups), the lists of consonant and vowel allophones (along with the languages in which they occur, the modification types characterizing them and the language groups), and

[2] It is interesting to note that, with the exception of Shina, almost all the Indic languages have predictable stress.

the patterns of vowel and consonant phonemes. The smaller tables, which are included within the chapters, are in fact based on the larger end-of-chapter tables. These are used to draw generalizations about the sounds and the relations amongst them in general as well as in relation to typological issues. For example, *Table 3.12* is about the Manners of Articulation that have voiceless consonants, and *Table 4.5* is about the distribution of vowel patterns in the Indic languages. Such tables are selected for discussion in the chapters on specific issues, which are by no means exhaustive. They have been especially limited, as the tables at chapter ends can be used for getting answers to other questions. Thus they can be expected to yield data from Indic languages for questions regarding implicational generalizations between segments, which characterize the work on universals in the tradition of Greenberg (1966), and fruitfully carried forward in Maddieson (1980) (for instance, the relation between the frequency of selected segments and the inventory size (p. 11)). The present study has been aimed at contributing to that tradition.

1.3 Language Groups

The languages being described here are listed below according to the language groups to which they belong. There are in all seven groups of these languages.

AUSTRO-ASIATIC

Bhumij, Bonda, Didayi, Gadaba, Gorum, Ho, Juang, Kharia, Khasi, Kisan, Korku, Mundari, Nancowry, Nicobarese-Car, Santali. (15)

DRAVIDIAN

Ave, Badaga, Gadaba-K, Gondi, Gondi-A, Irula, Kadar, Kannada, Kattunaicka, Kodagu, Kolami, Konda, Koraga, Kota, Koya, Kui, Kurux, Kuvi, Malayalam, Malto, Manda, Naiki, Ollari, Pengo, Tamil, Telugu, Toda, Tulu, Yerava. (29)

INDO-ARYAN

Assamese, Bagri (Rajasthani), Bengali, Bhili, Bhojpuri, Brokskat, Chakma, Dogri, Garhwali, Gojri, Gujarati, Haryanvi, Hindi, Jaunsari, Kacchi, Kashmiri, Konkani, Lahndi, Lamani, Magahi, Mahl, Maithili, Mandeali, Marathi, Nepali, Oriya, Punjabi, Rathvi, Shina, Sindhi, Urdu, Urdu-Dakhini-Hyderabadi. (32)

TIBETO-BURMAN

Adi, Angami, Ao-Naga, Apatani, Balti, Bantawa, Bodo, Byangsi, Chaudangsi, Chokri, Darma, Dimasa, Gallong, Galo, Galo-Lare, Garo, Hmar, Kabui, Kangri, Karbi, Kheza, Kinnauri, Kirnati-Koints, Kokborok, Koren, Lepcha, Ladakhi, Liangmei, Limbu, Lotha, Manchad, Mizo, Mao-Naga, Maring, Meitei, Mishmi, Monpa, Padaam, Paite, Phom, Purki, Raji, RangPo, Rawang, Sema-Naga, Spiti, Stod, Tamang, Tangsa, Tarao, Thaadou, Tibetan-Standard, Wancho, Zo. (55)

TAI-KADAI

Khampti, Turung (02)

ANDAMAN-NICOBAR

Great Andamanese, Jarawa, Onge (03)

CONTACT VARIETIES

Bishnupuria, Diu-Indo-Portugese, Halbi, Nagamese, Vagri Boli, Urdu-D-T, Indian English-Hindi (07)

HISTORICAL VARIETIES

Old Tamil, Old Telugu, Pali, Prakrit, Sanskrit-Classical (05)

The grounds on which the groups have been formed are discussed in Chapter 2 in the second volume of the book.

Chapter 2

Indic Languages and Language Groups

2.0 Introduction

This chapter deals with the details about the languages included in the present study. Section 2.1 brings up for a brief discussion the complex linguistic situation in India. Section 2.2 presents a straight list of the languages in an alphabetical order against the language groups to which they belong. Section 2.3 presents a rearranged list according to the internal relationship amongst the languages within the family to which they belong. We have followed Lewis (2009) for the most part in grouping the languages, avoiding a discussion of a large body of literature on classification, some of it controversial.

2.1 The linguistic situation in India

The languages described here are categorized as being of two general types in the political frame of reference in the Union Republic of India as of today, namely, SCHEDULED and NON-SCHEDULED languages. Scheduled languages are those languages that have official status in the country. The two most prominent Scheduled languages are the official languages of the Union. These are Hindi, recognized by the Constitution of India as the First Official Language, and English, recognized as the Second Official Language.

The other Scheduled languages which are the official languages of the States are the following: Assamese (Assam), Bengali (West Bengal, Tripura), Gujarati (Gujarat, Union territory of Dadra and Nagar Haveli, and Union territories of Daman and Diu), Hindi (Arunachal Pradesh, Bihar, Chattisgarh, Haryana, Madhya Pradesh, Rajasthan, Uttar Pradesh, and the Union Territories of Delhi, Andaman and Nicobar islands, Lakshadweep, Daman and Diu), Kannada (Karnataka), Khasi (Meghalaya), Konkani (Goa),

Malayalam (Kerala), Manipuri or Meitei (Manipur), Marathi (Maharashtra, Union territory of Dadra and Nagar Haveli, and Union territories of Daman and Diu), Mizo (Mizoram), Nepali (Sikkim), Oriya (Orissa), Punjabi (Punjab), Tamil (Tamil Nadu), Telugu (Andhra Pradesh), Urdu (Jammu and Kashmir, Bihar, and Uttar Pradesh). The last of these, Urdu, is the main official language of the Jammu and Kashmir State and the second official language of the other States.

Apart from these, there are other languages which are recognized as Scheduled languages by the Union, usually spoken by communities centred within a State. These include Bodo (Assam), Garo (Meghalaya), Kokborok or Tripuri (Tripura), Maithili (Bihar), and Santali (West Bengal). Only one of the Scheduled languages, Sindhi, has its speakers widely distributed in India, on account of the resettlement of the Hindu speakers post-Independence in 1947. One of the States, Nagaland, has English as its official State language.

Four languages are recognized as Classical languages, namely, Sanskrit, Old Tamil, Old Telugu and Old Kannada. Sanskrit has received official patronage for a very long time, and is used both as a subject of study as well as the medium of instruction in a large number of schools, colleges, and universities all over India.

All the other languages in the present book apart from the 24 languages mentioned above and the historical varieties are known as Non-Scheduled languages. The Constitution of India recognizes the use of the mother-tongue as a medium of instruction as a fundamental right. Many of the Non-Scheduled languages are being used as mediums of instruction at the primary level. As awareness about the mother tongue as a medium of instruction grows, and some of the languages are used as mediums of instruction, it is expected that they will have a better chance of survival than those which are not.

Apart from the variety of languages, there are also a variety of scripts in India. These are mainly of three types. The commonest is the alpha-syllabic or 'abugida' script (Daniels & Bright 1996) used for Sanskrit and other scheduled languages, with different names and symbols, but all derived from a common source, namely Brahmi (Patel et al. 2006). The Roman script is used for English and some of the non-scheduled languages such as Mizo. Some of the non-scheduled languages have adopted modified scripts, such as Ol-Chiki, an alphabetic script for Santali. [1]

[1] One of the goals of the present volume is to put together the sounds of the Indic languages for language technology solutions to problems such as the development of common scripts or better scripts.

2.1.1 Multilingualism in India or Indian multilingualism

The issues of the structure and use of language in India cannot be addressed without a close consideration of the multilingual character of its linguistic situation. Indic languages more often than not function in multilingual/ multidialectal settings. The situation often leads to problems of identification, especially in relation to their association with communities, and the prevalent use of multiple names for the languages and the communities (see e.g. Singh & Manoharan 1993, Lewis 2009). It is interesting to note that the 2001Census of India gives a total of 6661 names returned as 'mother tongue'. Of these, 3592 names were rationalized by the 2001 Census against the background information sought in its questionnaire. However, only 1635 names from the rationalized names could be recognized for classification, leaving out 1957 names still waiting to be classified. This gives a complex and rich picture of the linguistic universe for the speech communities of India, which must be looked into closely in relation to questions of literacy, language technology, language endangerment and preservation, and language development. On the basis of earlier work, especially Pattanayak (e.g. 1981, 1986, 2001), Khubchandani (1997), Breton (1997), Annamalai (2008), and NCERT (2006)[2], I try to present below some of the traits of Indian multilingualism, which together or in combination are assumed to characterize it.

a. Communicative fluidity.

   Multilingualism in India is not fixed, but fluid. Fluidity in Indian multilingualism is reflected in two ways. One – there is transparency and lack of fixed boundaries (Khubchandani 1977). Two – supported by considerable cultural commonness and added socio-political and economic changes, migration across regions and states occurs with unceasing continuity. This has led to the adoption of dominant languages of the region for necessary functionalities such as social interaction or education of the young generation. Languages that did not claim attention a decade ago, may begin to do so now[3].

b. Convergence.

   As a result of a prolonged contact amongst neighbouring languages, there is considerable convergence across them irrespective of their

[2] The report of the NCERT National Focus Group on the Teaching of Indian Languages, chaired by Ramakant Agnihotri.

[3] Ajit Mohanty (p.c.) informs that while he worked on the Bodo language about a decade ago, which is now recognized as a scheduled language of the country, speakers of Kui in Orissa did not raise issues about their language. They now assert for its use as a medium of instruction in school.

family allegiance, as can be found in the regions of thickly diverse groups as in southern Orissa. Learning languages is considerably facilitated by the features of convergence. Sridhar (2008) presents an insightful account of the tendency in Indic languages to absorb external influences without losing their essential character. Many other studies including Masica (1976), Sridhar (1981), Krishnamurti (1986), Ohala (1991), Annamalai (2004) and Subbarao (2008), among others, present syntactic, morphological, phonological and discourse features that are found across the Indian languages, supporting a strong case for ´India as a linguistic area´ as proposed by Emeneau (1956), a term that has gained popularity in relation to the Indian linguistic situation. On account of convergence, the speaker of one language, say, of a minority community in the midst of a majority community, is able to communicate in another language with minimal competence. This has to do both with linguistic as well as pragmatic convergence. The basic communicative contexts and styles are more often than not shared, and the effort of using another language is minimized. The forces of convergence have, not surprisingly, applied to Indian English as well. In spite of regional variation, there is a common core of grammatical and discourse structure found across the country and the South Asian region (see e.g. Mesthrie and Bhatt 2009).

c. Functional openness.

Use of language in India does not make an issue of a language being chosen for use in favour of another, because a language is seen as a vehicle of individual and collective functions. The language you speak at home is your inalienable right, as is the language you use in religion. There is a choice of language for education and of the print and audio-visual media. There is more than one official language anywhere. The language of social interaction is not less free than the language of the cinema. English in India is a language that can be found for almost any of the functions, except of religious rituals, where it is limited to Christianity. Pattanayak´s (2001) declaration is representative of a large number of Indians.

d. Constitutional and legal support.

Multilingualism in India is not only a collective reality; it is fully protected by law. As Annamalai (2008:233) points out, "Indian courts have deliberated and decided on ensuring that there is no discrimination in the equal treatment given to speakers of different languages and that there is no denial of opportunities to anyone because of the language they speak....This gives legal protection to distributed functions of languages and survival of multilingualism." Various bodies of educational and human rights commissions have been engaged in the recent past to further strengthen the multilingual rights of individuals and communities where political support for them has been hard to come by.

e. Language shift.

Another characteristic feature of Indian multilingualism is the phenomenon of language shift. As Breton (1997: 19) observes,

> In many places the language unit and ethnic group may not appear identical. This can be explained by the process of *language shift* which takes into account the process of acculturation-deculturation, wherein populations shift from one language to another, from one generation to the next, through various degrees of bilingualism. As a direct consequence, this sociocultural process simultaneously leads to a closely related sociogeographical process of the *spread of language* through new communities and in wider areas.

f. Non-dualistic attitude.

A less obvious feature that marks the South Asian attitude to reasoning in general and is manifested in language use is the non-dichotomous or non-dualistic attitude towards languages, diffusing the possibilities of language conflict. Most language movements in India are motivated by the need to assert the need *for* the use of specific languages rather than *against* the use of other languages. That is how new languages have kept being added to the list of scheduled languages recognized by the Constitution, such as Bodo, Dogri, Konkani, among others. Situations of conflict are in most cases motivated by electoral politics (see also King 2008), and are short-lived, or seen as tendentious and not of serious consequence. To quote King (1986: 141):

> The unique genius of south Asia, probably its greatest legacy from Vedic values, is the ability to absorb conflicting ideas and create harmony out of opposing views...These countries live every day with a degree of diversity unknown in the countries of the west. Language conflicts go against the grain of this tradition of tolerance.

2.2 Language groups

The language groups to which the languages being described here are assumed to belong are given below along with the languages.

Language Groups	Languages	No. of languages
Austro-Asiatic	Bhumij, Bonda, Didayi, Gadaba, Gorum, Ho, Juang, Kharia, Khasi, Kisan, Korku, Mundari, Nancowry, Nicobarese-Car, Santali.	15
Dravidian	Ave, Badaga, Gadaba-K, Gondi, Gondi-A, Irula, Kadar, Kannada, Kattunaicka, Kodagu, Kolami, Konda, Koraga, Kota, Koya, Kui, Kurux, Kuvi, Malayalam, Malto, Manda, Naiki, Ollari, Pengo, Tamil, Telugu, Toda, Tulu, Yerava.	29
Indo-Aryan	Assamese, Bagri (Rajasthani), Bengali, Bhili, Bhojpuri, Brokskat, Chakma, Dogri, Garhwali, Gojri, Gujarati, Haryanvi, Hindi, Jaunsari, Kacchi, Kashmiri, Konkani, Lahndi, Lamani, Magahi, Mahl, Maithili, Mandeali, Marathi, Nepali, Oriya, Punjabi, Rathvi, Shina, Sindhi, Urdu, Urdu-Dakhini-Hyderabadi.	32
Tibeto-Burman	Adi, Angami, Ao-Naga, Apatani, Balti, Bantawa, Bodo, Byangsi, Chaudangsi, Chokri, Darma, Dimasa, Gallong, Galo, Galo-Lare, Garo, Hmar, Kabui, Kangri, Karbi, Kheza, Kinnauri, Kirnati-Koints, Kokborok, Koren, Lepcha, Ladakhi, Liangmei, Limbu, Lotha, Manchad, Mizo, Mao-Naga, Maring, Meitei, Mishmi, Monpa, Padaam, Paite, Phom, Purki, Raji, RangPo, Rawang, Sema-Naga, Spiti, Stod, Tamang, Tangsa, Tarao, Thaadou, Tibetan-Standard, Wancho, Zo.	55

TAI-KADAI	Khampti, Turung	02
ANDAMAN-NICOBAR	Great Andamanese, Jarawa, Onge	03
CONTACT VARIETIES	Bishnupuria, Diu-Indo-Portugese, Halbi, Nagamese, Vagri Boli, Urdu-D-T, Indian English- Hindi	07
HISTORICAL VARIETIES	Old Tamil, Old Telugu, Pali, Prakrit, Sanskrit- Classical	05

Total Number of Indic languages in SPIL: 148

The languages listed above are given below along with their internal relations with other languages. Although there exists considerable literature on the classification of these languages (for example, see some of the references in Schiering and van der Hulst 2009), I have resorted to a simple decision of going as far as possible with the grouping in Ethnologue (Lewis 2009). I have of course checked the groupings with other generally accepted groupings, such as in Krishnamurti (2003) for Dravidian and Cardona and Jain (2003) for Indo-Aryan. Where a language variety is not included in the Ethnologue, and there is nothing controversial about it, I have grouped it on my own; such language varieties are, in the main, in the groups of Contact Varieties and Historical Varieties. The names of languages described in the sketches are in capital letters.

AUSTRO-ASIATIC

MON-KHMER (Malaysia, Combodia, Myanmar, Thailand)

NICOBAR

Car (1)

NICOBARESE-CAR [caq]

Chowra-Teressa

Chaura [crv]

Teressa [tef]

Great Nicobar

Nicobarese, Southern [nik]

Nancowry

NANCOWRY, Nicobarese, Central [ncb]

Shom Peng

Shom Peng [sii]

NORTHERN MON-KHMER

Khasian

KHASI [kha]

Lyngngam [lyg]

Pnar [pbv]

War [aml]

Khmuic (China, Lao, Thailand, Vietnam)

MUNDA

North Munda

Kherwari

Agariya [agi]

Bijori [bix]

Koraku [ksz]

KISAN[4]

Mundari

MUNDARI [unr]

HO [hoc]

BHUMIJ [muw]

SANTALI [sat]

Korku

KORKU [kfq]

South Munda

Kharia-Juang

JUANG [jun]

KHARIA [khr]

[4] There is no definite information about the classification of Kisan, as belonging to either the A-A or the Dravidian group. It is being classified here as belonging to the A-A group on the basis of its closeness to Korku and some other Munda languages.

Koraput Munda

Gutob-Remo-Gta'

GADABA-GUTOB [gau]

REMO/ BONDA [bfw]

DIDAYI/ GTA? [gaq]

Sora-Juray-Gorum

Sora [srb]

Juray [juy]

GORUM [pcj]

DRAVIDIAN

CENTRAL

Kolami-Naiki

KOLAMI, Northwestern [kfb]

NAIKI/ Kolami, Southeastern [nit]

Parji-Gadaba

Gadaba, Mudhili [gau]

GADABA, Pottangi Ollar [gdb]

GADABA, Konekor [not available]

Duruwa [pci]

NORTHERN

Brahui [brh] (Pakistan)

Kumarbhag Paharia [kmj]

MALTO [mjt]

KURUX [kru]

Kurux, Nepali [kxl] (Nepal)

Sauria Paharia [mjt]

SOUTH-CENTRAL

Gondi-Kui

Gondi

- Maria, Dandami [daq]
- Muria, Eastern [emu]
- Muria, Far Western [fmu]
- ABUJHMARIA Gondi, Southern [ggo]
- GONDI, Northern [gno]
- Khirwar [kwx]
- Maria [mrr]
- Muria, Western [mut]
- Nagarchal [nbg]
- Pardhan [pch]

Konda-Kui

- AVE [not available]
- KONDA [kfc]
- KOYA [kff]

Manda-Kui

- MANDA [mha]

Kui-Kuvi

- KUI [kvd]
- KUVI [kxv]

Manda-Pengo

- PENGO [peg]

Telugu

- Chenchu [cde]
- Manna-Dora [mju]
- Savara [svr]
- TELUGU [tel]
- Waddar [wbq]

SOUTHERN

- Tamil-Kannada
  - Kannada
    - BADAGA [bfq]
    - Holiya [hoy]
    - KANNADA [kan]
    - Urali [url]
  - Tamil-Kodagu
    - KODAGU [kfa]
  - Tamil-Malayalam
    - TAMIL [tam]
      - KATTUNAICKA [not available]
    - IRULA [iru]
    - MALAYALAM [mal]
      - KADAR [key]
      - YERAVA [yea]
  - Toda-Kota
    - TODA [tcx]
    - KOTA [kfe]
  - Tulu
    - Bellari [brw]
    - Kudiya [kfg]
  - Koraga
  - KORAGA, Korra [kfd]
    - Koraga, Mudu [vmd]
    - TULU [tcy]

UNCLASSIFIED

- Ullatan [ull]

Unclassified

Allar [all]

Bazigar [bfr]

Bharia [bha]

Kamar [keq]

Kanikkaran [kev]

Kurichiya [kfh]

Malankuravan [mjo]

Vishavan [vis]

INDO-ARYAN

CENTRAL ZONE

Bhili

BHILI [bhb]

Dom [dgo]

DOGRI [gju]

GOJRI [dgo]

GUJARATI [guj]

RATHVI [rtw]

HINDI [hin]

Khandesi [khn]

LAMANI [lmn]

PUNJABI [pan]

Powari [pwr]

HARYANVI [bgc]

Rajasthani [raj]

BAGRI [bgq]

Romani [not available]

URDU [urd]

East Central zone

Awadhi [awa]

Bagheli [bfy]

Dhanwar [dha]

Hindustani, Fijian [hif] (Fiji)

Chhattisgarhi [hne]

Eastern zone

ASSAMESE [asm]

BENGALI [ben]

CHAKMA [ccp]

BHOJPURI [bho]

MAGAHI [mag]

MAITHILI [mai]

ORIYA [ori]

Pahari

GARHWALI [gbm]

JAUNSARI [jns]

MANDEALI [mjl]

NEPALI [nep]

(Varieties in Nepal)

(Varieties in Bangladesh)

Northwestern zone

Dardic

BROKSKAT [bkk]

KASHMIRI [kas]

SHINA [plk]

LAHNDA [lah]

SINDHI [snd]

KACCHI [kfr]

Nuristani

Ashkun [ask]

(Varieties in Pakistan)

(Varieties in Afganistan)

Sinhalese-Maldivian

Maldivian [div]

MAHL [div][5]

Sinhala [sin] (Sri Lanka)

Veddah [ved] (Sri Lanka)

SOUTHERN ZONE

BHILI [bhb]

KONKANI [knn]

MARATHI [mar]

URDU-DAKHINI (HYDERABAD)

Usui [usi] (Bangladesh)

TIBETO-BURMAN

Himalayish

Mahakiranti

Chepang-Kham-Magar-Sunwari (mainly in Nepal)

Chepang [cdm]

Kham [kif]

MAGAR [mgp]

RAJI [rji]

Sunwari [sun]

Kiranti (mainly in Nepal)

[5] The Ethnologue entry for Maldivian includes Mahl as one of its dialects.

Eastern

BANTAWA [bap]

KIRANTI-KOINTS (Nepal, also India)

LIMBU [lif]

Western

Newari

Tibeto-Kanauri

LEPCHA [lep]

Tibetic

Bodish, Tshangla, Dhimal, Toto [txo] (India)

Tamangic

Chantyal [chx]

Gurung [gvr]

Ghale (Nepal)

Manangba [nmm] (Nepal)

Nar Phu [npa] (Nepal)

Seke [skj] (Nepal)

TAMANG [tai]

Thakali [ths] (Nepal)

Tibetan

Central

TIBETAN STANDARD [bod]

STOD [sbu]

Eastern

Northern

Southern

Unclassified

MONPA [twm]

Western

BALTI [bft]

LADAKHI [lbj]

PURKI [prx]

Western Himalayish (20)

Almora

BYANGSI [bee]

CHAUDANGSI [cdn]

DARMA [drd]

Rangkas [rgk]

Eastern (Nepal)

Janggali (Nepal)

Kanauri

Gahri [bfu]

Kinnauri, Chitkuli [cik]

Jangshung [jna]

KANGRI [xnr]

KINNAURI [kfk]

Kaike [kzq] (Nepal)

MANCHAD [lae]

Tinani [lbf]

Kinnauri, Bhoti [nes]

Shumcho [scu]

Sunam [ssk]

Tukpa [tpq])

Kanashi [xns]

RANGPO [rnp]

SPITI [spt]

JINGPHO-KONYAK-BODO

- Jingpho-Luish
  - Jingpho
    - Jingpho [kac] (Myanmar)
    - Singpho [sgp]
    - Taman [tcl] (Myanmar)
  - Luish (Myanmar)
- Konyak-Bodo-Garo
  - Bodo-Garo
    - Bodo
    - BODO [brx]
    - Deori [der]
    - DIMASA [dis]
    - Tiwa [lax]
    - Riang [ria]
    - KOK BOROK [trp]
    - Kachari [xac]
  - Garo
    - GARO [grt]
    - Megam [mef] (Bangladesh)
  - Koch
  - Konyak
    - Chang [nbc]
    - Konyak [nbe]
    - Nocte [njb]
    - Khiamniungan [nky]
    - WANCHO [nnp]
    - PHOM [nph]

TANGSA [nst] (also in Myanmar)

Tutsa [tvt]

Karen

Pa'o

Karen, Pa'o [blk] (Myanmar)

Pwo (Myanmar and Thailand)

KUKI-CHIN-NAGA

Kuki-Chin

Central

Bawm [bgr]

Haka [cnh] (Myanmar)

Ngawn [cnw] (Myanmar)

Zotung [czt] (Myanmar)

Darlong [dln] (Bangladesh)

HMAR [hmr]

MIZO [lus]

Pankhu [pkh] (Bangladesh)

Senthang [sez] (Myanmar)

Tawr [tcp] (Myanmar)

Northern

Aimol [aim]

Anal [anm]

Biete [biu]

Chiru [cdf]

Siyin [csy] (Myanmar)

Tedim [ctd] (Myanmar)

Falam [flm] (Myanmar)

Gangte [gnb]

Hrangkhol [hra] (Myanmar)

Kharam [kfw]

Kom [kmm]

Lamkang [lmk]

Chothe [nct]

Monsang [nmh]

Moyon [nmo]

PAITE [pck] (India)

Purum [pub] (Myanmar)

Purum [puz]

Ralte [ral] (Myanmar)

Sakechep [sch]

Simte [smt]

THADOU [tcz]

TARAO [tro]

Vaiphei [vap]

Yos [yos] (Myanmar)

ZO (also Myanmar)

Zome [zom] (Myanmar)

Southern (Myanmar)

Naga

Angami-Pochuri

ANGAMI [njm]

CHOKRI [nri]

KHEZHA [nkh]

MAO [nbi]

Rengma [nnl]

Pochuri [npo]

SEMA [nsm]

Sumi [nsm]

Poumei [pmx]

Ao

LOTHA [njh]

AO [njo]

Sangtam [nsa]

Yimchungru [yim]

Tangkhul

Naga, Khoibu [nkb]

Naga, Tangkhul [nmf]

Naga, MARING [nng]

Unclassified

Puimei [npu]

Zeme

KABUI [nkf]

LIANGMAI [njn]

KOIRENG [nkd]

Thangal [nki]

Maram [nma]

Mzieme [nme]

Rongmei [nbu]

Zeme [nzm]

Lolo-Burmese (China, Myanmar, Vietnam)

Meitei

MEITEI [mni] (India)

Mikir

Amri [ajz]

KARBI [mjw]

Mru (Bangladesh)

Tani

ADI [adi]

GALO [adl]

GALO- LARE[6]

GALLONG

APATANI [apt]

Bori

Bugun [bgg]

Hills-Miri [mrg][7]

Idu-Mishmi [clk]

Milang [adi][8]

Minyong [adi]

Mishmi [mhu]

Nyishi [dap]

Digaro-Miri [mrg]

MISHMI- Miju [mxj]

Na [nbt]

PADAAM [adi]

Pailibo [adi]

Sulung [suv]

Tagin [dap][9]

Yano [dap]

Nungish (mainly in Myanmar)

RAWANG

---

[6] Gallong- Lare and Gallong as described in this book are dialectal varieties of Galo.

[7] Hills-Miri is a dialect of Miri, spoken in Arunachal Pradesh.

[8] Milang, Minyong, Padaam and Pailibo are dialects of Adi.

[9] Tagin and Yano are dialect of Nyishi/Nisi, possibly different languages.

TAI-KADAI

Khampti, Turung (2)

Tai-Kadai

- Kam-Tai
  - Be-Tai
    - Tai-Sek
      - Tai
        - Central
        - East Central
          - Northwest
            - TURUNG [try]
        - Northern
        - Southwestern
          - East Central
          - Lao-Phutai
          - Northwest (9)
            - Ahom [aho]
            - Aiton [aio]
            - KHAMPTI [kht]
            - Phake
          - Southern
          - Unclassified

ANDAMANESE

- GREAT ANDAMANESE
  - Central
    - Aka-Bea [abj]
    - Akar-Bale [acl]
    - Aka-Kede [akx]

Aka-Kol [aky]

A-Pucikwar [apq]

Oko-Juwoi [okj]

Northern

Aka-Cari [aci]

Aka-Kora [ack]

Aka-Jeru [akj]

Aka-Bo [akm]

South Andamanese

JARAWA [anq]

ONGE [oon]

Sentinel [std]

CONTACT VARIETIES

Creole/ Pidgin varieties

Assamese- based

NAGAMESE [nag]

Meitei-based

BISHNUPURIA [bpy]

Oriya-based

HALBI [hlb]

Gujarati-based

VAGRI BOLI [vaa]

Urdu-based

DAKHINI URDU –TAMIL [not available]

Portugese-based

DIU-INDO-PORTUGESE [not available]

Second Language Variety

INDIAN ENGLISH-HINDI [not available]

HISTORICAL VARIETIES

- Austro-Asiatic
  - Proto- Munda
  - Proto Nicobarese
- Dravidian
  - OLD TAMIL
  - OLD TELUGU
- Indo-Aryan
  - SANSKRIT- CLASSICAL [san]
  - PALI [pli]
  - PRAKRIT [psu]
- Tibeto-Burman
  - Proto Tani
  - Proto- Kuki-Chin Naga
  - Proto Himalayish
  - Proto Tibetan
- Tai-Kadai
  - Proto Tai
  - Proto Kadai

Chapter 3

Segments: Consonants

3.0 Introduction

In this chapter we present facts and generalizations relating to consonantal segments and their patterns in three sub-sections: section 3.1 on consonant phonemes, section 3.2 on distributional constraints on consonant phonemes, and section 3.3 on consonant allophones. The discussion in section 3.1 and section 3.3 centres around four comprehensive tables – *Tables 3.1, 3.2, 3.4* and *3.28*. *Tables 3.1, 3.2* and *3.3* respectively contain a list of the phonemes, a complementary list of the frequently occurring phonemes with the languages in which they do not occur, and the patterns of the major classes of consonants in terms of laryngeal types.

3.1 Patterns of consonant phonemes

The list of the consonant phonemes in SPIL are presented in *Table 3.1* below.

Table 3.1 List of consonant phonemes in SPIL

MANNERS & PHONEMES	NO. OF SEGMENTS	*PHONEME LABELS* AND THEIR DISTRIBUTION IN LANGUAGES	LANGUAGE GROUPS
Plosives			
p	146	*Voiceless bilabial plosive*	
	15	Bhumij, Bonda, Didayi, Gadaba-G, Gorum, Ho, Juang, Kharia, Khasi, Kisan, Korku, Mundari, Nancowry, Nicobarese-C, Santali.	A-A

contd.

Table 3.1 *contd.*

	29	Ave, Badaga, Gadaba-K, Gadaba-O, Gondi, Gondi-A, Irula, Kadar, Kannada, Kattunaicka, Kodagu, Kolami, Konda, Koraga, Kota, Koya, Kui, Kurux, Kuvi, Malayalam, Malto, Manda, Naiki, Pengo, Tamil, Telugu, Toda, Tulu, Yerava.	DR
	32	Assamese, Bagri, Bengali, Bhili, Bhojpuri, Brokskat, Chakma, Dogri, Garhwali, Gojri, Gujarati, Haryanvi, Hindi, Jaunsari, Kacchi, Kashmiri, Konkani, Lahndi, Lamani, Magahi, Mahl, Maithili, Mandeali, Marathi, Nepali, Oriya, Punjabi, Rathvi, Shina, Sindhi, Urdu, Urdu-D-H.	I-A
	53	Adi, Angami, Ao-N, Apatani, Balti, Bantawa, Byangsi, Chaudangsi, Chokri, Darma, Dimasa, Gallong, Galo, Galo-L, Garo, Hmar, Kabui, Kangri, Karbi, Khezha, Kinnauri, Kiranti-K, Kokborok, Koren, Ladakhi, Lepcha, Liangmai, Limbu, Lotha, Magar, Manchad, Mao-N, Maring, Meitei, Mishmi, Mizo, Monpa, Padaam, Paite, Phom, Purki, Raji, RangPo, Sema-N, Spiti, Stod, Tamang, Tangsa, Tarao, Thaadou, Tibetan-St, Wancho, Zo.	T-B
	02	Khampti, Turung	T-K
	03	G-Andamanese, Jarawa, Onge	AN
	07	Bishnupuria, Diu-I-P, Halbi, IE-H, Nagamese, Urdu-D-T, Vagri-B.	C-V
	05	Sanskrit-Cl, Pali, Prakrit O-Tamil, O-Telugu	H-V
p^h	102	*Voiceless aspirated bilabial plosive*	
	08 (+2)	Bhumij, Bonda, Gadaba-G, (Ho), (Juang), Kharia, Khasi, Kisan, Korku, Santali	A-A
	06 (+1)	Gadaba-K, (Kannada), Kurux, Malayalam, Naiki, Telugu, Tulu.	DR
	30	Assamese, Bagri, Bengali, Bhili, Bhojpuri, Brokskat, Chakma, Dogri, Garhwali, Gojri, Gujarati, Haryanvi, Hindi, Jaunsari, Kacchi, Kashmiri, Konkani, Lahndi, Lamani, Magahi, Maithili, Mandeali, Marathi, Nepali, Oriya, Punjabi, Rathvi, Shina, Sindhi, Urdu, Urdu-D-H	I-A

contd.

Table 3.1 *contd.*

	43	Adi, Angami, Balti, Bantawa, Bodo, Byangsi, Chaudangsi, Chokri, Darma, Hmar, Kabui, Kangri, Karbi, Khezha, Kinnauri, Kiranti-K, Kokborok, Koren, Ladakhi, Limbu, Lotha, Magar, Manchad, Mao-N, Maring, Meitei, Mishmi, Mizo, Monpa, Phom, Purki, Raji, RangPo, Rawang, Spiti, Tibetan-St, Tamang, Tangsa, Tarao, Thaadou, Stod, Wancho, Zo.	T-B
	02	Khampti, Turung	T-K
	05 (+1)	Bishnupuria, DIU-I-P, Naga Pidgin, (Urdu-D-T), Vagri-B	C-V
	04	(O-Tamil), Pali, Prakrit, Sanskrit-Cl.	H-V
b	141	*Voiced bilabial plosive*	
	13	Bhumij, Bonda, Didayi, Gadaba-G, Gorum, Ho, Juang, Kharia, Khasi, Kisan, Korku, Mundari, Santali.	A-A
	29	Ave, Badaga, Gadaba-K, Gadaba-O, Gondi, Gondi-A, Irula, Kadar, Kannada, Kattunaicka, Kodagu, Kolami, Konda, Koraga, Kota, Koya, Kui, Kurux, Kuvi, Malayalam, Malto, Manda, Naiki, Pengo, Tamil, Telugu, Toda, Tulu, Yerava.	DR
	32	Assamese, Bagri, Bengali, Bhili, Bhojpuri, Brokskat, Chakma, Dogri, Garhwali, Gojri, Gujarati, Haryanvi, Hindi, Jaunsari, Kacchi, Kashmiri, Konkani, Lahndi, Lamani, Magahi, Mahl, Maithili, Mandeali, Marathi, Nepali, Oriya, Punjabi, Rathvi, Shina, Sindhi, Urdu, Urdu-D-H.	I-A
	53	Adi, Angami, Apatani, Balti, Bantawa, Bodo, Byangsi, Chaudangsi, Chokri, Darma, Dimasa, Gallong, Galo, Galo-L, Garo, Hmar, Kabui, Kangri, Karbi, Khezha, Kinnauri, Kiranti-K, Kokborok, Koren, Ladakhi, Lepcha, Liangmai, Limbu, Lotha, Magar, Manchad, Mao-N, Maring, Meitei, Mishmi, Mizo, Monpa, Padaam, Paite, Phom, Purki, Raji, RangPo, Rawang, Sema-N, Spiti, Tangsa, Tarao, Thaadou, Stod, Wancho, Zo.	T-B
	01	Turung	T-K

contd.

Table 3.1 *contd.*

	03	G-Andamanese, Jarawa, Onge.	AN
	07	Bishnupuria, Diu-I-P, Halbi, Nagamese, Vagri-B, Urdu-D-T, IE-H	C-V
	04	Sanskrit-Cl, Pali, Prakrit O-Telugu	H-V
$b^ʔ$		*Voiced glottalized bilabial plosive*	
		Bishnupuria	C-V
$b^ɦ$	58	*Voiced aspirated bilabial plosive*	
	08 (+2)	Bhumij, Bonda, Didayi, (Ho), (Juang), Kharia, Khasi, Kisan, Korku, Santali	A-A
	06 (+1)	Gadaba-K, (Kannada), Kurux, Malayalam, Naiki, Telugu, Tulu	DR
	23	Assamese, Bagri, Bengali, Bhili, Bhojpuri, Chakma, Garhwali, Gujarati, Haryanvi, Hindi, Jaunsari, Konkani, Lahndi, Lamani, Magahi, Maithili, Mandeali, Marathi, Nepali, Oriya, Rathvi, Sindhi, Urdu, Urdu-D-H	I-A
	06 (+2)	Bantawa, Chaudangsi, Karbi, Limbu, (Meitei), Raji, RangPo, (Stod)	T-B
	04 (+1)	Diu-I-P, (IE-H), Naga Pidgin, Urdu-D-T, Vagri-B	C-V
	04 (+1)	Pali, Prakrit, Sanskrit-Cl (O-Telugu)	H-V
t̪	135	*Voiceless dental plosive*	
	15	Bhumij, Bonda, Didayi, Gadaba-G, Gorum, Ho, Juang, Kharia, Khasi, Kisan, Korku, Mundari, Nancowry, Nicobarese-C, Santali.	A-A
	29	Ave, Badaga, Gadaba-K, Gadaba-O, Gondi, Gondi-A, Irula, Kadar, Kannada, Kattunaicka, Kodagu, Kolami, Konda, Koraga, Kota, Koya, Kui, Kurux, Kuvi, Malayalam, Malto, Manda, Naiki, Pengo, Tamil, Telugu, Toda, Tulu, Yerava.	DR
	31	Bagri, Bengali, Bhili, Bhojpuri, Brokskat, Chakma, Dogri, Garhwali, Gojri, Gujarati, Haryanvi, Hindi, Jaunsari, Kacchi, Kashmiri, Konkani, Lahndi, Lamani, Magahi, Mahl, Maithili, Mandeali, Marathi, Nepali, Oriya, Punjabi, Rathvi, Shina, Sindhi, Urdu, Urdu-D-H.	I-A

contd.

Table 3.1 *contd.*

	45	Adi, Angami, Ao-N, Balti, Bantawa, Byangsi, Chaudangsi, Chokri, Darma, Gallong, Galo, Garo, Hmar, Kabui, Kangri, Karbi, Khezha, Kinnauri, Kiranti-K, Kokborok, Koren, Lepcha, Limbu, Lotha, Magar, Manchad, Maring, Meitei, Mishmi, Mizo, Monpa, Padaam, Phom, Purki, Raji, RangPo, Sema-N, Spiti, Tibetan-St, Tamang, Tangsa, Tarao, Thaadou, Stod, Wancho.	T-B
	02	Khampti, Turung	T-K
	03	G-Andamanese, Jarawa, Onge	AN
	05	Bishnupuria, Halbi, Nagamese, Vagri-B, Urdu-D-T,	C-V
	05	Pali, Prakrit, Sanskrit-Cl O-Tamil, O-Telugu	H-V
d̪	124	*Voiced dental plosive*	
	13	Bhumij, Bonda, Didayi, Gadaba-G, Gorum, Ho, Juang, Kharia, Khasi, Kisan, Korku, Mundari, Santali.	A-A
	28	Ave, Badaga, Gadaba-K, Gadaba-O, Gondi, Gondi-A, Irula, Kannada, Kattunaicka, Kodagu, Kolami, Konda, Koraga, Kota, Koya, Kui, Kurux, Kuvi, Malayalam, Malto, Manda, Naiki, Pengo, Tamil, Telugu, Toda, Tulu, Yerava.	DR
	31	Bagri, Bengali, Bhili, Bhojpuri, Brokskat, Chakma, Dogri, Garhwali, Gojri, Gujarati, Haryanvi, Hindi, Jaunsari, Kacchi, Kashmiri, Konkani, Lahndi, Lamani, Magahi, Mahl, Maithili, Mandeali, Marathi, Nepali, Oriya, Punjabi, Rathvi, Shina, Sindhi, Urdu, Urdu-D-H.	I-A
	38 (+1)	Adi, Angami, Balti, Bantawa, Byangsi, Chaudangsi, Chokri, Darma, Gallong, Garo, Hmar, Kabui, Kangri, Karbi, Khezha, Kinnauri, Kiranti-K, Kokborok, Koren, Lepcha, (Limbu), Magar, Manchad, Maring, Meitei, Mishmi, Mizo, Monpa, Padaam, Phom, Purki, Raji, RangPo, Rawang, Sema-N, Spiti, Tarao, Thaadou, Stod, Wancho.	T-B
	01	Turung	T-K

contd.

Table 3.1 *contd.*

	03	G-Andamanese, Jarawa, Onge	AN
	05	Bishnupuria, Halbi, Nagamese, Urdu-D-T, Vagri-B	C-V
	05	Pali, Prakrit, Sanskrit-Cl O-Tamil, O-Telugu	H-V
t̪ʰ	96	*Voiceless aspirated dental plosive*	
	07 (+3)	Bhumij, Bonda, (Didayi), (Ho), (Juang), Kharia, Khasi, Kisan, Korku, Santali.	A-A
	06 (+1)	Gadaba-K, (Kannada), Kurux, Malayalam, Naiki, Telugu, Tulu.	DR
	29	Bagri, Bengali, Bhili, Bhojpuri, Brokskat, Chakma, Dogri, Garhwali, Gojri, Gujarati, Haryanvi, Hindi, Jaunsari, Kacchi, Kashmiri, Konkani, Lahndi, Lamani, Magahi, Maithili, Mandeali, Marathi, Nepali, Oriya, Punjabi, Rathvi, Shina, Sindhi, Urdu, Urdu-D-H.	I-A
	39	Adi, Angami, Ao-N, Balti, Bantawa, Byangsi, Chaudangsi, Chokri, Darma, Hmar, Kabui, Kangri, Karbi, Khezha, Kinnauri, Kiranti-K, Kokborok, Koren, Limbu, Lotha, Magar, Manchad, Maring, Meitei, Mishmi, Mizo, Monpa, Phom, Purki, Raji, Rawang, Spiti, Tibetan-St, Tamang, Tangsa, Tarao, Thaadou, Stod, Wancho.	T-B
	02	Khampti, Turung	T-K
	05	Bishnupuria, Halbi, Nagamese, Urdu-D-T, Vagri-B	C-V
	04	Pali, Prakrit, Sanskrit-Cl O-Telugu	H-V
d̪ʱ		*Voiced aspirated dental plosive*	
	07 (+2)	Bhumij, Bonda, (Ho), (Juang), Kharia, Khasi, Kisan, Korku, Santali.	A-A
	06 (+1)	Gadaba-K, (Kannada), Kurux, Malayalam, Naiki, Telugu, Tulu.	DR
	23	Bagri, Bengali, Bhili, Bhojpuri, Brokskat, Chakma, Garhwali, Gujarati, Haryanvi, Hindi, Jaunsari, Konkani, Lahndi, Lamani, Magahi, Maithili, Mandeali, Marathi, Nepali, Oriya, Rathvi, Sindhi, Urdu, Urdu-D-H	I-A

contd.

Table 3.1 *contd.*

	06 (+2)	Adi, Bantawa, Chaudangsi, Karbi, (Meitei), Raji, RangPo, (Stod).	T-B
	02 (+1)	Halbi, (Urdu-D-T), Vagri-B	C-V
	04	Pali, Prakrit, Sanskrit-Cl O-Telugu	H-V
t̠	21	*Voiceless alveolar plosive*	
	01	Nicobarese-C	A-A
	05	Irula, Kota, Malayalam, Tamil, Toda	DR
	02	Assamese, Brokskat	I-A
	10	Apatani, Balti, Galo-L, Lepcha, Liangmai, Mao-N, Mizo, Paite, Purki, Zo.	T-B
	02	Diu-I-P, Nagamese	C-V
	01	O-Tamil	H-V
d̠	21	*Voiced alveolar plosive*	
	03	Irula, Kota, Toda	DR
	02	Assamese, Brokskat	I-A
	13	Apatani, Balti, Bodo, Galo, Galo-L, Lepcha, Liangmai, Mao-N, Mizo, Paite, Purki, Tangsa, Zo	T-B
	03	Diu-I-P, IE-H, Nagamese	C-V
t̠ʰ	12	*Voiceless aspirated alveolar plosive*	
	02	Assamese, Brokskat	I-A
	08	Balti, Bodo, Liangmai, Mao-N, Mizo, Paite, Purki, Zo	T-B
	02	IE-H, Nagamese	C-V
d̠ˀ	01	*Voiced glottalised alveolar plosive*	
	01	Bishnupuria	C-V
d̠ʱ	04	*Voiced aspirated alveolar plosive*	
	03	Assamese, Dogri, Gojri	I-A
	(1)	(Nagamese)	C-V

contd.

Table 3.1 *contd.*

ṭ	01	*Voiceless post-alveolar plosive*	
	01	Dimasa	T-B
ḍ	01	*Voiced post-alveolar plosive*	
	01	Dimasa	T-B
ʈ	62 (+1)	*Voiceless retroflex plosive*	
	14	Bhumij, Bonda, Didayi, Gadaba-G, Gorum, Ho, Juang, Kharia, Khasi, Kisan, Korku, Mundari, Nicobarese-C, Santali.	A-A
	29	Bagri, Bengali, Bhili, Bhojpuri, Dogri, Garhwali, Gojri, Gujarati.Haryanvi, Hindi, Kacchi, Kashmiri, Konkani, Lahndi, Lamani, Magahi, Mahl, Maithili, Mandeali, Marathi, Nepali, Oriya, Punjabi, Rathvi, Shina, Sindhi, Urdu, Urdu-D-H.	I-A
	14 (+1)	Bantawa, Byangsi, Chaudangsi, Dimasa, Hmar, Kangri, Kinnauri, Kiranti-K, Ladakhi, Lepcha, (Limbu), RangPo, Tamang, Tibetan-St, Stod.	T-B
	03	G-Andamanese, Jarawa, Onge	AN
	02	Diu-I-P, Nagamese.	C-V
ɖ	96	*Voiced retroflex plosive*	
	13	Bhumij, Bonda, Didayi, Gadaba-G, Gorum, Ho, Juang, Kharia, Khasi, Kisan, Korku, Mundari, Santali.	A-A
	28	Ave, Badaga, Gadaba-K, Gadaba-O, Gondi, Gondi-A, Irula, Kannada, Kattunaicka, Kodagu, Kolami, Konda, Koraga, Kota, Koya, Kui, Kurux, Kuvi, Malayalam, Malto, Manda, Naiki, Pengo, Tamil, Telugu, Toda, Tulu, Yerava.	DR
	31	Bagri, Bengali, Bhili, Bhojpuri, Brokskat, Chakma, Dogri, Garhwali, Gojri, Gujarati, Haryanvi, Hindi, Jaunsari, Kacchi, Kashmiri, Konkani, Lahndi, Lamani, Magahi, Mahl, Maithili, Mandeali, Marathi, Nepali, Oriya, Punjabi,Rathvi,Shina,Sindhi,Urdu,Urdu-D-H.	I-A

contd.

Table 3.1 *contd.*

	11 (+1)	Bantawa, Byangsi, Chaudangsi, Dimasa, Hmar, Kangri, Kinnauri, Ladakhi, (Limbu), Lepcha, RangPo, Stod.	T-B
	03	G-Andamanese, Jarawa, Onge.	AN
	05	Bishnupuria, Halbi, IE-H, Urdu-D-T, Vagri-B.	C-V
	04	Pali, Prakrit, Sanskrit-Cl O-Telugu	H-V
ʈʰ	66	*Voiceless aspirated retroflex plosive*	
	07 (+2)	Bhumij, Bonda, (Ho), (Juang), Kharia, Khasi, Kisan, Korku, Santali.	A-A
	06 (+1)	Gadaba- K, (Kannada), Kurux, Malayalam, Naiki, Telugu, Tulu.	DR
	30	Bagri, Bengali, Bhili, Bhojpuri, Brokskat, Chakma, Dogri, Garhwali, Gojri, Gujarati, Haryanvi, Hindi, Jaunsari, Kacchi, Kashmiri, Konkani, Lahndi, Lamani, Magahi, Maithili, Mandeali, Marathi, Nepali, Oriya, Punjabi, Rathvi, Shina, Sindhi, Urdu, Urdu-D-H.	I-A
	12 (+1)	Bantawa, Byangsi, Chaudangsi, Hmar, Kangri, Kinnauri, Kiranti-K, Ladakhi, (Limbu), Lepcha, Tamang, Tibetan-St, Stod.	T-B
	01	G-Andamanese.	AN
	03	Bishnupuria, Halbi, Vagri-B.	C-V
	03 (+1)	Pali, Prakrit, Sanskrit-Cl. (O-Telugu).	H-V
ɖʱ	46 (+8)	*Voiced aspirated retroflex plosive*	
	08 (+2)	Bhumij, Bonda, Didayi, (Ho), (Juang), Kharia, Khasi, Kisan, Korku, Santali.	A-A
	06 (+1)	Gadaba-K, (Kannada), Kurux, Malayalam, Naiki, Telugu, Tulu.	DR
	24	Bagri, Bengali, Bhili, Bhojpuri, Brokskat, Chakma, Garhwali, Gujarati, Haryanvi, Hindi, Jaunsari, Konkani, Lahndi, Lamani, Magahi, Maithili, Mandeali, Marathi, Nepali, Oriya, Rathvi, Sindhi, Urdu, Urdu-D-H.	I-A
	04 (+2)	Bantawa, Chaudangsi, (Limbu), Raji, RangPo, (Stod).	T-B

contd.

Table 3.1 *contd.*

	02 (+2)	Halbi, (IE-H), (Urdu-D-T), Vagri-B.	C-V
	03 (+1)	Pali, Prakrit, Sanskrit-Cl. (O-Telugu).	H-V
ɖˀ	01	*Voiced glottalized retroflex plosive*	
	01	Bishnupuria.	C-V
c	01	*Voiceless palatal plosive*	
	01	Tibetan-St.	T-B
cʰ	01	*Voiceless aspirated palatal plosive*	
	01	Tibetan-St	T-B
k	146	*Voiceless velar plosive*	
	15	Bhumij, Bonda, Didayi, Gadaba-G, Gorum, Ho, Juang, Kharia, Khasi, Kisan, Korku, Mundari, Nancowry, Nicobarese-C, Santali.	A-A
	29	Ave, Badaga, Gadaba-K, Gadaba-O, Gondi, Gondi-A, Irula, Kadar, Kannada, Kattunaicka, Kodagu, Kolami, Konda, Koraga, Kota, Koya, Kui, Kurux, Kuvi, Malayalam, Malto, Manda, Naiki, Pengo, Tamil, Telugu, Toda, Tulu, Yerava.	DR
	32	Assamese, Bagri, Bengali, Bhili, Bhojpuri, Brokskat, Chakma, Dogri, Garhwali, Gojri, Gujarati, Haryanvi, Hindi, Jaunsari, Kacchi, Kashmiri, Konkani, Lahndi, Lamani, Magahi, Mahl, Maithili, Mandeali, Marathi, Nepali, Oriya, Punjabi, Rathvi, Shina, Sindhi, Urdu, Urdu-D-H.	I-A
	53	Adi, Angami, Ao-N, Apatani, Balti, Bantawa, Byangsi, Chaudangsi, Chokri, Darma, Dimasa, Gallong, Galo, Galo-L, Garo, Hmar, Kabui, Kangri, Karbi, Khezha, Kinnauri, Kiranti-K, Kokborok, Koren, Ladakhi, Lepcha, Liangmai, Limbu, Lotha, Magar, Manchad, Mao-N, Maring, Meitei, Mishmi, Mizo, Monpa, Padaam, Paite, Phom, Purki, Raji, RangPo, Sema-N, Spiti, Tibetan-St, Tamang, Tangsa, Tarao, Thaadou, Stod, Wancho, Zo.	T-B
	02	Khampti, Turung	T-K

contd.

Table 3.1 *contd.*

	03	G-Andamanese, Jarawa, Onge	AN
	07	Bishnupuria, Diu-I-P, Halbi, Nagamese, Vagri-B, Urdu-D-T, IE-H	C-V
	05	Sanskrit-Cl, Pali, Prakrit O-Tamil, O-Telugu	H-V
k^j	01	*Voiceless palatalized velar plosive*	
	01	Tibetan-St	T-B
k^w	01	*Voiceless labialized velar plosive*	
	01	Khezha.	T-B
k^h	92 (+5)	*Voiceless aspirated velar plosive*	
	05 (+3)	Bhumij, Bonda, (Didayi), (Ho), (Juang), Kharia, Kisan, Santali.	A-A
	05 (+1)	Gadaba-K, (Kannada), Kurux, Malayalam, Naiki, Tulu.	DR
	29	Assamese, Bagri, Bengali, Bhojpuri, Brokskat, Chakma, Dogri, Garhwali, Gojri, Gujarati, Haryanvi, Hindi, Jaunsari, Kacchi, Kashmiri, Konkani, Lahndi, Lamani, Magahi, Maithili, Mandeali, Marathi, Nepali, Oriya, Punjabi, Rathvi, Shina, Urdu, Urdu-D-H.	I-A
	45	Adi, Angami, Balti, Bantawa, Bodo, Byangsi, Chaudangsi, Chokri, Darma, Dimasa, Hmar, Kabui, Kangri, Karbi, Khezha, Kinnauri, Kiranti-K, Kokborok, Koren, Ladakhi, Liangmai, Limbu, Lotha, Magar, Manchad, Mao-N, Maring, Meitei, Mishmi, Mizo, Monpa, Phom, Purki, Raji, RangPo, Rawang, Spiti, Tibetan-St, Tamang, Tangsa, Tarao, Thaadou, Stod, Wancho, Zo.	T-B
	02	Khampti, Turung	T-K
	03	Bishnupuria, Naga Pidgin, Vagri Boli.	C-V
	03 (+1)	Pali, Prakrit, Sanskrit-Cl. (O-Telugu)	H-V
k^{hj}	01	*Voiceless aspirated palatalized velar plosive*	
	01	Tibetan-St	T-B
k^{hw}	01	*Voiceless aspirated labialized velar plosive*	

contd.

Table 3.1 *contd.*

	01	Khezha.	T-B
g	132 (+3)	*Voiced velar plosive*	
	12	Bhumij, Bonda, Didayi, Gadaba-G, Gorum, Ho, Juang, Kharia, Kisan, Korku, Mundari, Santali.	A-A
	28	Ave, Badaga, Gadaba-K, Gadaba-O, Gondi, Gondi-A, Irula, Kannada, Kattunaicka, Kodagu, Kolami, Konda, Koraga, Kota, Koya, Kui, Kurux, Kuvi, Malayalam, Malto, Manda, Naiki, Pengo, Tamil, Telugu, Toda, Tulu, Yerava.	DR
	32	Assamese, Bagri, Bengali, Bhili, Bhojpuri, Brokskat, Chakma, Dogri, Garhwali, Gojri, Gujarati, Haryanvi, Hindi, Jaunsari, Kacchi, Kashmiri, Konkani, Lahndi, Lamani, Magahi, Mahl, Maithili, Mandeali, Marathi, Nepali, Oriya, Punjabi, Rathvi, Shina, Sindhi, Urdu, Urdu-D-H.	I-A
	46 (+3)	Adi, Angami, Apatani, Balti, Bantawa, Bodo, Byangsi, Chaudangsi, Chokri, Darma, Dimasa, Gallong, Galo, Galo-L, Garo, Kabui, Kangri, Karbi, Kinnauri, Kiranti-K, Kokborok, (Koren), Ladakhi, Lepcha, Liangmai, (Limbu), Magar, Manchad, Mao-N, Meitei, Mishmi, Monpa, Padaam, Paite, Phom, Purki, Raji, RangPo, Rawang, Sema-N, Spiti, (Tarao), Thaadou, Stod, Wancho, Zo.	T-B
	01	Turung	T-K
	02	Jarawa, Onge.	AN
	07	Bishnupuria, Diu-I-P, IE-H, Halbi, Nagamese, Urdu-D-T, Vagri-B.	C-V
	04	Pali, Prakrit, Sanskrit-Cl. O-Telugu.	H-V
gˀ	01	*Voiced glottalized velar plosive*	
	01	Bishnupuria.	C-V
gʱ	43 (+7)	*Voiced aspirated velar plosive*	
	06 (+2)	Bhumij, Bonda, (Ho), (Juang), Kharia, Kisan, Korku, Santali.	A-A

contd.

Table 3.1 *contd.*

	05 (+1)	Gadaba- K, (Kannada), Kurux, Malayalam, Naiki, Tulu.	DR
	23	Assamese, Bagri, Bengali, Bhojpuri, Brokskat, Chakma, Garhwali, Gujarati, Haryanvi, Hindi, Jaunsari, Konkani, Lahndi, Lamani, Magahi, Maithili, Mandeali, Marathi, Nepali, Oriya, Rathvi, Urdu, Urdu-D-H.	I-A
	05 (+2)	Bantawa, Chaudangsi, Karbi, (Meitei), Raji, RangPo, (Stod).	T-B
	02 (+1)	Naga Pidgin, Vagri Boli, (IE-H).	C-V
	03 (+1)	Pali, Prakrit, Sanskrit-Cl. (OTelugu).	H-V
q	07 (+2)	*Voiceless uvular plosive*	
	01	Korku.	A-A
	01	Malto.	DR
	03 (+2)	Brokskat, Hindi, Urdu, (Punjabi), (Sindhi).	I-A
	02	Apatani, Purki.	T-B
G	01	*Voiced uvular plosive*	
	01	Malto.	DR
?	27 (+2)	*Voiceless glottal stop*	
	06	Bhumij, Bonda, Didayi, Khasi, Kisan, Nancowry.	A-A
	05	Gadaba- K, Konda, Kui, Kurux, Kuvi.	DR
	14 (+2)	Adi, Bantawa, (Dimasa), Gallong, (Galo-L), Garo, Kiranti-K, Limbu, Mizo, Paite, Phom, RangPo, Rawang, Tangsa, Tibetan-St, Stod.	T-B
	02	Khampti, Turung	T-K
Nasals			
m	148	*Voiced bilabial nasal*	
		All 148 languages	
m̥	02	*Voiceless bilabial nasal*	
	02	Byangsi, Chokri.	T-B

contd.

Table 3.1 *contd.*

^{h}m	02	*Preaspirated voiced bilabial nasal*	
	02	Chaudangsi, Darma.	T-B
m̥^{h}	02	*Voiceless aspirated bilabial nasal*	
	02	Angami, Mizo.	T-B
m^{ɦ}	08	*Voiced aspirated bilabial nasal*	
	03	Bhili, Bhojpuri, Magahi.	I-A
	04	Khezha, Lotha, Raji, RangPo.	T-B
	01	Vagri-B.	C-V
ɱ	01	*Voiced labio-dental nasal*	T-B
	01	Chokri.	
n̪		*Voiced dental nasal*	
	04	Didayi, Gorum, Juang, Mundaṛi.	A-A
	15	Badaga, Gadaba-K, Gondi-A, Irula, Kadar, Kattunaicka, Kolami, Malayalam, Manda, Naiki, Pengo, Tamil, Telugu, Toda, Tulu.	DR
	14	Bengali, Bhili, Bhojpuri, Brokskat, Dogri, Gojri, Haryanvi, Kacchi, Magahi, Mahl, Nepali, Oriya, Punjabi, Rathvi.	I-A
	10	Byangsi, Chokri, Hmar, Kabui, Kinnauri, Kokborok, Maring, Meitei, RangPo, Tangsa.	T-B
	01	Khampti	T-K
	02	Bishnupuria, Vagri-B.	C-V
	03	Sanskrit-Cl. O-Tamil, O-Telugu.	H-V
n̲		*Voiced alveolar nasal*	
	11	Bhumij, Bonda, Gadaba-G, Ho, Kharia, Khasi, Kisan, Korku, Nancowry, Nicobarese-C, Santali.	A-A
	17	Ave, Gadaba-O, Gondi, Kadar, Kannada, Kodagu, Konda, Koraga, Kota, Koya, Kui, Kurux, Kuvi, Malayalam, Malto, Tamil, Yerava.	DR

contd.

Table 3.1 *contd.*

	18	Assamese, Bagri, Chakma, Garhwali, Gujarati, Hindi, Jaunsari, Kashmiri, Konkani, Lahndi, Lamani, Maithili, Mandeali, Marathi, Shina, Sindhi, Urdu, Urdu-D-H.	I-A
	45	Adi, Angami, Ao-N, Apatani, Balti, Bantawa, Bodo, Chaudangsi, Darma, Dimasa, Gallong, Galo, Galo-L, Garo, Kangri, Karbi, Khezha, Kiranti-K, Koren, Ladakhi, Lepcha, Liangmai, Limbu, Lotha, Magar, Manchad, Mao-N, Mishmi, Mizo, Monpa, Padaam, Paite, Phom, Purki, Raji, Rawang, Sema-N, Spiti, Tibetan-St, Tamang, Tarao, Thaadou, Stod, Wancho, Zo.	T-B
	01	Turung	T-K
	03	G-Andamanese, Jarawa, Onge	AN
	05	Diu-I-P, IE-H, Halbi, Nagamese, Urdu-D-T.	C-V
	01	O-Tamil.	H-V
n̪̊	03	*Voiceless dental nasal*	
	03	Byangsi, Chokri, Mizo	T-B
n̥	02	*Voiceless alveolar nasal*	
	01	Jaunsari.	I-A
	01	Chokri.	T-B
ʰn	02	*Preaspirated voiced alveolar nasal*	
	02	Chaudangsi, Darma.	T-B
n̥ʰ	02	*Voiceless aspirated alveolar nasal*	
	02	Angami, Mizo.	T-B
nʱ	07 (+1)	*Voiced aspirated alveolar nasal*	
	02	Bhojpuri, Magahi.	I-A
	04 (+1)	Khezha, (Kiranti-K), Lotha, Raji, RangPo.	T-B
	01	Vagri-B.	C-V
ɳ		*Voiced retroflex nasal*	

contd.

Table 3.1 *contd.*

	6(+1)	Bhumij, Bonda, Ho, (Juang), Kisan, Mundari, Santali.	A-A
	21	Ave, Badaga, Gadaba- K, Gadaba- O, Kadar, Kannada, Kattunaicka, Konda, Koraga, Kota, Koya, Kui, Kuvi, Malayalam, Manda, Pengo, Tamil, Telugu, Toda, Tulu, Yerava.	DR
	16(+1)	Bagri, Haryanvi, Dogri, Garhwali, Gojri, Gujarati, Kacchi, Lahndi, Lamani, Mahl, (Maithili), Mandeali, Marathi, Oriya, Punjabi, Shina, Urdu-D-H.	I-A
	6(+1)	Chaudangsi, Kangri, Kinnauri, (Limbu), Raji, RangPo, Spiti,	T-B
	02	Urdu-D-T, Vagri-B.	C-V
	05	O-Tamil, O-Telugu, Pali, Prakrit, Sanskrit-Cl.	H-V
ŋ		*Voiced velar nasal*	
	15	Bhumij, Bonda, Didayi, Gadaba-G, Gorum, Ho, Juang, Kharia, Khasi, Kisan, Korku, Mundari, Nancowry, Nicobarese-C, Santali.	A-A
	20(+1)	Ave, Gadaba-K, Gadaba-O, Gondi, Gondi-A, Kadar, Kattunaicka, Kolami, Konda, Koraga, Kota, Kui, Kuvi, Malayalam, Malto, Manda, Naiki, Pengo, (Toda), Tulu, Yerava.	DR
	18(+2)	Assamese, Bengali, Bhojpuri, Brokskat, Chakma, Dogri, Gujarati, Haryanvi, (Hindi), Kacchi, Lahndi, Lamani, Magahi, (Marathi), Nepali, Oriya, Punjabi, Shina, Sindhi, (Urdu-D-H).	I-A
	47	Adi, Angami, Ao-N, Apatani, Balti, Bantawa, Bodo, Byangsi, Chaudangsi, Chokri, Darma, Gallong, Galo, Galo-L, Garo, Hmar, Kabui, Karbi, Khezha, Kinnauri, Kiranti-K, Kokborok, Koren, Ladakhi, Lepcha, Liangmai, Lotha, Mao-N, Maring, Meitei, Mishmi, Monpa, Padaam, Paite, Phom, Purki, Raji, RangPo, Sema-N, Tamanag, Tangsa, Tarao, Thaadou, Tibetan-St, Stod, Wancho, Zo.	T-B
	02	Khampti, Turung	T-K
	02	G-Andamanese, Onge.	AN
	05	Bishnupuria, DIU-I-P, IE-H, Nagamese, Vagri-B.	C-V
	02(+1)	(O-Tamil), O-Telugu, Sanskrit-Cl.	H-V

contd.

Table 3.1 *contd.*

ɲ̊ʰ	01	*Voiceless aspirated velar nasal*	
	01	Mizo.	T-B
ŋʱ	01	*Voiced aspirated velar nasal*	
	01	Lotha.	T-B
ɲ̊ʱ	01	*Voiceless aspirated palatal nasal*	
	01	Angami.	T-B
ɲʱ	01	*Voiced aspirated palatal nasal*	
	01	Lotha.	T-B
ɲ		*Voiced palatal nasal*	
	06 (+2)	Bonda, Ho, (Juang), Kharia, (Mundari), Nancowry, Nicobarese-C, Santali.	A-A
	06 (+1)	Kattunaicka, Koraga, Malayalam, Malto, (Gadaba-O), Tamil, Tulu, Yerava.	DR
	05 (+1)	(Dogri), Gojri, Lahndi, Lamani, Punjabi, Sindhi.	I-A
	16	Balti, Byangsi, Chokri, Gallong, Galo, Ladakhi, Lepcha, Lotha, Monpa, Padaam, Phom, Purki, RangPo, Koren, Sema-N, Stod.	T-B
	02	G-Andamanese, Onge.	AN
	01	Vagri Boli.	C-V
	02	O-Tamil, Sanskrit-Cl.	H-V
Rhotics			
ɾ		*Voiced dental/alveolar tap*	
	01	Nicobarese-C	A-A
	08	Kattunaicka, Konda, Koya, Kui, Malayalam, Malto, Toda, Tulu	DR
	16	Bagri, Bengali, Bhojpuri, Gujarati, Haryanvi, Hindi, Kacchi, Konkani, Lahndi, Lamani, Magahi, Maithili, Marathi, Rathvi, Urdu, Urdu-D-H.	I-A
	07	Ao-N, Byangsi, Chokri, Hmar, Spiti, Tangsa, Tarao.	T-B

contd.

Table 3.1 *contd.*

	01	G-Andamanese	AN
	01	IE-H	C-V
	04	O-Tamil, O-Telugu, Pali, Prakrit.	H-V
ɾ^{ɦ}	02	*Voiced aspirated alveolar tap*	
	02	Bhojpuri, Magahi.	I-A
ɾ$^{>}$	02	*Voiced post- alveolar tap*	
	02	Assamese, Chakma	I-A
r̪	12	*Voiced dental trill*	
	01	Didayi	A-A
	01	Pengo	DR
	03	Brokskat, Dogri, Sindhi,	I-A
	06	Byangsi, Galo, Kinnauri, Spiti, Tibetan-St, Tamang,	T-B
	01	Vagri-B	C-V
r̪^{ɦ}	01	*Voiced aspirated dental trill*	
	01	Vagri-B	C-V
r̪$^{>}$	03	*Voiced post-dental trill*	
	02	Kolami, Toda	DR
	01	Chakma	I-A
r		*Voiced alveolar trill*	
	14	Bhumij, Bonda, Gadaba-G, Gorum, Ho, Juang, Kharia, Khasi, Kisan, Korku, Mundari, Nancowry, Nicobarese-C, Santali,	A-A
	26	Ave, Badaga, Gad-K, Gad-O, Gondi, Gondi-A, Irula, Kadar, Kannada, Kaṭṭunaicka, Kodagu, Konda, Koraga, Kota, Kurux, Kuvi, Malaya, Malto, Manda, Naiki, Pengo, Tamil, Telugu, Toda, Tulu, Yerava	DR
	12	Bhili, Garhwali, Gojri, Jaunsari, Kacchi, Kashmiri, Mahl, Mandeali, Nepali, Punjabi, Shina, Urdu-D-H.	I-A

contd.

Table 3.1 *contd.*

	40	Adi, Angami, Apatani, Balti, Bantawa, Bodo, Chokri, Chaudangsi, Darma, Dimasa, Gallong, Galo-L, Garo, Kabui, Kangri, Karbi, Khezha, Kiranti-K, Kokborok, Koren, Ladakhi, Lepcha, Limbu, Lotha, Magar, Manchad, Mao-N, Maring, Meitei, Mishmi, Mizo, Monpa, Padaam, Purki, Raji, RangPo, Sema-N, Spiti, Tarao, Stod.	T-B
		Khampti	T-K
		Bishnupuria, Diu-I-P, Halbi, Nagamese, Urdu-D-T, Vagri-B.	C-V
		O-Telugu, Sanskrit-Cl	H-V
r̥	03	*Voiceless dental/ alveolar trill*	
	01	Konda.	DR
	02	Chokri, Mao-N.	T-B
ʰr̥	02	*Preaspirated voiceless alveolar trill*	
	02	Chaudangsi, Darma.	T-B
r̥ʰ	02	*Voiceless aspirated alveolar trill*	
	02	Angami, Mizo.	T-B
rʱ	07 (+01)	*Voiced aspirated (apico-)alveolar trill*	
	07	Byangsi, Khezha, Lotha, Magar, Manchad, Raji, RangPo.	T-B
	(01)	(Halbi)	C-V
r̠	02	*Voiced post-alveolar trill*	
	02	Kattunakicka, Tamil	DR
Ṙ		*Voiced retroflex trill*	
	01	Irula	DR
ʀ		*Voiced uvular trill*	
	02	Gondi, Gondi-A	DR
	01	Vagri-B	C-V
ɽ		*Voiced retroflex flap*	

contd.

Table 3.1 *contd.*

	08	Bhumij, Ho, Juang, Kharia, Kisan, Korku, Mundari, Santali.	A-A
	16	Ave, Gadaba-K, Gadaba-O, Kattunaicka, Konda, Koraga, Kota, Kui, Kurux, Kuvi, Malto, Manda, Pengo, Tamil, Toda, Yerava.	DR
	10(+2)	Bagri, Dogri, Gojri, Haryanvi, Jaunsari, Kacchi, (Kashmiri), Lahndi, Mahl, (Maithili), Punjabi, Sindhi.	I-A
		(Byangsi), Chaudangsi, Kangri, Manchad, Raji, RangPo, Rawang.	T-B
ɽʱ	02 (+1)	*Voiced aspirated retroflex flap*	
	(01)	(Juang).	A-A
	02	Manchad, RangPo.	T-B
Nasal flap			
ɽ̃	03	*Voiced retroflex nasal flap*	
	03	Gojri, Hindi, Urdu.	I-A
Fricatives	02		
ɸ	02	*Voiceless bilabial fricative*	
	01	G-Andamanese	AN
	01	Bishnupuria	C-V
β	03	*Voiced bilabial fricative*	
	03	Chokri, Tangsa, Wancho.	T-B
f		*Voiceless labio-dental fricative*	
	02	Nancowry, Nicobarese-C	A-A
	02(+4)	(Kannada), (Kodagu), (Malayalam), Tamil, (Telugu), Toda.	DR
	08(+2)	(Dogri), Gojri, Hindi, Lahndi, Mahl, (Marathi), Punjabi, Sindhi, Urdu, Urdu-D-H	I-A
	12(+3)	Adi, Angami, (Balti), Brokskat, Hmar, Khezha, Kinnauri, (Koren), Lepcha, Liangmai, Lotha, Mao-N, Mizo, (Purki), Sema-N.	T-B
	03	Diu-I-P, IE-H, Urdu-D-T	C-V

contd.

Table 3.1 *contd.*

v		*Voiced labio-dental fricative*	
	05	Gadaba-O, Kolami, Kota, Kuvi, Yerava.	DR
	02(+4)	(Hindi), Lahndi, Mahl, (Marathi), (Punjabi), (Urdu-D-H).	I-A
	14	Adi, Angami, Brokskat, Chokri, Hmar, Khezha, Kinnauri, Lepcha, Lotha, Mao-N, Mizo, Paite, Thaadou, Zo.	T-B
		Diu-I-P.	C-V
θ	02	*Voiceless inter-dental fricative*	
	02	Malto, Toda.	DR
s̪>	01	*Voiceless post-dental sibilant fricative*	
		Toda	DR
z̪>	01	*Voiced post-dental sibilant fricative*	
	01	Toda	DR
s		*Voiceless alveolar sibilant fricative*	
	15	Bhumij, Bonda, Didayi, Gadaba-G, Gorum, Ho, Juang, Kharia, Khasi, Kisan, Korku, Mundari, Nancowry, Nicobarese-C, Santali.	A-A
	25	Ave, Badaga, Gadaba-K, Gadaba-O, Gondi, Gondi-A, Irula, Kannada, Kattunaicka, Kodagu, Kolami, Konda, Koraga, Koya, Kui, Kurux, Kuvi, Malayalam, Malto, Manda, Naiki, Pengo, Telugu, Toda, Tulu.	DR
	3o	Assamese, Bagri, Bhili, Bhojpuri, Brokskat, Dogri, Garhwali, Gojri, Gujarati, Haryanvi, Hindi, Jaunsari, Kacchi, Kashmiri, Konkani, Lahndi, Lamani, Magahi, Mahl, Maithili, Mandeali, Marathi, Nepali, Oriya, Punjabi, Rathvi, Shina, Sindhi, Urdu, Urdu-D-H.	I-A
	53	Adi, Angami, Ao-N, Apatani, Balti, Bantawa, Byangsi, Chaudangsi, Chokri, Darma, Dimasa, Gallong, Galo, Galo-L, Garo, Hmar, Kabui, Kangri, Khezha, Kinnauri, Kiranti-K, Kokborok, Koren, Ladakhi, Lepcha, Liangmai, Limbu, Lotha, Magar, Manchad, Mao-N, Maring, Meitei, Mishmi, Mizo, Monpa, Padaam, Paite, Phom, Purki, Raji, RangPo, Sema-N, Spiti, Tibetan-St, Tamang, Tangsa, Tarao, Thaadou, Stod, Wancho, Zo.	T-B
	02	Khampti, Turung	T-K

contd.

Table 3.1 *contd.*

	02	G-Andamanese, Jarawa,	AN
	06	Bishnupuria, Diu-I-P, Halbi, IE-H, Nagamese, Urdu-D-T, Vagri-B.	C-V
	04	Sanskrit-Cl, Pali, Prakrit O-Telugu	H-V
z		*Voiced alveolar sibilant fricative*	
	06(+1)	Gadaba-K, (Kannada), Kattunaicka, Kolami, Gadaba-O, Pengo, Toda.	DR
	11(+3)	Assamese, Brokskat, (Dogri), Gojri, (Gujarati), Hindi, Kashmiri, Lahndi, Mahl, (Punjabi), Shina, Sindhi, Urdu, Urdu-D-H.	I-A
	22	Adi, Angami, Ao-N, Balti, Chokri, Dimasa, Hmar, Khezha, Kinnauri, Koren, Ladakhi, Lepcha, Liangmai, Lotha, Mao-N, Mishmi, Mizo, Monpa, Purki, Sema-N, Stod, Wancho.	T-B
	03(+2)	IE-H, Naga Pidgin, (Urdu-D-T), Vagri-B.	C-V
z^h	01	*Voiced aspirated alveolar sibilant fricative*	
	01	Monpa.	T-B
ʂ		*Voiceless retroflex sibilant fricative*	
	01	Santali.	A-A
	06(+3)	(Kannada), Kattunaicka, (Konda), (Kui), Malayalam, Tamil, Telugu, Toda, Tulu.	DR
	03(+1)	Brokskat, Mahl, (Maithili), Marathi.	I-A
	04	Byangsi, Kinnauri, Ladakhi, RangPo.	T-B
	01(+1)	(O-Telugu), Sanskrit-Cl.	H-V
ʐ		*Voiced retroflex sibilant fricative*	
	01	Toda.	DR
	02	Brokskat, Shina.	I-A
	15	Angami, Balti, Bodo, Byangsi, Chokri, Kinnauri, Ladakhi, Lepcha, Lotha, Mao-N, Phom, Purki, Sema-N, Stod, Wancho.	T-B
	01	Diu-I-P	C-V
ç<	03	*Voiceless pre-palatal sibilant fricative*	

contd.

Table 3.1 *contd.*

	01	Kannada	DR
	01	Bhili.	I-A
	01	Urdu-D-T	C-V
ʃ		*Voiceless post/palato-alveolar sibilant fricative*	
	05(+1)	(Kodagu), Koraga, Malayalam, Telugu, Toda, Tulu.	DR
	18(+1)	Bagri, Bengali, Brokskat, Chakma, Gojri, Gujarati, Hindi, Kashmiri, Lahndi, Lamani, (Maithili), Mandeali, Marathi, Punjabi, Shina, Sindhi, Urdu, Urdu-D-H.	I-A
	22	Adi, Angami, Balti, Bodo, Byangsi, Chokri, Kinnauri, Kiranti-K, Koren, Ladakhi, Lepcha, Lotha, Mao-N, Monpa, Phom, Purki, RangPo, Rawang, Sema-N, Tibetan-St, Stod, Wancho.	T-B
	03	Bishnupuria, Naga Pidgin, IE-H.	C-V
	01(+1)	(O-Telugu), Sanskrit-Cl.	H-V
ʒ		*Voiced palato-alveolar sibilant fricative*	
	01	Toda.	DR
	02	Brokskat, Shina.	I-A
	14	Angami, Balti, Bodo, Byangsi, Chokri, Kinnauri, Ladakhi, Lepcha, Lotha, Mao-N, Purki, Sema-N, Stod, Wancho.	T-B
	01	Diu-I-P	C-V
ç	05	*Voiceless palatal sibilant fricative*	
	01	Jaunsari	I-A
	04	Chaudangsi, Darma, Khezha, Tangsa.	T-B
ʝ	02	*Voiced palatal fricative*	
	01	Kolami.	DR
	01	Khezha.	T-B

contd.

Table 3.1 *contd.*

x		*Voiceless velar fricative*	
	02	Kurux, Toda.	DR
	09(+1)	Assamese, Brokskat, Dogri, Gojri, Hindi, Lahndi, (Punjabi), Shina, Sindhi, Urdu-D-H.	I-A
	09(+1)	Apatani, Balti, (Mao-N), Paite, Purki, Raji, Sema-N, Tangsa, Thaadou, Zo.	T-B
	01	G-Andamanese.	AN
ɣ		*Voiced velar fricative*	
	01	Malto.	DR
	08(+1)	Brokskat, Dogri, Gojri, Hindi, Lahndi, Mahl, (Punjabi), Shina, Sindhi.	I-A
	04	Balti, Chokri, Purki, Sema-N.	T-B
χ	03 (+1)	*Voiceless uvular fricative*	
	01	Lahndi.	I-A
	02(+1)	Chokri, Purki, (Tangsa).	T-B
ʁ	02 (+1)	*Voiced uvular fricative*	
	01	Malto.	DR
	(01)	(Lahndi).	I-A
	01	Chokri.	T-B
ħ	01	*Voiceless pharyngeal fricative*	
	01	Sanskrit-Cl.	H-V
ʕ	01 (+1)	*Voiced pharyngeal fricative*	
	01	Tulu.	DR
	(01)	(Tangsa)	T-B
h		*Voiceless glottal fricative*	

contd.

Table 3.1 *contd.*

	14 (+1)	Bhumij, Bonda, Didayi, Gadaba-G, Gorum, Ho, (Juang), Kharia, Khasi, Kisan, Korku, Mundari, Nancowry, Nicobarese-C, Santali.	A-A
	17 (+3)	Ave, Badaga, Gadaba-K, Gondi, (Gondi-A), Irula, Kannada, (Kodagu), (Konda), Koraga, Kui, Kurux, Kuvi, Malayalam, Malto, Manda, Naiki, Pengo, Tamil, Telugu.	DR
	28	Bagri, Bengali, Bhili, Bhojpuri, Brokskat, Chakma, Dogri, Garhwali, Gojri, Hindi, Jaunsari, Kashmiri, Konkani, Lahndi, Lamani, Magahi, Mahl, Maithili, Mandeali, Marathi, Nepali, Oriya, Punjabi, Rathvi, Shina, Sindhi, Urdu, Urdu-D-H.	I-A
	52 (+1)	Adi, Angami, Ao-N, Apatani, Balti, Bantawa, Byangsi, Chaudangsi, Chokri, Darma, Dimasa, Gallong, Galo-L, Garo, Hmar, Kabui, Karbi, Khezha, Kinnauri, Kiranti-K, Kokborok, Koren, Ladakhi, Lepcha, Liangmai, Lotha, Magar, Manchad, Mao-N, Maring, Meitei, Mishmi, Mizo, Monpa, (Padaam), Paite, Phom, Purki, Raji, RangPo, Sema-N, Spiti, Tibetan-St, Tamang, Tangsa, Tarao, Thaadou, Stod, Wancho, Zo.	T-B
	02	Khampti, Turung	T-K
	01	Jarawa	AN
	06	Diu-I-P, Halbi, IE-H, Nagamese, Urdu-D-T, Vagri-B.	C-V
	05	Sanskrit-Cl, Pali, Prakrit O-Telugu.	H-V
ɦ	08 (+1)	*Voiced glottal fricative*	
	02 (+1)	(Kolami), Koya, Tulu.	DR
	04	Assamese, Gujarati, Haryanvi, Kacchi.	I-A
	03	Galo, Khezha, Limbu.	T-B
	01	Bishnupuria.	C-V
Lat. Fricative			
ɮ		*Voiced alveolar lateral fricative*	
	01	Monpa.	T-B

contd.

Table 3.1 *contd.*

Approximants			
w		*Voiced labio-velar approximant*	
	09 (+2)	Bhumij, Bonda, Didayi, Gadaba-G, Gorum, Ho, Kharia, (Kisan), (Korku), Nicobarese-C, Santali.	A-A
	09	Gadaba-K, Irula, Koraga, Kurux, Malto, Pengo, Tamil, Telugu, Toda.	DR
	15 (+1)	Assamese, Bagri, Bengali, Bhojpuri, Chakma, Dogri, Garhwali, Gojri, Gujarati, Haryanvi, Jaunsari, Lamani, Magahi, (Maithili), Mandeali, Oriya.	I-A
	34 (+1)	Adi, Angami, Balti, Bantawa, Bodo, Byangsi, Chaudangsi, Chokri, Dimasa, Galo, Kabui, Kangri, Khezha, Kinnauri, Kokborok, Koren, Ladakhi, Limbu, Lotha, (Mao-N), Maring, Meitei, Mishmi, Mizo, Monpa, Phom, Purki, Raji, RangPo, Rawang, Sema-N, Tarao, Thaadou, Stod, Wancho.	T-B
	02	Khampti, Turung	T-K
	03	Bishnupuria, Diu-I-P, Nagamese.	C-V
	02	O-Tamil, O-Telugu.	H-V
^{h}w	02	*Pre-aspirated voiced labio-velar approximant*	
	02	Chaudangsi, Darma.	T-B
$w^{ɦ}$	01	*Voiced aspirated labia-velar approximant*	
	01	Khezha.	T-B
ʋ		*Voiced labio-dental approximant*	
	02	Mundari, Nancowry.	A-A
	13 (+3)	Ave, Badaga, Gondi-A, Kadar, (Kannada), Kattunaicka, Kodagu, (Konda), Koya, (Kui), Malayalam, Manda, Naiki, Tamil, Tulu, Yerava.	DR
	10(+1)	Bhili, (Gojri), Hindi, Kacchi, Kashmiri, Marathi, Nepali, Shina, Sindhi, Urdu, Urdu-D-H.	I-A
	01	Karbi.	T-B

contd.

Table 3.1 *contd.*

	03	Halbi, Urdu-D-T, Vagri Boli.	C-V
	03	Pali, Prakrit, Sanskrit-Cl.	H-V
ɹ	10	*Voiced alveolar lareral approximant*	
	02	Malayalam, Tulu.	DR
	05	Chaudangsi, Chokri, Darma, Liangmai, Raji.	T-B
	01	Turung	T-K
	02	O-Tamil, O-Telugu.	H-V
ɹ̥	01	*Voiceless alveolar lareral approximant*	
	01	Chokri	T-B
ɻ	02	*Voiceless retroflex approximant*	
	02	O-Tamil, O-Telugu	H-V
j	134 (+5)	*Voiced palatal approximants*	
	10 (+1)	Bhumij, Bonda, (Didayi), Gadaba-G, Gorum, Ho, Khasi, Kisan, Korku, Mundari, Nancowry.	A-A
	26 (+3)	Ave, Badaga, Gadaba-K, Gadaba-O, Gondi, Gondi-A, Irula, Kadar, Kannada, Kattunaicka, Kodagu, (Kolami), (Konda), Koraga, Kota, Koya, (Kui), Kurux, Kuvi, Malayalam, Malto, Manda, Naiki, Pengo, Tamil, Telugu, Toda, Tulu, Yerava.	DR
	31 (+1)	Assamese, Bagri, Bengali, Bhili, Bhojpuri, Brokskat, Chakma, Dogri, Garhwali, Gojri, Gujarati, Haryanvi, Hindi, Jaunsari, Kacchi, Kashmiri, Konkani, Lahndi, Lamani, Magahi, Mahl, (Maithili), Mandeali, Marathi, Nepali, Oriya, Punjabi, Rathvi, Shina, Sindhi, Urdu, Urdu-D-H.	I-A
	51	Adi, Angami, Ao-N, Apatani, Balti, Bantawa, Bodo, Byangsi, Chaudangsi, Chokri, Darma, Dimasa, Gallong, Galo, Galo-L, Kabui, Kangri, Karbi, Khezha, Kinnauri, Kiranti-K, Kokborok, Koren, Ladakhi, Lepcha, Liangmai, Limbu, Lotha, Magar, Manchad, Mao-N, Maring, Meitei, Mishmi, Mizo, Monpa, Padaam, Paite, Phom, Purki, Raji, RangPo, Rawang,Sema-N, Spiti, Tibetan-St, Tamang, Tarao, Thaadou, Stod, Wancho.	T-B
	02	Khampti, Turung	T-K

contd.

Table 3.1 *contd.*

	03	G-Andamanese, Jarawa, Onge	AN
	07	Bishnupuria, Diu-I-P, Halbi, IE-H, Nagamese, Urdu-D-T, Vagri-B.	C-V
	04	Sanskrit-Cl, Pali, O-Tamil, O-Telugu	H-V
ʰj	02	*Preaspirated voiced palatal approximant*	
	02	Chaudangsi, Darma.	T-B
jʱ	01	*Voiced aspirated palatal approximant*	
	01	Raji.	T-B
Lateral approximants			
l		*Voiced lateral approximant*	
	15	Bhumij, Bonda, Didayi, Gadaba-G, Gorum, Ho, Juang, Kharia, Khasi, Kisan, Korku, Mundari, Nancowry, Nicobarese-C, Santali.	A-A
	28	Ave, Badaga, Gadaba-K, Gadaba-O, Gondi, Gondi-A, Irula, Kadar, Kannada, Kattunaicka, Kodagu, Kolami, Konda, Koraga, Kota, Koya, Kui, Kurux, Kuvi, Malayalam, Malto, Manda, Naiki, Pengo, Tamil, Telugu, Toda, Tulu, Yerava.	DR
	32	Assamese, Bagri, Bengali, Bhili, Bhojpuri, Brokskat, Chakma, Dogri, Garhwali, Gojri, Gujarati, Haryanvi, Hindi, Jaunsari, Kacchi, Kashmiri, Konkani, Lahndi, Lamani, Magahi, Mahl, Maithili, Mandeali, Marathi, Nepali, Oriya, Punjabi, Rathvi, Shina, Sindhi, Urdu, Urdu-D-H.	I-A
	54 (+1)	Adi, Angami, Ao-N, Apatani, Balti, Bantawa, Bodo, Byangsi, Chaudangsi, Chokri, Darma, Dimasa, Gallong, Galo, Galo-L, (Garo), Hmar, Kabui, Kangri, Karbi, Khezha, Kinnauri, Kiranti-K, Kokborok, Koren, Ladakhi, Lepcha, Liangmai, Limbu, Lotha, Magar, Manchad, Mao-N, Maring, Meitei, Mishmi, Mizo, Monpa, Padaam, Paite, Phom, Purki, Raji, RangPo, Rawang,Sema-N, Spiti, Tibetan-St, Tamang, Tangsa, Tarao, Thaadou, Stod, Wancho, Zo.	T-B
	02	Khampti, Turung	T-K

contd.

Table 3.1 *contd.*

	03	G-Andamanese, Jarawa, Onge	AN
	07	Bishnupuria, Diu-I-P, Halbi, IE-H, Nagamese, Urdu-D-T, Vagri-B.	C-V
	05	Sanskrit-Cl, Pali, Prakrit O-Tamil, O-Telugu	H-V
ʰl	02	*Preaspirated voiced alveolar lateral approximant*	
	02	Chaudangsi, Darma.	T-B
l̥	04	*Voiceless alveolar lateral aproximant*	
	01	Toda.	DR
	03	Chokri, Maring, Zo.	T-B
l̥ʰ	02	*Voiceless aspirated lateral approximant*	
	02	Angami, Thaadou.	T-B
lʱ	09 (+1)	*Voiced aspirated lateral approximant*	
	02	Bhojpuri, Magahi.	I-A
	05 (+1)	Byangsi, Khezha, (Kiranti-K), Lotha, Mizo, RangPo.	T-B
	02	Halbi, Vagri-B.	C-V
ɭ		*Voiced retroflex lateral approximant*	
	03 (+1)	Bonda, Ho, (Juang), Korku.	A-A
	13	Badaga, Irula, Kadar, Kannada, Kattunaicka, Kodagu, Kota, Malayalam, Tamil, Telugu, Toda, Tulu, Yerava.	DR
	13	Bagri, Bhili, Gojri, Gujarati, Haryanvi, Kacchi, Lahndi, Lamani, Mahl, Mandeali, Marathi, Oriya, Punjabi.	I-A
	02	Kinnauri, Kangri.	T-B
	02	Urdu-D-T , Vagri Boli.	C-V
	03	O-Tamil, O-Telugu, Pali.	H-V
ɭ̥	01	*Voiceless retroflex lateral approximant*	
	01	Toda.	DR

contd.

Table 3.1 *contd.*

ɭʱ	01	*Voiced aspirated retroflex lateral approximant*	
	01	Pali.	H-V
Affricates			
pf	04	*Voiceless labio-dental affricate*	
	04	Angami, Chokri, Khezha, Mao-N.	T-B
pɸ	01	*Voiceless bilabial affricate*	
	01	Lotha.	T-B
bv	04	*Voiced labio-dental affricate*	
	04	Angami, Khezha, Lotha, Mao-N.	T-B
pfʰ	02	*Voiceless aspirated labio-dental affricate*	
	02	Angami, Khezha.	T-B
ts		*Voiceless dental/alveolar affricate*	
	05 (+1)	Gadaba-O, Kattunaicka, (Kolami), Kuvi, Gadaba-O, Toda.	DR
	06	Bhili, Brokskat, Jaunsari, Kashmiri, Nepali, Shina.	I-A
	23	Adi, Angami, Balti, Byangsi, Chaudangsi, Chokri, Darma, Karbi, Khezha, Kiranti-K, Ladakhi, Lepcha, Liangmai, Lotha, Mao-N, Mishmi, Mizo, Monpa, Purki, Rawang, Tangsa, Stod, Wancho, Zo.	T-B
	01	Khampti	T-K
dz		*Voiced dental/alveolar affricate*	
	04	Gadaba-O, Kattunaicka, Kuvi, Toda.	DR
	03	Bhili, Jaunsari, Nepali.	I-A
	17	Angami, Byangsi, Chokri, Darma, Karbi, Khezha, Kiranti-K, Ladakhi, Lepcha, Lotha, Mao-N, Mishmi, Monpa, Purki, Rawang, Stod, Zo.	T-B
tsʰ		*Voiceless aspirated dental/alveolar affricate*	
	04	Jaunsari, Kashmiri, Nepali, Shina.	I-A

contd.

Table 3.1 *contd.*

	12	Angami, Balti, Byangsi, Chaudangsi, Chokri, Darma, Karbi, Khezha, Ladakhi, Mishmi, Mizo, Stod.	T-B
dzʱ	02	*Voiced aspirated dental/alveolar affricate*	
	02	Bhili, Nepali.	I-A
ts>	01	*Voiceless post-alveolar affricates*	
	01	Limbu	T-B
dz>	01	*Voiced post-alveolar affricate*	
	01	Limbu	T-B
tsʰ>	01	*Voiceless aspirated post-alveolar affricate*	
	01	(Limbu)	T-B
ʧ>	02	*Voiceless pre-palatal affricate*	
	02	Paite, Turung.	T-B
ʤ>	02	*Voiced post-alveolar affricate*	
	02	Paite, Turung.	T-B
tʂ	01	*Voiceless retroflex affricate*	I-A
	01	Shina.	I-A
tʂʰ	01	*Voiceless aspirated retroflex affricate*	
	01	Shina.	I-A
tʃ		*Voiceless palato-alveolar affricate*	
	14	Bhumij, Bonda, Didayi, Gadaba-G, Gorum, Ho, Juang, Kharia, Kisan, Korku, Mundari, Nancowry, Nicobarese- C, Santali	A-A
	25 (+2)	Ave, Badaga, Gadaba-K, Gadaba-O, Gondi, Gondi-A, Irula, Kadar, Kannada, Kattunaicka, Kodagu, Kolami, (Konda), Koraga, Kota, Koya, (Kui), Kurux, Malayalam, Malto, Naiki, Pengo,Tamil, Telugu, Toda, Tulu, Yerava.	DR
	28	Bagri, Bengali, Bhili, Bhojpuri, Dogri, Gojri, Gujarati, Haryanvi, Hindi, Jaunsari, Kacchi, Kashmiri, Konkani, Lahndi, Lamani, Magahi, Mahl, Maithili, Mandeali, Marathi, Nepali, Oriya, Punjabi, Rathvi, Shina, Sindhi, Urdu, Urdu-D-H.	I-A

contd.

Table 3.1 *contd.*

	45	Adi, Angami, Ao-N, Apatani, Balti, Bantawa, Byangsi, Chaudangsi, Chokri, Darma, Dimasa, Gallong, Galo-L, Garo, Hmar, Kabui, Kangri, Karbi, Khezha, Kinnauri, Kiranti-K, Kokborok, Ladakhi, Liangmai, Limbu, Lotha, Magar, Manchad, Mao-N, Meitei, Monpa, Paite, Phom, Purki, RangPo, Rawang, Sema-N, Spiti, Stod, Tamang, Tarao, Thaadou, Tibetan-St, Wancho, Zo.	T-B
	02	Khampti, Turung	T-K
	03	G-Andamanese, Jarawa, Onge.	AN
	07	Bishnupuria, Diu-I-P, Halbi, IE-H, Nagamese, Urdu-D-T, Vagri-B	C-V
	05	O-Tamil, O-Telugu, Pali, Prakrit, Sanskrit-Cl.	H-V
tʃʰ		*Voiceless aspirated palato-alveolar affricate*	
	03 (+1)	Bhumij, Bonda, (Juang), Khasi.	A-A
	05 (+1)	Gadaba-K, Kurux, Malayalam, (Naiki), Telugu, Tulu.	DR
	26	Bagri, Bengali, Bhojpuri, Dogri, Garhwali, Gujarati, Haryanvi, Hindi, Jaunsari, Kacchi, Kashmiri, Konkani, Lahndi, Lamani, Magahi, Maithili, Mandeali, Marathi, Nepali, Oriya, Punjabi, Rathvi, Shina, Sindhi, Urdu, Urdu-D-H.	I-A
	31	Adi, Angami, Balti, Bantawa, Byangsi, Chaudangsi, Chokri, Darma, Dimasa, Galo-L, Hmar, Kangri, Karbi, Khezha, Kinnauri, Kiranti-K, Kokborok, Ladakhi, Liangmai, Limbu, Magar, Manchad, Monpa, Paite, Purki, RangPo, Spiti, Tibetan-St, Tamang, Stod, Zo.	T-B
	02	Khampti, Turung	T-K
	01	Jarawa	AN
	04/04	Halbi, Nagamese, Urdu-D-T, Vagri-B	C-V
		O-Telugu, Pali, Prakrit, Sanskrit-Cl.	H-V
ʤ		*Voiced palato-alveolar affricate*	
	13	Bhumij, Bonda, Didayi, Gadaba-G, Gorum, Ho, Juang, Kharia, Khasi, Kisan, Korku, Mundari, Santali	A-A

contd.

Table 3.1 *contd.*

	28	Ave, Badaga, Gadaba-K, Gadaba-O, Gondi, Gondi-A, Irula, Kadar, Kannada, Kattunaicka, Kodagu, Kolami, Konda, Koraga, Kota, Koya, Kui, Kurux, Malayalam, Malto, Manda, Naiki, Pengo, Tamil, Telugu, Toda, Tulu, Yerava.	DR
	28	Bagri, Bengali, Bhili, Bhojpuri, Dogri, Gojri, Gujarati, Haryanvi, Hindi, Jaunsari, Kacchi, Kashmiri, Konkani, Lahndi, Lamani, Magahi, Mahl, Maithili, Mandeali, Marathi, Nepali, Oriya, Punjabi, Rathvi, Shina, Sindhi, Urdu, Urdu-D-H.	I-A
	44	Adi, Angami, Apatani, Balti, Bantawa, Byangsi, Chaudangsi, Chokri, Darma, Dimasa, Gallong, Galo, Galo-L, Garo, Hmar, Kabui, Kangri, Karbi, Khezha, Kinnauri, Kiranti-K, Kokborok, Koren, Ladakhi, Lepcha, Liangmai, Limbu, Lotha, Magar, Manchad, Mao-N, Meitei, Monpa, Padaam, Paite, Purki, RangPo,Sema-N, Spiti, Tibetan-St, Tamang, Thaadou, Stod, Zo.	T-B
	02	Khampti, Turung	T-K
	03	G-Andamanese, Jarawa, Onge.	AN
		Bishnupuria, Diu-I-P, Halbi, IE-H, Nagamese, Vagri-B (05)	C-V
		O-Telugu, Pali, Prakrit, Sanskrit-Cl. (04)	H-V
ʤˀ	01	*Voiced glottalized palato-alveoalar affricate*	
	01	Bishnupuria.	C-V
ʤʱ		*Voiced aspirated palato-alveoalar affricate*	
	03 (+1)	Bhumij, Bonda, (Juang), Khasi.	A-A
	03 (+1)	Kurux, Malayalam, (Naiki), Telugu.	DR
	25	Bagri, Bengali, Bhili, Bhojpuri, Brokskat, Chakma, Garhwali, Gujarati, Haryanvi, Hindi, Jaunsari, Konkani, Lahndi, Lamani, Magahi, Maithili, Mandeali, Marathi, Nepali, Oriya, Rathvi, Shina, Sindhi, Urdu, Urdu-D-H.	I-A
	03	Bantawa, Chaudangsi, Raji.	T-B
	03 (+1)	Halbi, Nagamese, (Urdu-D-T), Vagri-B.	C-V

contd.

Table 3.1 *contd.*

	03 (+1)	(O-Telugu), Pali, Prakrit, Sanskrit-Cl.	H-V
Implosives			
ɓ	02	*Voiced bilabial implosive*	
	02	Kacchi, Sindhi.	I-A
ɗ>	01	*Voiced post-alveolar implosive*	
	01	Kacchi.	I-A
ᶑ	01	*Voiced retroflex implosive*	
	01	Sindhi.	I-A
ʄ	01	*Voiced palatal implosive*	
	01	Sindhi.	I-A
ɠ	01	*Voiced velar implosive*	
	01	Sindhi.	
Syllabic consonants[1]			
m̩	04	*Syllabic voiced bilabial nasal*	
	03	Angami, Chokri, Mao-N (?)	T-B
	01	Turung	T-K
b̩	01	*Syllabic voiced bilabial plosive*	
	01	Mao-N	T-B
n̩	04	*Syllabic voiced alveolar nasal*	
	03	Angami, Chokri, Mao-N (?)	T-B
	01	Turung	T-K
ɲ̩	01	*Syllabic voiced palatal nasal*	
	01	Angami	T-B
ŋ̩	04	*Syllabic voiced velar nasal*	

[1] Syllabic nasals have been noted in the source descriptions of the languages listed here, but they need to be better investigated.

Table 3.1 *contd.*

	03	Angami, Chokri, Mao-N (?)	T-B
	01	Turung	T-K
r̩	02	*Syllabic voiced dental trill*	
	02	Chokri, Mao-N (?)	T-B

Certain frequently occurring consonant phonemes in SPIL are not found to occur in some language listed in *Table 3.2.*

Table 3.2 Frequent consonant phonemes in SPIL, not occurring in some languages

*/p/:	*Voiceless bilabial plosive*	T-B
	Bodo, Rawang	
*/b/:	*Voiced Bilabial plosive*	T-B
	Ao, Khampti, Konyak, St Tibetan, Tamang	A-N
	Nancowry, Nicobarese-(C)	
	Old Tamil	H-V
*/t/:	*Voiceless alveolar plosive*	
	Assamese.	I-A
	Apatani, Bodo, Ladakhi, Mao, Rawang.	T-B
*/d/	*Voiced alveolar plosive*	
	Assamese.	I-A
	Apatani, Bodo, Galo, Khampti, Konyak, Ladakhi, Lotha, Mao, St Tibetan, Tamang, Tangsa.	T-B
	Nancowry, Nicobarese (Car)	A-N
	Old Tamil	H-V
*/ʈ/:	*Voiceless retroflex stop*	
	Assamese, Brokskat, Chakma	I-A
	Bantawa, Byangsi, Chaudangsi, Hmar, Kangri, Kinnauri, Kiranti-Koints,Ladakhi, Lepcha, RangPo, Tod.	T-B
	Great Andamanese, Jarawa, Onge, Nicobarese- Car.	A-N
	Naga Pidgin.	C-V
*/ɖ/:	*Voiced retroflex stop*	
	Assamese. Brokskat, Chakma	I-A

co

Table 3.2 *contd.*

	Bantawa, Byangsi, Hmar, Kangri, Kinnauri, Ladakhi, Lepcha, St Tibetan, Tamang Tod.	T-B
	Nancowry, Nicobarese- Car.	A-N
	Naga Pidgin.	C-V
	Old Tamil.	H-V
* /k/:	*Voiceless velar plosive*	
	Bodo, Rawang.	T-B
*/g/:	*Voiced velar plosive*	
	Khasi.	A-A
	Ao, Hmar, Khampti, Kheza, Konyak, (Koren), Lotha, Maring, Mizo, St Tibetan, Tamang Tangsa, (Tarao),	T-B
	Great Andamanese, Nancowry, Nicobarese- Car.	A-N
	Old Tamil.	H-V
*/m/:	*Voiced bilabial plosive*	
*/ɾ//r/:	*Voiced alveolar tap/ trill*	
	Koya, Kui	DR
	Haryanvi, Bengali, Bhojpuri, Chakma, Gujarati, Hindi, Lahndi, Mahl, Maithili.	I-A
	Ao, Gallong, Galo, Hmar, Konyak, Rawang, Tangsa, Thaadou.	T-B
	(Old Tamil), Pali, Prakrit.	H-V
*/s/:	*Voiceless alveolar sibilant fricative*	
	Kota, Yerava.	DR
	Bengali, Chakma.	I-A
	Bodo, Karbi	T-B
	Onge.	A-N
	Old Tamil.	H-V
*/h/:	*Voiceless glottal fricative*	
	(Juang).	A-A
	Gondi-A), Kattunaicka, (Kodagu), Kolami, (Konda), Kota, Koya, Ollari, Toda, Tulu, Yerava.	DR
	Assamese, Haryanvi, Gujarati, Kacchi.	I-A
	Galo, (Padaam), Singpho, Kangri.	T-B
	Great Andamanese, Onge.	A-N

contd.

Table 3.2 *contd.*

	Bishnupuria.	C-V
	Old Tamil.	H-V
*/j/:	*Voiced palatal approximants*	
	(Didayi), Juang, Kharia, Santali.	A-A
	(Kolami), (Konda), (Kui).	DR
	(Maithili).	I-A
	Garo, Hmar, Tangsa.	T-B
	Nicobarese- Car.	A-N
	Prakrit.	(H-C)
*/ʧ/	*Voiceless palatal affricate*	
	Khasi	A-A
	Kuvi, Malto	DR
	Bodo, Dimasa, Galo, Karbi, Khampti-Tai, Kiranti-K, Lepcha, Liangmai, Mishmi, Mizo, Padaam, Paite, St Tibetan, Tamang, Tangsa, Thaadou, Turung, Zo.	T-B
*/ʤ/	*Voiced palatal affricate*	
	Kadar, Kuvi, Malto	DR
	Ao, Bodo, Dimasa, Hmar, Karbi, Khampti-Tai, Kiranti-K, Liangmai, Limbu, Lotha, Maring, Mishmi, Mizo, Paite, Phom, Sema-Naga, St Tibetan, Tamang, Tangsa, Thaadou, Turung, Wancho, Zo.	T-B
	Jarawa, Nancowry, Nicobarese-C.	A-N
	Old Tamil	H-V

Table 3.3: Patterns of major classes of consonants in terms of laryngeal types.

ABBREVIATIONS

Laryngeal types: 1= voiceless unaspirated, 2= voiced unaspirated, 3= voiceless aspirated, 4= voiced aspirated,

Places of Articulation: Bilabial (A), Labio-Dental (B), Dental (C), Post-Dental (C1), Alveolar (D), Apico-Alveolar (D1), Post alveolar (E), Retroflex (F), Palato-Alveolar (G), Prepalatal (H), Palatal (I), Velar (J), Uvular (K), Pharyngeal (L), and Glottal (M).

Angled brackets <> indicate irregularity in pattern, parenthese ( ) indicate optionality of a Place of Articulation, and a slash (/) indicates either or between Places of Articulation.

P	PATTERN	PLACES	TOTAL	EXCEPTIONS	A-A	DR	I-A	T-B	T-K	AN	C-V	H-V
	1,2,3,4	ACFJM	17		Bhumij Gad-G Kisan	Kurux		Bantawa RaNPo				
	1,2,3,4	ADFJM	17		Bonda							
	1,2,3,4	ACFJK	17		Korku							
	1,2,3,4	ACFJ<K>	17	K has 1 only			Urdu					
	1,2,3,4	AC<D>FJ	17	D has no 3, 4		Malaya						
	1,2,3,4	ACFJ	16		Kharia Santali	Telugu Tulu	Bagri Bengali Bhojpuri Garhwali Gujarathi Haryanvi Hindi Lahndi Lamani Magahi Maithili Mandeali Marathi	Chaudan Manchad Raji			Bishnu Halbi VB	Pali Prakrit Sans

contd.

Table 3.3 *contd.*

							Nepali Oriya Rathvi Ur-D-H					
	1,2,3,4	AC/DEJ	16				Jaunsari					
	1,2,3,4	<A>CFJ	15	A has no 3			Konkani					
	1,2,3,4	ACF<J>	14	J has no 3, 4			Bhili					
	1,2,3,4	ACF<J><(K)> [12+2+1]	15	J has no 3, 4, K has 1 only as optional			Sindhi					
	1,2,3 (4)	ACFJ	12 +(4)	4 is optional				Spiti Stod				
	1,2(3) (4)	ACFIJ	10 (+10)								Ur-D-T	
	1,2(3) (4)	ACFJ	8+(8)	3, 4 are optional	Ho Juang	Kan-nada Naiki						O-Tel
	1,2,3,4	ADJ	12				Assame	Karbi			Na-game	
	1,2,3,4	ACJ	12				Chakma					
	1,2,3,4	AD1J	12					Magar				
	1,2,3,4	ACJ	12					Meitei				

contd.

Table 3.3 *contd.*

	1,2,3	ACDJ<K>	13	K has 1 only				Balti Purki				
	1,2,3	ACDJ<L>	13	L has 1 only			Brokskat					
	1,2,3	ACD<J>M	12	J has no 2				Mizo				
	1,2,3	ACFJ<(K)>	13	K has 1 only and is optional			Punjabi					
	1,2,3	ACFJ	12				Gojri Kacchi Kashmiri Shina	Kangri Kinnauri Ladakhi				
	1,2,3	<A><C>FJ	12+(2)	A C have optional 4				Byan				
	1,2,3	AC<F>JM	12	F has no 2				Kiran-K				
	1,2,3	ACF<J>	11	J has no 3				Hmar				
	1,2,3	A<C>JM	11	C also has 4				Adi				
	1,2,3	ADJM	10					Phom Thaadou				
	1,2,3	ADJ	9					Angami Chokri Mao-N Mishmi Zo				

contd.

Table 3.3 *contd.*

	1,2,3	ACJ	9					Darma Kabui Kokboro Monpa				
	1,2,3	AD(J)	8 +(1)	2 is optional in J				Tarao				
	1,2,3	AC<J>	8	J has no 2				Maring				
	1,2,3	AD<J>M	9	J has no 3				Paite				
	1,2,3	<A>DJ	8	A has no 3				Liangmai				
	1,2,3	AC/DJM	10						Turung			
	1,2,3	AC1JM	10		Khasi							
	1,2,3	AD(J)M	9 + (1)	2 is optional in J				Wancho				
	1,2,3	ACF<J>	11	J has no 3			Dogri					
	1,2,3	AD1 <J><J1>	10					Khezha				
	1,2,3	AC<(J)>M	10	2 is optional In J				Koren				
	1,2,4	A<C>F<J>M	11 + (2)	C and J have 3 as optional and no 4	Didayi							
	1,2,(4)	A<C>FJ	8 + (3)	C does not have optional 4							IE-H	
	1,2	A C D F I J	12			Toda						

contd.

Table 3.3 *contd.*

	1,2	A C F I J M	11					Tib-St				
	1,2	AD<F>J(K)(M)	11	K and M have 1 as optional and F has 4						Jara-wa		
	1,2	A C D F J	10			Irula Kota		Lepcha				
	1,2	ACFJK	10			Malto						
	1,2	ACFJ	8		Mundari	Ave Badaga Gad-K Gondi Gondi-A Kattu Kodagu Kolami Koraga Koya Manda Gad-O Pengo Yerava				Onge		
	1,2	AC<D>FJ	9	D has only 1		Tamil						
	1,2	ACFJM	9		Gorum	Konda Kui Kuvi	Mahl					

contd.

Table 3.3 *contd.*

	1,2	A<C>FJ	10	C has also 3 and J has not 2						G-A		
	1,2	ACJM	7					Garo Gallong				
	1,2	ADJ(M)	6 + (1)	M is optional				Galo- L				
	1,2	ADJ	6					Apatani Bodo Sema-N			Diu-IP	
	1,2	ACJ	6					Padaam				
	1,2	A<C><D>J	6	C has no 2 and D has no 1				Galo				
	1,2	AEJ	6					Dimasa				
	1,3	ACFJ	8					Tamang				
	1,3	ACJM	7						Khamp			
	1,3	<A>CJ	7	A has 2				Lotha				
	2,3	ADJM	7					Rawang				
	1	ACDFJ	5									O-Tam
	1	<A>CFJ	5	A also has 2		Kadar						
	1	ADJM	4		Nanco							
	1	ADFJ	4		Nico-C							
	1	ADJ	3					Ao-N				

contd.

Table 3.3 *contd.*

	Variant	ACFJM	8 + (7)					Limbu				
	Variant	AC/DJM	8					Tangsa				
	Nil				Nil	Nil	Nil	Nil	Nil	Nil	Nil	Nil
P-P	**Pattern**	**Places**	**Total**	**Exceptions**	**A-A**	**DR**	**I-A**	**T-B**	**T-K**	**AN**	**C-V**	**H-V**
	1 3	J	2					Tib- St				
L-P	**Pattern**	**Places**	**Total**	**Exceptions**	**A-A**	**DR**	**I-A**	**T-B**	**T-K**	**AN**	**C-V**	**H-V**
	1 3	J	2					Khezha				
G-P	**Pattern**	**Places**	**Total**	**Exceptions**	**A-A**	**DR**	**I-A**	**T-B**	**T-K**	**AN**	**C-V**	**H-V**
	2	A CFJ	4								Bishnu	
AF	**Pattern**	**Places**	**Total**	**Exceptions**	**A-A**	**DR**	**I-A**	**T-B**	**T-K**	**AN**	**C-V**	**H-V**
	1,2,3,4	I	4		Bhumij Bonda Gad-G Kharia Kisan Korku	Kurux Malaya Telugu Tulu	Bagri Bengali Bhojpuri Chakma Garhwali Gujarati Haryan Hindi Jaunsari Lahndi Lamani Magahi	Bantawa Chaudan Magar Raji RanPo			Halbi Na- game VB	Pali Prakrit Sans

contd.

Table 3.3 *contd.*

							Maithili Mandeali Marathi Nepali Oriya Rathvi Shina					
							Sindhi Urdu Ur-D-H					
	1 ,2,3,4	<C>I	6	C has only 1,3				Chaudan				
	1, 2,3,4	<C>I	7	C has no 3			Konkani					
	1,2,(3), (4)	I	2 + (2)		Juang	Kan-nada Naiki					Ur-D-T	O-Tel
	1,2,3	DI	7	I also has 4 as optional				Spiti Stod				
	1,2,3	AD1I	9					Khezha				
	1,2,3	ADI	9					Angami				
	1,2,3	<A>DI	7	A has only 1				Chokri				
	1,2,3	CI	6					Darma				
	1,2,3	<C>I	5	C has no 2			Kashmiri	Balti				
	1,2,3	DI	6					Byangsi Ladakhi				

contd.

Table 3.3 *contd.*

	1,2,3	<D>I	5	D has no3				Monpa Purki				
	1,2,3	<D>I	4	D has no 2 3			Brokskat					
	1,2,3	I	3				Dogri Gojri Kacchi Punjabi	Adi Kinnauri Kokbo Kangri				
	1,2,3	D	3					Karbi Mishimi				
	1,2(3)	E	3					Limbu				
	1,2,4	DH	6				Bhili					
	1,2(4)	I	2 (+1)					Meitei				
	1,2	ADI	6					Mao-N				
	1,2	DI	4					Rawang				
	1,2	CI	4			Kattu Gad-O						
	1,2	C1G	4			Toda						
	1,2	<D>I	3	D has no1		Koraga						
	1,2	(<C>)I	3	C has no2 and 1 is optional		Kolami						
	1,2	<C>I	3	C has no2				Tangsa				

contd.

Table 3.3 *contd.*

	1,2	I	2		Didayi Gorum Ho Mundari Santali	Ave Badaga Gad-K Gondi Gondi-A Irula Kodagu Kota Pengo Tamil Yerava Koya		Apatani Garo Thaadou Gallong Kabui Tarao Koiren		G-A Onge	Bishnu Diu-IP IE-H	
	1,2	C	2			Kuvi		Kiran-K Lepcha				
	1,2	D	2				Mahl					
	1,2	H	2					Paite	Turung			
	(1)2	I	2			Kui Konda						
	1,3	<A>DI	6	A has 2no3				Lotha				
	1,3	C(F)G	4 (+2)					Tib-St				
	1,3	D						Mizo				
	1,3	H	2					Tamang				
	1	I	1		Nanco Nico-C	Kadar		Ao-N Hmar Maring Phom Tarao				O-Tam

contd.

Table 3.3 *contd.*

	1	D	1					Liangmai Thaadou	Khamp			
	1	C	1					Tangsa				
	1	CI	2					Wancho		Jara- wa		
	2	I			Khasi	Manda		Galo Lepcha Padaam Sema-N				
	Nil				Nil	Nil	Assame	Nil	Nil	Nil	Nil	Nil
G-AF	**Pattern**	**Places**	**Total**	**Exceptions**	**A-A**	**DR**	**I-A**	**T-B**	**T-K**	**AN**	**C-V**	**H-V**
	2	I	1								Bishnu	
N	**Pattern**	**Places**	**Total**	**Exceptions**	**A-A**	**DR**	**I-A**	**T-B**	**T-K**	**AN**	**C-V**	**H-V**
	2,4	ADIJ	8					Lotha Sema- N				
	2,4	AD1 J	6					Magar				
	2,6	AD <J>	5	J has no 6				Darma				
	2,4	AD1 <J>	5	J has no 4				Khezha				
	2,4	AC<J>	5	J has no 4			Bhojpuri Magahi					
	1,2	ADI<J>	7	J has no 1				Angami				

contd.

Table 3.3 *contd.*

	1,2	AC<I><J>	6	IJ have no 1				Byangsi				
	2	<A><C>FIJ	7	A and C also have 4				RaNPo				
	2	<A>B<C>IJ	7	A and C also have 1				Chokri				
	2	<A><C>DIJ	7	A and C also have 4							VB	
	2	<A><D>FJ	6	A and D also have 4				Raji				
	2	ACDFIJ	6			Kadar Malaya						
	2	ACDFI(J)	5 + (1)	J is optional								O-Tam
	2	ACDFI	5			Tamil						
	2	ACFIJ	5			Tulu	Punjabi					
	2	ADFIJ	5		Bonda Ho Kharia Santali	Koraga Yerava Katttu	Gujarati Lahndi					Sans
	2	ADF(I)J	**5**	In I 2 is optional		Gad-O						
	2	AD(F)IJ	4 + (1)	F is optional				Spiti				
	2	ACF(I)J	4 + (1)	I is optional	Mundari		Dogri					

contd.

Table 3.3 *contd.*

	2	ADFJ	4		Bhumij Gad-G Kisan	Ave Konda Kota Kui Kuvi	Lamani Shina					
	2	ACFJ	4		Juang	Gad-K Manda Pengo	Haryanvi Kacchi Oriya	Kinnauri				O-Tel
	2	AC(F)J	3 (+1)					Limbu				
	2	ADFI	4			Kodagu						
	2	ADIJ	4		Khasi Nanco Nico-C	Malto		Gallong Galo-L Koiren Monpa Paadam Phom Purki Stod		G-A Jara- wa Onge		
	2	ACIJ	4				Sindhi	Balti Galo Ladakhi Lepcha Monpa Stod Tib-St				
	2	AC/DIJ	4						Turung			

contd.

Table 3.3 *contd.*

	2	A<C>J	4	C also has 4				Kiran-K				
	2	ADF(J)	3 + (1)	J is optional			Marathi Ur-D-H					
	2	ACF (J)	3 + (1)			Toda						
	2	ACF	3			Badaga Irula Telugu	Rathvi Gojri Mahl					
	2	ACJ	3		Didayi Gorum	Gondi Kolami Naiki	Bengali Brokskat Nepali	Hmar Kabui Kokbor Maring Meitei Tamang Tangsa	Khamp		Bishnu	
	2	<A><C>J	3(+2)	A and C also have 4							Halbi	
	2	ADJ	3			Gondi-A	Assame Chakma	Adi Ao-N Apatani Bantawa			Diu-IP IE-H Na-game	
								Bodo Dimasa Garo Liangmai				

contd.

Table 3.3 *contd.*

								Mishmi Mizo Paite Rawang Thaadou Torao Wancho Zo				
	2	ADF	3		Korku	Kan- nada Koya	Bagri Garhwali Mandeali	Kangri			Ur-D-T	
	2	A<D>F	4	D also has 1			Jaunsari					
	2	AD(F)	2 + (1)	F is optional			Maithili					
	2	AD(J)	2 + (1)	J is optional			Hindi Urdu					
	2	AF	2									Pali Prakrit
	2	AD	2			Kurux	Kashmiri					
	Variant	AD	3				Bhili					
		ADFIJ	7				Konkani					
		ADFJ	6					Chaudang				
	Pattern	**Places**	**Total**	**Exceptions**	**A-A**	**DR**	**I-A**	**T-B**	**T-K**	**AN**	**C-V**	**H-V**
TR												

contd.

Table 3.3 *contd.*

	1,2	D	2			Konda		Chokri Mao-N Lepcha				
	1,2	C	2					Byangsi Tib-St				
	2,3	D	2					Angami Mizo				
	2,4	D	2					Lotha Manchad Raji RaNPo				
	2,4	D1	2					Khezha Magar				
	2,(4)	D	1(+1)								Halbi	
	2,6	D	2					Chaudan Darma				
	2,4	C<K>	3	K has no 4							VB	
	2	DK	2			Gondi Gondi-A						
	2	DF	2			Irula						
	2	DE	2			Tamil						
	2	C1D	2			Toda						
	2	E	1			Kattu						

contd.

Table 3.3 *contd.*

	2	C	1		Didayi							
	2	D	1		Bhumij Bonda Gad-G Gorum Ho Juang Kharia Khasi Kisan Korku Mndari Nanco	Ave Badaga Gad-K Gad-O Kadar Kan- nada Kodagu Koraga Kota Kurux Kuvi	Bhili Garhwali Gojri Jaunsari Kacchi Kashmiri Mahl Mandeali Nepali Oriya Punjabi Shina.	Apatani Balti Bantawa Bodo Chokri Dimasa Gallong Galo-L Garo Kabui Kangri Karbi	Khamp	G-A Jara- wa Onge	Bishnu Diu-IP Na- game Ur-D-T	O-Tel Sans
					Nico-C Santali	Malaya Malto Manda Naiki Telugu Toda Tulu Yerava	Ur-D-H	Kiran-K Koren Kokbo Ladakhi Limbu Maring Meitei Mishmi Monpa Padaam Purki Sema-N Tarao Tod				
	2	C1	1			Kolami	Chakma					

contd.

Table 3.3 *contd.*

	2	C	1		Didayi	Pengo	Brokskat Dogri Sindhi	Galo Kinnauri Spiti Tamang				
	Pattern	**Places**	**Total**	**Exceptions**	**A-A**	**DR**	**I-A**	**T-B**	**T-K**	**AN**	**C-V**	**H-V**
TP												
	2,4	D	2				Bhojpuri Magahi					
	2	C1	1			Toda						
	2	C/D	1					Tangsa				
	2	D	1		Nico-C	Kattu Konda Koya Kui Malaya	Bagri Bengali Gujarati Haryanvi Hindi	Ao-N Byangsi Chokri Hmar Spiti		G- And	IE- H	O-Tamil O- Telugu Pali Prakrit
						Malto Tulu	Kacchi Konkani Lahndi Lamani Maithili Marathi Rathvi Urdu Ur-D-H	Tarao				

contd.

Table 3.3 *contd.*

	2	E	1				Assame Chakma					
	Pattern	**Places**	**Total**	**Exceptions**	**A-A**	**DR**	**I-A**	**T-B**	**T-K**	**AN**	**C-V**	**H-V**
FP												
	2,4	F	2					Manchad RaNPo				
	2,(4)	F	1 + (1)		Juang							
	2	F	1		Bhumij Ho Juang Kharia Kisan Korku	Ave Gad-K Gad-O Kattu Konda Koraga	Bagri Dogri Gojri Haryanvi Kacchi (Kashmi)	(Byang) Chaudan Kangri Raji Rawang		Jara- wa	VB	
					Mundar Santali	Kota Kui Kurux Kuvi Malto Manda Pengo Tamil Toda Yerava	Lahndi Mahl (Maithili) Punjabi Sindhi					
	Pattern	**Places**	**Total**	**Exceptions**	**A-A**	**DR**	**I-A**	**T-B**	**T-K**	**AN**	**C-V**	**H-V**
NF	2	F	1				Gojri Hindi Urdu					

contd.

Table 3.3 *contd.*

	Pattern	Places	Total	Exceptions	A-A	DR	I-A	T-B	T-K	AN	C-V	H-V
FR												
	1,2	BDEJ(K)M	11 + (1)	In K 2 is optional			Lahndi					
	1,2	BCEFJM	11	M has no 2			Brokskat					
	1,2	<B><Ci>C1DGF <J>	11	B CJ have no 2		Toda						
	1,2	<A><B>DG<J>K <M>	10	A B J have no 1 M has no 2				Chokri				
	1,2	BDGFM	9					Kinnauri				
	1,2	(B)DEJ<K><M>	9	BKM have no 2. B is optional.				Purki				
	1,2	(B)DG**J1**M	8 (+2)	B is optional				Balti				
	1,2	BD1IM	8					Khezha				
	1,2	BDE(J)M	8	J has no 2nd 1is optional				Mao-N				
	1,2	(B)DEJM	8	B is optional				Sema-N				
	1,2	DE<F>JM	8	F has no1			Shina					

contd.

Table 3.3 *contd.*

	1,2	BDEM	7	M has no 2				Angami Lepcha Lotha				
	1,2	BDEJM	8	E and M have only 1			Urdu					
	1,2	DEFM	7	M has no 2				Ladakhi				
	1,2	DE<F>M	7	F has no 2				Spiti				
	1,2	BDD2	5 (+1)	2 is optional in D2							Diu-IP	
	1,2	BDJM	6	J and M has no 2			Mahl					
	1,2	<A>DE<M>	6	A has no 1 M has no 2				Wancho				
	1,2	BD<E>M	6	F has no 2				Adi				
	1,2	DE<M>	5	M has only 1				Stod				
	1,2	CM	3			Pengo					VB	
	1,2	D<F>	3	F has no 2		Kattu						
	1,2	<B>D	3			Gada-O						
	1,2	EM	3	M has no 2			Chakma	Magar				
	1	B<D>E<J>M	7	D and J have also 2			Gojri					

contd.

Table 3.3 *contd.*

	1	<A>CIJ(<L>)M	6	A L have 2. L is optional				Tangsa				
	1	(B)<D>EM	5	D also has 2 B is Optional				Koren				
	1	DEFL<M>	5	M has 2		Tulu						Sans
	1	B<D>EM	5	D also has 2							IE-H	
	2	B<C1>I(M)	5	C1 has2 in M 2 optional		Kolami						
	1	(B) (C)<J>M	4 + (2)	B is optional D also has optional 2 J also has 2.			Dogri					
	1	(B)<D>FHM	6 +(2)	B is optional; D also has optional2		Kan-nada						
	1	<B>DEJM	6 +(2)	B has optional 2; D also has 2			Ur-D-H					
	1	(B)<D>FHM	4+ (2)	B is optional D has also 2 which is optional							Ur-D-T	
	1	(B)DEFM	4 + (1)	In B 1 is optional		Malaya Telugu						

contd.

Table 3.3 *contd.*

	1	<B>D(J)M	3 (+1)	B is 2 J is optional				Thaadou				
	1	<B>DJM	5	B has also 2			Konkani					
	1	C/DEIM	4				Jaunsari					
	1	BDIM	4		Khasi							
	1	ADEM	4								Bishnu	
	1	<D>EM	4	D also has 2							Na-game	
	1	<B>DEF<M>	4	B also has 2, and M has 2			Marathi					
	1	<D>EM	**4**	D also has 2			Kashmiri					
	1	CEFM	4					RaNPo				
	1	D(F)(I)M	4	2 is optional in Fand I								O-Tel
	1	CiD<K>M	4	K has no 1but 2		Malto						

contd.

Table 3.3 *contd.*

	1	<(B)><D>E(J)M	3 + (4)	B has 2 optional no 1; D has also 2as optional; J has 1 and 2 both optional			Punjabi					
	1	BDM	3		Nanco Nico-C							
	1	B<D>M	4	D also has 2				Liangmai				
	1	<B>DM	3	B has no1 but 2		Kuvi		Zo				
	1	E<F>M	3	F is 2.				Phom				
	1	DGM	3					Kiran- K				
	1	BDF	3			Tamil						
	1	DJM	3			Kurux		Apatani Raji				
	1	DEM	3			Koraga	Lamani Mandeali	Rawang Byangsi				
	1	DIM	3					Chaudan Darma				
	1	ADJ	3							G-A		
	1	DGM	3				Bhili					

contd.

Table 3.3 *contd.*

	1	CFM	3					Tib-St				
	1	DFM	3		Santali							
	1	A<(B)>(D)(E)M	2 +(4)	B also has 2 optionally						Jara- wa		
	2	BDM	3					Hmar Mizo				
	1	D(E)(F)M	2 + (2)	E and F are Optional			Maithili					
	1	D(F)M	2 + (1)	F optional		Kui						
	1	DM	2		Bhumij Bonda Didayi Gad-G	Ave Badaga Gondi Koya	Bagri Haryanvi Oriya	Ao-N Galo-L Bantawa Gallong	Khamp Turung		Halbi	
					Ho Kisan Korku Mundari	Manda Gad-K		Garo Kabui Kokbo Maring Meitei Mishmi				
	1	DJ	2				Rathvi					
	1	CM	2		Kharia		Bhojpuri Magahi	Galo Tamang				Pali Prakrit
	1	D(M)	2		Juang	Gondi-A		Padaam				

contd.

Table 3.3 *contd.*

	1	DI	2			Naiki		Tarao				
	2	BI	2			Yerava						
	1	(B)D(E)(M)	1 + (3)	B E M are optional		Kodagu						
	1	D(F)(M)	1 + (2)	F M optional		Konda						
	2	B	1			Kota						
	1	D	1		Gorum							
	1	I	1				Bengali					
	1	M	1					Karbi				
	Variant	ACEJM	7				Sindhi					
	Variant	BDEJM	6 (+2)				Hindi					
	Variant	DM	2				Nepali	Limbu				
	Variant	DM	3				Nepali	Dimasa				
	Variant	EM	2				Kacchi					
	Variant	EM	3				Kacchi	Bodo				
	Variant	DJM	5				Assa-mese					
	Variant	DEM	3(+1)				Gujarati					
	Variant	DEM	5					Monpa				

contd.

Table 3.3 *contd.*

	Pattern	Places	Total	Exceptions	A-A	DR	I-A	T-B	T-K	AN	C-V	H-V
AX												
	2,6	A <D> I	5	D has only 2				Chaudan Darma				
	2	ABFI	4			Tamil						
	2	A<D>I	4	D also has 2				Chokri				
	2	AEI	3				Assame	Liangmai				
	2	AFI	3									O-TEL
	2	BDI	3			Malaya						
	2	A(B)I	2(+1)				Gojri Punjabi					
	2	AI	2		Bhumij Bonda Gad-G Gorum Ho Kharia Khasi	Gad-K Irula Koragu Kurux Malto Pengo Telugu Toda	Bengali Chakma Dogri Garhwali Gujarati Haryanvi Jaunsari Lamani Magahi Oriya	Adi Angami Balti Batawa Bodo Byangsi Dimasa Kabui Kinnauri Kiran-K Koren	Khamp Turung	G-A Jar- wa Onge	Bishnu Diu-IP IE-H Na- game	

contd.

Table 3.3 *contd.*

								Kokboro Ladakhi Limbu Lotha Magar Maring Meitei Mishmi Mizo Monpa RaNPo Rawang Sema-N Spiti Tib-St Stod Tarao Thaadou Wancho				
	2	BI	2		Mundari Nancowry	Badaga Gondi	Bagri Bhili	Ao-N Karbi			Halbi IE-H	Pali Sanskr
						Gondi-A Kadar Kuttu Kodagu Koya Naiki Yerava	Bhojpuri Hindi Kacchi Kashmiri Marathi Rathvi Shina Sindhi Urdu Ur-D-H	Kangri			VB	

contd.

Table 3.3 *contd.*

	2	(AI)	(2)				Nepali	Tamang				
	2	AI	2		Kisan							
	2	FI	2									OTam
	2	D(I)	1 + (1)	D is optional	Juang							
	2	A(I)	1 + (1)	I is optional	Didayi							
	2	(A)I	1 + (1)	A is optional	Korku			Mao-N				
	2	A	1		Santali Nicoba- rese			Garo				Prakrit
	2	D	1				Shina					
	2	I	1			Kan- nada Kota Kuvi Gad-O	Brokskat Konkani Lahndi Marathi Mahl	Apatani Gallong Galo Galo-L Lepcha				
	2	(B)(I)	(2)	B and I are optional		Konda Kui						
	Pattern	**Places**	**Total**	**Exceptions**	**A-A**	**DR**	**I-A**	**T-B**	**T-K**	**AN**	**C-V**	**H-V**
LA												
	1,2	C1F	4			Toda						
	1,2	C	2					St Tib				

contd.

Table 3.3 *contd.*

	1,2	D	2					Angami Chokri Maring Byangsi				
	2,4	D	2				Bhojpuri Magahi	Lotha				
	2,(4)	D	1 (+1)								Halbi	
	2,4	D1	2					Magar Monpa Raji				
	2,4	F	2					Zo				
	2,6	D	2					Chaudan Darma				
	2	<C>F	3	C also has 4							VB	
	2	<D>F	3	D also has 4				RangPo				
	2	D<F>	3	F also has 4								Pali
	2	CF	2									O-Tam O-Tel
	2	DF	2		Bonda Ho Korku	Badaga Irula Kadar Kan- nada Kattu	Bagri Bhili Gujarati Haryanvi Kacci Lahndi	Kinnauri		Jara- wa	Ur-D -T	

contd.

Table 3.3 *contd.*

						Kodagu Kota Malaya Tamil Telugu Tulu Yerava.	Mahl Oriya Punjabi Ur-D-H					
	2	D(F)	1 + (1)	F is optional	Juang							
	2	C1(F)	1 + (1)	F is optional		Kolami						
	2	C	1		Kharia	Pengo	Brokskat Dogri Sindhi	Gallong Tamang Tangsa				
	2	D	1		Bhumij Didayi Gad-G Gorum Khasi Kisan Mundar Nanco Nicoba Santali	Ave Gad-K Gad-O Gondi Gondi-A Konda Koraga Koya Kui Kurux Kuvi	Assame Bengali Chakma Garhwali Rathvi Hindi Kashmiri Maithili Hindi Nepali Ur-D-H	Adi Ao-N Apatani Balti Bantawa Bodo Dimasa Garo-L Hmar Kabui Kiranti-K	Khamp Turung	G-A Onge	Bishnu Na- game Diu-IP IE-H	Prakrit Sanskr
						Malto Manda Naiki		Koiren Kokbo Ladakhi Lepcha Liangmai				

contd.

Table 3.3 *contd.*

								Limbu Meitei Mikir Mishmi Mizo Paadam Paite Phom Purki Rawang Sema-N Stod Tarao Thaadou Wancho				
	2	C/D	1					Turung				
	Pattern	**Places**	**Total**	**Exceptions**	**A-A**	**DR**	**I-A**	**T-B**	**T-K**	**AN**	**C-V**	**H-V**
LF												
	1	D	1					Thaadou				
	2	D	1					Ao-N				
IMP												
	2	AFIJ	4				Sindhi					
	2	AE	2				Kacchi					

The main properties of the patterning of consonant phonemes, as presented in *Tables 3.1–3.3* are discussed below.

3.1.1 Air-stream

All the 148 languages included here have speech sounds produced by the pulmonic egressive air-stream mechanism. Two of the languages, Sindhi and one of its varieties, Kacchi, both Indo-Aryan, have implosives, produced by the ingressive pulmonic air-stream mechanism.

3.1.2 Manners of articulation

Twelve types of MANNERS OF ARTICULATION are found for the consonant phonemes in Indic languages. These are – PLOSIVE (P, for short), NASAL (N), TRILL (TR), TAP (TP), FLAP (FL), NASAL FLAP (NF), FRICATIVE (FR), APPROXIMANT (AX), LATERAL APPROXIMANT (LA), LATERAL FRICATIVE (LF), AFFRICATE (AF), and IMPLOSIVE (IMP). Plosive and affricate are together referred to as STOP (S). Some other terms that are used here as found in the literature are OBSTRUENTS, SONORANTS, RHOTICS, DORSAL and SIBILANT FRICATIVES. There is one class of consonants that cuts across some of the sonorant manner types, such as the nasal and lateral approximant, namely, SYLLABIC CONSONANTS (SC). See, for example, *Table 3.8*.

Note that in the tables on frequency counts presented in this chapter, the twelve manners of articulation listed above are used exclusively for themselves. In other words, for example, a lateral approximant is not counted as an approximant. In the course of preparing the phonological sketches with reference to the sounds found in the languages, the following points about the manners of articulation have claimed our attention.

a. PLOSIVE/AFFRICATE in the palatal place of articulation. For PALATAL STOPS, it was difficult to decide whether they are plosives or affricates. Most descriptions classifying them either way do not give justification for their classification. Thus the IPA descriptions for Hindi by Ohala (1999) and for Sindhi by Nihalani (1995) classify them as plosives and affricates respectively. In languages in which palatal stops pattern in congruity with the plosives, as in a majority of the Indo-Aryan languages, the single classification of palatal and other stops as plosives is understandable, especially since the orthographic tradition in Brāhmī- derived scripts supports it. However, in the languages in which the palatal stops pattern differently from non-palatal stops, the issue of the classification of palatal stops as plosives or affricates is of interest. Because of the need to determine the issue on physical phonetic evidence, pending such evidence, we have chosen to classify all palatal stops as affricates, unless argued otherwise. The only cases here of palatal stops treated as plosives here are of Toda, which have been shown (Nara and Bhaskararao 2–2) to be stops, besides post-dental and alveo-palatal affricates, and of Classical Tibetan, which has also been claimed to have palatal stops, but alveo-palatal affricates. The decision to treat palatal stops as affricates can be considered to be less controversial for languages in which palatal stops have incongruous patterns in relation to the rest of the stop series. Some of the languages in which this is the case are Jarawa (A-N), Kabui , Koren, Lepcha (T-B), Didayi, Khasi, Santali (A-A) and Shina (I-A), among others.

b. TAP/TRILL distinction. One of the areas where the reader is likely to encounter a somewhat loose use of terms in some of the works is the TAP/TRILL/FLAP distinction and the use of the corresponding IPA symbols. The distinction however is important keeping in view the fact that languages may contrast them. There are languages in SPIL that contrast a trill and a tap in different places, e.g. Spiti (T-B), as well as in the same place, e.g. Tarao (T-B). There is at least one language variety that has contrasts between all the three manners- trill, tap and flap- namely, Old Telugu. Some languages have only a rhotic approximant, e.g. Liangmai (T-B) and Turung (T-K). There are also languages that don't have a rhotic at all, e.g., Wancho and Zo (T-B).

The different manners of articulation are listed in *Table 3.4* with their frequency of occurrence. This as well as the following tables may be read with the help of the legend reproduced below:

P= PLOSIVE, N= NASAL, TR= TRILL, TP= TAP, FL= FLAP, NF= NASAL FLAP, FR= FRICATIVE, AX= APPROXIMANT, LA= LATERAL APPROXIMANT, LF = LATERAL FRICATIVE, AF = AFFRICATE, and Imp= IMPLOSIVE.

Table 3.4 Frequency of occurrence of manners of articulation in Indic languages

Manners of articulation	P	N	TR	TP	FP	NF	FR	LF	AX	LA	AF	IMP
No. of languages (Total-148)	148	148	116	40	43	03	144	01	143	148	147	02

Table 3.4 has the Manners arranged in the order in which they appear in the sketches. *Table 3.5* rearranges the figures, with the frequency of the Manners in descending order.

Table 3.5 Frequency of occurrence of Manners of Articulation in Indic languages in descending order

Manners of articulation	P	N	LA	AF	FR	AX	TR	FP	TP	NF	IMP	LF
No. of languages (Total-148)	148	148	148	147	144	143	116	43	40	03	02	01
Percentage of frequency of occurrence	100	100	100	99.3	97.3	96.6	78.4	29.0	27.0	2.0	1.4	0.7

As can be seen, seven of the Manners have a fairly high frequency of occurrence; and three occur rarely, namely, Nasal Flaps (3 languages), Implosives (2 languages) and Lateral Fricative (1 language). The taps and the trills are in general complementary in the languages, but not necessarily[3] so.

The various manners of articulation are given below with break ups for their frequency of occurrence in different language groups.

Table 3.6 Frequency of manners of articulation in the language groups

	P	N	LA	AF	FR	AX	TR	FP	TP	NF	IMP	LF
A-A	15	15	15	15	15	14	15	09	01	–	–	–
DR	29	29	29	29	27	29	28	16	08	–	–	–
I-A	32	32	32	31	32	32	17	11	18	03	02	–
T-B	55	55	55	53	55	51	45	07	07	–	–	01
T-K	02	02	02	02	02	02	01	–	–	–	–	–
AN	03	03	03	03	02	03	03	01	01	–	–	–
C-V	07	07	07	07	07	07	06	01	01	–	–	–
H-V	05	05	05	05	04	05	02	–	04	–	–	–
TOTAL	148	148	148	147	144	143	117	45	40	03	02	01

[3] Had they been complementary, the number of languages would total to 157 languages. Since there are only 148 languages in the database, some of the languages can be clearly seen to have both trills and taps. Malayalam, Tulu and Tarao, for example, have both. For the reason that some languages have both trills and taps, they are treated as separate Manner types in the sketches.

The above table can help identify the language groups which have certain rare sounds, as for example, the implosives in the I-A group or the lateral fricative in the T-B group. *Table 3.2,* giving the detailed list of the occurrence of the consonant phonemes, of course, specifies the languages in which the sounds occur. *Table 3.6* can also help identify the group in which a certain manner type with a high frequency of occurrence is not found: for example, the lateral approximant is missing only in one language from the Dravidian group.

Table 3.6 also shows that the language groups can be ordered according to the number of Manners found in them thus: I-A (11 Manners), T-B (10), DR, A-A (9), AN, C-V, H-V (8), and T-K (7).

3.1.3 Places of articulation.

The following 15 places are found for the consonants: BILABIAL (Bil), LABIO-DENTAL (L-d), DENTAL (Den), POST-DENTAL (Po-den), ALVEOLAR (Alv), APICO-ALVEOLAR (Ap-alv), POST-ALVEOLAR (Po-alv), RETROFLEX (Retr), PALATO-ALVEOLAR (Pal-alv), PREPALATAL (Pr-pal), PALATAL (Pal), VELAR (Vel), UVULAR (Uvu), PHARYNGEAL (Phar), and GLOTTAL (Glot).

A point about the RETROFLEX as a place of articulation may be noted here. It has been used here as a place between post-alveolar and pre-palatal. The point for the articulation of the retroflex consonants as well as the manner in which the tongue is held is variable in the languages on many counts, including parameters of articulation, such as apicality (e.g. Chomsky & Halle 1968), retraction (e.g. Bhat 1974, Catford 1977), sub-lingual cavity (e.g. Keating 1991), etc. and contextual factors such as speaker dependency, vocalic context (e.g. Dixit & Flege 1991), language groups (e.g. Ladefoged & Maddieson 1996). Hamann (2–3) presents a useful survey of the studies on retroflex sounds. In the present study, however, the topic has been treated rather conventionally, as assumed in general by the authors of the descriptions of the languages.

All other places of articulation being in general uncontroversial, let us turn to the distribution of consonants for the various places in SPIL. These are given in *Table 3.7* below. The Table may be read with the help of the legend for places of articulation reproduced below:

Bil= BILABIAL (Bil), L-d = LABIO-DENTAL, Den= DENTAL, Po-den= POST-DENTAL, Alv= ALVEOLAR, Ap-alv= APICO-ALVEOLAR, Po-alv= POST ALVEOLAR, Retr= RETROFLEX, Pal-alv= PALATO-ALVEOLAR, Pr-pal= PREPALATAL, Pal= PALATAL, Vel= VELAR, Uvu= UVULAR, Phar= PHARYNGEAL, and Glot= GLOTTAL.

Table 3.7 Places of articulation for phonemes with frequency of occurrence

PLACES	SEG	MANNERS	NO. OF LANGUAGES	LANGUAGE GROUPS
Bil	18	6 (P, N, IMP,FR, AF, SylC)	148	All (8)
L-d	07	4 (N, FR, AF, AX)	68	A-A, DR, I-A, T-B C-V, H-V (6)
Den	09	3 (P, N, TR)	136	All (8)
Po-den	03	2(FR, TR)	03	DR, I-A (2)
Alv	23	7 (P, N, FR, Tp, TR, LA, LF)	148	All (8)
Ap-alv	01	1 (TR)	08	T-B, C-V (2)
Po-alv	07	4 (P, AF, TP, TR)	08	DR, I-A, T-B, T-K (4)
Retr	19	10 (P, N, FR, TR, FP, NF, AX, LA, IMP, AF)	118	A-A, DR, I-A, T-B, AN, C-V, H-V (7)
Pal-alv	07	2 (FR, AF)	142	All (8)
Po-alv/ Pal-alv	01	1 (FR)	51	DR, I-A, T-B, C-V, H-V (5)
Pr-pal	02	2 (FR, AF)	05	DR, I-A, T-B, T-K, C-V (5)
Pal	12	5 (P, N, FR, AX, IMP)	144	All (8)
Vel	14	4 (P, N, FR, IMP)	148	All (8)
Uvu	02	1 (FR)	15	A-A, DR, I-A, T-B, C-V (5)
Phar	02	1 (FR)	03	DR, T-B, H-V (3)
Glot	03	2 (P, FR)	137	All (8)

Table 3.7 gives the places of articulation, the number of phonemic segments found at the places, the number of the manners of articulation in which those places are found to occur, the number of languages in which the places are found and the language groups in which they are found. The table should be read as follows for the bottom row: In the Glottal place, there are three segments (/ʔ h ɦ/), out of two manners of articulation (P, FR); the segments are found to occur in 137 languages from all the 8 groups.

As for the manners in *Table 3.6*, the places are being given again in *Table 3.8* according to their frequency of occurrence in the languages. The table should be read as follows for the top row: In the alveolar place, 23 phonemic segments are found; they belong to one of the 7 manner types (P, N, FR, TP, TR, LA, LF); alveolar phonemic segments (belonging to any one or a combination of the 7 Manners) are found in all the 148 languages.

Table 3.8 Frequency of places of articulation

PLACES	SEG	MANNERS	NO. OF LGS	LANGUAGE GROUPS
Alv	23	7 (P, N, FR, TP, TR, LA, LF)	148	All (8)
Bil	18	6 (P, N, IMP, F, AF, SylC)	148	All (8)
Vel	14	4 (P, N, FR, IMP)	148	All (8)
Pal	12	5 (P, N, FR, AX, IMP)	144	All (8)
Pal-alv	07	2 (FR, AF)	142	All (8)
Glot	03	2 (P, FR)	137	All (8)
Den	09	3 (P, N, TR)	136	All (8)
Retr	19	10 (P, N, FR, TR, FP, NF, AX, LA, IMP, AF)	118	A-A, DR, I-A, T-B, AN, C-V, H-V (7)
L-d	07	4 (N, FR, AF, AX)	68	A-A, DR, I-A, T-B C-V, H-V (6)
P-alv/ Pal-alv	01	1 (FR)	51	DR, I-A, T-B, C-V, H-V (5)
Uvu	02	1 (FR)	15	A-A, DR, I-A, T-B, C-V (5)
Ap-alv	01	1 (TR)	08	T-B, C-V (2)
P-alv	07	4 (P, AF, TP, TR)	08	DR, I-A, T-B, T-K (4)
Pr-pal	02	2 (FR, AF)	05	DR, I-A, T-B, T-K, C-V (5)
P-den	03	2 (FR, TR)	03	DR, I-A (2)
Phar	02	1 (FR)	03	DR, T-B, H-V (3)

As can be seen from *Table 3.8*, the places according to their frequency of occurrence are as follows- Alveolar, bilabial, velar> palatal> palato-alveolar> glottal> dental> retroflex> labio-dental> dental/alveolar (on account of uncertainty in the descriptions)> uvular> apico-alveolar, post-alveolar> pre-palatal> post-dental, pharyngeal. Of these, alveolar, retroflex, bilabial, velar and palatal are the places where the largest number of contrasts, in that order, are found.

As many places of articulation are given for the languages overall, it is useful to show which of them are involved in contrast for different manner types within a language in these language groups. The most relevant positions are the coronal ones for which nine places have been noted in the descriptions of the Indic languages, from Dental to Palatal. While two-place coronal contrast is widely used in these languages, there are also three-place and four-place contrasts among coronals. These are given for the manner types in *Table 3.9*.

Table 3.9 Four-place coronal contrast in SPIL

			A-A (15)	DR (29)	I-A (32)	T-B (55)	T-K (02)	AN (03)	C-V (07)	H-V (05)
Places	Manners	Total (148)								
1. Den, Alv, Retr & Pal	P	01	–	01	–	–	–	–	–	–
	N	03	–	03	–	–	–	–	–	–
2. Po-den, Alv, Retr & Alv-pal	N	01	–	01	–	–	–	–	–	–
Total	02	05	–	05	–	–	–	–	–	–

Table 3.9 shows that five languages, all from the Dravidian group, have four-place contrast among coronals. The three-place contrasts are given in *Table 3.10*.

Table 3.10 Three-place contrast among coronal consonants in SPIL

			A-A (15)	DR (29)	I-A (32)	T-B (55)	T-K (02)	AN (03)	C-V (07)	H-V (05)
PLACES	MANNERS	TOTAL (148)								
Den, Retr & Pal	**P**	07	01	01	02	01	–	–	01	01
Alv, Retr & Pal	P	12	04	05	02	01	–	–	–	–
	N	01	–	–	01	–	–	–	–	–
Den/ Alv, Po-alv & Pal	FR	01	–	–	01	–	–	–	–	–
Den, Alv &Retr	**P**	05	–	04	–	01	–	–	–	–
Den, Po-alv & Retr	**FR**	01	–	–	01	–	–	–	–	–
Alv, Po-alv & Retr	**FR**	02	–	02	–	–	–	–	–	–
Alv, Retr & Alv-pal	**FR**	01	–	–	–	01	–	–	–	–
Alv, Retr & Alv-pal	**FR**	02	–	01	–	–	–	–	01	–
Total	03	32	05	13	07	04	–	–	02	01

Whereas four-place contrasts involve only plosives and nasals as manner types, three-place contrasts also involve fricatives to a greater extent. Two-place contrasts among coronals add two more manner types, namely, approximants and lateral approximants, as can be seen in *Table 3.11*:

Table 3.11 Two-place coronal contrasts in SPIL

			A-A (15)	DR (29)	I-A (32)	T-B (55)	T-K (02)	AN (03)	C-V (07)	H-V (05)
Places	**Manneers**	**Total (148)**	**A-A (15)**	**DR (29)**	**I-A (32)**	**T-B (55)**	**T-K (02)**	**AN (03)**	**C-V (07)**	**H-V (05)**
1. Den & Retr	**P**	91	12	24	28	15	–	02	05	05
	N	18	01	07	06	03	–	–	–	01
	FR	01	–	–	–	01	–	–	–	–
	LA	03	–	–	–	–	–	–	01	02
2. Po-Den & Retr	LA	02	–	02	–	–	–	–	–	–
3. Alv & Retr	**P**	03	02	–	–	–	–	01	–	–
	N	24	04	07	09	03	–	–	01	–
	TR	01	–	01	–	–	–	–	–	–
	FR	06	01	05	–	–	–	–	–	–
	LA	31	04	12	10	02	–	01	01	01
4. Den & Alv	**P**	03	–	–	01	02	–	–	–	–
5. Po-Den & Alv	**TR**	01	–	01	–	–	–	–	–	–
	FR	01	–	01	–	–	–	–	–	–
6. Alv & Po-alv	**TR**	01	–	01	–	–	–	–	–	–
	FR	30	–	03	09	13	–	01	04	–
7. Den /Alv & Po-alv	**P**	01	–	–	01	–	–	–	–	–
	FR	01	–	–	01	–	–	–	–	–
8. Po-alv & Retr	**FR**	01	–	–	–	01	–	–	–	–
9. Den/ Alv & Pa	**P**	26	–	04	04	17	–	01	–	–

contd.

Table 3.11 *contd.*

	N	20	03	01	01	20	01	03	–	–
	FR	08	01	02	–	05	–	–	–	–
	AX	05	01	01	–	03	–	–	–	–
10. Po-alv & Pal	**AX**	02	–	–	01	01	–	–	–	–
11. Retr & Pal	**AX**	03	–	01	–	–	–	–	–	02
12. Po-den & Pr-pal	**P**	01	–	01	–	–	–	–	–	–
13. Alv & Pr-pal	**P**	01	–	01	–	–	–	–	–	–
14. Alv & Pr-pal	**FR**	05	–	–	02	03	–	–	–	–

As an areal feature of Indic languages (see Emeneau 1956), retroflex is of greatest interest among the places for Indic sounds (see Pandey 2006 for details). It is found to occur in seven of the eight groups in *Table 3.11*, with the exception of Tai-Kadai, and in ten manners of articulation. There are 19 segmental retroflex phonemes, the second largest number for any place, after the alveolar. It should be noted that although clearly two different types of retroflex consonants have been noted in the Indic languages (Ladefoged & Bhaskararao 1983), an 'apical' and a 'sub-apical', produced with the tip (and the blade) of the tongue touching the roof of the mouth straight and curled back, respectively, for the two types, such a distinction is not maintained in the present study for lack of good phonetic details of the languages involved. The frequency data of retroflex consonants are given in *Table 3.12*.

Table 3.12 Frequency of retroflex consonant phonemes

Manners	Number of Languages	Language Groups
Plosives	103	A-A, DR, I-A, T-B, AN, C-V, H-V (7)
Nasals	59	A-A, DR, I-A, T-B, C-V, H-V (6)
Flap	43	A-A, DR, I-A, T-B (4)
Lateral Approx.	37	A-A, DR, I-A, T-B, C-V, H-V (6)
Fricatives	34	A-A, DR, I-A, T-B, C-V, H-V (6)

contd.

Table 3.12 *contd.*

Nasal Flap	03	I-A (1)
Approximant	02	H-V (1)
Trill	01	DR (1)
Implosive	01	I-A (1)
Affricate	01	I-A (1)
Any one of the Manners	148	

Apart from the retroflex consonants, glottal consonants also hold some interest. Both the glottal or laryngeal stop (LS) and glottal fricative, voiceless and voiced, are found to occur in the languages, as shown below.

Table 3.13 Frequency of glottal sounds

MANNERS	NUMBER OF LANGUAGES	LANGUAGE GROUPS
Plosives (LS)	29	A-A, DR, T-B, T-K (4)
Voiceless fricatives	126	A-A, DR, I-A, T-B, T-K, AN, C-V, H-V (8)
Voiced fricatives	11	DR, I-A, T-B, C-V (4)
Any one of the Manners	137	

Whereas the voiceless fricatives occur in all the eight groups, voiced fricatives and the laryngeal stop occur only in four of the groups. The laryngeal stop does not occur in I-A, AN, C-V, and H-V varieties. The fact that it occurs in the DR group, but not in Old Tamil or Old Telugu, implies that it is a later historical development in the languages of the group.

3.1.4 Laryngeal types.

Four main laryngeal types are found for the Indic sounds – voiceless unaspirated (Laryngeal Type1 or 1), voiced unaspirated (LT2 or 2), voiceless aspirated (LT3 or 3), and voiced aspirated (LT4 or 4). Of these, 1 and 2 are found for most Manners of Articulation. 2 is common to all the Manners.

Two additional laryngeal types are found: Voiceless Preaspirated (LT5 or 5), and Voiced Preaspirated (LT6 or 6), mainly for sonorants (nasals, trills, taps, laterals and approximants), in some of the languages of the T-B group.

Besides, for the stops (that is, plosives and affricates), there are unique instances of modified types in three of the languages- palatalized (Tibetan-Standard, T-B), labialized (Khezha, T-B) and glottalized (Bishnupuria, C-V). They are listed as plosives in the sketches, but separately in the table for consonant patterns.

The tables containing the frequency of occurrence of each of the four laryngeal types are given below in tandem: *Table 3.14* for voiceless unaspirated consonant phonemes, *Table 3.15* for voiced unaspirated consonant phonemes, *Table 3.16* for the voiceless aspirated consonant phonemes, and *Table 3.17* for the voiced aspirated phonemes.

A comparison of *Tables 3.14* and *3.15* reveals that voiced unaspirated consonants have greater frequency of occurrence than voiceless unaspirated consonants in terms of both the number of manners of articulation (12 vs. 6) and the number of segments (89 vs. 59).

Table 3.14 Frequency of voiceless unaspirated consonant phonemes

	No. of segments	No. of languages	Language groups
Total	59	148	All (08)
Plosives	19	148	All (08)
Fricatives	13	143	All (08)
Affricates	12	139	All (08)
Trills	03	07	DR, T-B (2)
Nasals	07	05	I-A, T-B (2)
Approximants	01	02	H-V (1)

Table 3.15 Frequency of voiced unaspirated consonant phonemes

	No. of segments	No. of languages	Language groups
Total	89	148	All (08)
Nasals	18	148	All (08)
Lateral Approx.	06	147	All (08)
Approximants	07	143	All (08)
Plosives	18	142	All (08)
Affricate	07	136	All (08)

contd.

Table 3.15 *contd.*

TRILL	09	114	ALL (08)
FRICATIVES	12	67	DR, I-A, T-B, C-V (4)
FLAPS	02	43	A-A, DR, I-A, T-B (4)
TAPS	03	40	A-A, DR, I-A, T-B, AN, C-V, H-V (7)
NASAL FLAP	01	03	I-A (1)
IMPLOSIVES	05	02	I-A (1)
LAT FRICATIVES	01	01	T-B (1)

A look at *Table 3.16* for voiceless aspirated consonants reveals that they are found in the largest number in the plosives. The presence of voiceless aspirated consonant of any other manner implies the presence of voiceless aspirated plosives in the language. Voiceless aspirated consonants have the lowest frequency of occurrence in the DR group, less than 25%. A-A and AN groups follow next.

Table 3.16 Frequency of voiceless aspirated consonants

	NO. OF LANGUAGES	P	AF	N	LA	TR
A-A	11	11	04	–	–	–
DR	07	07	06	–	–	–
I-A	31	31	26	–	–	–
T-B	49	49	33	02	02	02
T-K	02	02	02	–	–	–
AN	02	01	01	–	–	–
C-V	05	05	04	–	–	–
H-V	04	04	04	–	–	–
TOTAL	111	110	80	02	02	02

Table 3.17, like *Table 3.16*, reveals that the contrast for voiced aspirated consonants is found most commonly in plosives. A comparison between *Tables 3.16* and *3.17* shows that voiced aspirated consonants occur less frequently than voiceless aspirated consonants, in terms of the number of segments (70 vs. 111) and the number of language groups (6 vs. 8). However, voiced aspirated contrast is found in a larger number of manner types (8 vs. 5) than voiceless aspirated contrast. Both the tables show that the I-A group

has the largest number of aspirated consonant phonemes, both voiceless and voiced. A-A, DR, C-V and H-V have roughly the same number of voiceless and voiced aspirated contrasts, as compared to T-B, T-K and AN which have significantly more voiceless aspirated contrast than voiced aspirated contrast.

Table 3.17 Frequency of voiced aspirated consonants

	No. of languages	P	Af	N	LA	Tr	Ax	Fp	Tp
A-A	10	10	04	–	–	–	–	01	–
DR	07	07	04	–	–	–	–	–	–
I-A	28	27	25	03	02	–	–	–	02
T-B	17	09	03	05	06	07	02	02	–
T-K	–	–	–	–	–	–	–	–	–
AN	–	–	–	–	–	–	–	–	–
C-V	04	04	04	01	02	02	–	–	–
H-V	04	04	04	–	01	–	–	–	–
Total	70	61	44	09	11	09	02	03	02

Having noted the patterning of the individual laryngeal types above, we now turn to look at the pattern of their combination in the consonant inventories. We take up each manner type for a close picture of the shaping of the consonant inventories. To begin with, the plosives; the numbers for the laryngeal types stand for the values mentioned at the beginning of this section (Section 3.1.4), and reproduced as follows: 1= VOICELESS UNASPIRATED, 2= VOICED UNASPIRATED, 3= VOICELESS ASPIRATED, and 4= VOICED ASPIRATED.

Table 3.18 Laryngeal patterns of plosives

Sr no.	Laryngeal patterns	Total	Perc.	A-A	DR	I-A	T-B	T-K	AN	C-V	H-V
1	1,2,3,4	50	33.78	07	04	24	08	–	–	04	03
2	1,2,(3),(4)	06	4.05	02	02	–	–	–	–	01	01
3	1,2,3, (4)	02	1.35	–	–	–	02	–	–	–	–
4	1,2,3	37	25.–	01	–	07	28	01	–	–	–
5	1,2,4	01	0.68	01	–	–	–	–	–	–	–
6	1,2, (4)	01	0.68	–	–	–	–	–	–	01	–

contd.

Table 3.18 *contd.*

7	1,2	40	27.03	02	22	01	11	–	03	01	–
8	1,3	03	2.03	–	–	–	02	01	–	–	–
9	2,3	01	0.68	–	–	–	01	–	–	–	–
10	1	05	3.38	02	01	–	01	–	–	–	01
11	2	00	–	–	–	–	–	–	–	–	–
12	3	00	–	–	–	–	–	–	–	–	–
13	4	00	–	–	–	–	–	–	–	–	–
14	VARIANT	02	1.35	–	–	–	02	–	–	–	–
15	TOTAL	148	1–	15	29	32	55	02	03	07	05

As we can see above, plosives have a predominance of all the four laryngeal types (about 39 %), three laryngeal types (1,2,3- 25%, LT 1,2,4- 01.36%), and two laryngeal types (1,2- 27.03%, 1,3- 2.03%, LT 2.3- 0.68 %). Single feature pattern of only voiceless unaspirated sounds is low in frequency (3.38). No other single feature pattern for plosives is found. There is a highly restricted occurrence of variation in the laryngeal type patterns for plosives found in the T-B group.

The picture for affricates is fairly similar, except for two patterns- 1,2,3 patterns are less frequent for affricates; only voiced unaspirated affricates(2) occur in 6 languages in three groups.

Table 3.19 Laryngeal patterns for affricates

SR NO.	LARYNGEAL PATTERNS	TOTAL	%.	A-A	DR	I-A	T-B	T-K	AN	C-V	H-V
1	1,2,3,4	45	30.61	06	04	23	06	–	–	03	03
2	1,2,(3),(4)	05	3.40	01	02	–	–	–	–	01	01
3	1,2,3, (4)	00	00	–	–	–	–	–	–	–	–
4	1,2,3	23	15.65	–	–	06	17	–	–	–	–
5	1,2,(3)	01	0.68	–	–	–	01	–	–	–	–
6	1,2,4	01	0.68	–	–	01		–	–	–	–
7	1,2, (4)	01	0.68	–	–	–	01	–	–	–	–
8	1,2	43	29.25	05	18	01	13	01	02	03	–

contd.

Table 3.19 *contd.*

9	(1),2	02	1.36	–	02	–	–	–	–	–	–
10	1,3	04	2.72	–	–	–	04	–	–	–	–
11	2,3	00	00	–	–	–	–	–	–	–	–
12	1	16	10.88	02	02	–	09	01	01	–	01
13	2	06	4.08	01	01		04	–	–	–	–
14	3	00	00	–	–	–	–	–	–	–	–
15	4	00	00	–	–	–	–	–	–	–	–
16	VARIANT	00	00	–	–	–	–	–	–	–	–
17	TOTAL OCCURRING	147		15	29	31	55	02	03	07	05
18	NIL	01				01					
19	GRAND TOTAL	148		15	29	32	55	02	03	07	05

Table 3.20 shows that the ratio of voicelessness is much higher in relation to voicing in fricatives. Voiced fricatives do occur with voiceless fricatives in 29 of the144 languages (20.13 %), but voiced fricatives do not occur alone, as for plosives.

Table 3.20 Laryngeal patterns for fricatives

SR NO.	LARYNGEAL PATTERNS	TOTAL	%	A-A	DR	I-A	T-B	T-K	AN	C-V	H-V
1	1,2	29	19.59		04	07	16			02	
2	1	106	71.62	15	22	20	36	02	02	05	04
3	2	01	00.67		01						
4	VARIANT	08	05.40			05	03				
5	TOTAL OCCURRING	144	97.29	15	27	32	55	02	02	07	04

The opposite is the case for all the other manner types that belong to the major class of sonorants. The tables for the laryngeal patterns for them are produced in *Tables 3.21–3.24.*

Table 3.21 Laryngeal patterns for nasals

Sr no.	Laryngeal patterns	Total	%	A-A	DR	I-A	T-B	T-K	AN	C-V	H-V
1	1,2	02		–	–	–	02	–	–	–	–
2	2,4	07		–	–	02	05	–	–	–	–
3	2,6	01		–	–	–	01	–	–	–	–
4	1	–		–	–	–	–	–	–	–	–
5	2	135		15	29	28	46	02	03	07	05
6	Variant	03		–	–	02	01	–	–	–	–
7	Nil	–		–	–	–	–	–	–	–	–
8	Total	148		15	29	32	55	02	03	07	05

Table 3.22 Laryngeal patterns for trills

Sr no.	Laryngeal patterns	Total	Perc.	A-A	DR	I-A	T-B	T-K	AN	C-V	H-V
1	1,2	06		–	01	–	05	–	–	–	–
2	2,3	02		–	–	–	02	–	–	–	–
3	2,4	06		–	–	–	06	–	–	–	–
4	2,6	02		–	–	–	02	–	–	–	–
5	1	–		–	–	–	–	–	–	–	–
6	2	101		–	–	–	30	01	03	06	02
7	Variant	–		–	–	–	–	–	–	–	–
8	Total occurring	117		15	28	17	45	01	03	06	02
9	Nil	31		–	01	15	10	01	–	01	03
10	Grand total	148		15	29	32	55	02	03	07	05

Table 3.23 Laryngeal patterns for taps

Sr no.	Laryngeal patterns	Total	Perc.	A-A	DR	I-A	T-B	T-K	AN	C-V	H-V
1	1,2	–									
2	2,3	–									
3	2,4	02				02					

contd.

Table 3.23 *contd.*

4	2,6	–									
5	1	–									
6	2	38		01	08	16	07	–	01	01	04
7	Variant	–									
8	Total	40		01	08	18	07	–	01	01	04
9	Nil	108		14	21	14	48	02	02	06	01
10	Grand Total	148		15	29	32	55	02	03	07	05

Table 3.24 Laryngeal patterns for flaps

Sr no.	Laryngeal patterns	Total	Perc.	A-A	DR	I-A	T-B	T-K	AN	C-V	H-V
1	2,4	02					02				
2	2,(4)	01		01							
3	2	42		08	16	11	05	–	01	01	–
4	Total occurring	45		09	16	11	07	–	01	01	–
5	Total no. of languages	103		06	13	21	48	02	02	06	05
6	Grand Total	148		15	29	32	55	02	03	07	05

Table 3.25 Laryngeal patterns for lateral approximants

Sr no.	Laryngeal patterns	Total	%	A-A	DR	I-A	T-B	T-K	AN	C-V	H-V
1	1, 2	06			01		05				
2	2, 4	08				02	05			02	
3	2, 6	02					02				
4	1	–									
5	2	120		15	28	24	36	02	03	07	05
6	Variant	–									
7	Nil	–									
8	Total	136		15	29	32	48	02	03	07	05

3.1.5 Modification types

Modification types among consonant phonemes are limited in occurrence to the following: Pre-aspiration – 2 languages, Chaudangsi and Darma (T-B); Labialization- 1 language, Khezha (T-B); Palatalization- 1 language, Tibetan- Standard (T-B); and Glottalization- 1 language, Bishnupuria (C-V). In addition to these, there are syllabic consonants restricted in occurrence to plosives, nasals and trills, with different distributions in 4 languages, as mentioned earlier: Angami, Chokri, Mao-Naga (T-B) and Turung (T-K).

3.1.6 Generalizations on consonant phoneme inventory

In addition to the observations regarding the patterning of consonants made above, some generalizations are stated below, at the risk of repetition. These are divided into general and typological generalizations.

a. General features of consonant phoneme inventories

i. Laryngeal type 1, 2, 3, 4 patterns are found mainly among stops, and in some cases sonorants; Laryngeal type 5 pattern, pre-aspirated, is found among sonorants.

ii. Fricatives have the largest number of variant laryngeal patterns among the Manners of articulation in the languages, that is, while for one place only a voiceless fricative may occur, for another place only the voiced fricative may occur, as can be seen in *Table 3.3.*

iii. Nasal Flap, Lateral Fricative, and Implosive are rare manners of articulation.

iv. The average size of the consonant inventory in SPIL is 26.9. This figure is higher than the average for the world languages, 22.7 (see Maddieson 2–5: 10). Only the Andaman group has lower than the world average; its average consonant size is 19.3. The minimum and the maximum sizes of the consonant inventory in SPIL are 14 in Ao-N (T-B) and 48 in Chokri (T-B).

v. It is interesting to note that by and large, the hypothesis of "size principle" (Lindblom and Maddieson 1988) regarding the relation between smaller inventory sizes and inherently simpler sounds is attested in the languages such as Nancowry, Nicobarese-Car, Gorum (A-A), Kadar, Gondi, Koya (DR), Ao-N, Bodo, Garo (T-B), and Jarawa, and Onge (AN). The exceptions, such as a 6 place contrast in Kadar (with 16 consonants), and a lateral fricative in Ao-N (with 14 consonants), seem to have to do with these being predominant areal features. An exemplar case here is Nancowry (A-A), which has 16 consonant phonemes, 8 obstruents, and 8 sonorants, with all the obstruents voiceless, and all the sonorants voiced. Nicobarese (A-A) has an almost similar inventory with the identical voicing generalization. Some other languages also show similar traits, such as Tamil (DR) and Old Tamil.

b. Typological features of consonant phoneme inventories

Austro-Asiatic

i. Many of the frequently occurring consonant phonemes are not found to occur either in the Nicobar subgroup (Nancowry and Nicobarese-C), or in Khasi, as can be seen in *Table 3.2*.

ii. Two of the languages of the Nicobar subgroup do not have laryngeal contrast: The obstruents are all voiceless, and the sonorants are all voiced.

iii. The average inventory size of the A-A languages is 25, and the minimum and maximum sizes are 16 (Nancowry) and 32 (Bonda).

Dravidian

i. Aspirated plosives are rare in Dravidian languages.

ii. Two of the four languages in the database that do not have fricatives are from DR, namely, Irula and Kadar. Old Tamil (H-V) is another language, historically related to this group.

iii. Post-alveolar, retroflex and velar trills occur mainly in the Dravidian languages, with the exception of Vagri-B, a contact variety, which has a velar trill.

iv. Four-way coronal contrasts are found only in languages of this group.

v. Six of the 29 languages do not permit coda consonants at all and two of them permit a few, making it the language group with the highest percentage, about 27%, for not allowing coda consonants.

vi. The average consonant inventory size of Dravidian languages is 24.3, and the minimum and maximum sizes are 16 (Kadar) and 38 (Toda).

Indo-Aryan

i. Most I-A languages have the LT 1, 2, 3, 4 patterns among stops, 7 have 1,2,3 pattern, while 1 (Mahl) has 1,2 pattern.

ii. Except for Assamese, all languages have retroflex consonants.

iii. Nasal flaps are found only in the languages of this group.

iv. The average consonant inventory size of the languages of the group is 31.9, and the minimum and maximum sizes are 21 (Assamese) and Lahndi (40).

Tibeto-Burman

i. Retroflex consonants in T-B languages are mainly found in the Himalayan languages, plausibly on account of language contact with the neighboring I-A languages.

ii. While word-initially, just a few of the languages disallow classes of consonants, word-finally, a lot of the languages have restrictions on classes of consonants occurring. Seven languages do not allow coda consonants at all, and 3 disallow most of the consonants.

iii. The palatalized and labialized modified plosives are found only in the T-B group.

iv. The laryngeal type pre-aspirated occurs only in the Himalayish subgroup.

v. The average consonant size inventory of the languages of the group is 26.1, and the minimum and maximum sizes are 14 (Ao-N) and 48 (Chokri), which are also the minimum and maximum sizes of the database.

Tai-Kadai

i. The laryngeal types in the T-K group are in common with the T-B languages of the northeast region, Turung has voiceless aspirated plosives, while Khampti has only unaspirated plosives.

ii. The average consonant size inventory of the languages of the group is 23.5, and the minimum and maximum sizes are 20 (Khampti) and 27 (Turung).

Andamanese

i. Jarawa and Onge are more closely related in excluding aspirated sounds in their inventory, unlike G-Andamanese.

ii. Onge is one of the four languages in the database that do not have any fricative.

iii. All the languages have 4 nasals (bilabial, dental, palatal and velar), 1 trill (dental/alveolar), and 2 approximants (bilabial and palatal). They differ with regard to the other sonorants.

iv. The average consonant size inventory of the languages of the group is 19.3, and the minimum and maximum sizes are 18 (Jarawa) and 22 (G-Andamanese).

Contact Varieties

i. Glottalized plosives and affricate are found only in Bishnupuria.

ii. The languages of this group draw their consonantal features from the source languages, and in some cases add new features. Thus Bishnupuria, Halbi, Nagamese, Vagri Boli have voiceless aspirated stops as in their source languages, while Diu-I-P does not have aspirated stops. Indian English- Hindi has them marginally. Bishnupuria, instead of voiced aspirated stops has Glottalized stops instead.

iii. The average consonant size inventory of the languages of the group is 28.2, and the minimum and maximum sizes are a wide range from 23 (IE-H) to 38 (Vagri-B).

Historical Varieties

i. The languages of this group have structures with close affinity with the present-day languages of their group in the following features: laryngeal types, nasals, approximants and lateral approximants.

ii. The average consonant size of the languages of the group is 28.2, with 20 (Old Tamil) as the minimum and 33 (Sanskrit-Cl) as the maximum sizes.

3.2 Constraints on the distribution of single consonant phonemes

Each of the sketches in Volume II of the book contains details about distributional restrictions on the occurrence of singlet and geminate consonants. The restrictions are presented in section 1.2 in the sketch. In addition, section 5.2 in each sketch contains details regarding the co-occurrence restrictions on consonants. In what follows, I discuss the distributional restrictions on singlet consonants. The restrictions on both geminate consonants as well as consonant clusters are taken up for discussion in Chapter 5 (section 5.2.3).

The restrictions on singlet consonants are discussed in relation to their position in the word. The details on the restrictions in the word-medial position are rather scarce compared to the restrictions on word-initial and word-final positions. They are in the main the following: aspirated consonants, the glottal fricative h/ɦ, the dorsal nasal and liquid, /ʃ/ and affricates.

Details on the constraints for the word-initial and word-final positions are quite commonly available and clearly generalizable. The constraints on word-initial consonants are presented in *Table 3.26* below.

Table 3.26 Non-occurring consonants in the word-initial position in SPIL

LANGUAGE GROUPS	DORSAL SONORANTS	LARYNGEAL STOPS	ASPIRATED CONSONANTS	APPROXIMANTS	OTHERS
A-A	08	06	01	04	
DR	24	03	00	10	
I-A	22	00	02	01	
T-B	09	09	02	03	b, r (Limbu)
T-K	00	00	00	00	
AN	02	01	00	01	f, s, ʦ (Jarawa)
C-V	05	00	00	01	
H-V	04	00	00	00	
TOTAL	74	19	05	20	

The consonants that are not permitted to occur in the word-initial position have been grouped into four – Dorsal (retroflex to velar) Sonorants; Approximants; Glottal/ Laryngeal stop; Aspirated consonants. Two of the languages, Jarawa and Limbu, have other specifications. The constraints on the groups can be easily graded as follows: DORSAL SONORANTS > APPROXIMANTS, LARYNGEAL STOP > ASPIRATED CONSONANTS > OTHERS.

The consonants that are not permitted in the word-final position have a wider range from ALL to subgroups of obstruents. Only in a few cases are sonorants disallowed in that position[4]. The data on constraints on final consonants are given in *Table 3.27*.

[4] The cases of ALL consonants are those that follow the markedness constraint NOCODA in Optimality Theory.

Table 3.27 Non-occurring consonants in the word-final position in SPIL

LANGUAGES	I ALL Cs	II MOST Cs	III OBS	IV S	V SA	VI S-A-VD	VII S-VD	VII S-VL	VIII F	IX RH	X RETRO	XI PAL.	XII APPR. (w/J)	XIII H/ɦ	XIV ERRATIC
A-A	00	00	00	00	10	07	00	00	03	00	08	00	01	01	00
DR	06	02	01	03	02	00	00	00	00	00	00	00	00	03	07 Ave (ɖ g), Kadar (nasals)
I-A	01	00	00	00	04	00	01	00	00	00	00	00	06	04	01 Chakma (ʃ)
T-B	07	03	00	00	27	19	04	00	28	03	00	03	05	08	00 Limbu (k r ʦ˃)
T-K	00	00	00	00	01	00	01	00	01	00	00	01	01	01	00
AN	00	00	01	00	00	00	00	00	00	00	01	00	01	00	00
C-V	00	01	00	00	03	00	00	01	00	00	00	00	00	00	02 Nagamese (ʧ s z l)
H-V	02	00	00	01	01	00	00	00	00	00	00	01	00	00	00
Total	16	06	02	04	48	26	06	01	32	03	09	05	14	17	10

OBS= OBSTRUENTS, S= STOPS, S-A= ASPIRATED STOPS, S-A-VD= VOICED ASPIRATED STOPS, S-VL= VOICELESS STOPS, F= FRICATIVES, SON-A= ASPIRATED SONORANTS, RETRO= RETROFLEX CONSONANTS, RH= RHOTICS, PAL.= PALATALS, APPR.= APPROXIMANTS.

The groups disallowed in the word-final position can be graded thus:

(3/1) ASPIRATED STOPS > FRICATIVES (other than /hɦ/) > VOICED ASPIRATED STOPS > /hɦ/ > ALL CONSONANTS > RETROFLEX CONSONANTS > MOST CONSONATS, VOICED STOPS, PALATAL CONSONANTS, STOPS >OBSTRUENTS, VOICELESS STOPS > OTHERS.

From the above graded scale of constraints, we can generalize further in terms of the natural classes. We need to separate the category ALL and MOST from the list here, as the former is motivated by the permitted syllable structure in the languages, prohibiting coda consonants. These are 16 in number. If we add 6 more, we have in all 22 languages (14.86 %) that do not permit consonants in general to occur word-finally. Among those that can be said to belong to natural subclasses of consonants, we can grade them as follows: i. [+spread glottis] (to include aspirated stops, fricatives (other than /h ɦ/), voiced aspirated stops, /h ɦ/, with 123 languages or 81.40% languages), followed by [-syllabic, + vocalic, +sonorant] (for approximants, 14 languages) > [+ coronal, + distributed] (for retroflex consonants, 9 languages) > [+-sonorant, -continuant, +voice] (for voiced stops, 6 languages) > [-sonorant, -continuant] (for stops, 4 languages) > [-sonorant] (for obstruents, 2 languages) and [-syllabic, +consonantal, -voice] (for voiceless consonants,1 language). Many of the languages have constraints on more than one group, for example, Kharia (A-A) does not permit aspirated stops, retroflex consonants, h and approximants. The number of languages and the groups in which the constraints hold are given in *Table 3.27*.

3.3 Consonant Allophones

3.3.1 Aspects of allophonic inventory of consonants

This section presents in brief some of the main aspects of the allophonic inventory of consonants in the Indic languages. The list of the allophones along with the specification of the processes of modification involved, and the languages as well as the language groups in which they occur are given in *Table 3.28*.

In the sketches in Volume II of the book, only those allophonic processes are included which find mention in the source descriptions. Almost all the source descriptions have been written in the mold of the traditional categorical approach with the notion of contrast being of central importance. The data on allophones thus must be seen as representing output spoken forms of the languages only in a general way. A positive aspect of the issue is that the most noticeable features of allophonic representation are included here, and our generalizations based on them are likely to be well grounded.

Table 3.28 Consonant allophones

Read: Allo = Allophone, M = Modification type, L = Language, LG = Language group

Manners and phones	Allo	M	L	LG
Plosives				
p		*voiceless bilabial plosive*		
	p̥	devoiced	Gondi	DR
			Meitei, Mishmi, Monpa, Spiti, Stod	T-B
			Diu-I-P, Bishnupuriya	C-V
		deaspirated	Kashmiri	I-A
			Bishnupuriya	C-V
	p̂	tensed	Gondi-A, Irula	DR
	p´	weakly aspirated (strengthening) (< p)	Toda, Tulu	DR
	p´	weakly aspirated (lenition) (< p^h)	Tulu	DR
			Haryanvi	I-A
	ˀp	preglottalized		
	pˀ	glottalized	Santali	A-A
			Bodo	T-B
	p̆	lax	Koraga, Koya	DR
			Limbu	T-B
	p̂´	tense and weakly aspirated (strengthening)	Koraga	DR
	p^w	labialized	Haryanvi, Kashmiri	I-A
			Mishmi	T-B

contd.

Table 3.28 *contd.*

	p^j	palatalized	Haryanvi, Kashmiri	I-A
	pˑ	lengthened	Bengali, Haryanvi	I-A
	pː	lengthened	Bengali, Chakma, Hindi	I-A
			Phom	T-B
p^h		*aspirated voiceless bilabial plosive*		
	p^h	aspirated	Gondi, Toda	DR
			Ao-N, Dimasa, Garo	T-B
			Nagamese	C-V
	p^{hw}	labialized	Haryanvi, Kashmiri	I-A
	p^{hj}	palatalized	Haryanvi, Kashmiri	I-A
	$\breve{p}^h$	laxed	Tibetan-St	
	p^hˑ	slightly lengthened	Haryanvi	I-A
	p^hː	lengthened	Bengali, Hindi	I-A
b		*voiced bilabial plosive*		
	b	voiced	Kadar, Malayalam, Tamil	DR
			Ao-N, Chaudangsi, Darma, Gallong, Galo-L, Karbi, Liangmai, Lepcha, Limbu, Meitei, Raji, Spiti, Tibetan-St	T-B
			Bishnupuriya, Nagamese	C-V
		aspirated		
		occluded	Bhojpuri (< /w/)	I-A
		denasalized (< /m/)		
		free variation	Sanskrit-Cl (~ ʋ)	H-V
	b̆	lax	Koya	DR
	b̂	tensed	Gondi-A	DR

contd.

Table 3.28 *contd.*

	b´	weakly aspirated (strengthening) (< b)	Tulu	DR
	b´	weakly aspirated (lenition) (< bʱ)	Tulu	DR
			Haryanvi	I-A
	ˀb	preglottalized	Mundari	A-A
	bˀ	glottallized	Kharia	A-A
	ˀbᵐ	preglottalized with nasal release	Mundari	A-A
	bʷ	labialized	Koya	DR
			Haryanvi, Kashmiri	I-A
			Mishmi	T-B
	bʲ	palatalized	Haryanvi, Kashmiri	I-A
	bˑ	slightly lengthened	Bengali, Haryanvi	I-A
	bː	lengthened	Bengali, Hindi	I-A
	ᵐb	prenasalized voiced bilabial plosive- free variation	Rawang (b ~ ᵐb~ p)	T-B
bʱ		*voiced aspirated bilabial plosive*		
	bʱ	voiced	Limbu	T-B
		aspirated	Spiti, Stod	T-B
	bgʷ	labialized	Haryanvi	I-A
	bʱʲ	palatalized	Haryanvi	I-A
	bʱˑ	slightly lengthened	Haryanvi	I-A
	bʱː	lengthened	Bengali, Hindi	I-A
t̪		*voiceless dental plosive*		
	t̪	advanced	Nancowry (< t)	AN
		occluded and advanced	Koya (< ʧ)	DR
		occluded, devoiced and advanced	Irula (<ʀ)	DR

contd.

Table 3.28 *contd.*

		devoiced	Gondi, Kannada (assim.)	DR
			Meitei, Monpa, Spiti, Stod	T-B
			Bishnupuriya	C-V
		deaspirated	Kashmiri	I-A
			Bishnupuriya	C-V
		inserted (< ø)	Sanskrit-Cl	H-V
	t̪̆	lax	Koraga, Koya	DR
	t̪̂	tensed	Gondi-A, Irula	DR
	t´	weakly aspirated (strengthening) (< t̪)	Toda, Tulu	DR
	t´	weakly aspirated (lenition) (< t̪ʰ)	Tulu	DR
			Haryanvi	I-A
	t̪̂´	tensed and weakly aspirated	Koraga	DR
	ˀt̪	preglottalized	Stod	T-B
	t̪ˀ	Glottalized	Mundari	A-A
	t̪ʷ	labialized	Haryanvi, Kashmiri	I-A
	t̪ʲ	palatalized	Haryanvi, Kashmiri	I-A
	t̪ˑ	slightly lengthened	Haryanvi	I-A
	t̪ː	lengthened	Bengali, Chakma, Hindi	I-A
t̪ʰ		*voiceless aspirated dental plosive*		
	t̪ʰ	aspirated	Gondi, Toda	
			Garo	T-B
	t̪ʰʷ	labialized	Haryanvi, Kashmiri	I-A
	t̪ʰʲ	palatalized	Haryanvi, Kashmiri	I-A
	t̪ʰˑ	slightly lengthened	Haryanvi	I-A
	t̪ʰː	lengthened	Bengali, Hindi	I-A
	tˇʰ	laxed	Tibetan-St	T-B

contd.

Table 3.28 *contd.*

d̪		*voiced dental plosive*		
	d̪	voiced	Kadar, Malayalam, Tamil	DR
			Ao-N, Chaudangsi, Darma, Gallong, Galo-L, Karbi, Liangmai, Lepcha, Lotha, Limbu, Meitei, Raji, Spiti, Tibetan-St	T-B
			Bishnupuriya	C-V
		occluded	Dimasa (< z),	T-B
		occluded and advanced	Irula (<R̥), Naiki (< ʤ)	DR
	t̪̆	lax	Koya	DR
	t̪̂	tensed	Gondi-A	DR
	d̪̊	devoiced	Bhili	I-A
	^{ʔ}d̪	preglottalized	Mundari	A-A
	^{ʔ}d̪^{N}	preglottalized with nasal release	Mundari	A-A
	d̪^{ʔ}	glottalized	Kharia	A-A
	d̪´	weakly aspirated (strengthening) (<d)	Tulu	DR
	d̪´	weakly aspirated (lenition) (< d^{ɦ})	Tulu	DR
			Haryanvi	I-A
	d̪^{w}	labialized	Haryanvi, Kashmiri	I-A
	d̪^{j}	palatalized	Haryanvi, Kashmiri	I-A
	d̪ˑ	slightly lengthened	Haryanvi	I-A
	d̪ː	lengthened	Bengali, Hindi	I-A
d̪^{ɦ}		*voiced aspirated dental plosive*		
	d̪^{ɦ}	voiced	Limbu	T-B
		aspirated	Spiti, Stod	T-B
	d̪^{ɦw}	labialized	Haryanvi	I-A

contd.

Table 3.28 *contd.*

	d̪ʱʲ	palatalized	Haryanvi	I-A
	d̪ʱˑ	slightly lengthened	Haryanvi	I-A
	d̪ʱː	lengthened	Bengali, Hindi	I-A
t		*voiceless alveolar plosive*		
	t	devoiced	Diu-I-P	C-V
			Mishmi	t-B
	tˀ	glottalized	Limbu	T-B
			Bodo	T-B
	tʲ	palatalized	Liangmai	T-B
	t	occluded	Malayalam (< r)	DR
	t̟	retracted	Zo	T-B
	t̠	advanced	Gondi (< ʈ)	DR
	tː	lengthened	Phom	T-B
tʰ		*voiceless aspirated alveolar plosive*		
	tʰ	aspirated	Gondi	DR
			Ao-N	T-B
			Nagamese	C-V
	t̟ʰ	retracted	Zo	T-B
	tʰʲ	palatalized	Liangmai	T-B
d		*voiced alveolar plosive*		
	d	voiced	Tamil	DR
			Liangmai	T-B
			Nagamese	C-V
		occluded	Nancowry (< r), Nicobarese (< r)	A-A
			Ave (< ʤ), Malayalam (< r)	DR
		assimilated	Sanskrit-Cl (< t, tʰ)	H-V

contd.

Table 3.28 *contd.*

		inserted (< ø)	Nancowry (/_r)	AN
	d̠	retracted (post-alveolar)	Liangmai, Zo	T-B
	d̲	advanced	Gondi (< ɖ)	DR
	d^j	palatalized	Liangmai	T-B
	^{n}d	prenasalized voiced alveolar plosive- free variation	Rawang (d~ ^{n}d ~t)	T-B
ʈ		*voiceless retroflex plosive*		
	ʈ	assimilated to place	Malayalam (< k/ __ʃ)	DR
		retracted	Assamese (< t), Brokskat	I-A
			Nancowry (< t)	AN
		devoiced	Gondi	DR
			Bishnupuriya	C-V
		deaspirated	Kashmiri	I-A
			Bishnupuriya	C-V
		inserted	Sanskrit-Cl	H-V
	ʈ̂	tensed	Gondi-A, Irula	DR
	ʈ´	weakly aspirated (strengthening) (< ʈ)	Tulu	DR
	ʈ´	weakly aspirated (lenition) (< ʈ^h)	Tulu	DR
			Haryanvi	I-A
	ʈ̂´	tensed and slightly aspirated	Koraga	DR
	ʈ^w	labialized	Haryanvi, Kashmiri	I-A
	ʈ^j	palatalized	Haryanvi, Kashmiri	I-A
	ʈː	lengthened	Chakma	I-A
ʈ^h		*voiceless aspirated retroflex plosive*		
	ʈ^h	aspirated	Toda	DR
	ʈ^{hw}	labialized	Haryanvi, Kashmiri	I-A

contd.

Table 3.28 *contd.*

	ʈʰʲ	palatalized	Haryanvi, Kashmiri	I-A
ɖ		*voiced retroflex plosive*		
	ɖ	retracted	Assamese (< d), Brokskat	I-A
		voiced	Kadar, Malayalam, Tamil	DR
			Bishnupuriya	C-V
	ɖ̊	devoiced	Bhili	I-A
	ɖ̂	tensed	Gondi-A	DR
	ɖ´	weakly aspirated (strengthening) (< ɖ)	Tulu	DR
	ɖ´	weakly aspirated (lenition) (< ɖʱ)	Tulu	DR
			Haryanvi	I-A
	ɖʷ	labialized	Haryanvi, Kashmiri	I-A
	ɖʲ	palatalized	Haryanvi, Kashmiri	I-A
	ɖˑ	slightly lengthened	Haryanvi	I-A
	ɖ	lenited and voiced	Kadar (ʈ)	DR
ɖʱ		*voiced aspirated retroflex plosive*		
	ɖʱ	aspirated	Spiti	T-B
	ɖʱʷ	labialized	Haryanvi	I-A
	ɖʱʲ	palatalized	Haryanvi	I-A
	ɖʱˑ	slightly lengthened	Haryanvi	I-A
k		*voiceless velar plosive*		
	k	devoiced	Gondi	DR
			Meitei, Mishmi, Monpa, Spiti, Stod	T-B
			Bishnupuriya, Diu-I-P	C-V
		deaspirated	Kashmiri	I-A
			Bishnupuriya	C-V

contd.

Table 3.28 *contd.*

		inserted (< ø)	Sanskrit-Cl	H-V
	$^{?}k$	preglottalized	Bonda	A-A
			Stod	T-B
	$k^{?}$	glottalized	Santali	A-A
			Bodo, Limbu	T-B
	k̆	lax	Koraga, Koya, Telugu	DR
	k̭	tensed	Gondi-A, Irula	DR
	k´	weakly aspirated (strengthening) (< k)	Toda, Tulu	DR
	k´	weakly aspirated (lenition) (< k^h)	Tulu	DR
			Haryanvi	I-A
	k̭´	tensed and slightly aspirated	Koraga	DR
	k^j	palatalized	Malayalam, Irula	DR
			Liangmai	T-B
	k^w	labialized	Koya	DR
			Haryanvi, Kashmiri	I-A
	k^j	palatalized	Haryanvi, Kashmiri	I-A
	kˑ	slightly lengthened	Haryanvi	I-A
	kː	lengthened	Chakma, Hindi	I-A
			Phom	T-B
	k̟	advanced	Shina	I-A
k^h		*voiceless aspirated velar plosive*		
	k^h	aspirated	Toda	DR
			Ao-N, Dimasa, Garo	T-B
			Nagamese	C-V
		free variation	Zo (~ x)	T-B
			Khampti (~ x)	T-K

contd.

Table 3.28 *contd.*

			Sanskrit-Cl (~ ṣ)	H-V
	$\breve{k}^{h}$	laxed	Tibetan-St	T-B
	k^{hw}	labialized	Kashmiri	I-A
	k^{hj}	palatalized	Kashmiri	I-A
			Liangmai	T-B
	k^{h}ˑ	slightly lengthened	Haryanvi	I-A
	k^{h}ː	lengthened	Hindi	I-A
	$k^{<}$	advanced	Shina	I-A
	$k^{>}$	retracted	Kinnauri, Sema-N	T-B
g		*voiced velar plosive*		
	g	voiced	Kadar, Malayalam	DR
			Ao-N, Chaudangsi, Darma, Gallong, Galo-L, Karbi, Liangmai, Lepcha, Limbu, Lotha, Meitei, Raji, Spiti, Tibetan-St	T-B
			Bishnupuriya, Nagamese	C-V
	ğ	lax	Koya, Telugu	DR
	g´	weakly aspirated (strengthening) (< g)	Tulu	DR
	g´	weakly aspirated (lenition) (< $g^{ɦ}$)	Tulu	DR
			Haryanvi	I-A
	g̊	devoiced	Bhili	I-A
	ĝ	tensed	Gondi-A	DR
	^{ʔ}g	preglottalized	Bonda	A-A
	$g^{ʔ}$	glottalized	Kharia	A-A
	g^{w}	labialized	Koya	DR
		labialized	Haryanvi, Kashmiri	I-A

contd.

Table 3.28 *contd.*

	g^{j}	palatalized	Haryanvi, Kashmiri	I-A
			Liangmai	T-B
	gˑ	slightly lengthened	Haryanvi	I-A
	gː	lengthened	Hindi	I-A
	$g^{<}$	advanced	Shina	I-A
	$g^{>}$	retracted	Kinnauri, Ladakhi, Sema-N	T-B
	^{ŋ}g	prenasalized velar plosive – free variation	Rawang (g~^{ŋ}g~k)	
$g^{ɦ}$		*voiced aspirated velar plosive*		
	$g^{ɦ}$	voiced	Limbu	T-B
		aspirated	Spiti, Stod	T-B
	$g^{ɦw}$	labialized	Haryanvi	I-A
	$g^{ɦj}$	palatalized	Haryanvi	I-A
	$g^{ɦ}$ˑ	slightly lengthened	Haryanvi	I-A
	$g^{ɦ}$ː	lengthened	Hindi	I-A
q		*voiceless uvular plosive*		
	q	retracted	Chokri	T-B
			Khampti	T-K
q^{h}		*voiceless aspirated uvular plosive*		
	q^{h}	retracted	Chokri	T-B
ʔ		*voiceless glottal plosive*		
	ʔ	debuccalized (< p, t, d, k, g, h)	Juang (< t,k), Korku (< h), Mundari (< g)	A-A
			Mandeali (< h)	I-A
			Lushai (< p, t, k), Thaadou (< k), Zo (< h), Spiti (< d, g)	T-B
		inserted (< ø)	Assamese	I-A

contd.

Table 3.28 *contd.*

			Galo-L, Garo, Tibetan-St, Wancho	T-B
	$ʔ^{ə}$	released	Khasi	A-A
Nasals				
m		*voiced bilabial nasal*		
	m	assimilated	Apatani (< ŋ), Gallong (< p, b)	T-B
	ɱ	dissimilated (place)	Chokri (< /_u)	T-B
	m̥	devoiced	Toda	DR
	$m^{ɦ}$	aspirated	Spiti	T-B
	m̩	syllabic[2]	Chokri	T-B
	m^{w}	labialized	Haryanvi, Kashmiri	I-A
	m^{j}	palatalized	Haryanvi, Kashmiri	I-A
	mˑ	slightly lengthened	Haryanvi	I-A
	mː	lengthened	Bengali, Hindi	I-A
	m̤	breathy voiced	Hindi	I-A
n		*voiced dental/ alveolar nasal*		
	n	assimilated	Gallong (< t, d)	T-B
			Meitei	T-B
	n˃	advanced	G-Andamanese	AN
	n̥	devoiced	Toda	DR
	$n^{ɦ}$	aspirated	Spiti	T-B
	n^{w}	labialized	Haryanvi, Kasmiri	I-A
	n̩	syllabic	Chokri	T-B
	nˑ	slightly lengthened	Haryanvi	I-A
	nː	lengthened	Bengali, Hindi	I-A
	n̤	breathy voiced	Hindi	I-A

[2] Syllabic consonants emerge as allophones on account of a loss of the following vowel in these languages.

contd.

Table 3.28 *contd.*

ɳ		*voiced retroflex nasal*		
	ɳ	assimilation (place)	general	All groups
		retroflexed	Garhwali	I-A
			Sanskrit-Cl	H-V
ɲ		*voiced palatal nasal*		
	ɲ	palatalized	Bhumij (< ŋ)	A-A
			Malto (< ŋ)	DR
			Haryanvi, Kasmiri	I-A
			Apatani, Chokri, Liangmai	T-B
			Bhumij (< ŋ)	A-A
	ɲ^{ɦ}	aspirated	Spiti	T-B
	ɲ^{ɦ}	palatalized	Khezha (< ŋ^{h})	T-B
		palatalized and aspirated	Spiti	T-B
	ɲˑ	slightly lengthened	Haryanvi	I-A
ŋ		*voiced velar nasal*		
	ŋ	assimilated	Mahl (< m, n)	I-A
			Chokri (< n/u__u), Gallong (< k, g) Limbu (< m)	T-B
			Gallong	T-B
	ŋ^{ɦ}	aspirated	Spiti	T-B
	ŋ^{ʔ}	glottalized	Bodo	T-B
	ŋ^{j}	palatalized	Malayalam	DR
			Liangmai	T-B
	ŋˑ	slightly lengthened	Haryanvi	I-A
	ŋː	lengthened	Bengali	I-A
			Mishmi	T-B

contd.

Table 3.28 *contd.*

Rhotics				
ɾ		*Voiced dental/alveolar tap*		
	ɾ	tapped	Kadar (< r), Telugu	DR
			Diu-I-P (< r)	C-V
	ɾʷ	labialized	Haryanvi	I-A
	ɾʲ	palatalized	Haryanvi	I-A
	ɾː	lengthened	Hindi	I-A
ɽ		*Voiced retroflex flap*		
		flapped	Mundari (< ɖ)	A-A
			Badaga, Kodagu, Koraga, Naiki, (< ɖ) Pengo (< ʈ, ɖ)	DR
			Bengali, Bhili, Dogri, Gujarati, Hindi, Lahndi, Maithili, Mandeali, Oriya	I-A
			Apatani, Purki (< d)	T-B
			Vagri-B (< ɖ)	C-V
		free variation	Kharia (ɽ ~ ɖʱ)	A-A
ɽʱ		*Voiced aspirated retroflex flap*		
	ɽʱ	flapped	Telugu	DR
			Bhili, Hindi, Maithili, Mandeali, Oriya	I-A
ɾʱ		*Voiced aspirated alveolar tap*		
	ɾʱ	aspirated	Spiti	T-B
r		*Voiced dental/alveolar trill*		
	r	trilled	Tamil (< t̲)	DR
			Hindi	I-A
			Limbu, Meitei (< l)	T-B
		desyllabified	Sanskrit-Cl (<¨)	H-V

contd.

Table 3.28 *contd.*

	r˃	advanced	G-Andamanese	AN
	r̥	devoiced	Khezha, Kiranti-K	T-B
	rʷ	labialized	Kashmiri	I-A
	rʲ	palatalized	Kashmiri	I-A
	rˀ	glottalized	Bodo	T-B
	r̩	syllabic	Chokri	T-B
R		*Voiced uvular trill*		
	R	retracted	Gondi-A	DR
			Malto (< r/_q,G)	DR
Fricatives				
ɸ		*Voiceless bilabial fricative*		
	ɸ	spirantized	Assamese, Bengali, Garhwali	I-A
β		*Voiced bilabial fricative*		
	β	spirantized	Irula (< b), Koya (< ʋ)	DR
			Assamese, Bengali (<bʱ), Garhwali, Shina (<b)	I-A
			Bodo, Chokri, Ladakhi	T-B
		voiced and spirantized	Kadar, Malayalam (< p)	DR
f		*Voiceless labio-dental fricative*		
	f	devoiced	Diu-I-P	C-V
	f	spirantized	Kharia (< pʰ)	A-A
			Dogri (< p), Mandeali, Marathi (< pʰ)	I-A
			Angami (< p, w)	T-B
		free variation	Kharia (~pʰ)	A-A
			Kashmiri (~pʰ)	I-A
v		*Voiced labio-dental fricative*		

contd.

Table 3.28 *contd.*

	v	voiced	Toda	DR
			Lamani	I-A
		spirantized	Kattunaicka (< ʋ), Irula, Kuvi, Telugu (< w)	DR
			Gujarati, Lamani (< w)	I-A
			Angami , Sema-N (< w)	T-B
		free variation	Koren (< w)	T-B
ð		*Voiced dental fricative*		
	ð	spirantized	Irula, Kodagu (< d)	
			Balti, Purki (< d)	T-B
		voiced	Toda (< T)	
		voiced and spirantized	Kadar, Malayalam (< tʃ)	DR
z		*Voiced post-dental sibilant fricative*		
	z	voiced	Toda	T-B
s		*Voiceless dental/ alveolar sibilant fricative*		
	s	spirantized	Irula, Kota, Tamil (< tʃ)	DR
		devoiced	Malayalam	DR
			Sema-N	T-B
			Diu-I-P	C-V
		assimilated (dental)	Bengali (< ʃ)	I-A
			Bishnupuriya	C-V
		free variation (~tʃ)	Ave	DR
	s^w	labialized	Haryanvi, Kasmiri	I-A
	s^j	palatalized	Haryanvi, Kasmiri	I-A
			Liangmai	T-B
	$s^ʔ$	devoiced and glottalized	Bodo (< z)	T-B
	sˑ	slightly lengthened	Haryanvi	I-A

contd.

Table 3.28 *contd.*

	sː	lengthened	Hindi	I-A
z		*Voiced alveolar sibilant fricative*		
	z	voiced	Toda	DR
		spirantized	Thaadou (< ʤ)	T-B
	z^w	labialized	Kashmiri	I-A
	z^j	palatalized	Kashmiri	I-A
			Liangmai	T-B
ʂ		*Voiceless retroflex sibilant fricative*		
	ʂ	spirantized and assimilated (retr.)	Irula	DR
		flapped	Naiki (< ʃ)	DR
			Purki (< ʃ)	T-B
			Bishnupuriya (< ʃ)	C-V
			Sanskrit-Cl (< ṣ)	H-V
ʐ		*Voiced retroflex sibilant fricative*		
	ʐ	voiced	Toda	DR
ʃ		*Voiceless post/palato-alveolar sibilant fricative*		
	ʃ	spirantized	Kota (< ʧ)	DR
		devoiced	Sema-N (< Z)	T-B
		assimilated (-back)	Korku	A-A
			Koya	DR
			Bodo	T-B
			Nagamese, Bishnupuria	C-V
		free variation	Koren (~ z)	T-B
	ʃː	lengthened	Hindi	I-A
ʒ		*Voiced palato-alveolar sibilant fricative*		
	ʒ	voiced	Toda	T-B
		assimilated (-back)	Bodo	T-B

contd.

Table 3.28 *contd.*

		free variation	Koren (< z)	T-B
ç		*voiceless palatal fricative*		
	ç	assimilated (-back)	Bodo, Raji	T-B
x		*Voiceless velar fricative*		
	x	spirantized	Tamil (< k), Toda (< k^h)	DR
			Garhwali	I-A
		free variation	Zo (~k^h)	T-B
ɣ		*Voiced velar fricative*		
	ɣ	*spirantized and voiced*	Malayalam (< k)	DR
			Dogri (< k)	I-A
		spirantized	Irula (g)	DR
			Garhwali	I-A
			Ladakhi, Shina	T-B
		voiced	Toda (< x)	T-B
		free variation	Chokri (~ɹ)	T-B
χ		*Voiceless uvular fricative*		
	χ	free variation	Chokri (~ɹ̥)	T-B
ħ		*Voiceless pharyngeal fricative*		
	ħ	devoiced	Tulu (< ʕ)	DR
		free variation	Chokri, Koren (~ h)	T-B
h		*Voiceless glottal fricative*		
	h	devoiced	Koya	DR
			Haryanvi, Marathi	I-A
			Bishnupuriya	C-V
		spirantized and debuccalized (< k)	Kadar	DR
ɦ		*Voiced glottal fricative*		
	ɦ	voiced	Bhili, Hindi, Kashmiri	I-A

contd.

Table 3.28 *contd.*

			Bodo	T-B
Approximants				
w		*Voiced labio-velar approximant*		
	w	approximantized	Limbu (< b)	T-B
			Kuvi (< v)	DR
			Bodo (< v)	T-B
		disyllabified (< /u u:/)	Khampti	T-K
			Tamang	T-B
		labialized	Tulu (< ʋ)	DR
			Shina (< ʋ)	I-A
			Urdu-D-T (< ʋ)	C-V
		inserted (< ø)	Galo-L	T-B
		devocalized	Gondi (< i̯, u̯)	DR
	w̥	devoiced	Toda	DR
w̃		*Nasalized voiced labio-velar approximant*		
	w̃	nasalized and approximantized	Telugu (< m)	DR
ʋ		*Voiced labio-dental approximant*		
	ʋ	approximantized	Tamil (< p)	DR
		assimilated	Gadaba-K (< w)	DR
		desyllabified	Sanskrit-Cl	H-V
ɹ		*Voiced alveolar lareral approximant*		
	ɹ	approximantized	Raji	T-B
	ɹʲ	palatalized	Liangmai	T-B
j		*Voiced palatal approximants*		
	j	disyllabified	Khampti (< i)	T-K
			Tamang (< i)	T-B
			Sanskrit-Cl(< i i:)	H-V

contd.

Table 3.28 *contd.*

	jˀ	glottalized	Koya	DR
	ĵ	tensed	Korku	A-A
	j̊	devoiced	Toda	DR
	jᶻ	spirantized	Kattunaicka	DR
		free variation	Koren, Tangsa (~ ʤ)	T-B
ɰ		*voiced velar approximant*		
	ɰ	denasalized and approximantized	Diu-I-P (< ŋ)	C-V
	ɰ	inserted (<ø)	Galo-L	T-B
Lateral approximants				
l		*Voiced alveolar lateral approximant*		
	l	voiced	Toda (< /l̥/)	DR
		assimilated	Kannada (< /ɭ/)	DR
			Limbu (< m n ŋ)	T-B
	l˃	retracted	G-Andamanese	AN
			Hindi	I-A
	ɬ	devoiced and spirantized	Kiranti-K, Purki	T-B
	ˀl	preglottalized	Limbu	T-B
	lˀ	glottalized	Bodo	T-B
	ɮˠ	spirantized and velarized	Koya	DR
	lʱ	aspirated	Spiti	T-B
	lʷ	labialized	Haryanvi, Kasmiri	I-A
	lʲ	palatalized	Haryanvi, Kashmiri	I-A
			Liangmai	T-B
	l̥	devoiced	Kiranti-K, Lepcha	T-B

contd.

Table 3.28 *contd.*

	l·	slightly lengthened	Haryanvi	I-A
	lː	lengthened	Hindi	I-A
	l̤	breathy voiced	Hindi	I-A
ɭ		*Voiced retroflex lateral approximant*		
	ɭ	voiced	Toda (< ɭ̊)	DR
	ɭ	flapped and retracted (< /l/)	Gondi, Kannada, Kolami	DR
Affricates			Assamese	I-A
pf		*Voiceless labio-dental affricate*		
	pf	affricated	Gadaba-K (< p)	DR
			Chokri (<p^h)	T-B
p^hɸ		*voiceless aspirated labio-dental affricate*		
		aspirated	Bodo (< /pf/)	T-B
pɸ		*Voiceless bilabial affricate*		
	pɸ	affricated (< /p^h/)	Gadaba-K (<p)	DR
bv		*Voiced labio-dental affricate*		
	bv	affricated	Gadaba-K (< /b/)	DR
t^hθ		*Voiceless aspirated dental affricate*		
	t^hθ	affricated	Bodo (< /t^h/)	T-B
ts		*Voiceless dental/alveolar affricate*		
	ts	advanced (< /tʃ/)	Ave, Gadaba-O, Koya, Telugu	DR
			Lamani, Marathi	I-A
			Ao-N, Kokborok	T-B
			Bishnupuriya, Nagamese	C-V
			O-Telugu	H-V
	ts^w	labialized	Kashmiri	I-A

contd.

Table 3.28 *contd.*

	tsʲ	palatalized	Kashmiri	I-A
		affricated	Dimasa (< s)	T-B
dz		*Voiced dental/alveolar affricate*		
	dz	advanced (< /dʒ/)	Ave, Gadaba-O, Koya, Telugu	DR
			Lamani, Marathi	I-A
			Kokborok	T-B
			O-Telugu	H-V
	dzʷ	labialized	Kashmiri	I-A
	dzʲ	palatalized	Kashmiri	I-A
		affricated (< /z/)	Kolami	DR
	dˑz	lengthened and affricated (< /z/)	Assamese	I-A
	dzʲ	affricated and palatalized	Assamese	I-A
tθ		*Voiceless dental affricate*		
	tθ	affricated	Toda (< /t/)	DR
dð		*Voiced dental affricate*		
	dð	affricated	Toda (< /d/)	DR
dʃ		*voiceless palatal affricate*		
	dʃ	devoiced (< dʒ)	Khasi	A-A
			Gondi	DR
			Monpa, Spiti, Stod	T-B
			Bishnupuriya, Diu-I-P	C-V
		affricated	Bishnupuriya (< /t/)	C-V
		affricated and devoiced	Gadaba-O (< g)	
		palatalized (< /ts/)	Kui	DR
			Chokri, Karbi	T-B
		deaspirated	Kashmiri	I-A

contd.

Table 3.28 *contd.*

		free variation (~ s)	Ave	DR
		lengthened	Hindi	I-A
	tʃ̂	tensed	Gondi-A	DR
	tʃ̆	laxed (< /tʃ/)	Koraga, Malayalam	DR
	tʃ^{ʔ}	glottalized	Santali	A-A
	tʃˑ	slightly lengthened	Haryanvi	I-A
	tʃː	lengthened	Hindi	I-A
	tʃ^{w}	labialized	Kashmiri	I-A
	tʃ^{j}	palatalized	Kashmiri	I-A
tʃ^{h}		*voiceless aspirated palatal affricate*		
	tʃ^{h}	aspirated	Gondi, Toda	DR
		palatalized (< /ʦ^{h}/)	Karbi	T-B
		affricated (< /s/)	Lepcha, Limbu	T-B
	tʃ̆^{h}	laxed	Tibetan-St	T-B
	tʃ^{h}ˑ	slightly lengthened	Haryanvi	I-A
	tʃ^{hw}	labialized	Kashmiri	I-A
	tʃ^{hj}	palatalized	Kashmiri	I-A
dʒ		*voiced palatal affricate*		
	dʒ	voiced	Kadar, Malayalam, Tamil	DR
			Ao-N, Galo-L, Limbu, Meitei, Spiti, Tibetan-St	T-B
			Bishnupuriya, Nagamese	C-V
		affricated and voiced (< t)	Bishnupuriya	C-V
		palatalized (< ʣ)	Kui	DR
			Chokri, Karbi	T-B
		free variation	Sanskrit-Cl (~ ʋ)	H-V
	dʒ^{ʔ}	glottalized	Kharia	A-A

contd.

Table 3.28 *contd.*

	ʤ̂	tensed	Gondi-A	DR
		occluded	Bhojpuri, Magahi (< j)	I-A
	ʤˑ	slightly lengthened	Haryanvi	I-A
	ʤː	lengthened	Hindi	I-A
	$ʤ^w$	labialized	Kashmiri	I-A
	$ʤ^j$	palatalized	Kashmiri	I-A
		free variation (~ /j/)	Bhojpuri, Kacchi, Magahi	I-A
$ʤ^ɦ$		*voiced aspirated palatal affricate*		
	$ʤ^ɦ$	aspirated	Spiti, Stod	T-B
	$ʤ^{ɦ}$ˑ	slightly lengthened	Haryanvi	I-A
k^hx		*voiceless aspirated velar affricate*		
	k^hx	affricated (< /k^h/)	Bodo (< /k^h/)	T-B

3.4 Allophonic modifications of consonants

3.4.1 Features

Before we proceed to discuss the features of allophonic modifications of consonants in the Indic languages, some points need to be noted here.

a. The inventory excludes the common allophones of voiced nasal /n/ phoneme, for the sake of parsimony. These are found commonly across the languages- nasals before stops are homorganic with the stops in the following places- bilabial, dental/alveolar, retroflex, palatal and velar. In most cases, the basic or underlying nasal is dental/alveolar. Its allophones on account of place assimilation with stops are excluded from the descriptions. However, the allophones of an underlying nasal other than a dental/alveolar nasal are taken into account, as for example, the palatal nasal [ɲ] allophone of the underlying velar nasal /ŋ/ in Bhumij and Malto. Similarly, the allophones of an underlying dental/alveolar nasal are taken into account if the context in which they occur is not of a following homorganic stop, as for example, in Chokri in which a velar nasal is derived from an alveolar nasal when flanked by /u/.

b. Tense consonants, half-long consonants, long consonants and geminates. There is considerable variation in the use of the terms 'tense' 'long' 'half-long' and 'geminate' for consonant allophones in the source descriptions of the Indic languages. In SPIL, the following symbols are used to distinguish between the terms:

(3/2) [p] = a consonant [p] that is neither tense nor lax nor long,

[pˑ] = a half-long or slightly long [p] allophone,

[pː] = a [p] allophone that is fully long or geminated,

[p̂] =a tense [p] allophone, and

[p̆] = a lax [p] allophone.

Note that on the surface geminated consonants are represented as long, like vowels.

c. Gradience. Some consonantal modifications require that they be represented in terms of gradience. One of them, length, has just been shown to be so represented above, following the practice in IPA representations (see the IPA chart). The other modification type is aspiration. Some of the languages, such as Toda and Tulu, distinguish between two degrees of aspiration- weakly aspirated and aspirated.

3.4.2 Processes of modification of consonants

Table 3.28 contains in all 37 processes of modification of consonants. The list of the modified segments in the table does not include nasal and sibilant allophones that assimilate to a neighboring stop in place for the reasons given above. The modification processes, similarly, exclude free variant allophones. We have classified the processes into five main classes, as shown in *Table 3.29* below. The main classes are ASSIMILATORY, MANNER, LARYNGEAL, SYLLABLE-BASED, and ARTICULATORY/ QUANTITATIVE. These labels are for convenience of presentation, and in general valid for the processes characterizing them. Thus, the manner processes deal with modifications in the segments involving change of manner of articulation. The laryngeal processes deal with modifications in terms of the laryngeal features of the consonant phonemes, such as voicing or glottalization. Syllable-based processes are motivated by the syllable-structure requirements of the language, and not merely by the environment stated in terms of the syllable and its parts. (What is meant here can be illustrated with an example. In Garo (Burling 1961), the voiceless plosives are aspirated in the syllable onset position. Aspiration in Garo takes place in a certain position within the syllable. In Wancho (Burling & Wangsu 1999), a glottal stop is inserted before a vowel initial syllable. The glottal stop insertion in Wancho not only takes place in a certain position in a syllable, but that position is part of the requirement of a phonetic syllable in Wancho. The syllable-based processes included in that category are like Wancho glottal stop insertion.) The articulatory/ quantitative class includes processes with the modification in the articulatory base, connected in certain cases with the quantity of the segment, as for example, slight lengthening, which may go with tense articulation. All other processes are categorized under co-occurrence, a term that can well apply to some of the other processes such as nasalization.

Table 3.29 Processes of allophonic modification of consonants in SPIL

CO-OCCURRENCE (07)	MANNER (12)	LARYNGEAL (09)	SYLLABLE-BASED (04)	ARTICULATORY/ QUANTITATIVE (05)
Assimilated	Affricated	Aspirated	Desyllabified	Laxed
Dissimilated	Approximantized	Wk. aspirated	Devocalized	Lenited
Advanced	Debuccalized	Deaspirated	Inserted	Tensed
Labialized	Denasalized	Devoiced	Syllabicated	Lengthened
Palatalized	Flapped	Glottalized		Sl. lengthened
Retracted	Nasalized	Preglottalized		
Retroflexed	Occluded	Preglottalized w. NR		
	Prenasalized	Voiced		
	V-Released	Breathy voiced		
	Spirantized			
	Tapped			
	Trilled			

The 37 processes of consonantal modification yield a total of 323 allophones, both systematic and novel. The tables below give a break up of the processes of modification under the main five classes in terms of the number of the segments each process gives rise to and the manners of articulation it affects in general and in each of the language groups. The following abbreviations are used in the table: SEG= SEGMENT and MNR= MANNERS. The abbreviations for the manners are as given in section 3.1.

Table 3.30 Modification processes of co-occurrence for consonants in SPIL

MODIFICATION TYPE 1: CO-OCCURRENCE	SEG	MNR		A-A	DR	I-A	T-B	T-K	AN	C-V	H-V
ASSIMILATED[3]	14	06	P, N, F, TR, AX, LA	01	06	02	07	–	–	02	01
DISSIMILATED	01	01	N	–	–	–	01	–	–	–	–
ADVANCED	09	04	P, N, TR, AF	–	05	05	02		02	01	02
LABIALIZED	28	08	P, N, F, TP, TR, AX, LA, AF	–	04	28	03	–	–	01	–
PALATALIZED	32	07	P, N, F, TP, TR, LA, AF	01	05	27	14	–	–	–	–
RETRACTED	11	03	P, TR, LA	–	02	04	07	01	02	–	–
RETROFLEXED (NON-IDENT PLACE)[4]	01	01	N	–	–	01	–	–	–	–	01
TOTAL	96	30		02	22	67	34	01	04	04	04

Table 3.31 Modification processes of manner for consonants in SPIL

MODIFICATION TYPE 2: MANNER	SEG	MNR		A-A	DR	I-A	T-B	T-K	AN	C-V	H-V
AFFRICATED	11	01	AF (<P, F)	–	06	01	05	–	–	02	–
APPROXIMANTIZED	05	02	AX, LA (<P, F, TR, N)	–	03	–	02	–	–	01	–
DEBUCCALIZED	02	02	P (<P, F), F (<P)	01	01	01	01	–	–	–	–

contd.

Table 3.31 *contd.*

DENASALIZED	01	01	AX	–	01	–	–	–	–	–	–
NASALIZED	01	01	AX	–	–	–	–	–	–	–	–
PRENASALIZED	03	01	P	–	–	–	03	–	–	–	–
PED	04	03	FP (< P), F, LA	01	04	03	02	–	–	02	01
CLUDED	05	02	P (F, TR, AF), AF (<AX)	–	03	02	01	–	–	01	–
V-RELEASED	01	01	P	01	–	–	–	–	–	–	–
SPIRANTIZED	14	03	F (<P, AF, AX), AX, LA	–	11	06	07	–	–	–	–
TAPPED	01	01	TP (<TR)	–	01			–	–	–	–
TRILLED	01	01	TR (P, TP, LA)	–	01	01	01	–	–	–	–
TOTAL	49	19		03	31	14	22	–	–	09	01

Table 3.32 Laryngeal modification processes for consonants in SPIL

MODIFICATION TYPE 3: LARYNGEAL	**SEG**	**MNR**		**A-A**	**DR**	**I-A**	**T-B**	**T-K**	**AN**	**C-V**	**H-V**
ASPIRATED	17	05	P, N, TP, LA, AF		05	–	16	–	–	03	–
DEASPIRATED	04	02	P, AF	–	–	04	–	–	–	–	–
BREATHY VOICED	03	02	N, LA	–	–	03	–	–	–	–	–
DEVOICED	19	07	P, N, F, TR, AX, LA, AF	01	11	04	08	–	–	08	–
GLOTTALIZED	13	07	P, N, F, TR, AX, LA, AF	07	01	–	07	–	–	–	–
PREGLOTTALIZED	05	02	P, LA	04	–	–	02	–	–	–	–
PREGLOTTALIZED (W. NR)	02	01	P	02	–	–	–	–	–	–	–

contd.

Table 3.32 *contd.*

Voiced	21	04	P, F, LA, Af	–	14	03	13	–	–	06	–
Weakly aspirated (Lenition)	07	01	P	–	07	–	–	–	–	–	–
Weakly aspirated (strengthening)	07	01	P	–	07	–	–	–	–	–	–
Total	98	32		14	45	21	46	–	–	20	–

Table 3.33 Syllable-based modification processes for consonants in SPIL

Modification type 4: Syllable-based	**SEG**	**MNR**		**A-A**	**DR**	**I-A**	**T-B**	**T-K**	**AN**	**C-V**	**H-V**
Desyllabicized	04	02	Tr, Ax	–	–	–	02	02	–	–	03
Devocalized	01	01	Ax	–	01	–	–	–	–	–	–
Inserted	06	02	P, Ax	–	–	01	03	–	–	–	–
Syllabicized	03	02	N, Tr	–	–	–	03	–	–	–	–
Total	14	07		–	01	01	08	02	01	–	05

Table 3.34 Quantitative modification processes for consonants in SPIL

Modification type 5: Quantitative	**SEG**	**Mnr**		**A-A**	**DR**	**I-A**	**T-B**	**T-K**	**AN**	**C-V**	**H-V**
Laxed	10	02	P, Af	–	06	01	04	–	–	–	–
Tensed	10	03	P, Ax, Af	01	09	–	–	–	–	–	–
Lenited	01	01	P	–	01	–	–	–	–	–	–

contd.

[5] The assimilation for nasals does not include the common place assimilation between stops and alveolar nasals, but non-alveolar nasals and any consonant.

[6] This mentions only that instance of retroflexion which is not assimilatory to an adjacent retroflex segment.

Table 3.34 *contd.*

Lengthened	23	06	P, N, F, Tp, LA, AF	–	–	22	04	–	–	–	–
Sl. lengthened	22	05	P, N, F, LA, Af	–	–	22		–	–	–	–
Total	66	17		01	16	45	08	–	–	–	–

The table below summarizes the modification processes applying to consonants in SPIL. Column 1 mentions the main five classes of modification types, column 2 specifies the number of allophonic segments, column 3 gives the number of processes within each main modification type (e.g. aspiration, glottalization, voicing etc. within the LARYNGEAL type), column 4 mentions the count of the number of the manners of articulation affected by the general class of modification type, and columns 5–12 give the numbers of the segments, processes and the total number of the manners of articulation mentioned against the general modification type for each of the language groups.

Table 3.35 **Summary of the modification processes for consonants in SPIL**

Modification types	**No. of processes (segments)**	**A-A proc (seg)**	**DR Proc (seg)**	**I-A proc (seg)**	**T-B proc (seg)**	**T-K proc (seg)**	**AN proc (seg)**	**C-V proc (seg)**	**H-V proc (seg)**
Co-occurrence	07 (96)	02 (02)	05 (22)	06 (67)	06 (34)	01 (01)	03 (04)	02 (04)	03 (04)
Manner	12 (49)	05 (03)	09 (31)	06 (14)	08 (22)	– (–)	– (–)	06 (09)	01 (01)
Laryngeal	09 (98)	04 (14)	06 (45	05 (21)	05 (46)	– (–)	– (–)	04 (20)	– (–)
Syllable-based	04 (14)	– (–)	01 (01	01 (01)	03 (08)	01 (02)	01 (01)	– (–	01 (05)
Articulatory Quantitative	05 (66)	01 (01)	03 (16)	03 (45)	02 (08)	– (–)	– (–)	– (–)	– (–)
Total	37 (323)	12 (20)	24 (115)	21 (148)	24 (118)	02 (03)	04 (05)	12 (33)	05 (10)

As is apparent from the above tables, especially *Table 3.35*, the five classes of modification processes yield 323 allophonic segments thus:

(3/3)	Modification processes	Number of segments	% out of 323

Co-occurrence	96	29.7
Manner	49	15.2
Laryngeal	98	30.3
Syllable-based	14	04.3
Articulatory/ Quantitative	66	20.4

As can be seen from the above figures, laryngeal and co-occurrence processes give rise to the largest number of segments, while syllable-based processes are the lowest. The latter may have to do with the nature of these languages, which are traditionally considered to be relatively 'syllable-timed'. This certainly seems to be the case with most of the Tibeto-Burman languages, which have monosyllabic roots. This account is closely supported by the productivity average of the processes, which is for all the processes 8.72. For the individual classes, the average figures of productivity are as follows:

(3/4)

Modification processes	Number of processes	Number of segments	Productivity average rate
Co-occurrence	07	96	13.7
Manner	12	49	04.1
Laryngeal	09	98	10.9
Syllable-based	04	14	03.5
Articulatory/ Quantitative	05	66	13.2

The syllable-based processes and the manner processes have the lower rates of productivity. The co-occurrence, quantitative and laryngeal processes have the higher productivity average. It is interesting to observe that while the co-occurrence and quantitative modification processes are predominantly found for the Indo-Aryan group, the laryngeal processes are found more frequently for the Dravidian and Tibeto-Burman groups. These data may be useful in further investigating the phonetic properties of the language groups. We noticed the relevance of the notion of syllable-timed speech rhythm above. Another feature that seems relevant here to account for the phonetic properties of the language groups is quantity-sensitivity. The fact that quantitative processes are predominantly found in the languages of the Indo-Aryan group may have to do with these languages having quantity-sensitive rhythm (see the discussion in section 5.3.1).

Chapter 4

Segments: Vowels

4.0 Introduction

In this chapter we are concerned with presenting details about the patterning of the inventories of vowels in Indic languages. Vowel phoneme patterns are of interest in more than one area of linguistic inquiry: universals and typology (e.g. Crothers 1978, Maddieson 1984, Lindblöm 1986), phonological theory (e.g., Clements and Hume 1995), linguistic evolution (e.g. De Böer 2001), speech perception (e.g. Liljencrants and Lindblöm 1972, Stevens 1989) and speech acquisition (e.g. Jusczyk 1986), to name a few.

The chapter is organized, on parallel with the preceding chapter on consonant phonemes and allophones, in three sections. Section 4.1 deals with the vowel phoneme patterns; section 4.2 discusses the constraints on the occurrence of vowels in the languages; and section 4.3 presents an overview of the allophonic modifications in the vowel phonemes of the languages, on the basis of the limited data in the source descriptions. The discussions around the three topics are based on the data presented in *Tables 4.1, 4.4* and *4.11*. The tables present exhaustive lists of the vowel phoneme patterns, vowel phonemes and vowel allophones, respectively. *Table 4.3* contains a list of the frequently occurring vowel phonemes found not to occur in some of the languages.

4.1 Vowel Phonemes

The organizational facts about the vowel phonemes in the Indic languages are discussed in two sub-sections – section 4.1.1 deals with the patterns of the vowel phonemes in the languages described in terms of the major categories. Section 4.1.2 deals with the occurrence of the phonemes in the languages. We begin with the vowel patterns first.

4.1.1 Vowel patterns

Table 4.1 is a comprehensive inventory of vowel patterns in Indic languages, organized keeping in view the following types of vowels: short monophthongs[4] (SV), long monophthongs (LV), diphthongs (DV), triphthongs (TV)[5] and nasal vowels (NV). The last include all the types of nasal vowels in the languages.

The table does not take into account the classification of vowels into further sub-types. One of the interesting subtypes is that of diphthongs in which either the first or the second vowel is prominent. This fact has been noted for the following languages: Liangmai, Mao-Naga, Paite and Wancho. These are termed here as Class I (with the first member more prominent than the second) and Class II (with the second member more prominent than the first). While a majority of the languages have diphthongs only of Class I type, two of them have the diphthongs only of Class II type, namely, Angami and Ao-Naga.

The Table should be read keeping the following points in mind. The first column gives the serial numbers of the patterns. The second column gives the numbers of the types of vowels according to the pattern of SV-LV-DV-TV-NV. The seven columns that follow list the languages according to their families that exemplify the patterns. Finally, the last column gives the vowels attested in the languages.v

The patterns are presented in terms of increasing complexity, as far as possible. Thus the first pattern of 5-0-0-0-0 consists only of five short vowels. The last pattern 7-8-7-0-19 for the Indo-Aryan language Shina consists of a total of 41 vowels. The notion of complexity however is based on two factors: one, the types of vowels- the greater the number of types, the more complex a system is; two, the number of vowels within each pattern type- 7-5-0-0-4 is less complex than 7-4-0-0-7. This only gives a general assessment of the relative complexity of the patterns, not an absolute one.

The vowel patterns have the following order: SV-LV-DV-TV-NV. Thus, the pattern for Shina, i.e. 7-8-7-0-19, should be read as 7 short monophthongs, 8 long monophthongs, 7 diphthongs, nil triphthongs, and 19 nasal vowels. All the vowels found in the language are given in the final column.

Note that in the final column there are slashes for those patterns which illustrate more than one language. The slashes specify the alternative

---

[4] Unless specified, the vowels are oral vowels.

[5] Triphthongs are limited to two languages of the T-B group. Generalizations about all vowels do not take these into account, unless mentioned otherwise.

instantiations of the pattern. Thus the six vowel pattern found for nine of the Indic languages, eight from the T-B group, in serial no. 3, has two of the vowels, namely, /i/ and /a/ constant, but the remaining four belong to one of the alternatives, e or ɛ, u or ɯ, o or ɔ, and ɨ or ə. By implication, there is no language with a six vowel pattern that has, for example, the vowels /i e ɛ u o a/ or /i e u ɯ o a/.

Table 4.1: Vowel patterns in SPIL

Main groups	Vowel Pattern S-L-D-T-N	A-A	DR	I-A	T-B	T-K	AN	C-V	H-V	Vowels
A: Oral Vowels Only	**i. Short monophthongs only**									
	5-0-0-0-0	Mundari Santali	Gondi		Chokri Karbi Ladakhi Monpa Spiti					SV: i/I e/ɛ u/ʊ/ɨ o/ɔ a/ə/ɐ
	6-0-0-0-0				Apatani Boro Kokborok Lotha Meitei Sema-N Tod Tarao			Halbi		SV: i e/ɛ u/ɯ o/ɔ ɨ/ə a
	7-0-0-0-0				Bantawa Galo- L Khezha Rawang		Onge			SV: i e u o ɯ/ɤ/ɨ/ɜ ə a
	7-0-0-0-0				Maring					SV: i e u o ə a ɑ
	5(+1)-0-0-0-0				Magar					SV: i e u o (ə) a

contd.

Table 4.1 *contd.*

	5(+2)-0-0-0-0	Juang								SV: i e (ɛ) u (o) ɔ a
	8-0-0-0-0				Thaadou					SV: i e ɛ u o ɔ ɐ a
	9-0-0-0-0					Khampti				SV: i e ɛ u ɯ o ɔ ɨ a
	ii. Short and long monophthongs									
	3-5-0-0-0								Prakrit	SV: i u ə LV: iː eː uː oː aː
	3-7-0-0-0								Sans-Cl[1]	SV: i u ə LV: iː eː æː uː oː ɑːː aː
	4-5-0-0-0				Darma					SV: ɛ u ɔ ə LV: iː eː uː oː aː
	5-5-0-0-0		Ave Badaga Gondi-A Kolami Konda Kota Koya Kui Malto Manda Naiki Gadab-O Yerava	Mahl Brokskat	Balti Chaudang Purki Tamang Zo				OTa OTe	SV: i e/ɛ u/ɯ o/ɔ a/ə LV: iː eː uː oː aː/ɑː

contd.

Table 4.1 *contd.*

	5(+1)-5-0-0-0		Kannada							SV: i e (æ) u o a LV: iː eː uː oː aː
	5-6-0-0-0				Hmar					SV: i e u ɔ ɐ LV: iː eː uː oː ɔː aː
	6-1-0-0-0	Gorum			Kabui Tangsa					SV: i e u o ə/ɔ a LV: əː/uː/ɒː
	8-1-0-0-0				Galo					SV: i e ɛ u o ɔ ɨ a LV: ɒː
	6-5-0-0-0		Malaya* Telugu			Turung				SV: i e u o ɨ/ə/æ a LV: iː eː uː oː aː
	6-6-0-0-0		Kadar							SV: i e u o ə a LV: iː eː uː oː əː aː
	6-7-0-0-0				Limbu[2]					SV: i ɛ u ʌ ə ɐ LV: iː eˑ ɛː uː ʌː oˑ ɐː
	7-4-0-0-0				Gallong					SV: i e œ u o ɨ a LV: iː uː oː aː
	7-7-0-0-0		Koraga							SV: i e ɛ u o ɨ a LV: iː eː ɛː uː oː ɨː aː
	7-7-0-0-0						G-A*			SV: i e ɛ u o ɔ a LV: iː eː ɛː uː oː ɔː aː
	8-8-0-0-0		Kodagu Toda							SV: i ʏ/ɛ e u ɯ o ɤ/ə e a LV: iː ʏː/ɛː eː uː ɯː oː ɤː/əː aː

contd.

Table 4.1 *contd.*

	9-3-0-0-0				Byangsi					SV: i e ɛ u ɯ o ɔ ɨ a LV: iː uː aː
	9-4-0-0-0				Padam					SV: i e u o ɔ ʌ ɑ ɨ ə LV: iː uː oː ɑː
	10-10-0-0-0		Irula							SV: i ï e ë u ü o ö a ä LV: iː ïː eː ë uː üː oː öː aː äː
	11-9-0-0-0				Adi					SV: i e ɛ æ u o ɔ ɨ ü ə a LV: iː eː ɛː uː oː ɔː ɨː əː aː
	iii. Short monophthongs, Diphthongs									
	5-0-8-0-0				Mizo					SV: i e u o a DV: ai au ɔu ɔi ei eu ia ua
	5-0-9-0-0				Liangmai					SV: i ɛ u ɔ a DV: ai̯ iu̯ au̯ ui̯ ɔi̯; i̯a i̯o i̯e ɔ̯a
	5-0-5-0-0				Garo					SV: i e u o a DV: ai au oi/ou/ ei ui
	6-0-3-0-0	Ho								SV: i e u o ɔ a DV: ai au ɔĩ
	6-0-5(+1)-0-0				Angami*			Nagame		SV: i e u o ə/ɞ a DV: i̯e i̯o (e̯o) ə̯i o̯u u̯o

contd.

Table 4.1 *contd.*

	6-0-6-0-0				Mao-Naga					SV: ie u o ɨ a DV: əi̯ ou̯ i̯u ə̯i ə̯u ə̯e
	8-0-5-0-0							Bishnu		SV: i e ɛ u o ɔ ɑ a DV: ei ai ɑu ɔi ɔu
	6-0-6-0-0				Dimasa					SV: ɪ ɛ ʊ ɔ ə a DV: ei ai oi ui əo ao
	7-0-5(+1)-0-0				Ao-Naga*					SV: i e u ɰ o ə ɑ DV: i̯e i̯o (e̯o) ə̯i o̯u u̯o
	10-0-6-0-0				Phom					SV: i e ɛ æ u ɰ o ɔ e a DV: aI ʌI aɰ ɛɰ aʊ oI
	6-0-5-0-0			Chakma						SV: i e æ u o ɒ DV: ɛi ai ɒi oi ui
	iv. Short monophthongs, Long monophthongs, Diphthongs									
	4-7-3-0-0							IE-H		SV: i e u ə LV: i:e: ɛ: u: o: ɔ: a: DV: ai au ɔe
	5-5-3-0-0	Khasi								SV: i e u o a LV: i:e: u: o: a: DV: ia ie uo

contd.

Table 4.1 *contd.*

	5-5-4-0-0		Pengo							SV: i e u o a LV: i:e: u: o: a: DV: ej aj oj uj
	v. Short monophthongs, Diphthongs, Triphthongs									
	6-0-10-4-0				Paite					SV: i e u o ə a DV: əj ai ej oj uj ew əw aw i̯a u̯a TV: i̯aj u̯aj i̯aw u̯aw
	vi. Short monophthongs, Diphthongs, Triphthongs Diphthongs, Triphthongs									
	6-5-12-3-0				Koren					SV: i e u o ə a LV: i: e: u: o: a: DV: iu io ia ie iu uo uə ui ou oi ei ai TV: uoi uia uəi
B. Oral and Nasal vowels	**vii. Short monophthongs, Nasals**									

contd.

Table 4.1 *contd.*

	5-0-0-0-5	Kharia		Gujarati*						SV: i e u o a NV: ĩ ẽ ũ õ ã
	6-0-0-0-3				Manchad					SV: i e u o ə ɑ NV: ẽ õ ã
	6-0-0-0-5				Nepali					SV: i e u o ʌ a NV: ĩ ẽ ũ ʌ̃ ã
	6-0-0-0-6	Kisan Gada-G								SV: i e u o ɞ/ɔ a NV: ĩ ẽ ũ õ ɞ̃/ɔ̃ ã
	6-0-0-0-7			Oriya						SV: i e u o ɔ a NV: ĩ ẽ ɛ̃ ũ ɔ̃ ə̃ ã
	7-0-0-0-7			Bengali	Raji					SV: i e æ/ɛ u o ɞ/ə a NV: ĩ ẽ æ̃ ũ õ ɞ̃/ə̃ ã
	8-0-0-0-5			Bhili						SV: i e ɛ u o ɨ ə a NV: ĩ ɛ̃ ũ ə̃ ã
	8-0-0-0-7			Assame-se						SV: i e ɛ u o ɞ ɒ a NV: ĩ ẽ ɛ̃ ũ õ ɒ̃ ã
	8-0-0-0-8			Maithili						SV: i e æ u o ɔ ə a NV: ĩ ẽ æ̃ ũ õ ɔ̃ ə̃ ã
	viii. Short monophthongs, Long monophthongs, Nasals									

contd.

Table 4.1 *contd.*

	3-5-0-0-3								Pali	SV: I ʊ ə LV: i: e: u: o: a: NV: ĩ ʊ̃ ã:
	3-7-0-0-5(+2)			Dogri						SV: I ʊ ə LV: ï: e: ɛ: u: o: ɔ: a: NV: ĩ: ẽ: (ɛ̃:) ũ: õ: (ɔ:) ã:
	3-7-0-0-7			Punjabi						SV: I ʊ ə ; LV: ï: e: æ: u: o: ɶ: a: NV: ĩ: ẽ: æ̃: ũ: õ: ɶ̃: ã:
	3-7-0-0-8			Kacchi						SV: I ʊ ə LV: ï: e: ɛ: u: o: ɔ: a: NV: ĩ: ẽ: ɛ̃: ũ: õ: ɔ̃: ə ã:
	3-7-0-0-9			Gojri Lahndi						SV: I ʊ ə/ɐ LV: ï: e: ɛ: o: ɔ:/ɶ: a:/ɑ: NV: ĩ ĩ: ẽ: ɛ̃: ũ: ʊ̃ õ: ɔ̃:/ɶ: ã:/ɑ:
	3-5-0-0-8			Urdu-D-H						SV: I ʊ ə LV: ï: e: u: o: a: NV: ĩ ĩ: ẽ: ũ: ũ õ: ə̃ ã:
	3-5(+2)-0-0-8(+2)			Sindhi						SV: I ʊ ə LV: ï: e: (ɛ:) u: o: (ɔ:) a: NV: ĩ ĩ: ẽ: (ɛ̃:) ũ: ũ õ: (ɔ̃:) ə̃ ã:
	3-7-0-0-10			Bagri Hindi* Urdu						SV: I ʊ ə LV: ï: e: ɛ: (æ:) u: o: ɶ: a: NV: ĩ ĩ: ẽ: ɛ̃: ũ: ʊ̃ õ: ɔ̃: ɶ̃ ã:

contd.

Table 4.1 *contd.*

	4-7-0-0-8				RangPo					SV: I ʊ ə a LV: ï: e: ɛ: u: o: ɔ: a: NV: ĩ: ẽ: ɛ̃: ũ: õ: ɔ̃: ã:
	5-3-0-0-8			Garhwali						SV: i e u o a LV: i: u: a: NV: ĩ ĩ: ẽ ũ ũ: õ ã ã:
	5-1-0-0-6			Lamani						SV: i e u o ə LV: ɑ: NV: ĩ ẽ ũ õ ɑ̃: ə̃
	5-5-0-0-1	Korku	Gadaba-(K)							SV: i e u o a/ɐ LV: i: e: u: o: a:/ɐ: NV: ã:
	5-5-0-0-6		Tamil							SV: i e u o a LV: i: e: u: o: a: NV: ẽ/ ẽ: õ / õ: ã / ã:
	5(+1)-5-0-0-6			Tibetan-St						SV: i e u o a (ɔ) LV: i: e: u: o: a: NV: ỹ: ø̃: œ̃: ũ: õ: ã:
	5-5-0-0-10		Kurux Kuvi		Kangri					SV: i e u o a LV: i: e: u: o: a: NV: ĩ ĩ: ẽ ẽ: ũ ũ: õ õ: ã ã:
	5-5-0-0-09							Urdu-D-T		SV: i ɛ u ɔ a LV: i: e: u: o: a: NV: ĩ ĩ: ẽ: ũ ũ: ɔ̃ õ: ã ã:

contd.

Table 4.1 *contd.*

	5-7-0-0-12			Bangru						SV: ï: I ü ʊ ə LV: ï: e: æ: u: o: a: NV: Ĩ ĩ̈: ĩ: ẽ: ɛ̃: ũ: ũ̈: ʊ̃ õ: ɔ̃ ə̃ ã:
	6-5-0-0-8							Vagri-B		SV: i e u o ɨ a LV: i: e: u: o: a: NV: ĩ: ẽ ẽ: ũ ũ: õ: ã ã:
	6-6-0-0-3	Bhumij			Mishimi					SV: i e u o ɔ a LV: i: e: u: o: ɔ: a: NV: ẽ õ ã
	6-6-0-0-12			Mandeali						SV: i e u o ə a LV: ĩ: e: æ: u: o: ɞ: a: NV: ĩ ĩ: ẽ ẽ: ũ ũ̈ : õ õ: ɞ: ɞ: ã ã:
	6-6-0-0-10		Kattu							SV: i e u o ɨ ɐ LV: i: e: u: o: ɨ: a: NV: ĩ ĩ: ẽ ũ̈: ũ: õ ɨ̃ ə̃ ɐ̃ ã:
	7-6-0-0-1		Tulu							SV: i e ɛ u ɯ o ɐ LV: i: e: ɛ: u: o: a: NV: ã
	8-9-0-0-(3)	Nico*								SV: i e u ɯ o ɔ ɒ LV: i: e: ɛ: u: o: ɔ: ɒ: ə:
	9-4-0-0-6	Bonda								SV: i I e u ʊ o ɔ a ə LV: i: e: u: a: NV: ĩ ẽ ũ õ ɔ̃ ã

contd.

Table 4.1 *contd.*

	8-3-0-0-12		Konkani							SV: i e ɛ u o ɔ ə a LV: i: u: a: NV: ĩ ĩ: ẽ ɛ̃ ũ ũ: õ ɔ̃ ã ã:
	8-5-0-0-7		Rathvi							SV: i e ɛ u o ɔ ə a LV: i: e: u: o: a: NV: ĩ ẽ ɛ̃ ũ õ ə̃ ã
	9-6-0-0-15			Kinnauri						SV: i e ɛ u o ɔ ɨ ə a LV: i: e: ɛ: u: o: a: NV: ĩ ĩ: ẽ ẽ̃: ɛ̃ ɛ̃: ũ̃ ũ: õ õ: ɔ̃ ɨ̃ ə̃ ã ã:
	10-10-0-0-3		Lepcha							SV: i e ɛ u ɯ o ɤ ɔ ə a LV: i: e: ɛ: u: ɯ: ɤ: o: ɔ: ə: a: NV: ɔ̃ ɔ̃: ã:
	ix. Short monophthongs, Diphthongs, Nasals									
	6-0-3-0-(6)	Didayi								SV: i e ɛ u o a; DV: a̯i̯ au̯ ɔi̯ NV: (ĩ ẽ ɛ̃ ũ õ ã)
	7-0-8-0-(1)				Wancho*					SV: i e u ɯ o ə a DV: aI əI aʊ i̯ei̯a u̯i u̯a u̯o NV: (ã)

contd.

Table 4.1 *contd.*

	9-0-3-0-9	Nanco*								SV: i e ɛ æ u o (ɔ) ɨ ə a DV: ia ua ɨa NV: ĩ ẽ ɛ̃ æ̃ ũ õ ɨ̃ ə̃ ã
	7(+1)-0-11-0-9							DI-P		SV: i e ɛ æ u o ɔ (ə) DV: iw ew ɛw aw ej ɛj əj aj ɔj oj uj NV: ĩ ẽ ɛ̃ æ̃ ũ õ ɨ̃ ə̃ ã ẽj ɔ̃j ãj ãw
	6-0-10-0-10				Kiranti-K					SV: i ɛ u o ə a DV: ai ɛi əi oi ui au ɛu əu iu əɛ NV: ĩ ɛ̃ ũ õ ə̃ ã ə̃ĩ ãĩ ũĩ õi
	x. Short monophthongs, Long monophthongs, Diphthongs, Nasals									
	3-7-4-0-10			Jaunsari						SV: ɪ ʊ a LV: iː eː ɛː uː oː ɔː aː DV: ai̯ au̯ i̯u u̯a NV: ĩ ʊ̃ ã ĩː ẽː ɛ̃ː ũː õː ɔ̃ː ãː
	5-1-2-0-8			Bhojpuri Magahi						SV: i e u o ə LV: aː DV: əi əu NV: ĩ ẽ ũ õ ə̃ ãː əĩ əũ

contd.

Table 4.1 *contd.*

	7-3-2-0-4			Marathi						SV: i e æ ʊ o ɔ a LV: iː uː aː DV: əi ə u NV: ẽ ũ ə̃ ã
	8-8-4-0-13			Kashmiri						SV: i e u o ɑ ɨ ə a LV: ĩː eː ɛː uː ɔː ɨː əː aː DV: uI uːI oə ɑaː NV: Ĩ ĩː ẽ ẽː ʊ̃ ũː õ ɔ̃ː ɨ̃ː ə̃ ə̃ː ɐ̃ ãː
	7-8-7-0-19			Shina						SV: i e ɛ u o ə a LV: iː eː ɛː uː oː ɔː əː aː DV: ei ɛi ai ui oi au eə NV: Ĩ ĩː ẽ ẽː ɛ̃ ɛ̃ː ũ ũː õ õː ə̃ ə̃ː ã ãː ẽĩ ɛ̃ĩ ãĩ ũĩ õĩ ãũ ẽə̃

The generalizations from the data presented in *Table 4.1* are presented in two parts – general and typological.

General features of the vowel patterns

The general features of the vowel patterns in the languages of India can be stated as follows.

a. The total number of vowels in the languages reported here range between 5 (pattern 5-0-0-0) and 41 (pattern 7-8-7-0-19, Shina).

b. There are languages with only short vowels, but there is no language with only long vowels, diphthongs, triphthongs or nasal vowels.

c. Nasal vowels have corresponding oral vowels in the language, and do not exceed the number of oral vowels in a language.

d. Unlike the nasal vowels, long vowels and diphthongs are found to have no restriction on their inventory in relation to the short oral vowels.

e. Most languages have instances of vowels undergoing change among all types[6] found across the language groups, mentioned in parentheses. A majority of them appear to be cases of emerging vowels, for example, nasal vowels in Dravidian and T-B languages.

f. The main patterns of the vowels are as follows:

(4/1)	Short vowels only	27
	Short + Long vowels	46
	Short vowels + Diphthongs	12
	Short vowels + Long vowels + Diphthongs	03
	Short vowels + Diphthongs + Triphthongs	01
	Short vowels + Long vowels + Diphthongs + Triphthongs	01
	Short vowels + Nasal vowels	12
	Short vowels + Long vowels + Nasal vowels	35
	Short vowels + Diphthongs + Nasal vowels	04
	Short vowels + Long vowels + Diphthongs + Nasal vowels	07
	Total no. of vowel patterns	148

g. The total number of languages with the different vowel types are as follows:

(4/2)	Total no. of languages:	148
	No. of languages with short oral vowels:	148
	No. of languages with long oral vowels:	92

[6] As mentioned above, the generalization does not apply to triphthongs.

No. of languages with oral diphthongs: 28
No. of languages with oral triphthongs: 02
No. of languages with Nasal vowels: 56
Note that all languages have short vowels.

Typological features

The typological features of phonemic vowel patterns in Indian languages can be derived from *Table 4.2* and *Table 4.3*. The features are discussed following the tables below.

Table 4.2 distribution of vowel patterns in Indic languages

VOWEL PATTERNS	ALL	A-A	DR	I-A	T-B	T-K	AN	C-V	H-V
SV	**28**	03	01	01	**20**	01	01	01	–
SV + LV	**47**	02	**21**	02	15	01	02	00	04
SV + DV	**12**	01	–	01	**08**	–	–	02	–
SV + LV + DV	**03**	01	01	–	00	–	–	01	–
SV + DV + TV	**01**	–	–	–	**01**	–	–	–	–
SV + LV+ DV + TV	**01**	–	–	–	**01**	–	–	–	–
SV + NV	**11**	02	–	**06**	03	–	–	–	–
SV + LV+ NV	**34**	04	06	**15**	06	–	–	02	01
SV + DV + NV	**04**	02	–	–	01	–	–	01	–
SV + LV+ DV + NV	**07**	–	–	**07**	–	–	–		–
Total languages	**148**	15	29	32	55	02	03	07	05

Table 4.3 Distribution of vowel types in Indic languages

VOWEL TYPES	ALL	A-A	DR	I-A	T-B	T-K	AN	C-V	H-V
SV:	148	13	29	32	55	02	03	07	05
LV:	92	06	**28**	**24**	23	01	**02**	03	**05**
DV:	28	04	01	08	11	–	–	**04**	–
TV:	02	–	–	–	**02**	–	–	–	–
NV:	56	08	06	**28**	10	–	–	03	01

a. Austro-Asiatic languages exemplify all the vowel patterns, except for triphthongs, which are limited to two languages of the T-B group.

b. Dravidian languages are characterized by (a) the presence of long vowels, and (b) an equation between the numbers of short and long vowels. Most commonly, they observe the 5-5 pattern for short and long vowels. Some of the languages of the southern group have larger than 5-5 patterns, especially Irula (10-10) and Kodagu and Toda (8-8 pattern). Gondi, a central Dravidian language, is alone in being without long vowels.

c. I-A languages are characterized by the presence of nasal vowels. 28 out of 32 languages have nasal vowels in them. A majority of them also have long vowels- 24 out of 32. The pattern with the largest number of types of vowels- SV-L-D-N- -s also found only in the Indo-Aryan group. 7 languages have it.

d. The T-B group has the following predominant patterns:

   i. Short vowels only. Out of a total of 28 languages with only short vowels, 21 belong to the T-B groups, while 3 belong to Austro-Asiatic and 1 each to Dravidian, Indo-Aryan, Andamanese and Contact Varieties.

   ii. Diphthongs and triphthongs without long vowels.

   iii. Triphthongs.

   iv. Nasal vowels found mainly in the northern or north western (but not north-eastern, except Mishmi, with only 3 nasal vowels).

e. The T-K group has short only and short and long vowel patterns.

f. The AN group has only oral vowels: 2 of the 3 languages have long vowels.

g. The C-V languages do not have noticeable features in the patterns of vowels. Most of them have features related to their source language languages. Thus T-B based languages have patterns of their T-B sources: Naga Pidgin and Bishnupuria have S-D, S-L-D patterns. Similarly VB and Diu have a large number of nasal vowels like their source languages.

h. The H-V languages, too, like the C-V varieties, pattern like the languages of the groups to which they belong, Dravidian and I-A.

4.1.2 Vowel phoneme inventory

The list of the vowel phonemes and their occurrence in the Indic languages are given in *Table 4.4*. While a consideration of Table *4.1* presents a general view of the patterns of the vowel types in the languages, *Table 4.4* can help us look at the pattern of the organization of the vowel types in terms of their qualities on the parameters of tongue height, tongue position and lip-rounding. The facts of the organization of vowels and vowel types in Indic languages are discussed below.

Table 4.4 Vowel phoneme inventory in SPIL

SVs	No. of vowels	Description & languages	LG
i	126	*Short, unrounded, close, front vowel*	
	12	Bhumij, Bonda, Didayi, Gadaba-G, Gorum, Ho, Juang, Kharia, Kisan, Korku, Mundari, Nancowry, Nicobarese-C, Santali	A-A
	27	Ave, Badaga, Gadaba-K, Gadaba-O, Gondi, Gondi-A, Irula, Kadar, Kattunaicka, Kodagu, Kolami, Konda, Koraga, Kota, Koya, Kui, Kuvi, Malayalam, Malto, Manda, Naiki, Pengo, Tamil, Telugu, Toda, Tulu, Yerava	DR
	19	Assamese, Bengali, Bhili, Bhojpuri, Brokskat,Garhwali, Gujarati, Haryanvi, Konkani, Lahndi, Lamani, Magahi, Mahl, Maithili, Mandeali, Nepali, Oriya, Rathvi, Shina	I-A
	50	Adi, Angami, Ao-N, Apatani, Balti, Bantawa, Bodo, Byangsi, Chokri, Dimasa, Gallong, Galo, Galo-L, Garo, Hmar, Kabui, Karbi, Kheza, Kinnauri, Kiranti-K, Kokborok, Koren, Lepcha, Ladakhi, Liangmai, Limbu, Lotha, Magar, Manchad, Mao-N, Maring, Meitei, Mishmi, Mizo, Monpa, Padaam, Phom, Purki, Raji, RangPo, Rawang, Sema-N, Tibetan-St, Spiti, Tamang, Tangsa, Tarao, Thaadou, Stod, Wancho, Zo.	T-B
	02	Khampti, Turung	T-K
	05	G-Andamanese, Jarawa, Onge	AN
	06	Bishnupuria, Diu-I-P, Halbi, Nagamese, Vagri-B, IE-H	C-V
	05	Sanskrit-Cl, Pali, Prakrit, O-Tamil, O-Telugu	H-V
ɪ		*Short, unrounded, between close and close-mid, front vowel*	
		Khasi	A-A
		Kannada, Kurux	DR
		Bagri, Dogri, Gojri,Haryanvi,Hindi,Jaunsari,Kacchi,Kashmiri,Marathi,Punjabi,Sindhi,Urdu,Urdu-D-H	I-A
		Chaudangsi, Kangri, Dimasa, Paite	T-B
		Urdu-D-T	C-V
ï		*Short, unrounded, close, centralized front vowel*	

contd.

Table 4.4 *contd.*

		Irula	DR
		Haryanwi	I-A
Y		*Short, rounded, close, front vowel*	
		Toda	DR
e	127	*Short, unrounded, close-mid, front vowel*	
	12	Bhumij, Bonda, Didayi, Gadaba-G, Gorum, Ho, Juang, Kharia, Khasi, Kisan, Korku, Nancowry, Nicobarese-C, Santali.	A-A
	28	Ave, Badaga, Gadaba-K, Gadaba-O, Gondi, Gondi-A, Irula, Kadar, Kannada, Kattunaicka, Kodagu, Kolami, Konda, Koraga, Kota, Koya, Kui, Kuvi, Malayalam, Malto, Manda, Naiki, Pengo, Tamil, Telugu, Toda, Tulu, Yerava	DR
	19	Assamese, Bagri, Bengali, Bhili, Bhojpuri, Garhwali, Gujarati, Kashmiri, Konkani, Lamani, Magahi, Mahl, Maithili, Mandeali, Marathi, Nepali, Oriya, Rathvi, Shina,	I-A
	50	Adi, Angami, Ao-N, Apatani, Balti, Bantawa, Bodo, Brokskat, Byangsi, Chokri, GalShort, Galo, Galo-L, Garo, Hmar, Kabui, Kangri, Karbi, Kheza, Kinnauri, Kiranti-K, Koren, Lepcha, Ladakhi, Limbu, Lotha, Magar, Manchad, Mao-N, Maring, Meitei, Mishmi, Mizo, Monpa, Padaam, Paite, Phom, Purki, Raji, Rawang, Sema-N, Tibetan-St, Spiti, Tamang, Tangsa, Tarao, Thaadou, Stod, Wancho, Zo.	T-B
	02	Khampti, Turung	T-K
	05	G-Andamanese, Jarawa, Onge	AN
	06	Bishnupuria, Diu-I-P, Halbi, Nagamese, Vagri-B, IE-H	C-V
	05	Sanskrit-Cl, Pali, Prakrit, O-Tamil, O-Telugu	H-V
œ		*Short, rounded, close-mid, front vowel*	
		Gallong	T-B
ë		*Short, unrounded, close-mid, centralized front vowel*	
		Irula	DR
ɛ		*Short, unrounded, open-mid, front vowel*	
		Bonda, Didayi, (Juang), Kharia, Mundari, Nicobarese-C	A-A
		Kodagu, Koraga, Kurux, Telugu, Tulu	DR

contd.

Table 4.4 *contd.*

		Assamese, Bhili, Chakma,(Gujarati), Konkani,Mahl, Rathvi, Shina, (Sindhi)	I-A
		Adi, Byangsi, Chaudangsi, Darma, Dimasa, Galo, Kinnauri, Kiranti-K,Kokborok, Lepcha, Liangmai, Limbu, Phom, Raji, Rangpo, Thaadou	T-B
		Khampti	T-K
		G-A, Onge	AN
		Bishnupuria, Diu-I-P, Urdu-D-T	C-V
æ		*Short, unrounded, just below open-mid, front vowel*	
		Nicobarese	A-A
		(Kannada), (Malayalam), Telugu	DR
		Bengali, Chakma, Maithili, Marathi,	I-A
		Phom	T-B
		G-Andamanese	AN
ä		*Short, open, centralized front vowel*	
		Irula	DR
ɨ		*Short, unrounded, close, central vowel*	
		Khasi, Nancowry	A-A
		Kattunaicka, Koraga	DR
		Bhili, Kashmiri	I-A
		Adi, Apatani,Byangsi, Chokri, Gallong, Galo, Galo-L, Kinnauri.Mao-N, Mishmi, Padaam, Rawang, Sema-N	T-B
		Khampti	T-K
		Jarawa *(close-mid),* (Onge)	AN
		Vagri-B	C-V
ʉ		*Short, rounded, close, central vowel*	
		Adi	T-B
ɵ		*Short, rounded, close-mid, central vowel*	
		Toda	DR

contd.

Table 4.4 *contd.*

ə	72 (+1)	*Short, unrounded, mid, central vowel*	
	04	Bonda, Juang, Korku, Nancowry	A-A
	09	Gadaba-K, Kadar, Kannada, Kattunaicka, Kodagu, Kolami, Kui, Malayalam,Tulu	DR
	24	Bagri, Bhili, Bhojpuri, Dogri, Gojri, Gujarati, Haryanvi, Hindi, Kacchi, Kashmiri, Konkani, Lahndi, Lamani, Magahi, Maithili, Mandeali, Marathi, Punjabi, Rathvi, Shina, Sindhi, Urdu, Urdu-D-H.	I-A
	24 (+1)	Adi, Angami, Bantawa, Bodo, Brokskat, Byangsi, Chaudangsi, Darma, Dimasa, Galo-L, Hmar, Kabui, Kheza, Kinnauri, Kiranti-K, Kokborok, Koren, Lepcha, Ladakhi, Limbu, Lotha, Magar, Manchad, Maring, Meitei, Padaam, Paite, Phom, Raji, RangPo, Rawang, (Spiti), Tarao, Stod, Wancho, Zo	T-B
	01	Turung	T-K
	05	G-Andamanese, Jarawa, Onge	AN
	03	Diu-I-P, Halbi, IE-H	C-V
	03	Sanskrit-Cl, Pali, Prakrit	H-V
ɞ		*Short, rounded, open-mid, central vowel*	
		Gadaba-G, Gorum	A-A
		Assamese, Bengali	I-A
		Khezha,	T-B
		Nagamese	C-V
ɐ		*Short, unrounded, between open-mid and open, central vowel*	
		Korku	A-A
		Kattunaicka, Telugu	DR
		Kashmiri, Lahndi	I-A
		Hmar, Limbu, Monpa	T-B
		Urdu-D-T	C-V
a	109 (+1)	*Short, unrounded, open, central vowel*	

contd.

Table 4.4 *contd.*

	12	Bhumij, Bonda, Didayi, Gadaba-G, Gorum, Ho, Juang, Kharia, Khasi, Kisan, Mundari, Nancowry, (Nicobarese-C), Santali.	A-A
	23	Ave, Badaga, Gadaba-K, Gadaba-O, Gondi, Gondi-A, Irula, Kadar, Kannada, Kodagu, Kolami, Konda, Koraga, Kota, Koya, Kui, Kuvi, Malayalam, Malto, Pengo, Tamil, Telugu, Yerava.	DR
	16	Assamese, Bengali, Bhili, Garhwali, Gujarati, Jaunsari, Konkani, Mahl, Maithili, Mandeali, Marathi, Nepali, Oriya, Rathvi, Shina, Urdu-D-H	I-A
	44	Adi, Angami, Apatani, Balti, Bantawa, Bodo, Brokskat, Chokri, Dimasa, Gallong, Galo, Galo-L, Garo, Kabui, Kangri, Karbi, Kheza, Kinnauri, Kiranti-K, Kokborok, Koren, Lepcha, Liangmai, Lotha, Magar, Manchad, Mao-N, Maring, Meitei, Mishmi, Mizo, , Padaam, Paite, Phom, Purki, Raji, RangPo, Rawang, Sema-N, Tibetan-St, Tamang, Tangsa, Tarao, Thaadou, Wancho .	T-B
	2	Khampti, Turung	T-K
	4 (+1)	G-Andamanese, Jarawa, Onge	AN
	05	Bishnupuria, Diu-I-P, Halbi, Nagamese, Vagri-B	C-V
	03	Sanskrit-Cl, O-Tamil, O-Telugu	H-V
u	126	*Short, rounded, close, back vowel*	
	12	Bhumij, Bonda, Didayi, Gadaba-G, Gorum, Ho, Juang, Kharia, Kisan, Korku, Mundari, Nancowry, (Nicobarese-C), Santali.	A-A
	27	Ave, Badaga, Gadaba-K, Gadaba-O, Gondi, Gondi-A, Irula, Kadar, Kattunaicka, Kodagu, Kolami, Konda, Koraga, Kota, Koya, Kui, Kuvi, Malayalam, Malto, Manda, Naiki, Pengo, Tamil, Telugu, Toda, Tulu, Yerava.	DR
	18	Assamese, Bengali, Bhili, Bhojpuri, Garhwali, Gujarati, Konkani, Lahndi, Lamani, Magahi, Mahl, Maithili, Mandeali, Nepali, Oriya, Rathvi, Shina,Urdu-D-H	I-A
	51	Adi, Angami, Ao-N, Apatani, Balti, Bantawa, Bodo, Brokskat, Byangsi, Chokri, Gallong, Galo, Galo-L, Garo, Hmar, Kabui, Karbi, Kheza, Kinnauri, Kiranti-K, Kokborok, Koren, Lepcha, Ladakhi, Liangmai, Limbu, Lotha, Magar, Manchad, Mao-N, Maring, Meitei, Mishmi, Mizo, Monpa, Padaam, Phom, Purki, Raji, RangPo, Rawang, Sema-N, Tibetan-St, Spiti, Tamang, Tangsa, Tarao, Thaadou, Stod, Wancho, Zo.	T-B
	02	Khampti, Turung	T-K
	05	G-Andamanese, Jarawa, Onge	AN

contd.

Table 4.4 *contd.*

	05	Bishnupuria, Diu-I-P, Halbi, Nagamese, Vagri-B, IE-H.	C-V
	05	Sanskrit-Cl, Pali, Prakrit, O-Tamil, O-Telugu	H-V
ʊ		*Short, rounded, between close and close-mid, back vowel*	
		Khasi	A-A
		Kannada, Kurux	DR
		Bagri, Dogri, Gojri, Haryanwi, Hindi, Jaunsari, Kacchi, Kashmiri, Marathi, Punjabi, Sindhi,Urdu,Urdu-D-H	I-A
		Dimasa, Kangri, Paite	T-B
		Urdu-D-T	C-V
ü		*Short, rounded, close, centralized back vowel*	
		Irula	DR
		Hariyanvi	I-A
ɯ		*Short, unrounded, close, back vowel*	
		Nicobarese-C	A-A
		Kodagu, Toda, Tulu	DR
		Ao-N, Bantawa, Boro, Byangsi, Darma, Lepcha, Phom, Wancho	T-B
		Khampti	T-K
o	*25(+1)	*Short, rounded,close-mid, back vowel*	
	11(+1)	Bhumij, Bonda, Didayi, Gadaba-Gutob, Gorum, Ho, (Juang), Kharia, Khasi, Kisan, Korku, Nancowry, Nicobarese-C, Santali.	A-A
	28	Ave, Badaga, Gadaba-K, Gadaba-O, Gondi, Gondi-A, Irula, Kadar, Kannada, Kattunaicka, Kodagu, Kolami, Konda, Koraga, Kota, Koya, Kui, Kuvi, Malayalam, Malto, Manda, Naiki, Pengo, Tamil, Telugu, Toda, Tulu, Yerava.	DR
	19	Assamese, Bagri, Bengali, Bhili, Bhojpuri, Chakma, Garhwali, Gujarati, Kashmiri, Konkani, Lamani, Magahi, Maithili, Mandeali, Marathi, Nepali, Oriya, Rathvi, Shina	I-A
	48	Adi, Angami, Ao-N, Apatani, Balti, Bantawa, Bodo, Brokskat, Byangsi, Chokri, GalShort, Galo, Galo-L, Garo, Kabui, Kangri, Karbi, Kheza, Kinnauri, Kiranti-K, Koren, Lepcha, Ladakhi, Lotha, Magar, Manchad, Mao-N, Maring, Meitei, Mishmi, Mizo, Monpa, Padaam, Paite, Phom, Purki, Raji, Rawang, Sema-N, Spiti, Stod, Tamang, Tangsa, Tarao, Thaadou, Tibetan-St, Wancho, Zo	T-B
	02	Khampti, Turung	T-K
	05	G-Andamanese, Jarawa, Onge	AN

contd.

Table 4.4 *contd.*

	05	Bishnupuria, Diu-I-P, Halbi, Nagamese, Vagri-B, Urdu-D-T	C-V
	02	O-Tamil, O-Telugu	H-V
ö		*Short, rounded, close-mid, centralized back vowel*	
		Irula	DR
ɤ		*Short, unrounded, close-mid, back vowel*	
		Kodagu	DR
		Lepcha	T-B
		Onge	AN
ɔ		*Short, rounded, open-mid, back vowel*	
		Bhumij, Bonda, Ho, Juang, Kharia, Kisan, Mundari, (Nancowry), Nicobarese-C	A-A
		Kurux	DR
		Assamese, (Gujarati), Oriya, Rathvi	I-A
		Adi, Byangsi, Chaudangsi, Darma, Dimasa, Galo, Hmar, Kinnauri, Kiranti-K, Kokborok, Liangmai, Lepcha, Phom, Tangsa, Thaadou, (Tibetan-St)	T-B
		Onge, G-A	AN
		Bishnupuria, DIU-I-P, Urdu-D-T	C-V
ɘɔ		*Short, late rounded, open-mid, back vowel*	
		Maithili	I-A
ʌ		*Short, unrounded, open-mid, back vowel*	
		Nicobarese	A-A
		Kurux	DR
		Nepali	I-A
		Limbu	T-B
ɒ		*Short, rounded, open, back vowel*	
		Assamese, Chakma, Mahl	I-A
		G-Andamanese	AN
ɑ		*Short, unrounded, open, back vowel*	
		Kolami, Kurux, Naiki, Manda, Toda	DR
		Ao-N, Byangsi, RangPo, Spiti, Stod	T-B
		Bishnupuria	C-V

contd.

Table 4.4 *contd.*

LVs			
i:	89	*Long, unrounded, close, front vowel*	
	04	Bhumij, Bonda, Juang, Korku, Nicobarese-C	A-A
	28	Ave, Badaga, Gadaba-K, Gadaba-O, Gondi-A, Irula, Kadar, Kannada, Kattunaicka, Kodagu, Kolami, Konda, Koraga, Kota, Koya, Kui, Kurux, Kuvi, Malayalam, Malto, Manda, Naiki, Pengo, Tamil, Telugu, Toda, Tulu, Yerava.	DR
	19	Bagri, Dogri, Garhwali, Gojri, Haryanvi, Hindi, Jaunsari, Kacchi, Kashmiri, Konkani, Lahndi, , Mahl, Mandeali, Marathi, Punjabi, Rathvi, Shina, Sindhi, Urdu, Urdu-D-H.	I-A
	23	Adi, Balti, Brokskat, Byangsi, Chaudangsi, Darma, Gallong, Hmar, Kangri, Kinnauri, Kiranti-K, Koren, Lepcha, Limbu, Magar, Manchad, Mishmi, Padaam, Purki, RangPo, Tamang, Tibetan-St, Zo	T-B
	01	Turung	T-K
	04	G-Andamanese, Jarawa, Onge	AN
	05	Diu-I-P, Halbi, Vagri-B, Urdu-D-T, IE-H	C-V
	05	Sanskrit-Cl, Pali, Prakrit, O-Tamil, O-Telugu	H-V
Y:		*Long, rounded, close, front vowel*	
		Kodagu, Toda	DR
ï:		*Long, unrounded, close, centralized front vowel*	
		Irula	DR
e:	88	*Long, unrounded, close-mid, front vowel*	
	04	Bhumij, Bonda, Khasi, Korku, Nicobarese-C	A-A
	28	Ave, Badaga, Gadaba-K, Gadaba-O, Gondi-A, Irula, Kadar, Kannada, Kattunaicka, Kodagu, Kolami, Konda, Koraga, Kota, Koya, Kui, Kurux, Kuvi, Malayalam, Malto, Manda, Naiki, Pengo, Tamil, Telugu, Toda, Tulu, Yerava.	DR
	18	Bagri, Dogri, Gojri, Haryanvi, Hindi, Jaunsari, Kacchi, Kashmiri, Konkani, Lahndi, Mahl, Mandeali, Punjabi, Rathvi, Shina, Sindhi, Urdu, Urdu-D-H.	I-A
	23	Adi, Balti, Brokskat, Byangsi, Chaudangsi, Darma, Galo, Hmar, Kangri, Kinnauri, Kiranti-K, Koren, Lepcha, Limbu, Magar, Manchad, Mishmi, Padaam, Purki, RangPo, Tamang, Tibetan-St, Zo.	T-B
	01	Turung	T-K
	04	G-Andamanese, Jarawa, Onge	AN
	05	Diu-I-P, Halbi, Vagri-B, Urdu-D-T, IE-H	C-V
	05	Sanskrit-Cl, Pali, Prakrit, O-Tamil, O-Telugu	H-V
ë:		*Long, unrounded, close-mid, centralized, front vowel*	

contd.

Table 4.4 *contd.*

		Irula	DR
ɛː		*Long, unrounded, open-mid, front vowel*	
		Nicobarese-C, Nancowry	A-A
		Kodagu, Koraga, Tulu	DR
		Bagri, Dogri, Gojri, Haryanvi, Hindi, Jaunsari, Kacchi, Kashmiri, Konkani, Lahndi, Punjabi, Rathvi, Shina, Sindhi	I-A
		Adi, Kangri, Kinnauri, Kiranti-K, Lepcha, Limbu, RangPo	T-B
		G-Andamanese	AN
æː		*Long, unrounded, just below open-mid, front vowel*	
		Nancowry	A-A
		Haryanwi, (Hindi), Lahndi, Punjabi, (Urdu)	I-A
		Sanskrit-Cl	(H-V)
äː		*Long, unrounded, open, centralized, front vowel*	
		Irula	DR
ɨː		*Long, unrounded, close, central vowel*	
		Khasi	A-A
		Kattunaicka,Koraga,	DR
		Bhili, Kashmiri	I-A
		Adi, Mishmi, Padaam	T-B
əː		*Long, unrounded, between close-mid and open- mid, central vowel*	
		Nicobarese-C	A-A
		(Kolami)	DR
		Brokskat, Kashmiri, Mandeali	I-A
		Adi, Kabui, Kiranti-K, Lepcha, Padaam, RangPo	T-B
ɐː		*Long, unrounded, between open-mid and open, central vowel*	
		Limbu	T-B
aː	88	*Long, unrounded, open, central vowel*	
	04	Bhumij, Bonda, Khasi, Korku, Nicobarese-C	A-A
	24	Ave, Badaga, Gadaba-K, Gondi-A, Irula, Kadar, Kannada, Kattunaicka, Kodagu, Kolami, Konda, Koraga, Kota, Koya, Kui, Kuvi, Malayalam, Malto, Manda, Pengo, Tamil, Telugu, Tulu, Yerava.	DR

contd.

Table 4.4 *contd.*

	22	Bagri, Bhojpuri, Dogri, Garhwali, Gojri, Haryanvi, Hindi, Jaunsari, Kacchi, Kashmiri, Konkani, Lahndi, Magahi, Mahl, Mandeali, Marathi, Punjabi, Rathvi, Shina, Sindhi, Urdu, Urdu-D-H	I-A
	23	Adi, Balti, Brokskat, Byangsi, Chaudangsi, Darma, GalLong, Hmar, Kangri, Kinnauri, Kiranti-K, Koren, Lepcha, Magar, Manchad, Mishmi, Padaam, Purki, Raji, RangPo, Tamang, Tibetan-St, Zo	T-B
	01	Turung	T-K
	04	G-Andamanese, Jarawa, Onge	AN
	05	Diu-I-P, Halbi, Vagri-B, Urdu-D-T, IE-H	C-V
	05	Sanskrit-Cl, Pali, Prakrit O-Tamil, O-Telugu	H-V
u:	89	*Long, rounded, close, back vowel*	
	04	Bhumij, Bonda, Khasi, Korku, Nicobarese-C	A-A
	28	Ave, Badaga, Gadaba-K, Gadaba-O, Gondi-A, Irula, Kadar, Kannada, Kattunaicka, Kodagu, Kolami, Konda, Koraga, Kota, Koya, Kui, Kurux, Kuvi, Malayalam, Malto, Manda, Naiki, Pengo, Tamil, Telugu, Toda, Tulu, Yerava.	DR
	19	Bagri, Dogri, Garhwali, Gojri, Haryanvi, Hindi, Jaunsari, Kacchi, Kashmiri, Konkani, Lahndi, Mahl, Mandeali, Marathi, Punjabi, Rathvi, Shina, Sindhi, Urdu, Urdu-D-H.	I-A
	23	Adi, Balti, Brokskat, Byangsi, Chaudangsi, Darma, GalLong, Hmar, Kangri, Kinnauri, Kiranti-K, Koren, Lepcha, Limbu, Magar, Manchad, Mishmi, Padaam, Purki, RangPo, Tamang, Tibetan-St, Zo.	T-B
	01	Turung	T-K
	04	G-Andamanese, Jarawa, Onge	AN
	05	Diu-I-P, Halbi, Vagri-B, Urdu-D-T, IE-H	C-V
	05	Sanskrit-Cl, Pali, Prakrit O-Tamil, O-Telugu	H-V
ü:		*Long, rounded, close, centralized, back vowel*	
		Irula	DR
ɯ:		*Long, unrounded, close, back vowel*	
		Nicobarese-C	A-A
		Kodagu, Toda	DR
		Lepcha, Wancho	T-B
o:	86	*Long, rounded, close-mid, back vowel*	

contd.

Table 4.4 *contd.*

	03	Bhumij, Khasi, Korku, Nicobarese-C	A-A
	28	Ave, Badaga, Gadaba-K, Gadaba-O, Gondi-A, Irula, Kadar, Kannada, Kattunaicka, Kodagu, Kolami, Konda, Koraga, Kota, Koya, Kui, Kurux, Kuvi, Malayalam, Malto, Manda, Naiki, Pengo, Tamil, Telugu, Toda, Tulu, Yerava.	DR
	17	Bagri, Dogri, Gojri, Haryanvi, Hindi, Jaunsari, Kacchi, Kashmiri, Konkani, Lahndi, Mandeali, Punjabi, Rathvi, Shina, Sindhi, Urdu, Urdu-D-H.	I-A
	23	Adi, Balti, Brokskat, Byangsi, Chaudangsi, Darma, Galo, Hmar, Kangri, Kinnauri, Kiranti-K, Koren, Lepcha, Limbu, Magar, Manchad, Mishmi, Padaam, Purki, RangPo, Tamang, Tibetan-St, Zo.	T-B
	01	Turung	T-K
	04	G-Andamanese, Jarawa, Onge	AN
	05	Diu-I-P, Halbi, Vagri-B, Urdu -D-T, IE-H	C-V
	05	Sanskrit-Cl, Pali, Prakrit, O-Tamil, O-Telugu	H-V
ö:		*Long, rounded, close-mid, centralized, back vowel*	
		Irula	DR
ɤ		Long, unrounded, close-mid, back vowel	
		Kodagu	DR
		Lepcha	T-B
ɔ:		*Long, rounded, open-mid, back vowel*[3]	
		Bhumij, Nicobarese-C	A-A
		Bagri, Dogri, Gojri, Haryanwi, Jaunsari, Kacchi.Kashmiri, Lamini, Punjabi, Rathvi, Shina, Sindhi	I-A
		G-Andamanese	AN
ʌ:		*Long, unrounded, open-mid, back vowel*	
		Limbu	T-B
ɘo:		*Long, late rounded, open-mid, back vowel*	
		Hindi, Lahndi, Punjabi, Urdu	I-A
		Sanskrit-Cl	(H-V)
ɒ:		*Long, rounded, open, back vowel*	
		Nicobarese-C	A-A
		Mahl	I-A
		Galo, Tangsa	T-B

contd.

Table 4.4 *contd.*

ɑ:		*Long, unrounded, open, back vowel*	
		Gadaba-K, Kolami, Kurux, Manda, Naiki, Toda, Yerava	DR
		Chakma, Lahndi, Lamani	I-A
		Byangsi, RangPo	T-B

Diphthongs

DVs			
ai		*Unrounded, open, central to unrounded, close, front diphthong*	
		Didayi	A-A
		Shina	I-A
		Dimasa, Galo-L, Garo, Koren, Liangmai,Mizo, Paite, Zo	T-B
		Bishnupuria	C-V
a:i		*Long, unrounded, open, central to unrounded, close, front diphthong*	
		Zo	T-B
ae		*Unrounded, open, central to unrounded, close-mid, front diphthong*	
		Didayi	A-A
		Mao-N	T-B
		Unrounded, open, central to rounded, close-mid, back diphthong	
ao		Didayi	A-A
		Dimasa, Mao-N	T-B
au		*Unrounded, open, central to rounded, close, back diphthong*	
		Khasi	A-A
		Bhojpuri, Magahi, Nepali, Shina	I-A
		Galo-L, Garo, Liangmai, Mizo, Phom, Wancho	T-B
a:u		*Short, unrounded, open, central to rounded, close, back diphthong*	
		Zo	T-B
aw		*Unrounded, open, central to bilabial, approximant, diphthong*	
		Paite	T-B
		Diu-I-P	C-V

contd.

Table 4.4 *contd.*

ɑu		*Unrounded, open, back to rounded, close, back diphthong*	
		Bishnupuria	C-V
aɯ		*Unrounded, open, central to unrounded, close, back, diphthong*	
		Phom	T-B
aj		*Unrounded, open, central to palatal, approximant, diphthong*	
		Diu-I-P	C-V
ɛi		*Unrounded, open-mid ,front to unrounded ,close, front diphthong*	
		Shina	T-B
ɛɯ		*Unrounded, open-mid, front to unrounded, close, back diphthong*	
		Phom	T-B
		Diu-I-P	C-V
ɛj		*Unrounded, open-mid, central to palatal, approximant diphthong*	
		Diu-I-P	C-V
ei		*Unrounded, close-mid, front to unrounded, close, front diphthong*	
		Didayi	A-A
		Shina,	I-A
		Dimasa, Garo, Koren, Mizo, Zo	T-B
		Bishnupuria	C-V
eə		*Unrounded, close-mid, front to unrounded betwee close-mid and open-mid, central diphthong*	
		Shina	I-A
eo		*Unrounded, close-mid, front to rounded, close-mid, back diphthong*	
		Didayi	A-A
		Dimasa,	T-B
		Nagamese	C-V
e̯o		*Less prominent, unrounded, close-mid, front to more prominent, rounded, close-mid, back diphthong*	
		(Angami), Ao-N	T-B
		(Nagamese)	C-V
eu		*Unrounded, close-mid, front to rounded, close, back diphthong*	

contd.

Table 4.4 *contd.*

		Didayi	A-A
		Zo	T-B
eːu		*Short, unrounded, close-mid, front to rounded, close, back diphthong*	
		Zo	T-B
ew		*Unrounded, close-mid, front to bilabial, approximant diphthong*	
		Paite	T-B
		Diu-I-P	C-V
ej		*Unrounded, close-mid, front to palatal, approximant diphthong*	
		Paite	T-B
		Diu-I-P	C-V
ɔi		*Rounded, open-mid, back to unrounded, close, front diphthong*	
		Bishnupuria	C-V
ɔːi		*Long, rounded, open-mid, back to unrounded, close, front diphthong*	
		Zo	T-B
ɔu		*Rounded, open-mid, back to rounded, close, back diphthong*	
		Bishnupuria	C-V
ɔ̯a		*Less prominent, rounded, open-mid, back to more prominent, unrounded, open, central diphthong*	
		Liangmai	T-B
ɔj		*Rounded, close-mid, back to palatal, approximant diphthong*	
		Diu-I-P	C-V
ʌɪ		*Unrounded, open-mid, back to unrounded, between close-mid and close, front diphthong*	
		Phom	T-B
oi		Rounded, close-mid, back to unrounded, close, front diphthong	
		Khasi	A-A
		Shina	I-A
		Garo, Koren, Zo	T-B
oɪ		*Rounded, close-mid, back to unrounded, between close-mid and close, front diphthong*	

contd.

Table 4.4 *contd.*

		Phom	T-B
oe		*Rounded, close-mid, back to unrounded, close-mid, front diphthong*	
		Mao-N	T-B
oə		*Rounded, close-mid, back to unrounded, between open-mid and close-mid, central diphthong*	
		Kashmiri	I-A
ou		*Rounded, close-mid, back to rounded, close, back diphthong*	
		Koren, Zo	T-B
o̭u		*Less prominent, rounded, close-mid, back to more prominent, rounded, close, back diphthong*	
		Angami, Ao-N, Liangmai, Mao-N	T-B
		Nagamese	C-V
oj		*Rounded, close-mid, back to palatal, approximant diphthong*	
		Paite	T-B
		Diu-I-P	C-V
ia		*Unrounded, close, front to unrounded, open, central diphthong*	
		Didayi	A-A
		Koren, Zo	T-B
iu		*Unrounded, close, front to unrounded, close, back diphthong*	
		Koren, Zo	T-B
ie		*Unrounded, close, front to unrounded, close-mid, central diphthong*	
		Koren, Mao-N, Zo	T-B
		Nancowry	AN
i̭a		*Less prominent, unrounded, close, front to more prominent, unrounded, open, central diphthong*	
		Liangmai, Paite	T-B
i̭e		*Less prominent, unrounded, close, front to more prominent, unrounded, close-mid, front diphthong*	
		Angami, Ao-N, Liangmai	T-B
		Nagamese	C-V

contd.

Table 4.4 *contd.*

i̯o		*Less prominent, unrounded, close, front to more prominent, unrounded, close-mid, back diphthong*	
		Angami, Ao-N, Liangmai	T-B
		Nagamese	C-V
ui		*Rounded, close, back to unrounded, close, front diphthong*	
		Zo	T-B
u:i		*Long rounded ,close, back to short, unrounded, close, front diphthong*	
		Zo	T-B
ue		*Rounded, close, back to unrounded, close-mid, front diphthong*	
		Mao-N	T-B
ua		*Rounded, close, back to unrounded, open, front diphthong*	
		Zo	T-B
uo:		*Rounded, close, back to long, rounded, close-mid, back diphthong*	
		Zo	T-B
uj		*Rounded, close, back to palatal, approximant diphthong*	
		Paite	T-B
		Diu-I-P	C-V
ʊ̯i		*Less prominent, rounded, between close-mid and close, back to more prominent, unrounded, close, front diphthong*	
		Wancho	T-B
ʊ̯a		*Less prominent, rounded ,between close-mid and close, back to more prominent, unrounded, open, central diphthong*	
		Wancho	T-B
ʊ̯o		*Less prominent, rounded, between close-mid and close, back to more prominent, rounded, close-mid, back diphthong*	
		Wancho	T-B
u̯a		*Less prominent, rounded, close, back to more prominent, unrounded, open, central diphthong*	
		Jaunsari	I-A
		Paite	T-B
u̯o		*Less prominent, rounded, close, back to more prominent, rounded, close-mid, back diphthong*	

contd.

Table 4.4 *contd.*

		Angami, Ao-N	T-B
		Nagamese	C-V
ɨa		*Unrounded, close, central to unrounded, open, front diphthong*	
		Nancowry	A-A
əi		*Unrounded, mid central to unrounded, close, front diphthong*	
		Khasi	A-A
		Bhojpuri, Magahi, Marathi	I-A
		Wancho	T-B
əu		*Unrounded, mid, central to unrounded, close, front diphthong*	
		Bhojpuri, Magahi, Marathi	I-A
əj		*Unrounded, mid, central to palatal, approximant diphthong*	
		Diu-I-P	C-V
ji		*Palatal, approximant to unrounded, close, front diphthong*	
		Wancho	T-B

Triphthongs

TVs			
iaj		*Unrounded, close, front to unrounded, open, central to palatal, approximant triphthong*	
		Paite	T-B
uaj		*Rounded, close, back to unrounded, open, central to palatal, approximant triphthong*	
		Paite	T-B
iaw		*Unrounded, close, front to unrounded, open central to labial approximant triphthong*	
		Paite	T-B
uaw		*Rounded, close, back to unrounded, open, central to labial, approximant triphthong*	
		Paite	T-B
uoi		*Rounded, close, back to rounded close-mid back to unrounded,close, front triphthong*	
		Koren, Zo	T-B

contd.

Table 4.4 *contd.*

uia		*Rounded, close, back to unrounded, close, front to unrounded, open, central triphthong*	
		Koren	T-B
uəi		*Rounded, close, back to unrounded, mid, central to palatal, approximant triphthong*	
		Koren	T-B
uou		*Rounded, close, back to rounded, close-mid, back to rounded, close, back triphthong*	
		Zo	T-B

Nasal vowels

NVs			
ĩ		*Short, unrounded, close, front nasal vowel*	
		Bonda, Didayi, Gadaba-G, Kharia, Kisan, Nancowry	A-A
		Kattunaicka, Kurux, Kuvi	DR
		Assamese, Bengali, Bhili, Bhojpuri, Garhwali, Gojri, Gujarati, Konkani, Lahndi, Lamani, Magahi, Maithili, Mandeali, Nepali, Oriya, Rathvi, Shina	I-A
		Raji, RangPo,	T-B
		Pali, Prakrit	H-V
ɪ̃		*Short, unrounded, between close and close-mid, front nasal vowel*	
		Bagri, Haryanvi, Hindi, Jaunsari, Kacchi, Kashmiri, Sindhi, Urdu, Urdu-D-H,	I-A
		Kangri	T-B
		Urdu-D-T	C-V
ĩ:		*Long, unrounded, close, front, nasal vowel*	
		Kattunaicka, Kurux, Kuvi, Tamil,	DR
		Bagri, Dogri, Garhwali, Gojri, Haryanvi, Hindi, Jaunsari, Kacchi, Kashmiri, Konkani, Lahndi, Mandeali, Punjabi, Shina, Sindhi, Urdu, Urdu-D-H,	I-A
		Diu-I-P, Vagri-B	C-V
ỹ		*Short, rounded, close, front, nasal vowel*	
		Assamese	I-A
ỹ:		*Long, rounded, close, front, nasal vowel*	
		Tibetan-St	T-B

contd.

Table 4.4 *contd.*

ẽ		*Short, unrounded, close-mid, front, nasal vowel*	
		Bhumij, Bonda, (Didayi), Gadaba-G, Kharia, Kisan, Nancowry	A-A
		Kattunaicka, Kuvi, Tamil,	DR
		Assamese, Bengali, Bhojpuri, Garhwali,Gujarati, Kashmiri, Konkani, Lamani, Magahi, Maithili, Mandeali, Marathi, Nepali, Oriya, Rathvi, Shina	I-A
		Kangri, Kinnauri, Mishmi, Raji	T-B
		Diu-I-P, Vagri B	C-V
ẽ:		*Short, unrounded, close-mid, front, nasal vowel*	
		Kurux, Kuvi,	DR
		Bagri, (Dogri), Gojri, Haryanvi, Hindi,Jaunsari, Kacchi,Kashmiri,Lahndi, Mandeali, Punjabi, Shina, Sindhi, Urdu,Urdu-D-H	I-A
		Vagri-B,	C-V
ø̃:		*Long, rounded, close-mid, front, nasal vowel*	
		Tibetan-St	T-B
ɛ̃		*Short, unrounded, open-mid, front, nasal vowel*	
		(Didayi), Kharia, Nancowry	A-A
		Kurux	DR
		Assamese, Bhili, (Gujarati), Konkani, Oriya, Shina, (Sindhi)	I-A
		Kinnauri, Raji	T-B
ɛ̃:		*Long, unrounded, open-mid, front, nasal vowel*	
		Nancowry	A-A
		Bagri, Dogri, Gojri, Hindi, Jaunsari, Kacchi, Kashmiri, Shina, (Sindhi), Urdu	I-A
		Kinnauri, Rangpo	T-B
æ̃		*Short, unrounded, just below open-mid, front, nasal vowel*	
		Bengali, Maithili	I-A
æ̃:		*Long, unrounded, just below open-mid, front, nasal vowel*	
		Gojri, Haryanwi, Lahndi, Punjabi	I-A
ɨ̃		*Short, unrounded, close, central, nasal vowel*	
		Nancowry	A-A

contd.

Table 4.4 *contd.*

		Kattunaicka	DR
		Kashmiri	I-A
		Kinnauri	T-B
		Diu-I-P	C-V
ɨ̃:		*Long, unrounded, close, central, nasal vowel*	
		Kashmiri	I-A
ʉ̄		*Short, rounded, close, central, nasal vowel*	
		Assamese	I-A
ɵ̃		*Short, rounded ,close-mid, central, nasal vowel*	
		Assamese	I-A
ʉ̃		*Short, rounded ,close, central, nasal vowel*	
		Assamese	I-A
ə̃		*Short, unrounded, mid, central, nasal vowel*	
		Bagri, Bhili, Bhojpuri, Gujarati, Haryanvi, Hindi, Kacchi, Kashmiri, Konkani, Lamani, Magahi, Maithili, Mandeali, Marathi, Oriya, Rathvi, Sindhi, Urdu, Urdu-D-H	I-A
		Kinnauri, Raji, RangPo,	T-B
ə̃:		*Long, unrounded, mid, central, nasal vowel*	
		Kashmiri, Mandeali	I-A
ɞ̃		*Short, rounded, mid, central, nasal vowel*	
		Gadaba-G	A-A
		Bengali, Mandeali	I-A
ɞ̃:		*Long, rounded, mid, central, nasal vowel*	
		Mandeali	I-A
ɐ̃		*Short, unrounded, open-mid, central, nasal vowel*	
		Kashmiri	I-A
ã		*Short, unrounded, open, central, nasal vowel*	
		Bhumij, Bonda, Gadaba-G, Korku, (Nicobarese-C)	A-A
		Gadaba-K, Tamil, Tulu	DR
		Bhili, Dogri, Garhwali, Jaunsari, Konkani, Mandeali, Marathi, Nepali, Rathvi, Shina	I-A
		Lepcha, Mishmi, Raji, Tibetan-St, (Wancho)	T-B
		Diu-I-P, Vagri-B	C-V

contd.

Table 4.4 *contd.*

ã:		*Long, unrounded, open,central, nasal vowel*	
		Tamil	DR
		Assamese, Bagri, Bhojpuri, Garhwali, Gojri, Gujarati, Hindi, Jaunsari, Kacchi, Kashmiri, Konkani, Magahi, Maithili, Mandeali, Oriya, Punjabi, Rathvi, Shina, Sindhi, Urdu-D-H	I-A
		Vagri-B	C-V
		Pali	H-V
ũ		*Short, rounded, close, back, nasal vowel*	
		Bonda, Didayi, Gadaba-G, Kharia, Kisan, Nancowry	A-A
		Kattunaicka, Kurux, Kuvi	DR
		Assamese, Bengali, Bhili, Bhojpuri, Garhwali, Gojri, Gujarati, Konkani, Lahndi, Lamani, Magahi, Maithili, Mandeali, Nepali, Oriya, Rathvi, Shina	I-A
		Raji, RangPo	T-B
		Pali, Prakrit	H-V
ʊ̃		*Short, rounded, between close and close-mid, back, nasal vowel*	
		Bagri, Haryanvi, Hindi, Jaunsari,Kacchi, Kashmiri, Sindhi, Urdu, Urdu-D-H	I-A
		Kangri	T-B
		Urdu-D-T	C-V
ũ:		*Long, rounded, close, back, nasal vowel*	
		Kurux, Kuvi	DR
		Bagri, Garhwali, Gojri, Haryanvi, Hindi, Jaunsari, Kacchi, Kashmiri, Konkani, Lahndi, Mandeali, Shina, Sindhi, Urdu D-H	I-A
		Vagri-B	C-V
		Tibetan- St	T-B
ʊ̃:		*Long, rounded, between close and close-mid, back, nasal vowel*	
		Kurux	DR
		Dogri	I-A
õ		*Short, rounded, close-mid, back, nasal vowel*	
		Bhumij, Bonda, Gadaba-G, Nancowry, (Nicobarese-C)	A-A
		Kuvi	DR
		Assamese, Bhojpuri, Garhwali, Gujarati, Kashmiri, Konkani, Lamani, Magahi, Maithili, Mandeali, Shina	I-A
		Kangri, Kinnauri, Mishmi, Raji, RangPo, Tibetan-St	T-B

contd.

Table 4.4 *contd.*

õ		*Long, rounded, close-mid, back, nasal vowel*	
		Kurux, Kuvi, Tamil	DR
		Bagri, Dogri, Gojri, Haryanvi, Jaunsari, Kacchi, Kashmiri, Lahndi, Mandeali, Punjabi, Shina, Sindhi, Urdu-D-H	I-A
		Diu-I-P, Vagri-B	C-V
		Kangri, Kinnauri, RangPo, Tibetan-St	T-B
ɔ̃		*Short, rounded, open-mid, back, nasal vowel*	
		Bonda, (Nicobarese-C), Nancowry	A-A
		Kurux	DR
		Assamese, Gujarati, Konkani, Oriya, Rathvi	I-A
		RangPo	T-B
ɔ̃:		*Long, rounded, open-mid, back, nasal vowel*	
		Bagri, Dogri, Gojri, Haryanvi, Jaunsari, Kashmiri, Punjabi, (Sindhi)	I-A
		RangPo	T-B
ʌ̃		*Short, rounded, open-mid, back, nasal vowel*	
		Nepali	I-A
ɒ̃		*Short, rounded, open, back, nasal vowel*	
		Kurux	DR
		Assamese	I-A
ɒ̃:		*Long, rounded, open, back,nasal vowel*	
		Kurux	DR
ɑ̃:		*Long, unrounded, open, back, nasal vowel*	
		Gadaba-K, Kattunaicka, Kurux	DR
		Lahndi, Lamani	I-A
œ̃		*Short, late-rounded, open-mid, nasal vowel*	
		Maithili	I-A
œ̃:		*Long, late-rounded, open-mid, nasal vowel*	
		Gojri, Hindi, Kacchi, Lahndi, Urdu	I-A
ẽi		*Unrounded, close-mid, front to unrounded, close, front, nasal diphthong*	
		Shina	T-B
ɛ̃ĩ		*Unrounded, open-mid, front to unrounded, close, front, nasal diphthong*	
		Shina	T-B

contd.

Table 4.4 *contd.*

ãĩ		*Unroundeo, open, central to unrounded, close, front, nasal diphthong*	
		Shina	I-A
		Kiranti-K	T-B
õĩ		*Rounded, close-mid, back to unrounded, close, front, nasal diphthong*	
		Shina	I-A
		Kiranti-K	T-B
ũĩ		*Rounded, close, back to unrounded, close, front, nasal diphthong*	
		Shina	I-A
		Kiranti-K	T-B
ə̃ĩ		*Unrounded, mid, central to unrounded, close, front, nasal diphthong*	
		Bhojpuri, Magahi	I-A
ə̃ũ		*Unrounded, mid, central to rounded, close, back, nasal diphthong*	
		Bhojpuri, Magahi	I-A
ãũ		*Unrounded, open, central to rounded, close, back, nasal diphthong*	
		Shina	I-A
ẽə̃		*Unrounded, mid, front to unrounded, mid, central, nasal diphthong*	
		Shina	I-A
ãj		*Unrounded, open, central to palatal, approximant, nasal diphthong*	
		Diu-I-P	C-V
ɔ̃j		*Unrounded, open-mid ,back to palatal, approximant, nasal diphthong*	
		Diu-I-P	C-V
ãw		*Unrounded, open, central to labial, approximant, nasal diphthong*	
		Diu-I-P	C-V

The total number of vowels according to their types and the number of languages in which they occur are presented again below for the sake of ease of reference.

(4/3) Total number of vowel types (161) Total number of languages (148)

Monophthong vowels: 51 148

Diphthong vowels:	55	27
Triphthong vowels:	08	03
Nasal vowels:	48	99

The monophthong vowels are divided further into short and long vowels:

(4/4)	i. Short vowels:	28	148 languages
	ii. Long vowels:	23	102 languages

They represent the vowel qualities of the monophthongs in the Indic languages. Together, they are divided into the following classes:

(4/5)	Total vowel positions:	51
	Front vowel positions:	17
	Central vowel positions:	11
	Back vowel positions:	23

As is the general case (see e.g. Maddieson 1980:) the peripheral vowels have much greater frequency of occurrence than the core vowels:

(4/6)	Peripheral vowels:	40
	Central vowels:	11

Similarly, the unrounded vowels have much wider distribution than rounded vowels, which are more commonly found with back vowels only than with the front and central vowels:

(4/7)	Unrounded vowels:	30
	Rounded vowels:	21

The distributional details of the peripheral and core vowels as well as the unrounded and rounded vowels are given in *Table 4.5* below.

Table 4.5 Distribution of oral monophthong vowels in SPIL according to tongue and lip positions

		Total 51	A-A	DR	I-A	T-B	T-K	AN	C-V	H-V
Front unrounded		14	08	13	09	07	04	06	05	04
	Close	04	02	04	03	02	02	02	02	02
	Bet. close and close-mid	01	01	01	01	01	–	–	01	–

contd.

Table 4.5 *contd.*

	Close-mid	03	01	03	01	01	01	01	01	01
	Open-mid	02	02	02	02	02	01	02	02	01
	Just below open-mid	02	02	02	02	01	–	01	–	–
	Open	01	00	01	00	00	00	00	00	00
Front rounded		03	–	–	–	01	–	–	–	–
	Close	02	–	–	–	–	–	–	–	–
	Close-mid	01	–	–	–	01	–	–	–	–
	Open-mid	00	–	–	–	–	–	–	–	–
	Open	00	–	–	–	–	–	–	–	–
Central unrounded		08	07	07	07	08	04	04	05	03
	Close	02	02	02	02	02	01	01	01	00
	Close-mid	–	–	–	–	–	–	–	–	–
	Open-mid	–	–	–	–	–	–	–	–	–
	Bet. open-mid and open	02	01	01	01	02	–	–	01	–
	Open	02	02	02	02	02	02	02	02	02
	Mid	01	01	01	01	01	01	01	01	01
	Bet. close-mid & open-mid	01	01	01	01	01	–	–	–	–
Central rounded		03	01	01	01	02	–	–	01	–
	Close	01	–	–	–	01	–	–	–	–
	Close-mid	01	–	01	–	–	–	–	–	–
	Open-mid	01	01	–	01	01	–	–	–	–
	Open	00	–	–			–	–	–	–
Back unrounded		08	03	07	02	08	01	01	01	00
	Close	02	02	02	–	02	–	–	–	–
	Close-mid	02	01	02	–	02	–	–	–	–
	Open-mid	02	01	01	01	02	–	–	–	–

contd.

Table 4.5 *contd.*

	Open	02		02	01	02	–	–	01	–
Back rounded		13	08	10	10	07	04	07	06	04
	Close	04	02	04	03	02	02	02	02	02
	Close-mid	04	02	04	02	02	02	02	02	02
	Open-mid	02	02	01	02	01	–	02	01	–
	Open	02	01	–	02	01	–	01	–	–
Back late rounded	Open-mid	02	–	–	02	–	–	–	01	–

The above table gives the distribution of the vowel positions according to the position of the tongue (Front, Central, Back) and the position of the lips (rounded, unrounded, late rounded). The facts are presented below according to the height of the vowels, that is Close, Close-mid, Open-mid, Open, etc. in *Table 4.6*.

Table 4.6 Distribution of monophthong oral vowels in SPIL according to height

	TOTAL	A-A	DR	I-A	T-B	T-K	AN	C-V	H-V
Close vowels									
No. of vowels	**15**	08	14	08	09	06	05	05	04
No. of languages	**147**	15	29	31	55	02	03	07	05
Close-mid vowels									
No. of vowels	**11**	03	10	03	06	03	04	03	03
No. of languages	**144**	14	29	32	52	02	03	07	05
Mid vowels									
No. of vowels	**02**	01	02	02	02	01	02	01	01
No. of languages	**83**	05	09	24	35	01	03	03	03
Open-mid vowels									
No. of vowels	**09**	06	04	08	06	01	04	03	02
No. of languages	**71**	12	05	25	21	01	02	04	01
Open vowels									
No. of vowels	**08**	03	06	05	05	02	03	03	02
No. of languages	**145**	15	29	32	52	02	03	07	05

contd.

Table 4.6 *contd.*

Just below open-mid vowels									
No. of vowels	**02**	02	02	02	01		01		
No. of languages	**10**	01	03	04	01		01		
Bet. close and close-mid vowels									
No. of vowels	**02**	02	02	02	02			02	
No. of languages	**21**	01	02	13	0			01	
Bet. open and open-mid vowels									
No. of vowels	**02**	01	01	01	02			01	
No. of languages	**09**	01	02	02	03			01	

Without going into the articulatory details of the vowel types other than short and long monophthongs, that is, the diphthongs, the triphthongs and the nasal vowels, their distribution in the different language groups is given in *Table 4.7*.

Table 4.7 Distribution of vowel glides and nasal vowels in SPIL

	TOTAL	**A-A**	**DR**	**I-A**	**T-B**	**T-K**	**AN**	**C-V**	**H-V**
Diphthongs									
No. of vowels	55	11	–	09	45	–	01	20	–
No. of languages	27	03	–	07	14	–	01	03	–
Triphthongs									
No. of vowels	08	–	–	–	08	–	–	–	–
No. of languages	03	–	–	–	03	–	–	–	–
Nasal vowels									
Short monophthong NVs									
No. of vowels	20	09	09	20	11	–	–	05	02
No. of languages	56	09	06	28	08	–	–	03	02
Long monophthong NVs									
No. of vowels	16	01	07	13	06	–	–	04	01
No. of languages	37	01	05	24	04	–	–	02	01
Diphthong NVs									

contd.

Table 4.7 *contd.*

No. of vowels	12			07	05	–	–	03	
No. of languages	06			03	02	–	–	01	

Some of the frequently occurring vowels are found not to occur in some languages, as shown in *Table 4.8*.

Table 4.8 Frequently occurring vowel phonemes in Indic languages, found not to occur in the languages listed herein.

SVs	No. of Vs		LG
*i	*22	*Short, unrounded, close, front vowel*	
	*01	Khasi	A-A
	*02	Kannada, Kurux	DR
	*13	Bagri, Chakma, Dogri, Gojri, Hindi, Jaunsari, Kacchi, Kashmiri, Marathi, Punjabi, Sindhi, Urdu, Urdu-D-H	I-A
	*05	Chaudangsi, Darma, Dimasa, Kangri, Paite	T-B
	*01	Urdu-D-T	C-V
*e	*21	*Short, unrounded, close, front vowel*	
	*01	Mundari	A-A
	*01	Kurux	DR
	*12	Chakma, Dogri, Gojri, Haryanvi, Hindi, Jaunsari, Kacchi, Lahndi, Punjabi, Sindhi, Urdu, Urdu-D-H	I-A
	*06	Chaudangsi, Darma, Dimasa, Kokborok, Liangmai, RangPo	T-B
	*01	Urdu-D-T	C-V
*a	40 (+1)	*Short, unrounded, open, central vowel*	
	01 (+1)	Korku, (Nicobarese-C)	A-A
	06	Kattunaika, Kurux, Manda, Naiki, Toda, Tulu	DR
	17	Bagri, Bhojpuri, Chakma, Dogri, Gojri, Haryanvi, Hindi, Kacchi, Kashmiri, Lahndi, Lamani, Magahi, Manda, Nepali, Punjabi, Sindhi, Urdu	I-A
	12	Ao-N, Byangsi, Chaudangsi, Darma, Hmar, Galo-L, Ladakhi, Limbu, Monpa, Spiti, Tod, Zo	T-B
	02	IE-H, Urdu-D-T	C-V
	02	Pali, Prakrit	H-V

contd.

Table 4.8 *contd.*

*o	*25(+1)	*Short, rounded,close-mid, back vowel*	
	*01(+1)	(Juang), Mundari	A-A
	*01	Kurux	DR
	*12	Dogri, Gojri, Haryanvi, Hindi, Jaunsari, Kacchi, Lahndi, Mahl, Punjabi, Sindhi, Urdu, Urdu-D-H	I-A
	*08	Chaudangsi, Darma, Dimasa, Hmar, Kokborok, Liangmai, Limbu, RangPo	T-B
	*01	IE-H	C-V
	*03	Pali, Prakrit, Cl-Sanskrit	H-V
*u	*22	*Short, rounded, close, back vowel*	
	*01	Khasi	A-A
	*02	Kannada, Kurux	DR
	*13	Bagri, Chakma, Dogri, Gojri, Haryanvi, Hindi, Jaunsari, Kacchi, Kashmiri, Marathi, Punjabi, Sindhi, Urdu	I-A
	*05	Chaudangsi, Darma, Dimasa, Kangri,Paite	T-B
	*01	Urdu-D-T	C-V
*ə	65 (+1)	*Short, unrounded, between close-mid and open- mid, central vowel*	
	11	Bhumij, Didayi, Gadaba-G, Gorum, Ho, Kharia, Khasi, Kisan, Mundari, Nicobarese-C, Santali	A-A
	20	Ave, Badaga, Gadaba-O, Gondi, Gondi-A, Irula, Konda, Koraga, Kota, Koya, Kurux, Kuvi, Malto, Manda, Naiki, Pengo, Tamil, Telugu, Toda, Yerava	DR
	07	Assamese, Bengali, Chakma, Garhwali, Jaunsari, Mahl, Oriya	I-A
	20 (+1)	Ao-N, Apatani, Balti, Chokri, Gallong, Galo, Garo, Karbi, Kangri, Liangmai, Mao-N, Mishmi, Mizo, Monpa, Purki, Sema-N, (Spiti), St Tibetan, Tamang, Tangsa, Thaadou	T-B
	01	Khampti	T-K
	04	Bishnupuriya, Naga-P, Urdu-D-T, Vagri-B	C-V
	02	OTamil, OTelugu	H-V
LVs			
*iː	*59	*Long, unrounded, close, open vowel*	
	*09	Didayi, Gadaba-G, Gorum, Ho, Juang, Kharia,Kisan, Mundari, Nancowry, Santali	A-A
	*01	Gondi	DR

contd.

Table 4.8 *contd.*

	*12	Assamese, Bengali,Bhili, Bhojpuri, Chakma, Garhwali, Gujarati, Lamani, Magahi, Maithili, Nepali, Oriya	I-A
	*33	Angami, Ao-N, Apatani, Bantawa, Bodo, Chokri, Dimasa, Galo, Galo-L, Garo, Kabui, Karbi, Kheza, Kokborok, Ladakhi, Liangmai, Lotha, Mao-N, Maring, Meitei, Mizo, Monpa, Paite, Phom, Raji,Rawang, Sema-N, Spiti, Tangsa, Tarao, Thaadou, Tod, Wancho.	T-B
	*01	Khampti	T-K
	*02	Bishnupuriya, Naga-P	C-V
*e:	*60	*Long, unrounded, close-mid, front vowel*	
	*09	Didayi, Gadaba-G, Gorum, Ho, Juang, Kharia, Kisan, Mundari, Nancowry, Santali	A-A
	*01	Gondi	DR
	*13	Assamese, Bengali, Bhili, Bhojpuri, Chakma, Garhwali, Gujarati, Lamani, Magahi, Maithili, Marathi, Nepali, Oriya	I-A
	*33	Angami, Ao-N, Apatani, Bantawa, Bodo, Chokri, Dimasa, Gallong, Galo-L, Garo, Kabui, Karbi, Kheza, Kokborok, Ladakhi, Liangmai, Lotha, Mao-N, Maring, Meitei, Mizo, Monpa, Paite, Phom, Raji, Rawang, Sema-N, Spiti, Tangsa, Tarao, Thaadou, Tod, Wancho.	T-B
	*01	Khampti	T-K
	*02	Bishnupuriya, Naga-P	C-V
*a:	*60	*Long, unrounded, open, central vowel*	
	*09	Didayi, Gadaba-G, Gorum, Ho, Juang,Kharia, Kisan, Mundari, Nancowry, Santali	A-A
	*05	Gondi, Kurux, Naiki, Gadaba-O, Toda,	DR
	*09	Assamese, Bengali, Bhili, Chakma, Garhwali, Gujarati, Lamani, Maithili, Oriya	I-A
	*33	Angami, Ao-N,Apatani,Bantawa, Bodo, Chokri, Dimasa, Galo, Galo-L, Garo, Kabui, Karbi, Kheza, Kokborok, Ladakhi, Liangmai, Limbu, Lotha, Mao-N, Maring, Meitei, Mizo, Monpa, Paite, Phom, Rawang, Sema-N, Spiti, Tangsa, Tarao, Thaadou, Tod, Wancho.	T-B
	*01	Khampti	T-K
	*02	Bishnupuriya, Naga-P	C-V
*o:	*62	*Long, rounded, close-mid, back vowel*	

contd.

Table 4.8 *contd.*

	*10	Bonda, Didayi, Gadaba-G, Gorum, Ho, Juang, Kharia, Kisan, Mundari, Nancowry, Santali	A-A
	*01	Gondi	DR
	*14	Assamese, Bengali, Bhili, Bhojpuri,Chakma, Garhwali, Gujarati, Lamani, Magahi, Mahl, Maithili, Marathi, Nepali, Oriya	I-A
	*33	Angami, Ao-N, Apatani, Bantawa, Bodo, Chokri, Dimasa, Gallong, Galo-L, Garo, Kabui, Karbi, Kheza, Kokborok, Ladakhi, Liangmai, Lotha, Mao-N, Maring, Meitei, Mizo, Monpa, Paite, Phom, Raji, Rawang, Sema-N, Spiti, Tangsa, Tarao, Thaadou, Tod, Wancho.	T-B
	*01	Khampti	T-K
	*02	Bishnupuriya, Naga-P	C-V
*u:	*59	*Long, rounded, close, back vowel*	
	*09	Didayi, Gadaba-G, Gorum, Ho, Juang, Kharia, Kisan, Mundari, Nancowry, Santali	A-A
	*01	Gondi	DR
	*12	Assamese, Bengali, Bhili, Bhojpuri, Chakma, Garhwali, Gujarati, Lamani, Magahi, Maithili, Nepali, Oriya	I-A
	*33	Angami, Ao-N, Apatani, Bantawa, Bodo, Chokri, Dimasa, Galo, Galo-L, Garo, Kabui, Karbi,Kheza, Kokborok, Ladakhi, Liangmai, Lotha, Mao-N, Maring, Meitei, Mizo, Monpa, Paite, Phom, Raji, Rawang, Sema-N, Spiti, Tangsa, Tarao, Thaadou, Tod, Wancho.	T-B
	*01	Khampti	T-K
	*02	Bishnupuriya, Naga-P	C-V

4.2 Constraints on the distribution of vowel phonemes

Details about distributional restrictions on the occurrence of singlet vowels and sequences of vowels in the languages are presented in section 2.2 of each sketch. We discuss here the regularities regarding distributional restrictions on singlet vowels. The restrictions on vowel sequences are discussed in section 5.2.3.

Constraints on singlet vowels should be considered under three heads: a. position in the word, namely, initial, medial and final; b. vowel segments that have restricted occurrence; c. co-occurrence restrictions among vowels.

4.2.1 Position in the Word

Constraints on the occurrence of vowels in the word concern mainly the initial and final positions. The word-medial position usually allows free occurrence of vowels. There are only three instances of languages mentioned with restrictions on vowels in the medial positions, namely, Kuvi (DR), Purki (T-B) and Vagri Boli (C-V), which do not allow /u:/, /e: o: u/ and /ẽ: ũ:/ respectively, in word-medial position.

Constraints on the occurrence of vowels in the initial position include the following cases.

a. A language that requires an onset in the lexical representation does not permit vowels in the word-initial position. The one language that has such a requirement is *Nancowry* (A-A). *Nicobarese* (A-A) and *Purki* (T-B) also have vowels occurring rarely in the word-initial position.

b. Constraints on vowels in terms of the final syllables are intricately linked with vowel quantity and show parametric variation – languages that prohibit mainly short vowels and languages that prohibit long vowels in the word-final position. The difference appears to be metrically conditioned. The languages that prohibit long vowels in the final position are usually the Dravidian languages that have usually word-initial stress, e.g. *Tamil, Kannada.* The northern-central Indo-Aryan languages, such as Hindi and Punjabi, which prohibit short vowels in the final position have bounded trochaic systems in general. Most eastern T-B languages have word-final stress. These do not have vowels prohibited from occurring in the final position. Only the Himalayan T-B languages, such as *Balti* and *Purki,* are found not to permit long vowels in the final position.

4.2.2 Vowel segments

Restrictions on the occurrence of vowel segments are presented below.

The commonest vowels that are prohibited from occurring in a word in any position are the middle vowels /e E o/ and the central vowels /ö ə/, in that order. The fact can be stated in terms of an implicational constraint (4/8):

(4/8) MIDDLE VOWELS

*V > * M

[A constraint on the occurrence of vowels must include middle vowels]

Middle vowels are found included in constraints on vowels of all types – short, long, nasal- as can be seen in *Table 4.9* below.

Table 4.9 constraints on the distribution of vowels in the word-initial position in SPIL

WORD-INITIAL	A-A	DR	I-A	T-B	AN	C-V
All Vowels	Nico-C					
ẽ õ	Bhu					
I e: Ɛ o	Bon					
Ɛ Ɛ: ɨ		Koraga				
ĩ ũ õ		Kurux				
ə		Malaya		Lotha		Halbi
ɨ ɔ: ɒ			Kashmiri			
o:			Lahndi			
ɨ ü u				Adi		
e o				Angami		
e: o:				Balti		
ɨ ə ɔ				Kinnauri		
ɨ ə u				Mao-N		
a e				Meitei		
Λ ɔ				Padaam		
o				Tarao		
e: Ɛ: u: o					G-A	
ĩ: ẽ ẽ: ã õ: ɨ						Vagri-B

4.2.3 Co-occurrence restrictions among vowels

Three types of co-occurrence restrictions are found among vowels. These are of three types, namely, vowel sequences, vowel consonant sequences, and vowels and other phonological phenomena, such as tone.

The constraints on vowel sequences are postponed for discussion in Chapter 5 (section 5.2.2), where other such co-occurrence constraints, such as onset and coda clusters and geminates are discussed.

Restrictions on the co-occurrence of vowels with consonants are more often than not erratic. These are being presented in *Table 4.10*. As can be seen in it, generalizations such as in *Galo, Kabui* and *Kodagu*, are hard to come by.

Table 4.10 Constraints on vowels in varied contexts in SPIL

Vowel phonemes	Context: After	Context: Before	Permitted Context:	Prevented context	A-A	DR	I-A	T-B	T-K	C-V	H-V
All vowels				after /ŋ j/							O-Tamil
All vowels				before and after /b/		Kadar					
LV				before CC							Pali Prakrit
LV			initial syllable			Ave					
LV			--1-Initial syll in poly; 2-stresed syll --1- Initial syll in poly; 2-monosyllable			Kolami Gad-O					
i: u:	c ɟ					Kodagu					
i e		Retroflex Cs				Kodagu					
ɛ			in Closed syllable				Assame				
e o			in gram. morpheme					Byngsi			
ẽ õ			word-medially		Bhumij						

contd.

Table 4.10 *contd.*

ə e o			When no NC in coda					Mishimi			
ə ɛ ɔ				stressed syll						Diu-I-P	
ɛ ɛ̃ ɔ ɔ̃			borrowed words				Sindhi				
I e: ə ʊ u:				final syll	Bonda						
I e: ɛ o				initial syll	Bonda						
ɨ				u, ɛ in following syllable		Koraga					
i			Unstressed First syllable				Lahndi				
ə			stressed syll						Turung		
Word-final ɨ				V- initial morpheme				Apatani			
DV			Open syl & closed Syll with LS					Phom			
DV								Wancho			
LV		Single C						RangPo			
Stressed V and NV			Root morpheme		Nanco						
Final LV			Open syl			Kodagu					

Constraints on the occurrence of vowels in relation to other phonological properties in the languages are commoner. These relate to (i) syllabic structure, (ii) pitch levels, and (iii) stress. Examples of these are presented below:

(i) *Assamese*: /ɛ/ occurs in closed syllables.

Mishmi: /ə, e, o/ do not occur of a nasal consonant is present in the coda position.

Phom: diphthongs occur only in open syllables, or in closed syllables with /ʔ/ in the coda position.

Koraga: /ɨ, u/ /ɨ, ɛ:/ do not occur in consecutive syllables.

(ii) *Mizo*: Short vowels occur with L tones.

Lahndi: /i, i:, u, u:/ have high pitch.

/e, ɐ, o/ have mid pitch.

/æ, œ, a:/ have low pitch

(iii) *Kolami*: Long vowels do not occur in non-stressable positions, i.e. medially and finally in polysyllabic words.

Most of the constraints on the co-occurrence restrictions on vowels in relation to other phonological properties are idiosyncratic and language-specific and not generalizable.

4.3 Vowel Allophones

This section presents in brief some of the main aspects of the allophonic inventory of vowels in the Indic languages. The list of the allophones along with the specification of the processes of modification involved and the languages as well as the language groups in which they occur are given in *Table 4.11*, as mentioned in the beginning.

Table 4.11 Allophonic inventory of vowels in SPIL

[Abbreviations: SV= Short vowels, LV= Long vowels, DV= Diphthongs, NV= Nasal vowels, Allo= allophones, M= Modifications, L= Language, LG= Language group]

SVs	Allo	M	L	LG
i		*Short, unrounded, close, front vowel*		

contd.

Table 4.11 *contd.*

	i	shortened (< /iː/)	Khasi	A-A
	i	raised (< /ɪ/)	Kurux	DR
			Dimasa	T-B
	ĭ	extra short	Kharia, Mizo	T-B
	i·	half-long and shortened	Dogri, Kacchi	I-A
	iˑ	half-long and lengthened	Nancowry	A-A
			Gondi, Konda,Tulu	DR
			Balti, Bodo, Khampti, Ladakhi, Meitei, Mishmi, Purki, Rangpo	T-B
	i	desyllabified	Juang, Nicobarese-C	A-A
			Kota	DR
			Bodo, Kabui, Khampti, Meitei,Thaadou	T-B
		vocalized	Gadaba-O, Kodagu, Malayalam	DR
			Bhili	I-A
	ị	retroflexed	Koya	DR
	ï	centralized	Assamese, Oriya	I-A
	ĭ̥	extra-short and devoiced	Bodo	T-B
	i̤	breathy	Gujarati	I-A
			Tamang	T-B
	i̟	advanced	Bodo	T-B
	i̟˔	advanced, raised and shortened	Khasi	A-A
	ḭ	creaky	Khampti	T-K
	ʲi	on-glided	Gondi- A, Kadar, Konda, Kui, Tamil	DR
			Bhili, Kashmiri	I-A
			G-Andamanese	AN
	ʲi·	on-glided with half length	Bhili	I-A
	ˀi	preglottalized	Gondi-A, Koya	DR

contd.

Table 4.11 *contd.*

			Assamese	I-A
			Mishmi	T-B
	ij	off-glided/ diphthongized	Toda	DR
ɪ		*Short, unrounded, between close and close-mid, front vowel*		
	ɪ	lowered (< /i/)	Khasi	A-A
	ɪ̞	lowered (< /ɪ/)	Bhumij, Didayi	A-A
			Irula, Kodagu, Koraga, Kota, Koya, Naiki, Telugu	DR
			Gujarati, Jaunsari	I-A
			Karbi, Lotha, Mao-N, Phom	T-B
			Vagri-B	C-V
	ɪ̞̈	lowered and centralized	Gadaba-O	DR
	ɪ̯	desyllabified	Kurux	DR
			Urdu-T	C-V
	ɪ̣	Retroflexed	Toda	DR
ʏ		*Short, rounded, close, front vowel*		
	ʏ̣	retroflexed	Toda	DR
e		*Short, unrounded, close, front vowel*		
	e	shortened	Hindi	I-A
			Pali, Prakrit	H-V
		lowered (</i)	Nancowry	A-A
			Kokborok, Stod	T-B
		raised (</ɛ/)	Krurux	DR
			Dimasa	T-B
			I-P-Diu	C-V
	eˑ	Lowered and half-long (</i/)	Bodo	T-B
	ẹ̞	lowered	Ao-N, Ladakhi	T-B
	ẹ̞	lowered	Khasi (< /i/)	A-A

contd.

Table 4.11 *contd.*

	ĕ̞	extra-short and lowered	Byangsi	T-B
	e̞	lowered	Ao-N, Ladakhi	T-B
	e̞·	advanced	Bhili	I-A
	e̟	advanced	Bhili	I-A
			Bodo	T-B
	e̟·	advanced and half-long	Bhili	I-A
	ĕ	extra-short	Dogri	I-A
			Mizo	T-B
	ĕ̥	extra-short and devoiced	Bodo	T-B
	ë	centralized	Kolami	DR
			Assamese, Oriya	I-A
	ḛ	creaky	Khampti	T-B
	e̤	breathy	Tamang	T-B
	e̯	desyllabified	Nicobarese-C	A-A
			Bodo, Meitei	T-B
	ẹ	retroflexed	Toda	DR
	ˀe	preglottalized	Gondi-A, Koya	DR
			Assamese	I-A
			Mishmi	T-B
	ʲe	on-glided	Kadar, Konda, Kui, Tamil	DR
			Ao-N	T-B
			G-Andamanese	AN
			Nagamese	C-V
	ʲe̞	lowered and on-glided	Tulu	DR
ɛ		*Short, unrounded, open-mid, front vowel*		
	ɛ	lowered	Bhumij, Didayi, Khasi, Korku, Santali	A-A
			Gadaba-K, Irula, Kadar, Kodagu, Koraga, Kota, Naiki, Telugu, Toda, Tulu	DR

contd.

Table 4.11 *contd.*

			Bengali	I-A
			Balti, Byangsi, Karbi, Mao-N, Purki, Sema-N, (Spiti), Stod, Tibetan-St	T-B
			Vagri-B	C-V
		fronted	Apatani (</ə/)	T-B
	ɛ̆	extra short	Kharia	A-A
			Dogri	I-A
	ɛ·	half-long	Nancowry	A-A
			Khampti	T-K
		half-long and shortened	Kacchi (</ɛː/)	I-A
		half-long and lowered	Bodo (</e/)	T-B
	ɛ̯	desyllabified	Nicobarese-C	A-A
			Kurux	DR
	ɛ̈	centralized	Assamese	I-A
	ɛ̤	breathy	Gujarati	I-A
	ɛ̰	creaky	Khampti	T-K
	ʲɛ	onglide	G-Andamanese	AN
	ˀɛ	preglottalized	Assamese	I-A
æ		***Short, unrounded, just below open-mid, front vowel***		
	æ	fronted	Mandeali (</a/)	I-A
	æ·	half-long	Nancowry	A-A
	æ̈	lowered and centralized	Koya	DR
	æ̯	desyllabified	Maithili	I-A
ɨ		***Short, unrounded, close, central vowel***		
	ɨ	centralized	Gondi-A (</i/), Irula (</u/), Kodagu (</ɯ/, /i/), Tulu (</ɯ/)	DR
			Kangri, Khezha	T-B
		centralized and raised	Korku (< /e/)	A-A
		raised	Mandeali (< /ə/)	I-A

contd.

Table 4.11 *contd.*

	ɨ·	half-long	Nancowry	A-A
			Mishmi	T-B
	ɨ̰	creaky	Khampti	T-K
ʉ		*Short, rounded, close, central vowel*		
	ʉ	centralized	Kangri	T-B
ɵ		*Short, rounded, close-mid, central vowel*		
	ɵ̣	retroflexed	Toda	DR
ə		*Short, unrounded, mid, central vowel*		
	ə	centralized	Kodagu (</ɸ/)	DR
		raised	Nancowry	A-A
			Kodagu, Konda, Telugu, Yerava	DR
			Assamese, Lahndi (</ɐ/)	I-A
			Liangmai, Kangri, Karbi, Sema-N, Spiti, Tibetan-St	T-B
			G-Andamanese	AN
		lowered	Apatani, Chokri (< /ɨ/)	T-B
		lowered and centralized	Lahndi (< /u/)	I-A
	ə̟	advanced	Bodo	T-B
		raised and advanced	Phom (< /a/)	T-B
	ə̝	raised	Karbi	T-B
	ə̯	desyllabified	Nicobarese-C	A-A
			Meitei	T-B
	ə̥	devoiced	Angami	T-B
	ə̆	extra short	Kharia	A-A
	ə̥˘	devoiced and extra short	Bodo	T-B
			Bodo, Meitei, RangPo	T-B

contd.

Table 4.11 *contd.*

	ə̤	breathy voiced	Gujarati	I-A
			Galo-L	T-B
	ə·	half-long	Nancowry	
	ˀə	preglottalized	Kattunaicka	DR
ɜ		*Short, unrounded, open-mid, central vowel*		
	ɜ	raised	Korku (< /ɐ/)	A-A
		lowered	Kadar	DR
			Gujarati (< /ə/)	I-A
ɞ		*Short, rounded, open-mid, central vowel*		
	ɞ	lowered	Toda (< /ɵ/)	DR
ɐ		*Short, unrounded, between open-mid and open, central vowel*		
	ɐ	raised	Bhumij	A-A
			Naiki, Tulu	DR
			Jaunsari, Oriya	I-A
			Brokstat, Liangmai, Mishmi, Phom, Sema-N, Tibetan-St	T-B
			Vagri-B, I-P-Diu	C-V
		raised and advanced	Kadar (< /ɑ/), Toda (</a/)	DR
		lowered	Tulu (< /ə/)	DR
	ɐ̰	raised and creaky	Sema-N	T-B
a		*Short, unrounded, open, central vowel*		
	ä	centralized	Irula	DR
	a	lowered	Kurux (< /ɐ/)	DR
	a̟	advanced	Bhili	I-A
			Apatani, Bodo	T-B
	a̟·	advanced and half-long	Bhili	I-A
	a̯	desyllabified	Nicobarese-C	A-A

contd.

Table 4.11 *contd.*

			Meitei	T-B
	a	extra short	Dogri	I-A
			Mizo	T-B
	ḁ̆	devoiced and extra short	Bodo	T-B
	a̤	breathy voiced	Gujarati	I-A
			Tamang	T-B
	a̰	creaky	Khampti	T-K
	ạ	retroflexed	Koya	DR
	ˀa	preglottalized	Gondi-A, Kattunaicka, Koya	T-B
			Assamese	I-A
			Mishmi	T-B
	ạ	retroflexed	Koya	DR
u		*Short, rounded, close, back vowel*		
	u	shortened	Khasi	A-A
	ü	centralized	Assamese, Oriya	I-A
	u	raised	Kurux (< /ʊ/)	
			Dogri	I-A
			Dimasa, Kokborok	T-B
	u̟	advanced	Monpa	T-B
	u̯	desyllabified	Juang, Nicobarese-C	A-A
			Kota, Malayalam	DR
			Bhili	I-A
			Bodo, Kabui, Meitei, Sema, Thaadou	T-B
			Khampti	T-K
		vocalized (< /w/, /ʋ/)	Gondi-A, Irula, Kodagu, Malayalam	DR
	u	extra short	Kharia	A-A
			Mizo	T-B

contd.

Table 4.11 *contd.*

	ṳ	breathy voiced	Gujarati	I-A
			Galo-L, Tamang	T-B
	ṵ	creaky	Khampti	T-K
	ụ	retroflexed	Toda	DR
	ˀu	preglottalized	Gondi-A	DR
			Assamese	I-A
			Mishmi	T-B
	u·	lengthened- half-long	Nancowry	A-A
			Gondi, Konda, Tulu	DR
			Bhili	I-A
			Balti, Ladakhi, Mishmi, Rangpo, Monpa	T-B
		shortened- half-long	Khasi	A-A
	ʷu	on-glided	Kadar, Konda, Kui, Tamil	DR
	ü:	vocalized, centralized and lengthened (< /w)	RangPo	T-B
ɯ		*Short, unrounded, close, back vowel*		
	ɯ	unrounded(<u)	Gondi-A, Kadar, Naiki, Tamil	DR
	ɯ	retracted	Apatan (< /ɨ/), Sema-N	T-B
		raised and retracted	Kokborok (< /ə/)	T-B
	ɯ̞	lowered and retracted	Sema-N (< /ɨ/)	T-B
	ɯ̟	advanced	Bodo	T-B
	ɯ̥̆	extra short and devoiced	Bodo	T-B
	ɯ·	half-long	Bodo	T-B
			Khampti	T-K
	ɯ̰	creaky	Khampti	T-K
ʊ		*Short, rounded, between close and close-mid, back vowel*		
	ʊ	lowered	Bhumij, Didayi, Khasi, Korku	A-A

contd.

Table 4.11 *contd.*

			Irula, Kodagu, Koraga, Kota, Telugu	DR
			Karbi, Lotha, Mao-N, Raji	T-B
			Vagri-B	C-V
	ʊ̯	desyllabified	Kurux	DR
			Urdu-D-T	C-V
	ʊ	raised	Tulu (< /o/)	DR
o	ö	centralized	Assamese, Oriya	I-A
			Wancho	T-B
	o	raised	Kurux	DR
			Oriya	I-A
			Dimasa, Kokborok	T-B
			I-P-Diu	C-V
		vocalized	Raji	T-B
	o̞	lowered	Khasi	A-A
	o̥	desyllabified	Juang, Nicobarese-C	A-A
			Kurux	DR
			Bodo, Meitei, Mishmi, Thaadou	T-B
	o·	half-long	Nancowry	A-A
			Gondi, Konda, Tulu	DR
			Bhili	I-A
			Balti, Ladakhi, Mishmi, Rangpo, Monpa	T-B
	ŏ	extra short	Hindi	I-A
			Mizo	T-B
	o̤	breathy voiced	Gujarati	I-A
			Galo-L, Tamang	T-B
	o̰	creaky	Khampti	T-K
	o̟	retroflexed	Koya, Toda	DR
	ˀo	preglottalized	Gondi-A, Koya	DR
			Assamese	I-A

contd.

Table 4.11 *contd.*

	ʷo	on-glided	Kadar, Konda, Kui, Tamil, Tulu	DR
			Bhili	I-A
			Ao-N	T-B
			Nagamese	C-V
	ʷo	on-glided and half-long	Bhili	I-A
	ö:	vocalized, centralized and lengthened (< /w)	RangPo	T-B
ɤ		*Short, unrounded, close-mid, back vowel*		
	ɤ	unrounded	Koya (< /o/)	DR
ɔ		*Short, rounded, open-mid, back vowel*		
	ɔ̈	centralized	Assamese	I-A
	ɔ	lowered	Bhumij, Didayi, Khasi, Santali	A-A
			Gadaba-O, Irula, Koraga, Kota, Naiki, Telugu, Tulu, Toda	DR
			Bengali	I-A
			Angami, Ao-N, Balti, Byangsi, Karbi, Mao-N, Monpa, Raji, Tibetan-St	T-B
		backed and raised	Tamil	DR
			Mandeali (< /a/)	I-A
		desyllabified		
		half-long	Bodo	T-B
			Khampti	T-K
	ɔ̟	advanced	Bodo	T-B
	ɔ̆	extra short	Kharia	A-A
	ɔ̥̆	extra short and devoiced	Bodo	T-B
	ɔ̤	breathy and lowered	Gujarati	I-A
		breathy	Tamang	T-B
	ɔ̰	creaky	Khampti	T-K
	ˀɔ	preglottalized	Assamese	I-A

contd.

Table 4.11 *contd.*

ʌ		*Short, unrounded, open-mid, back vowel*		
	ʌ	raised	Kadar (< /ɑ/), Toda (<ɑ/)	DR
			Ao-N	T-B
		raised and retracted (< /a/)	Kodagu, Tamil	DR
			Purki, Nagamese	T-B
ɑ		*Short, unrounded, open, back vowel*		
	ɑ	retracted	Kodagu (< /a/)	DR
			Karbi	T-B
		retracted and lowered	Ladakhi (< /ə/)	T-B
	ɑˑ	half-long	RangPo	T-B
LVs				
iː		*Long, unrounded, close, front vowel*		
	iː	lengthened	Kharia, Mundari, Nancowry	A-A
			Gadaba-K, Gondi, Kui, Naiki, Gondi-A/	DR
			Bhili, Gujarati, Hindi, Lamani, Kashmiri	I-A
			Bodo, Galo-L, Liangmai, Meitei, Mizo, Monpa, Tod	T-B
			Khampti,	T-K
		raised and lengthened	Jaunsari	I-A
			Khampti	T-K
	i̥ː	devoiced	Koya, Toda	DR
	ˀiː	preglottalized	Gondi-A	DR
	ʲiː	on-glide	Kui, Konda, Tamil	DR
			Lotha	T-B
		on-glided and lengthening	Bhili	I-A
	iːʲ	off-glided/ diphthongized	Toda	DR

contd.

Table 4.11 *contd.*

e:		*Long, unrounded, close-mid, front vowel*		
	e:	lengthened (</e/)	Kharia, Nancowry	A-A
			Gadaba-K, Gondi, Kui, Naiki	DR
			Assamese, Gujarati, Lamani	I-A
			Bodo, Galo-L, Liangmai, Mizo, Monpa, Stod	T-B
		lengthened and lowered	Bodo (< /i/)	T-B
		lengthened and raised	Khampti	T-B
	ë:	centralized	Kolami	DR
	ẹ:	retroflexed	Toda	DR
	ẹ̟:	fronted and lengthened	Bhili	I-A
	ʲe:	on-glided	Kui	DR
	e·	shortened	Kacchi	I-A
	ˀe:	preglottalized	Gondi-A	DR
	~e:ə	diphthongized (free variation)	RangPo	T-B
ɛ:		*Long, unrounded, open-mid, front vowel*		
	ɛ:	lowered	Khasi	A-A
		lowered	Toda, Yerava	DR
			Vagri-B	C-V
		lengthened	Nancowry	A-A
			Bhili	I-A
			Galo-L, Liangmai	T-B
		lengthened and lowered	Bodo (< /e/)	T-B
	ɛ̞:	lengthened and lowered	Dogri (< /ɛ/)	I-A
	ɛ·	shortened	Kacchi	I-A
	ɛ:ʲ	off-glided	Kashmiri	I-A
æ:		*Long, unrounded, open-mid, central vowel*		

contd.

Table 4.11 *contd.*

	æ:	lengthened	Nancowry	A-A
		fronted	Mandeali (< /a:/)	I-A
ɨ:		*Long, unrounded, close, central vowel*		
	ɨ:	lengthened	Nancowry	A-A
			Galo-L, Liangmai	T-B
	ɨ:	centralized	Tulu (< /i/)	DR
ɵ:		*Long, rounded, close-mid, central vowel*		
	ɵ̣:	retroflexed	Toda	DR
ɞ:		*Long, rounded, open-mid, central vowel*		
	ɞ:	rounded	Toda (< / ɵ:/)	DR
ə:		*Long, unrounded, between close-mid and open-mid, central vowel*		
	ə:	lengthened	Nancowry	A-A
			Bhili, Gujarati	I-A
			Bodo, Stod	T-B
a:		*Long, unrounded, open, central vowel*		
	a:	lengthened	Nancowry	A-A
			Gadaba-K, Kuvi, Naiki	DR
			Bhili	I-A
			Bodo, Galo-L, Liangmai, Meitei, Mizo	T-B
		lengthened and lowered	Monpa (< /ɐ/)	T-B
		centralized	Irula	DR
		retroflexed	Koya	DR
	a̟:	fronted and lengthened	Bhili	I-A
		on-glided		
	a·	shortened (half-long)	Kacchi	I-A
	ˀa:	preglottalized	Gondi-A	DR

contd.

Table 4.11 *contd.*

uː		*Long, rounded, close, back vowel*		
	uː	lengthened	Kharia, Nancowry	A-A
			Gadaba-K, Gondi, Kui, Naiki	DR
			Bhili	I-A
			Galo-L, Liangmai Mizo, Monpa, Stod	T-B
			Khampti	T-K
	uː	lengthened and raised	Khampti (< /o/)	T-K
	u̝ː	lengthened and raised	Jaunsari (< /u/)	I-A
	üː	centralized and vocalized	RangPo (< /w/)	T-B
	ụː	retroflexed	Toda	DR
	uː	fronted and lengthened		
	ʷuː	on-glided	Kui, Konda, Tamil	DR
	uː	shortened (half-long)	Kacchi	I-A
	ˀuː	preglottalized	Gondi-A	DR
ɯː		*Long, unrounded, close, back vowel*		
	ɯː	lengthened	Bodo	T-B
			Khampti	T-K
ʊː		*Long, rounded, between close and close-mid, back vowel*		
	ʊː	lowered	Tulu	DR
oː		*Long, rounded, close-mid, back vowel*		
	oː	lengthened (</e/)	Kharia, Nancowry	A-A
			Gadaba-K, Gondi, Kui, Naiki	DR
			Bhili	I-A
			Galo-L, Liangmai Meitei, Mizo, Monpa, Stod	T-B

contd.

Table 4.11 *contd.*

		lengthened and raised	Khampti	T-B
	o̝:	raised and lengthened	Dogri	I-A
	ö:	centralized and vocalized	RangPo (< /w/)	T-B
	ọ:	retroflexed	Koya, Toda	DR
	ʷo:	onglide	Kui, Konda, Tamil	DR
		onglide with lengthening	Bhili	I-A
	oˑ	shortened	Kacchi	I-A
	ˀo:	preglottalized	Gondi-A	DR
	o:ə	diphthongized (free variation)	RangPo	T-B
ɔ:		*Long, rounded, open-mid, back vowel*		
	ɔ:	lengthened	Bodo, Galo-L, Liangmai	T-B
	ɔ:	lowered	Telugu, Yerava	DR
			Khasi	A-A
		retracted and raised	Mandeali (< /a:/)	I-A
	ɔ̝:	raised	Dogri	I-A
ɤ:		*Long, unrounded, close-mid, back vowel*		
	ɤ:	unrounded and lengthened	Koya (< /o/)	DR
ɒ:		*Long, rounded, open, back vowel*		
	ɒ:	raised and rounded	Telugu	DR
ɑ:		*Long, unrounded, open, back vowel*		
	ɑ:	lengthened	Stod	T-B
	ɑ̣:	retroflexed	Toda	DR
DVs				
ĭă		*Unrounded close front to unrounded open central diphthong*		
		shortened	Khasi (< /ia/)	A-A

contd.

Table 4.11 *contd.*

i̯e		*Unrounded close front to unrounded close-mid central diphthong*		
		diphthongized	Kolami	DR
əi		*Unrounded, mid, central to unrounded close front diphthong*		
		diphthongized	Telugu (< /æː/)	DR
			Maithili, Hindi	I-A
ɔːə		*Long, rounded, open-mid, back to unrounded, mid, central diphthong*		
		diphthongized	Kashmiri (< /ɔː/)	I-A
əʊ̯		*Unrounded, mid, central to rounded, between close and close-mid back diphthong*		
		diphthongized (fully)	Maithili, Hindi (< /ꜵ/)	I-A
ꜵ		*Unrounded, mid, central to rounded, close-mid, back diphthong*		
		half-long	Hindi, Kacchi	I-A
ʊə̯		*rounded, between close and close-mid, back to unrounded, mid, central*		
		diphthongized	Assamese (< /ʊ/)	I-A
oe̯		*Rounded, close-mid back to unrounded close-mid front diphthong*		
		diphthongized	Assamese (</o/)	I-A
ọo̯		*Rounded, just above close-mid back to unrounded close-mid front diphthong*		
		lowered	Khasi	A-A
ɞe̯		*Rounded, open-mid, central to unrounded close-mid front diphthong*		
		diphthongized	Assamese (< /ɞ/)	I-A
ɒe̯		*Rounded, open, back to unrounded close-mid front diphthong*		

contd.

Table 4.11 *contd.*

		diphthongized	Assamese (< /ɒ/)	I-A
ae̯		*Unrounded open central to unrounded close-mid front diphthong*		
		diphthongized	Assamese (< /a/)	I-A
ɛə̯		*Unrounded open-mid front to unrounded between close-mid and open-mid central diphthong*		
		diphthongized	Assamese (< /ɛ/)	I-A
ei̯		*Unrounded close-mid front to unrounded close front diphthong*		
		diphthongized	Assamese (< /e/)	I-A
e̝e̯		*Unrounded just above close-mid front to unrounded close-mid front diphthong*		
		lowered	Khasi	A-A
NVs[1]		Nasal Vowels		
ĩ		*Short, unrounded, close front nasal vowel*		
	ĩ	raised	Kurux	DR
ĩ:		*Long, unrounded, close front nasal vowel*		
		lengthened	Bhili	I-A
ẽ		*Short, unrounded, close-mid front nasal vowel*		
		raised	Kurux	DR
ɛ̃:		*Long, unrounded, open-mid front nasal vowel*		
	ɛ̃:	lengthened	Bhili (< /ɛ̃/)	I-A
ə̃		*Short, unrounded, between close-mid and open-mid central nasal vowel*		
	ə̃	raised	Lahndi (< /ɐ/)	I-A

[1] The list of nasal vowels here does not include the vowels which have contextual nasalization, as mentioned in the introduction, but only those nasal vowels that are variants of nasal vowel phoneme. We assume that all oral vowels can be contextually nasalized, and thus need not be specified in the present list.

contd.

Table 4.11 *contd.*

	ə̃	raised and centralized	Lahndi (< /ũ/)	I-A
ə̃:		*Long, unrounded, between close-mid and open-mid central nasal vowel*		
	ə̃:	lengthened	Bhili (< /ə̃/)	I-A
ã:		*Long, unrounded, open central nasal vowel*		
	ã:	lengthened	Bhili < /ã/)	I-A
ũ		*Short, rounded, close back nasal vowel*		
	ũ	raised	Kurux (< /ʊ̃/)	DR
ũ:		*Long, rounded, close back nasal vowel*		
	ũ:	lengthened	Bhili < /ũ/)	I-A
õ		*Short, rounded, close-mid back nasal vowel*		
		raised	Kurux (< /ɔ̃/)	DR

4.3.1 Allophonic modifications of vowels

A look at the allophonic inventory of vowels in *Table 4.11* gives a total of 24 modification processes involved in yielding the allophones in the Indic languages. These are classifiable into four main types, namely, QUALITATIVE, QUANTITATIVE, LARYNGEAL, AND SYLLABLE-BASED, and presented in *Table 4.12* below.

Table 4.12 Allophonic modification types in SPIL

QUALITATIVE (10)	**QUANTITATIVE (05)**	**LARYNGEAL (04)**	**SYLLABLE-BASED (05)**
Advanced	Extra-short	Breathy voiced	Desyllabified
Retracted	Lengthened half-long	Creaky	Diphthongized
Centralized	Shortened half-long	Devoiced	Vocalized
Fronted	Lengthened	Pre-glottalized	Off-glided

contd.

Table 4.12 *contd.*

Backed	Shortened		Onglided
Lowered			
Raised			
Rounded			
Unrounded			
Retroflexed			

These modification processes together give 224 allophones. The syllable-based vocalic allophonic processes are syllable-based on account of either being dependent on a syllable structure context (for example, on-glided vowels in the Onset position) or leading to a change in the syllable structure (for example desyllabified vowels that lose their status as the Nucleus). The desyllabified vowels in these cases, it should be noted, are those that lose their function as independent nuclei (e.g. a+i>ai̯).

The tables below give a breakup of the segments resulting from the processes in general and in the language groups.

Table 4.13 Qualitative modification of vowels in SPIL

MODIFICATION TYPE: QUALITATIVE				A-A	DR	I-A	T-B	T-K	AN	C-V	H-V
ADVANCED	07	Front	01	1	–	1	1	–	–	–	–
		Central	03	–	1	1	2	–	–	–	–
		Back	03	–	–	–	3	–	–	–	–
RETRACTED	04	Back	04	–	2	1	3	–	–	–	–
CENTRALIZED	17	Front	05	–	4	2		–	–	–	–
		Central	07	1	5	2	2	–	–	–	–
		Back	05	–	–	3	4	–	–	–	–
FRONTED	06	Front	03	–	–	2	1	–	–	–	–
		Central	02	–	–	2	–	–	–	–	–
		Back	01	–	1	–	–	–	–	–	–
BACKED	01	Back	01	–	1	1	–	–	–	–	–
LOWERED	20	Front	08	6	5	3	5	–	–	3	–

contd.

		Central	06	–	4	2	2	–	–		–
		Back	06	3	4	1	4	–	–	1	–
RAISED	20	Front	04	1	3	–	2	–	–	1	–
		Central	05	4	3	4	2	–	1	1	–
		Back	11	–	6	6	5	1	–	1	–
ROUNDED	02	Central	01	–	1	–	–	–	–	–	–
		Back	01	–	1	–	–	–	–	–	–
UNROUNDED	03	Back	03	–	3	–	–	–	–	–	–
RETROFLEXED	13	Front	04	–	4	–	–	–	–	–	–
		Central	04		4	–	–	–	–	–	–
		Back	05		5	–	–	–	–	–	–
Total	93		93	16	57	31	36	1	1	7	0

Table 4.14 Quantitative modification processes in SPIL

MODIFICATION TYPE: QUANTITATIVE				**A-A**	**DR**	**I-A**	**T-B**	**T-K**	**AN**	**C-V**	**H-V**
EXTRA-SHORTENED	08	Front	02	1	–	2	1	–	–	–	–
		Central	02	1	–	1	2	–	–	–	–
		Back	04	2	–	1	4	–	–	–	–
LENGTHENED HALF-LONG	11	Front	03	3	1	–	–	–	–	–	–
		Central	02	1			2	–	–	–	–
		Back	06	2	2	3	5	2	–	–	–
SHORTENED HALF-LONG	05	Front	02	–	–	2	–	–	–	–	–
		Central	01	–	–	1	–	–	–	–	–
		Back	02	1	–	1	–	–	–	–	–
LENGTHENED	29	Front	08	6	3	5	5	3	–	–	–
		Central	08	5	1	4	5	-	–	–	–
		Back	13	4	5	6	10	4	–	–	–

contd.

SHORTENED	09	Front	4	2	4	–	–	–	–	–	1
		Central	02	1	–	1	–	–	–	–	–
		Back	03	1	-	2	–	–	–	–	–
TOTAL	62		62	30	16	29	34	9	0	0	1

Table 4.15 Laryngeal modification processes for vowels in SPIL

MODIFICATION TYPE: LARYNGEAL				A-A	DR	I-A	T-B	T-K	AN	C-V	H-V
BREATHY VOICED	07	Front	02	–	–	2	1	–	–	–	–
		Central	02	–	–	2	2	–	–	–	–
		Back	03	–	–	3	3	–	–	–	–
CREAKY	09	Front	02	–	–	–	1	2	–	–	–
		Central	03	–	–	–	1	2	–	–	–
		Back	04	–	–	–	–	4	–	–	–
DEVOICED	06	Front	02	–	1	–	1	–	–	–	–
		Central	02	–	–	–	2	–	–	–	–
		Back	02	–	–	–	2	–	–	–	–
PRE-GLOTTALIZED	12	Front	04	–	3	2	1	–	–	–	–
		Central	03	–	2	1	1	–	–	–	–
		Back	05	–	4	3	1	–	–	–	–
TOTAL	34		34	0	10	13	16	8	0	0	0

Table 4.16 Syllable-based modification processes for vowels in SPIL

MODIFICATION TYPE: SYLLABLE-BASED				A-A	DR	I-A	T-B	T-K	AN	C-V	H-V
DESYLLABIFIED	08	Front	04	2	3	1	1	–	–	1	–
		Central	02	2	–	–	2	–	–	–	–
		Back	02	2	2	1	2	1	–	1	–

contd.

Table 4.16 *contd.*

DIPHTHONGIZED	15	Front	09	–	3	6	1	–	–	–	–
		Central	04	–	1	3	–	–	–	–	–
		Back	02	–		1	1	–	–	–	–
VOCALIZED	05	Front	01	–	1	1	–	–	–	–	–
		Back	04	–	1		3	–	–	–	–
OFF-GLIDED	03	Front	03	–	2	1	–	–	–	–	–
ON-GLIDED	08	Front	04	–	1	2	2	–	–	1	–
		Back	04	–	4	2	1	–	–	1	–
TOTAL	39		39	6	18	18	13	1	2	4	0

Tables 4.10–4.14 show that the four types of modification processes give rise to the number of allophones as given below.

(4/9) MODIFICATION PROCESS	NUMBER OF SEGMENTS	% OUT OF 228
Qualitative (10)	93	40.78
Quantitative (05)	62	27.19
Laryngeal (04)	34	14.91
Syllable-based (05)	39	17.10

Each process gives an average of 9.5 allophones. The largest number of allophonic segments are on account of the qualitative processes (93/228), and the smallest number are on account of laryngeal processes (34/228). The figures of the productivity of these processes are different: the quantitative processes, with only 5 of them yielding 62 segments, are the most productive, and the syllable-based processes, with 5 of them yielding 39 segments, are the least productive in the present data.

Chapter 5

Above Segments

5.0 Introduction

In this chapter we discuss four main aspects of the word phonology of the Indic languages above the segment, namely, syllable structure (**section** 5.1), permissible segment sequences (**section** 5.2), including consonant clusters, geminate consonants, and vowel sequences, suprasegementals (**section** 5.3), including word-stress and tone, and phonological cues for grammatical structure (**section** 5.4). Of these, word stress has not been included for description in the sketches, and thus it has been only touched upon in this chapter.

5.1 Syllable Structures

5.1.1 Canonical syllable structures

We briefly discuss here the main types of syllable structures found in the Indic languages. We have chosen to restrict the descriptions to canonical syllable structures in the languages. The canonical syllable structures are listed in *Table 5.1*.

Table 5.1 should be read with the following points in mind:

i. Languages having restricted types of consonants or consonant clusters are marked as O/- and C/- for restricted onsets and codas.

ii. Languages marked with an asterisk should be read with the footnote explanations given below the chart.

iii. The abbreviations in parentheses against the names of the languages stand for different types of asymmetries in syllables in them: I= Initial, NI= Non-initial, F= Final, NF= Non-final, SF= Stem-final, WF= Word-final, R= Root

Table 5.1 Canonical syllable structures in Indic languages

No	Canonical syllable structure type	A-A	DR	I-A	T-B	T-K	A-N	C-V	H-V
1	(C) V:		Kodagu (F/NF) Kolami* (In)						
2	C V (C)	Nancowry-N	Kodagu (F)		Bodo(NI)				
3	(C) V/NV								Pali (F)
4	C V (C)		Kolami*(F-1)						
5	C V (C) (C)		Naiki (NF)						
6	C V (C) (N) (C) (C) (C)		Kolami*(F-2)						
7	(C) CV (C) (C)	Khasi			Garo				
8	(C) V (C)	Gadaba-G (F) Gorum Ho Khar, Mundari Nicobarese-C Parengi Santhali	Gadaba-K (In) Gondi* Kodagu (NF) Koya Yerava (Wd)	Lahndi Magahi Mahl (In) Sindhi	Adi Gallong Galo-L* Hmar Ho Mizo Kok Thadou Padaam Rawang* Phom Wancho		G-A Onge Jarawa	Bishnu	OTa (In) Pali (NF) Prakrit (NF)
9	(C) V (m)								Prakrit (F)

contd.

Table 5.1 *contd.*

10	(C) V (C) (C)	Kisan	Gondi Tulu Ollari Kurux (In)	Bhili (In) Bhojpuri	Mizo Paite				
11	(C) V (N) (C)							Halbi	
12	(C) V (C) (C) (C)		Yerava (St)						
13	(C) V (C) (C) (C) (C)		Malto(R)						
14	(C) (C) V		Malto(WdF) Kuvi (F)	Mahl (NI)	Khezha				
15	(C) (C) V/ C`				Chokri*				
16	(C) (r) V/ C`				Angami*				
17	(C) (r) V		Koraga		Mao-N				
18	(C) (C) V (C)	Did Juang	Ave Badaga (NF) Kattu Kui (F) Kuvi (NF) Irula Telugu (F) Tulu		Bodo(In) Byangsi Chakma Chaudang Darma Koren Maring Meitei Raji Spiti Tangsa Tarao			Nagamese* Vagri-B	
19	(C) (C) V (LS)		Kui (F)						
20	(C) (C) V (j)		Badaga (F)						

contd.

Table 5.1 *contd.*

21	(C) (L/j) V (C)	Gadaba (NF)		Urdu-D-H	Karbi Kiranti-K			Urdu-D-T	
22	(C) (G/l) V (C)				Bantawa Meitei	Khampti			
23	(C) (L) V (C)				Dimasa* Tarao				
24	(C) (w/r) V (C)				Khezha				
25	(C) (r) V (C)			Shina		Turung			O-Telu
26	(C) (G) V (C)				Kabui Magar O/-Spiti				
27	(C) (G/r) V (C)			Nepali	Stod				
28	(C) (j) V (C)				Apatani Darma Raji				
29	(N) (C) V (C)				Lotha				
30	(C) V (C) (C)				Lotha			Nagamese*	
31	(C) (C) V (C) (C)	Bhumij	Tamil Gadaba-K (NI) Kui (NF) Kurux (NI) Manda Pengo Telugu (NF)	Bhili(NI) Dogri Kacchi Punjabi	Kinnauri Kiranti-K Monpa Purki		G-And		O-Ta (NI)

contd.

Table 5.1 *contd.*

32	(C) (Sn) V (C) (C)				Koren (Wd)				
33	(C) (L/G) V (C) (C)				Mishmi				
34	(C) (G) V (C) (C)	Korku		Bagri Lamani					
35	(C) (G/r) V (C) (C)			Gojri Rathvi	Manchad RangPo				
36	(C) (L) V (L) (C)							Diu-I-P	
37	(C) (r) V (C) (C)		Naiki (NF)	Kashmiri					
38	(C) (ɬ) V (j/ʔ) (C)				Ao-N				
39	(C) (C) V (C) (C) (C)		Naiki (F)						
40	(C) (Sn) V (C) (C) (C)				Koren (R)				
41	(C) (L) V (C) (C) (C)		Kota						
42	(C) (r/j) V (C) (C) (C)		Gond-A						
43	(C) (G) V (C) (C) (C) (C)		Toda*						
44	(C) (C) (C) V (C)		Malayalam Kannada (WF)	Bengali Marathi	Lepcha				
45	(C) (C) (C) V (C) (C)		Bonda Manda	Assamese Gujarati Maithili Mandeali	Balti O/C- Brokskat O/C- Garo Ladakhi				

contd.

Table 5.1 *contd.*

46	(C) (C) (C) V (N) (C)			Oriya					
47	(C) (C) (C) V (r) (C)								Sans
48	(C) (C) (G) V (C) (C)	Khasi							
49	(C) (C) (C) V (C) (C) (C)		Kannada (SF)	Haryanvi Hindi					
50	(C) (C) (C) V (C) (C) (C) (C)							IE-H	

Note:

- A majority of languages have restrictions on the onsets and codas generally stated in terms of Cs. The restrictions are found in the tables of consonant clusters.
- Angami, Chokri and Ladakhi permit a syllabic consonant in the place of a vowel.
- Angami, Chokri, Rawang, Zo: word-final consonants are also coda consonants.
- Dimasa: monovocalic words are not attested; a monosyllabic word must have either an onset or a coda.
- Gondi: a sequence of up to five consonants are permitted word-medially; the syllable structure divisions are not clear.
- Kolami: 3 canonical syllable structures are found (see the list in 5.2.1), and a minimal word requirement- CV:/CVC.
- Nagamese: A consonant cluster can occur either “in the onset or in the coda and not in both” (Sridhar 1985:61).
- Toda: multiple final consonants have been noted in the analyses of Emeneau (1957,1984) and Saktivel (1976), as having release; the consonants are assumed to have arisen from the loss of short vowels.
- Many languages show asymmetrical syllable structures within words. The asymmetries are classified into five types:

a. Initial (In) and Non-initial(NIn),
b. Final (F) and Non-final (NF),
c. Initial (In), Final-1 (F-1), and Final-2 (F-2),
d. Roots (R) and Word-final (WdF), and
e. Stem-initial (StI) and Word-final (WdF).
f. Stem level (St) and Word level (Wd)

The asymmetrical syllable structures are listed in the last point of section 5.1.2.

5.1.2 Properties of the syllable structure types

A close look at *Table 5.1* brings out the following general and typological properties of the syllable structure types.

General properties

The general properties of the syllable structures in these languages can be stated as follows:

a. Syllable structures with simple and complex onsets and codas are found in all language groups.
b. While there are languages with obligatory simple onsets, mainly from the Dravidian and the AN groups, there is no language with obligatory codas.
c. Languages with asymmetrical complex onsets and complex codas are found. There are languages with more complex onsets than codas, especially from the Tibeto-Burman group, and with more complex codas than onsets, especially from the Dravidian group.
d. The maximum number of complex onsets is found to be three, from the Indo-Aryan group, and the Tibeto-Burman languages of the Himalayan subgroup.
e. The maximum number of complex codas is found to be four, in Toda, a South Dravidian language. The complex codas are assumed to have arisen from the loss of vowels.
f. Most languages permitting complex onsets and codas have restrictions on the co-occurring segments, specified in the sketches.
g. Given the canonical syllable structure requirement, a majority of languages permit free combinations of medial clusters. However,

many languages from the various groups require the medial clusters to conform to the restrictions on the codas and the onsets in them.

h. Many languages show asymmetrical syllable structures within words. The asymmetries are classified into five types:
   i. Initial (In) and Non-initial(NIn),
   ii. Final (F) and Non-final (NF),
   iii. Initial (In), Final-1 (F-1), and Final-2 (F-2),
   iv. Roots (R) and Word-final (WdF),
   v. Stem-initial (StI) and Word-final (WdF), and
   vi. Stem level (St) and Word level (Wd).

The asymmetrical syllable structures are listed below:

Asymmetrical syllable structures in Indic languages

a.

Initial (In)	**Non-initial (NIn)**	**Language**
(C) V (C) (C)	(C) (C) V (C) (C)	Bhili (I-A)
(C) V (C)	(C) (C) V (C) (C)	Gadaba-K (DR)
(C) V (C)	(C) (C) V	Mahl (I-A)
(C) V (C) (C)	(C) V (C) (C) (C)	Kurux (DR)
(C) V (C)	(C) (C) V (C)	O-Tamil (H-V)

b.

Final (F)	**Non-final (NF)**	**Language**
(C) (C) V (j)	(C) (C) V (C)	Badaga (DR)
(C) V (C)	(C) (L/j) V (C)	Gadaba-G (A-A)
C V (C) /(C) VV	(C) V (C) / (C) VV	Kodagu (DR)
(C) (C) V	(C) (C) V (C)	Kuvi (DR)
(C) (C) V (C)	(C) (C) V (C) (C)	Kui (DR), Telugu (DR)
(C) (C) V (C) (C) (C)	C V (C) (C)	Naiki (DR)
(C) V / NV	(C) V (C)	Pali (H-V)
(C) V (m)	(C) V (C)	Prakrit (H-V)

c.

Inial (I) (bisyllabic)	**Final-1 (F-1)** (Polysyllabic)	**Final-2 (F-2)**	**Language**
C V(:)	C V (N) (C) (C) (C)	C V (C)	Kolami (DR)

d. **Roots (R)**	**Word-final (WdF)**	**Language**
(C)V(C) (C)(C) (C)	(C) (C) V	Malto (DR)
(C) V (C_F/ Vi)	(C) V (Vi) (C)	Galo-L (T-B)

(C_F = a permitted coda consonant, Vi = the second vowel position of a diphthong.)

e. **Stem- final (StF)**	**Word-final (WdF)**	**Language**
(C) (C) (C)V(C) (C)(C)	(C) (C)(C)V(C)	Kannada (DR)

f. **Stem level (St)**	**Word level (Wd)**	**Language**
(C) V (C) (C) (C)	(C) V (C)	Yerava (DR)

Typological Properties:

The salient typological properties of the syllable structures in the individual language groups are given below.

a. Austro-Asiatic:

   i. The languages of the Austro-Asiatic group permit the middle range of restricted syllable structures: (C)V(C), (C) V(C)(C), (C) (C)V(C), and (C)(C)V(C)(C).

   ii. With the exception of Mundari, complex codas in the A-A languages must have either a glottal stop or a nasal (n ŋ ɳ) as the first member.

b. Dravidian:

   i. Many Dravidian languages permit more complex codas than onsets.

   ii. While some Dravidian languages, especially from the southern subgroup, have an obligatory onset requirement at the level of the lexical representation, many others have it at the level of phonetic representation, leading to the insertion of word-initial on-glides in words beginning with vowels. The obligatory onset requirement is also found in Garo, a Tibeto-Burman language of the Bodo subgroup, and Nancowry-N of the Nicobarese sub-group of the A-A group.

   iii. Many Dravidian languages have positional asymmetrical structures. The positional asymmetries are of various types, as given below.

   - Initial versus non-initial positions: Kurux and Kodagu permit complex onsets non-initially, but simple onsets initially.

- Final versus non-final positions: Kuvi permits a coda only non-finally. Telugu permits complex codas non-finally, but simple codas finally.
- Medial versus word-edge positions: Gondi permits up to 5 consonants word-medially, but a simple consonant initially and finally. Gadaba-K permits syllables of the (C)V(C) (C) structure initially, (C) (C) V(C) (C) structure medially, and (C) (C) V (C) finally, thus restricting complex clusters to the medial position.

c. Indo-Aryan:

   i. Indo-Aryan languages have a preference for complex onsets and codas. Bengali and Marathi are an exception in permitting asymmetrical cluster configurations: up to three consonants in the onset but a single consonant in the coda position. This may have to do with the languages preserving the earlier syllable structure of the Indo-Aryan languages.

d. Tibeto-Burman:

   i. Tibeto-Burman languages show a preference for simple codas. Of the 11 out of the 55 languages in the data that permit complex codas, 3 have severe restrictions on the codas, while the others are also restricted. Balti is an exception in permitting free combinations of complex onsets and codas.

   ii. Syllabic consonants occur as nuclei in a few Tibeto-Burman languages, mainly, Angami, Chokri, and Mao-N, and Ladakhi, and a Tai-Kadai language, Turung. Ladakhi permits word- and morpheme-initial syllabic consonants; while in the other languages, syllabic consonants are assumed to have arisen from the loss of a following vowel.

   iii. Medial clusters in the Naga subgroup conform to the constraints on word-initial and word-final clusters. For example, Mao-Naga permits word-initial onsets with the first member as one of the following, namely, /p p^h k k^h /, and the second member as /r/. The word-medial clusters follow the same restriction.

e. Andamanese:

   i. The Andamanese languages have the commonest canonical syllable structure: (C) V (C).

f. Tai-Khampti:

The two languages of the T-K group permit complex onsets, Turung allows only the trill to constitute a complex onset, (C) (r) V (C), as compared to Khampti, which allows slightly more general complex onset, (C) (L/G) V (C).

g. Contact-Varieties:

i. The languages of the Contact Varieties share a common feature amongst them- they all have more simplified canonical syllable structures than their sources. They may share their simplified structures with their neighboring languages.

Bishnupuria: (C) V (C). More like Meitei and less like Assamese with complex onset and coda clusters.

Diu-I-P: (C) (L) V (L) (C). The complex onset is as in Portugese (see Mateus & d'Andrade 2000: 40-41); the coda cluster is influenced by Gujarati.

Halbi: (C) V (N) (C) Like Oriya, in Coda structure, but simplified onset structure.

IE-H: (C) (C) (C) V (C) (C) (C) (C). The syllable structure is as in native English, which it shares with Hindi.

Nagamese: i. (C)(C)V (C) ii. (C)V (C) (C). Note that a consonant cluster can occur either "in the onset or in the coda and not in both". (Sridhar 1985:61).

In common with Assamese, it has complex onset and coda clusters, but the canonical structure is still simplified in allowing either the onset or the coda to be complex.

Urdu-D-T: (C) (L/j) V (C). Considerably more simplified than Urdu.

Vagri-B: (C) (C) V (C). More like the surrounding Dravidian language varieties than like Gujarati in having a more simplified syllable structure from its source, Gujarati.

h. Historical Varieties:

i. A common feature of all the Historical varieties is that, with the exception of Sanskrit, all have more simplified canonical syllable forms than their descendents. Even for Sanskrit, instances of later languages (Hindi, Haryanvi) having more complex canonical structures can be found.

5.2 Segment Sequences

5.2.1 Consonants

Constraints on consonant sequences are discussed under two heads in this section: consonant clusters and geminate consonants.

5.2.1.1 Consonant clusters

The table of canonical syllable structures is complemented with tables of permitted consonant clusters in the Indic languages. These can be found under three main sub-heads – word-initial clusters (*Tables 5.2, 5.3*), word-medial clusters (*Tables 5.4, 5.5*) and word-final clusters (*Tables 5.6, 5.7*). Each of them is presented in terms of two-consonant clusters and three consonant clusters.

The tables present facts about specific cluster types. For word-initial and word-final clusters, languages that allow any two consonants to occur are shown to permit C+C consonant clusters. For word-medial positions, such languages are listed under the category 'general', as mentioned in the sketches. A few of the sketches do not contain information on consonant clusters for lack of adequate data; Kodagu is one of them.

Tables 5.2–5.7 introduce new terms and corresponding abbreviations for them for the specification of cluster types. Thus the terms Sonorant (for manners other than plosives, affricates and fricatives), Obstruent (for plosives, affricates and fricatives), Liquid (for taps, trills, flaps and lateral approximants), Glide, and Geminate are used to characterize general classes. The full forms of the abbreviations of these terms are given with the tables.

Table 5.2 Word-initial two-consonant clusters

Abbreviations:
C=Consonant, O=Obstruent, S=Stop, P=Plosive, Pvl=Voiceless Plosive, Pvd=Voiced Plosive, PA= Aspirated Plosive, PU=Unaspirated Plosive, F=Fricative, Sib= Sibilant, Sn= Snorant, Ax= Approximant, N=Nasal, G=Glide, L=Liquid, LS=Laryngeal Stop, G=Geminate (e.g., NG=Geminate Nasal), H=Homorganic with the preceding consonant (e.g., SH= Homorganic Stop)

Column 1	Column 2	Column 3	A-A	DR	I-A	T-B	T-K	AN	C-V	H-V
C+C			Didayi							
C+Sn				Kannada Naiki		Koren				Sanskrit
	PU/m +r/ɽ/ɳ			Kuvi						
	S/m +r/ɽ/ɳ/j			Ave						
C+G/L				Malaya (Lit) Telugu (Lit) Tulu	Assamese Gujarati Hindi Marathi Oriya Punjabi Mandeali	Tamang	Khamp		IE-H	
	S+G/L					Purki				
	S/L+G/L				Jaunsari					
	N+G/L									

contd.

Table 5.2 *contd.*

C+G/l						Bantawa				
C+w/r						Khezha				
C+j/r				Kattunaicka						
C+L/j/h						Lepcha				
C+ L/j			Gadaba-G	Kui		Kiranti-K				
C+L				Gadaba-O Irula Kadar Kota		Tarao				
	O+L								Diu-I-P	
	O+w				Jaunsari					
	S+L					Byangsi				
	S/m/s+L					Dimasa				
	N+L				Maithili					
C+r				Koraga	Gojri Kacchi Kashmiri	Chokri Stod Karbi	Turung			
	S/F/L+r									
	S/F/N+ j					Byangsi				

contd.

Table 5.2 *contd.*

		kr, lr, sr	Bonda							
	Obs + r					Garo				
		p/s + r	Bhumij							
	P /m/w/s + r									O-Tel
	S + r		Juang		Jaunsari	Monpa				
	S + r/ɽ			Pengo						
		p/ph/k/ kh/ + r				Mao-N Angami				
		p/k + r				Kinnauri				
		tr		Gon-A						
		hr			Maithili	Hmar				
C + l										
		pl, tl				Ao-N				
		sl								
		tl, hl,				Hmar				
		kl, gl	Bonda							

contd.

Table 5.2 *contd.*

C + G			Korku	Toda	Bagri Gojri Kacchi Lamani	Bodo Kabui Karbi Limbu Purki RangPo Stod Spiti Chaudan Magar				
	Pl + r/l/j								Nagamese	
C + w										
	S/F/ + w					Byangsi				
		sw	Bhumij							
C + j				Gadaba-O	Haryanvi	Apatani Darma Raji				
	S/F/N + j					Byangsi				
	P/N + j					Ladakhi				
	P + j									
		pj	Bhumij							
		gj	Gondi-A							

contd.

Table 5.2 *contd.*

		p								
	Sib + j			Kannada						
	N + j									
		m, nj						Gr-An		
		mr, kj, gj,							Vagri-B	
C + N										
C + n/m						Bodo				
		sn	Bonda	Irula						
		kn	Bonda							
		hm				Hmar				
C + F										
		kʃ, ps								Sanskrit
		ps				Monpa				
C + h				Kannada	Haryanvi Mandeali					
	N + h				Marathi					
N + C						Lotha				
		nd, nt		Tulu						

contd.

Table 5.2 *contd.*

		mb	Bonda							
	N/r/s + S				Bagri					
S + C										
	S + ţ/ʋ			Kattunaicka						
	S + d					Lepcha				
	S + r/ʃ/ʂ				Brokskat					
F + C						Purki				
s + C					Assamese Gujarati Hindi Marathi Oriya				IE-H Nagamese	Sanskrit
	s/ʂ + P/N					Ladakhi				
	s + S				Maithili					
	S + kʂ			Kannada						
	z + Pl					Ladakhi				
		s + p/t/k				Garo				
		sk				Kinnauri				

contd.

Table 5.2 *contd.*

h+C						Chokri				Sans
	L+O					Purki				
	L+S					Ladakhi				
	r+O/Ax					Purki				

Note: 1. In Kattunaicka, instances of C are restricted to /p, b, k, g, m, n /.

2. In Chaudangsi clusters (C+G), the first consonant is among those permitted to occur initially.
3. In Derma, (C+j), /r/ and /w/ also occur as the second member, in two or three lexical items.
4. In Kiranti-Koints, the following consonants do not occur as the first member: /n ɲ ʥ z ʃ ʒ j/.
5. In Lepcha, the following consonants do not occur as the first member: /n ɲ ʥ ʤ z ʃ ʒ j/.
6. In Raji, the first consnant is among those permitted to occur initially.

Table 5.3 Word-initial three-consonant clusters

Column 1	Column 2	Column 3	A-A	I-A	T-B	H-V
C+C+C						
	N+S+G/L					
	N+S+L					
		ntr nɖr	Bonda			
	N+N+S					
		ŋŋk	Bonda			
	N+S+S					
		ɳɖɖ	Bonda			
	F+S+G/L					
	s+S+r			Marathi		
		s+p/t/k/m+r		Assamese		
		s+p/t/k/m			Garo	
		s+p/t/m+r		Gujarati Hindi Oriya		Sanskrit
		S+t/m+r		Maithili		
		str		Bengali		
		stj	Bonda			
		s/ʂ + kj			Ladakhi	
	G/L+S+ G/L					
		rgj			Ladakhi	
C+l/h+j					Mandeali	
C+L+j/h					Kiranti-K Lepcha	

Table 5.4 Word-medial two-consonant clusters[1]

			A-A	DR	I-A	T-B	T-K	A-N	C-V	H-V
			Bhumij	Ave	Assamese	Adi	Khampti	GA	Diu-P	Sanskrit
			Bonda	Badaga	Bagri	Ao-N	Turung		Halbi	OTelugu
			Gadaba-G	Gadaba-O	Bengali	Apatani			IE-H	
			Gorum	Gondi	Bhili	Bodo			Nagamese[1]	
			Ho	Gondi-A	Bhojpuri	Byangsi			Urdu-D-T	
			Juang	Irula	Brokskat	Chaudangsi			Vaagri-B	
			Kharia	Kannada	Chakma	Darma				
			Khasi	Kattunaicka	Dogri	Dimasa				
			Kisan	Kolami	Garhwali	Galo-L				
			Korku	Konda	Gojri	Galo				
			Nancowry	Koraga	Gujarati	Garo				
			Nicoba-C	Koya	Haryanvi	Hmar				
			Santali	Kui	Kacchi	Kabui				
				Kurux	Kashmiri	Kangri				
				Kuvi	Konkani	Karbi				
				Malto	Lahndi	Kinnauri				
				Manda	Lamani	Kiranti-K				
				Naiki	Magahi	Koren				
				Pengo	Mahl	Ladakhi				
				Tamil	Maithili	Lepcha				
				Telugu	Mandeali	Limbu				
				Toda	Marathi	Lotha				
				Tulu	Nepali	Magar				
				Yerava	Oriya	Manchad				

[1] Exception: /s z/ do not occur as C1.

Table 5.4 *contd.*

					Punjabi Rathvi Shina Sindhi Urdu Urdu-D-H	Mao-N Maring Mishmi Monpa Padaam Paite Phom Purki Raji RangPo Sema-N Spiti Stod Tamang Tangsa Tarao Wancho				
Coda+ Onset						Bodo Koren Liangmai Thaadou Zo				
C+C										
		pd- , -ṭb-, -fv-, -nb-,-sj-								
C+N/S				Malayalam						

contd.

Table 5.4 *contd.*

C+G/L										
		C+w/j/r				Meitei				
		C+j				Apatani				
C+L/F				Malayalam						
C+L/j/h						Kiranti-K				
C+L										
		C+r				Chokri				
S+C			Mundari							
	S+G									
		S+w						Onge		
	S+L		Mundari							
		p/ph/k/ kh+r				Angami (=In), Mao (=In)				
F+C										
		h+C				Chokri (=Initial)				
L+C			Mundari	Kota						
		r+C		Kota		Apatani				
		ɽk		Kota						
N+C				Telugu		Apatani				O-Telugu Prakrit

contd.

Table 5.4 *contd.*

		m+c				Kheza				
		JN+S						Jarawa		
	N+N			Kota						
		n + m								
	N+S			Kota				Onge		O- Tamil

Note: The following languages have been noted as allowing two consonants to occur medially in general, but with restrictions:

Konda: O+O clusters have identical voicing word internally; across words, they can have disparate voicing; Ao-Naga and Nagamese: any two consonants occur medially (except (/s z / do not occur as C1).

Table 5.5 Word-medial three-consonant clusters

			A-A	DR	I-A	T-B	C-V	H-V
General				Kolami Kurux Malto Telugu	Bengali Brokskat Dogri Gujarati(?) Haryanvi[2] Hindi Mandeali Marathi	Garo Ladakhi	IE-H	Sanskrit
Coda+Onset					Gojri (C_1 C_2 =word-final)	Bodo Hmar Paite Spiti		
C+C+C						Lepcha		
	Sn+O+Sn			Konda				
C+ʔ+C			Bonda					
C+C+?				Kui				
C+CH+C					Gojri			
NH+CH+C			Kharia					
C+C+G/L						Mishmi		
C+C+G						Kabui		
C+C+j						Apatani		
C+C+L						Karbi		
C+C+r					Jaunsari			

contd.

Table 5.5 *contd.*

	S+S+Sn			Kannada				
	S+S+j				Bhili			
		kʈr, ɳɖr		Irula				
		kʈ^{h}r				Manchad RangPo		
		bdr		Gadaba-K				
	F+S+G/L							
		str		Gadaba-K	Maithili			
NH+CH+r			Bonda					
CH+CH+j				Koraga				
N+C+C				Gadaba-K Koraga				
n+C+C					Bhili			
N/L/j+C_i +C_i N/j/r/l/v				Kadar				
N/r/l/j/v +C + N/j/r/l/v					Kacchi			
	N/r + Vd Pl/N/S + C(k g ʈ ɖ r l n ɳ j)			Manda				
N+C+G/L								
N+C+j/r					Assamese			

contd.

Table 5.5 *contd.*

	N/b/s + t/d/ḍ + L/j		Gadaba-G					
	NH + P + c/s /r, rtj, rșt.			Kattunaicka				
		ŋkn				Kinnauri		
N+C+r/j					Oriya			
NH+S+C								Halbi
	N+SH+S			Pengo				
	N+SH+L/G			Ave				
	N + S/s + L					Dimasa[4]		
	Any one C= N/G/L		Korku					
	C_1= N/s/j/r			Tulu				
	If C_1 = ḍ, then C_3 = j/r/ʋ			Tulu				
N+S+C				Kuvi Kui				
	N+S+S							
		ɳḍk	Bonda					
	N+S+F							
		nts				Adi		
	S+S+S							

contd.

Table 5.5 *contd.*

		ʔtt, ʔtk	Bhumij					
	N+S+S				Oriya			
	n+S+S			Ave				
		mbg			Marathi			
		nɖk	Bonda					
		ndt, nɖp, nɖt	Gadaba-G					
		ndk, ndg, ŋgt						
		prj, mnd, ndr ŋgl						Vagri-B
	N+S+r		Juang					
	N+S+F							
		ŋgz				Manchad RangPo		
C+N+C				Koraga	Kacchi			
	S+N+S	dnk						
G/L+N+C								
j/r/l+N+C				Koraga				
	N+S+G/L							
	N+S+l/r/ɽ				Punjabi			
	N/b/s +t/d/ɖ+L/j		Gadaba-G					

contd.

Table 5.5 *contd.*

	N+S+G	ŋtj		Gadaba-K				
		mtj			Marathi			
	N+S+L	ntj, ndr, ɳɖr ɳɖl		Gadaba-K				
		ndr, nɖr, mpr	Bonda					
		ŋgl		Kota				
		nɖr	Didayi					
		ndr, ŋgr	Juang					
		ŋgr, mbr	Mundari					
		ndr, nzr			Kashmiri			
		mdr				Adi		
		ndr, npr				Kinnauri		
		mɖr, ŋɖr				Manchad RangPo		
		ntr, ntl, $nt^{h}l$				Tarao		
	L+N+S		Ave					
		rrnɖ	Bonda					
		rnd		Yerava				

contd.

Table 5.5 *contd.*

		rndʒ, ɭmb			Bhili			
	G+N+S							
		jɳɖ		Irula				
		jŋt, jŋp		Gadab-O				
		jŋg, jmb		Yerava				
G/L+C+C								
j+C+C				Gadab-K		Mishmi		
r+C+C				Kuvi				
		rpt		Kota				
r+C+j					Oriya			
G/L+G/L+C		rjk, lrc		Kota				
C+G/L+G/L								
		glɒ		Kota				
		plj			Marathi			
G/L+C+G/L								
		rpj				Manchad RangPo		

Note: 1. Brokskat: 4 consonant clusters may occur in the medial position.

2. Dimasa: N+S/s+L medial clusters, there is a syllable division following N.
3. Kannada: there are more than 3 consonants in the medial position.
4. Kheza: medial clusters with m+C are found in fast speech pronunciations of words with morphemes –mi, a connective.
5. Kiranti-Koints: 4 consonant clusters may occur in the medial position, with the following restriction: the final consonant is /j/ and the third consonant is l/r/h.
6. Konda: consonant clusters usually occur across morphemes, as many affixes have an onset.
7. Koren: in the medial position, permitted codas + onsets occur in complex words.
8. Kota has 4 consonant clusters in medial and 5 consonant clusters in final positions.
9. Lepcha: in the medial position some clusters occur with the following restriction, as in Kiranti-Koints: the final consonant is /j/ and the third consonant is l/r/h.
10. Naiki: in the medial position, permitted codas+onsets (complex words) occur.
11. Pengo: the 3 consonant clusters in the medial position are found in morphologically complex forms.
12. Zo: in the medial C_1 C_2, C_1 is the permitted coda in monosyllables (i.e. /p t h l m n ŋ/), and C_2 is any consonant, with syllable division between them. E.g. /po : l.pi/, /təŋ.va : l/, /mən.na :/.

Table 5.6 Word-final two-consonant clusters

Column 1	Column 2	Column 3	A-A	DR	I-A	T-B	T-K	A-N	C-V	H-V
C+C					Hindi Punjabi				IE-H	
	O+Sn			Konda Naiki		Koren				
	C_1=N/r/l/f/x				Gojri					
	C_2= k/ʧ/m/ n/l/ɭ			Kota						
	Sn+Sn			Konda Naiki						
	Sn+ Sn/O					Koren				
	O+O			Konda						
		ɖɖ, nn			Lamani					
N+C				Kolami	Kacchi Mandeali Oriya	Kiranti-K				
n+C					Bhili					
		n+d/j/s							Nagamese	
		mp, nt, nd, ndh, ns			Assamese					
		nz, nd				Manchad				
		nt	Bhumij							

contd.

Table 5.6 *contd.*

		ŋk, nd, nɖ	Bonda							
		ɳɖ, ŋg		Kui						
		ɳɖ		Gadaba-O						
	N+Hvd	mb, nd, ɳɖ, g		Manda						
		mb							Nagamese	
	N+S			Kota Kurux Pengo	Haryanvi Kashmiri Bhojpuri					
	N+SH					Purki			Halbi	
		nɖ ɲɟ ŋg	Korku							
	N+P				Lamani					
		ŋk ŋp	Bonda			Monpa				
		ɳʈ ŋk	Kisan							
	N+F					Purki				
S+C										
	S+Sn				Maithili					
	S+S				Maithili					
		kt tk				Kinnauri				

contd.

Table 5.6 *contd.*

	Pvl+t			Irula						
	S+s				Maithili					
LS+C										
	LS+P									
		ʔp, ʔt	Bhumij							
		ʔp				Ao-N				
		ʔp, jp							Nagamese	
	ʔ + N/r					Garo				
		ʔŋ	Bonda							
F+C						Purki				
	S + Sn				Maithili					
	s + S				Kashmiri					
		s + k/p/m/j				Ladakhi				
		st		Irula	Lamani	Manchad			Nagamese	
		ss								
		hḍ hn hl			Mandeali					

contd.

Table 5.6 *contd.*

L+C						Kiranti-K				
		ɭd ɭh			Mandeali					
r/ɽ +C				Kota						
r+C										Sanskrit
	r+S					Purki				
		rs			Assamese Gujarati Kacchi					
		rt, rz, rɦ								
		rt	Bonda							
		rd				Bodo				
		rp^h				Manchad				
	L+O								Diu- I-P	
		l+ʔ				Paite				
G+C				Kurux						
		w+ɖ/r/s/ɭ			Mandeali					
j+C					Bhili					

contd.

Table 5.6 *contd.*

		j + ʤ/s							Nagamese	
		jc	Korku							
		jl jn								
		jp				Ao-N		G-A		
		jr				Mandeali				
		jk, jg, jŋ				Mishmi				
		w + r/n							Nagamese	
C+j					Haryanvi					
C+F										
C+s						Brokskat[4]				
	P/N+s					Ladakhi				
	S+s				Bhojpuri					
		ks			Lamani					
		ts, ns				Garo				
C+h					Haryanvi					
C+LS						Mizo				

[4] The initial C for Brokskat is restricted to b/k/g/h/m/ŋ in a limited number of words.

Table 5.7 Word-final three-consonant clusters

				DR	I-A	T-B	C-V
	C+C+C						
		C+C+CH		Gondi-A			
		C+C+s/z/t/d/θ					IE-H
		C+CH+C		Gondi-A			
		C_2/C3=nasal		Kota[5]			
		F+S+G/L					
			str ndr rdr		Hindi		
			ʈlt ɖlt nɭt ʈln ɖln	Kolami			
		C+h+j			Haryanvi		
		N+S+C (in mono- syllables)		Naiki		Koren	

The tables below that draw upon *Tables* 5.2–5.7 should be read as follows. Each cluster type is listed in the first column, followed by the remark whether it applies in general (gen) or specifically to some instances of the general type. The total number of languages found mentioned for the cluster types are also given along with the number of times the languages of the groups are mentioned in the following columns. Information about the total number of cluster types and the Indic languages actually found to have them is mentioned in the rows below the first line.

Table 5.8 Word-initial two-consonant clusters

CLUSTER GEN OR SPEC	TOTAL (148)	A-A (15)	DR (29)	I-A (32)	T-B (55)	T-K (02)	AN (03)	C-V (07)	H-V (05)
	13	04	07	04	12	01	01	01	04
			(No. of Cluster types)						
	(72)	(07)	(18)	(14)	(34)	(02)	(01)	(04)	(02)
			(No. of languages)						
1. C+C gen	01	01	–	–	–	–	–	–	–
2. C+Sn gen + spec	05	–	04	–	01	–	–	–	01

[5] In Kota, there must be a nasal as C2 or C3.

contd.

Table 5.8 *contd.*

3. C+G/L gen + spec	83	09	17	16	32	02	01	04	01
4. C+N spec	03	01	01	–	01	–	–	–	–
5. C+F spec	05	–	01	02	02	–	–	–	01
6. N+C gen + spec	04	01	01	01	01	–	–	–	–
7. S+C spec	03	–	01	–	02	–	–	–	–
8. F+C gen	01	–	–	–	01	–	–	–	–
9. /s/+C gen + spec	13	–	01	06	03	–	–	02	01
10. /h/+C gen	01	–	–	–	01	–	–	–	–
11. L+O gen	01	–	–	–	01	–	–	–	–
12. L+S gen	01	–	–	–	01	–	–	–	–
13. /r/+O/Ax gen	01	–	–	–	01	–	–	–	–
	___	___	___	___	___	___	___	___	___
Frequency of mention of languages:									
	122	12	26	25	47	02	01	06	03

Table 5.9 Word-initial three-consonant clusters

CLUSTERS GEN OR SP		TOTAL (148)	A-A (15)	DR (29)	I-A (32)	T-B (55)	T-K (02)	AN (03)	C-V (07)	H-V (05)
		07	03	01	01	04	00	00	00	01
(No. of Cluster types)										
		(14)	(01)	(00)	(07)	(05)	(00)	(00)	(00)	(01)
(No. of languages)										
1. N+S+L	sp	01	01	–	–	–	–	–	–	–
2. N+N+S	sp	01	01	–	–	–	–	–	–	–
3. N+S+S	sp	01	01	–	–	–	–	–	–	–
4. F+S+G/L	sp	11	–	–	07	02	–	–	–	01
5. G/L+S+G/L	sp	01	–	–	–	01	–	–	–	–
6. C+l/h+j	sp	01	–	–	–	01	–	–	–	–
7. C+L+j/h	sp	02	–	–	–	02	–	–	–	–
		___	___	___	___	___	___	___	___	___
Frequency of mention of languages										
		17	03	00	07	06	00	00	00	01

Table 5.10 Word-medial two-consonant clusters

(Note: 1. The data exclude geminates. 2. Languages that do not have constraints on medial clusters allow any two consonants to occur medially, if permitted by the syllable structure, that is, if they have closed syllables.)

CLUSTER	GEN OR SP	TOTAL (148)	A-A (15)	DR (29)	I-A (32)	T-B (55)	T-K (02)	AN (03)	C-V (07)	H-V (05)
		08	02	04	00	06	00	02	00	01
		(No. of cluster types)								
		(19)	(01)	(03)	(00)	(10)	(00)	(02)	(00)	(03)
		(No. of languages)								
Coda+Onset	gen	04	–	–	–	04	–	–	–	–
C+N/S	gen	01	–	01	–	–	–	–	–	–
C+G/L	sp	04	–	–	–	04	–	–	–	–
C+L/Fr	gen	01	–	01	–	–	–	–	–	–
S+C	gen + sp	05	01	–	–	03	–	01	–	–
/h/+C	sp	01	–	–	–	01	–	–	–	–
L+C	gen + sp	03	01	01	–	01	–	–	–	–
N+C	gen + sp	09	–	02	–	02	–	02	–	03
		___	___	___	___	___	___	___	___	___
Frequency of mention of languages:										
		28	02	05	00	15	00	03	00	03

Table 5.11 Word-medial three-consonant clusters

CLUSTER	GEN OR SP	TOTAL (148)	A-A (15)	DR (29)	I-A (32)	T-B (55)	T-K (02)	AN (03)	C-V (07)	H-V (05)
		11	05	05	04	05	00	00	01	00
		(No. of cluster types)								
		(50)	(09)	(14)	(10)	(15)	(00)	(00)	(02)	(00)
		(No. of languages)								
Coda+ Onset	gen	04	–	–	–	04	–	–	–	–
C+C+C	gen	01	–	–	–	01	–	–	–	–
C+ʔ+C	gen	01	01	–	–	–	–	–	–	–

contd.

Table 5.11 *contd.*

C+C+?	gen	01	–	01	–	–	–	–	–	–
C+CH+C	gen	01	–	–	01	–	–	–	–	–
NH+CH+C	gen	01	01	–	–	–	–	–	–	–
NH+CH+r	gen	01	01	–	–	–	–	–	–	–
CH+CH+j	gen	01	–	01	–	–	–	–	–	–
N+C+C	gen+sp	30	05	11	07	05	–	–	02	–
C+N+C	gen+sp	23	05	08	05	05	–	–	–	–
G/L+C+C	gen+sp	08	–	03	02	03	–	–	–	–
Frequency of mention of languages:										
		72	13	24	15	18	00	00	02	00

Table 5.12 **Word-final two-consonant clusters**

CLUSTER	GEN OR SP	TOTAL (148)	A-A (15)	DR (29)	I-A (32)	T-B (55)	T-K (02)	AN (03)	C-V (07)	H-V (05)
		13	05	08	07	10	00	01	06	01
		(No. of cluster types)								
		(48)	(04)	(09)	(15)	(15)	(00)	(01)	(03)	(01)
		(No. of languages)								
C+C	gen	03	–	–	02	–	–	–	01	–
O+O	gen	01	–	01	–	–	–	–	–	–
O+Sn	gen	03	–	02	–	01	–	–	–	–
Sn+Sn	gen	02	–	02	–	–	–	–	–	–
Sn+Sn/O	gen	01	–	–	–	01	–	–	–	–
N+C	gen+sp	27	04	07	09	04	–	–	02	–
S+C	sp	03	00	01	01	01	–	–	–	–
LS+C	sp	05	02	–	–	02	–	–	01	–
F+C	gen+sp	09	–	01	04	03	–	–	01	–
L+C	gen+sp	13	01	01	04	05	–	–	01	01
G+C	gen+sp	09	01	01	02	03	–	01	01	–

contd.

Table 5.12 *contd.*

C+LS	gen	01	–	–	–	01	–	–	–	–
C+ /s/	gen+sp	05	–	–	02	03	–	–	–	–
		___	___	___	___	___	___	___	___	___
Frequency of mention of languages:										
		82	08	16	24	24	00	01	07	01

A fair idea about the comparative properties of the Indic languages is available from these tables. For example, the table of word-initial three consonant clusters shows that only a certain type of cluster occurs in the Dravidian group, namely, F+S+G/L, but none occurs in the Tibeto-Burman group, compared to the word-initial two-consonant clusters, which have a variety in the Tibeto-Burman group.

In order to get a picture of the cluster types in relation to the languages, two smaller tables giving two types of composite data are given below. One of them is about the consonant cluster types in the language groups vis-à-vis all the languages, and the other is about the number of Indic languages in which the cluster types are permissible vis-à-vis the number of times the languages are mentioned. These are being produced below.

(Read: E.g., out of a total of 13 types of word-initial two-consonant clusters, 4 apply to the A-A languages, 7 to the DR languages, 12 to the I-A languages, and so on; and out of a total of 19 types of word-medial consonant clusters, 11 apply to T-B languages, none to T-K languages, 2 to AN languages, 1 to C-V languages and 1 to H-V languages)

Abreviations: W-I= word-initial, W-M= word-medial, W-F= word-final, 2C= two-consonant, 3C= three-consonant.

Table 5.13 Composite figures of consonant clusters in Indic language groups

CLUSTERS	TOTAL (148)	A-A (15)	DR (29)	I-A (32)	T-B (55)	T-K (02)	AN (03)	C-V (07)	H-V (05)
W-I: 2C	13	04	07	04	12	01	01	01	01
W-I: 3C	07	03	01	01	04	00	00	00	01
Total	20	07/20	08/20	05/20	16/20	01/20	01/20	01/20	02/20
W-M: 2C	08	02	04	00	06	00	02	00	01
W-M: 3C	11	05	05	04	05	00	00	01	00
Total	19	07/19	09/19	04/19	11/19	00/19	02/19	01/19	01/19

contd.

Table 5.13 *contd.*

W-F: 2C	13	05	08	07	10	00	01	06	01
W-F: 3C	07	00	05	02	01	00	00	01	00
Total	20	05/20	13/20	09/20	11/20	00/20	01/20	07/20	01/20
	—	—	—	—	—	—	—	—	—
Grand total	59	19/59	30/59	18/59	38/59	01/59	04/59	09/59	04/59

(Read: E.g., 7 of the A-A languages are mentioned for a total of 12 times for the word-initial two-consonant clusters, and 1 is mentioned 3 times for word-initial three-consonant clusters)

Table 5.14 Composite figures of the Indic languages and their mention in the tables for the constraints on consonant clusters

	TOTAL	A-A	DR	I-A	T-B	T-K	AN	T-B	H-V
W-I: 2C	122/72	12/07	26/18	25/14	47/34	02/02	01/01	06/04	03/02
W-I: 3C	17/14	03/01	00/00	07/07	06/05	00/00	00/00	00/00	01/01
Total	139/86	15/08	26/18	32/21	53/39	02/02	01/01	06/04	04/03
W-M: 2C	28/19	02/01	05/03	00/00	15/10	00/00	03/02	00/00	03/03
W-M: 3C	72/50	13/09	24/14	15/10	18/15	00/00	00/00	02/02	00/00
Total	100/69	15/10	29/17	15/10	33/25	00/00	03/02	02/02	03/03
W-F: 2C	82/48	08/04	16/09	24/15	24/15	00/00	01/01	07/03	01/01
W-F: 3C	08/07	00/00	05/04	02/02	01/01	00/00	00/00	01/01	00/00
W-F: 4C	04/04	00/00	03/03	00/00	00/00	00/00	00/00	01/01	00/00
Total	94/59	08/04	24/16	26/17	25/16	00/00	01/01	09/05	01/01
	—	—	—	—	—	—	—	—	—
Grand total	333/214	38/22	79/51	73/48	111/80	02/02	05/04	17/11	08/07

5.2.1.2 Geminate consonants

Geminate consonants may occur word-initially, medially and finally. The initial and final positions are the

There are only two examples of geminates in the INITIAL position, presented below:

Didayi (A-A): Geminates of /t ɖ k g tʃ m n l r s h/ occur initially. Geminates of /p r n/ occur medially. Geminate of /p/ does not occur initially.

Lahndi (I-A): of / b d g|/, especially in the Multani dialects.

Geminates in the FINAL position occur in the following languages, all belonging to the I-A group:

Kisan: Geminates of /b ʧ ʤ t m n l r s/ are attested word medially and finally.

Lamani: Geminates of /ɖ n/ occur finally.

Punjabi: Geminates of /k g ʧ t^h/ occur finally.

Geminate consonants occur predominantly in the intervocalic position, either within a morpheme (intra-morphemic) or across morphemes (inter-morphemic), or both. Languages may however prohibit geminate consonants intra-morphemically, but allow them inter-morphemically, or prohibit them in both contexts, giving rise to alternative repair strategies when two identical consonants occur adjacently on account of word-formation. *Table 5.15* is a detailed table of the geminates in SPIL in terms of the classes of consonants and domains (across the board or across morphemes) that occur in the different language groups.

Table 5.15 Permitted geminate consonants in SPIL

Language Groups	No. of Languages with Geminates	All	Most	Major Class	NCs	Erratic	Mixed	Rd	Rare	AM	Yes, Inad. Data	None
A-A	06	–	–	–	02			03	–	01	–	09
DR	28	04	09	07	01	01	01	01	–	03	01	01
I-A	28	–	05	07	03	01	04	01	01	01	04	04
T-B	36	–	–	05	08	04	–	02	02	--	16	19
T-K	01	–	–	–	–	–	–	–	–	–	01	01
AN	03	–	–	–	02	–	–	–	–	–	01	–
C-V	06	–	02	01	03	–	–	–	–	–	–	01
H-V	03	–	01	01	01	–	–	–	–	–	–	02
Total	111	04	18	21	16	06	04	07	03	03	30	37

The main categories for the geminate consonants in the Indic languages are the following:

> (i) all consonants, (ii) most consonants, (iii) major classes, (iv) nasal consonants, (v) erratic, (vi) mixed, (vii) restricted, (viii) rare, (ix) across morphemes, (x) present, but inadequate data, and (x) none.
>
> These categories exhaust the characterization of the geminates in the languages, and are helpful in typological differentiation of the language groups, briefly discussed below:

AUSTRO-ASIATIC:

> The majority of the languages (9/15) do not permit consonant germination. The 6 languages which do permit them in one of the following ways: 1- across morphemes only, 2- restricted number, 3- nasal consonants.

DRAVIDIAN:

> Dravidian presents an opposite picture of the A-A group in allowing most of the languages with geminate consonants. Only 1 of the 29 languages does not allow geminates. 4 languages permit all consonants, and these are the only languages that permit all consonants to have geminates. 16 allow either most or major classes, 3 allow only across morphemes. The other 8 languages have other categories of geminates.

INDO-ARYAN:

> The Indo-Aryan group of languages allows the entire range of categories- 5- 'most', 7- 'major classes', 4- 'none', and 4- 'inadequate data'. The remaining 12 languages fall in the range of 'nasal consonants' as a group to 'rare'.

TIBETO-BURMAN:

> Tibeto-Burman languages are more like the A-A group in in having negative data for geminates. 35 of the languages either don't allow geminates (19) or have inadequate data (16); 17 of the languages allow groups of consonants, and 4 allow restricted geminates.

T-K

> 1 of the 2 languages does not allow geminates, and for 1 there is inadequate data.

AN

> 2 of the 3 languages allow nasal consonants to have geminates.

C-V

3 of the 7 languages allow most or major classes, 3 allow nasal consonants, and 1 does not allow geminates.

H-V

2 of the 5 languages do not allow geminates, 2 allow major classes and 1 nasal consonants.

5.2.2 Vowel sequences

Constraints on vowel sequences are not crucially sensitive, unlike constraints on consonant sequences, to the position within the word. They are, however, sensitive to the structure of the word. Essentially, four main types of systems are found among the Indic languages with regard to the constraints on vowel sequences. These are interpreted in terms of the languages permitting hiatus between syllabic nuclei. We assume that vowel sequences do not surface at all in a language, if hiatus is required in it throughout the word. If hiatus is not required in the word, then vowel sequences surface. There are two other logical possibilities, which arise on account of the distinction between simple and complex/compound words- one is of a system in which hiatus is required within a morpheme, but not across morphemes, giving rise to vowel sequences resulting from word-formation, and the other is of a system in which hiatus is required across morphemes, but not within a morpheme, in which case, vowel sequences are permitted within a morpheme, but not across morphemes. All these types of systems are found in the Indic languages, with different degrees of frequency, and presented in *Table 5.16*, at the end of the chapter.

The different systems found in SPIL with regard to constraints on vowel sequences have the percentage of occurrence as given below:

Constraint on vowel sequence	Languages	Percentage
a. Hiatus (i.e. vowel sequences) throughout	102/148	68.91 %
b. No-hiatus throughout (i.e. no vowel sequences at all):	36/148	24.32 %
c. Hiatus intra-morphemic	01/148	.67 %
d. Hiatus cross-morphemic	09/148	6.08 %

Of these four types, the first evidently is the commonest. All language groups have instances of languages that belong to this class – thus, all language groups have languages in which vowel sequences are permitted to occur.

All the other three types are restricted. Languages of the Austro-Asiatic, Indo-Aryan and historical varieties allow hiatus in the word, resulting in vowel sequences in all of them; a majority of the Dravidian languages do not allow hiatus in the word, disallowing vowel sequences in them. There is just one instance of a Tibeto-Burman language, Koren, which allows hiatus across morphemes, but not within morphemes. Three of the groups have instances of languages that allow hiatus within a morpheme, but not across morphemes, namely, DR, T-B and H-V, giving rise to vowel sequences to come up on account of word-formation.

Two points need to be noted with regard to hiatus. One, phonological descriptions of languages generally do not investigate prosodic phonological structures. Thus we have information about hiatus within and across morphemes, but we do not have information about hiatus across morphemes within a phonological phrase or an intonational phrase. All generalizations regarding across morphemes need to be investigated with regard to their application in prosodic domains (phonological word, phonological phrase, intonational phrase). Two, in languages in which when vowel sequences come up on account of word-formation (H-T type languages), different repair strategies are resorted to, such as vowel deletion, segment (typically, a semi-vowel or glottal stop) insertion or vowel sandhi (see e.g. Casali 1996, Calabrese 2005:75–117).

Table 5.16 Vowel sequences permitted in the languages in SPIL

ABBREVIATIONS: H-T= HIATUS THROUGHOUT (i.e. vowel sequences both within and across morphemes), NH-T= NOHIATUS THROUGHOUT, H-IM= HIATUS INTRA-MORPHEMIC, H-AM= HIATUS CROSS-MORPHEMIC.

[This classification is aimed to classify each language uniquely to a class. For languages, that allow vowel sequences cross-morphemically, but not within a morpheme, for example, the Dravidian language Pengo, it is possible to alternatively put it to both categories – NH and H-AM. This may create confusion, which is avoided by resorting to the categories chosen here. The classification is restricted to the domain of the phonological word.]

	A-A	DR	I-A	T-B	T-K	AN	C-V	H-V
NH-T	Nil	Ave Badaga Gadaba–K Gadaba–O Gondi Gondi –A Irula Kadar Kannada Kattunaicka Kolami Koraga Kuvi Malto Manda Naiki		Ao-N Balti Bodo Dimasa Kabui Ladakhi Liangmai	Turung	Onge G-A	Bishnupuria Nagamese Urdu-D-T Vagri-B	Nil

contd.

Table 5.16 *contd.*

		Tamil Telugu Toda Tulu Yerava						
H-T	Bhumij Bonda Didayi Gadaba-G Gorum Ho Juang Kharia Khasi Kisan Korku Mundari Nancowry Nicobarese Santali	Kodagu Kota Kui Kurux	Assamese Bagri Bengali Bhili Bhojpuri Brokstat Chakma Dogri Garhwali Gojri Gujarati Haryanvi Hindi Jaunsari Kacchi Kashmiri Konkani Lahndi Lamani Magahi Mahl Maithili Mandeali	Adi Angami Apatani Bantawa Byangsi Chaudangsi Darma Gallong Galo Galo-L Garo Hmar Kangri Khezha Kinnauri Kiranti-K Lepcha Limbu Lotha Magar Manchad Mao-N Maring	Khampti	Jarawa	Diu-I-P Halbi IE-H	O-Ta O-Te Pali Prakrit

contd.

Table 5.16 *contd.*

			Marathi Nepali Oriya Punjabi Rathvi Shina Sindhi Urdu Urdu-D-H	Mishmi Monpa Padaam Paite Phom Raji RangPo Rawang Sema-N Spiti Tamang Tangsa Tarao Thadou Tibetan-St Stod Wancho Zo				
H-IM	Nil	Nil		Koren			Nil	Nil
H-AM	Nil	Konda Koya Malayalam Pengo	Nil	Chokri Karbi Kokborok Meitei			Nil	Sans-Cl

5.3 Suprasegmentals

The two prominent suprasegmental or prosodic features at the word level are stress and tone. We briefly discuss them in this section.

5.3.1 Word-stress

As discussed in the introduction in Chapter 1, word-stress is one of the topics that is more noticeable in its absence than presence in the descriptions of the Indic languages. For the sake of consistency of presentation, the description of word-stress has been left out in the present sketches. It is however pertinent here to put together the general features of word-stress in Indic languages on the basis of the available literature[1].

Some features of word-stress in the Indic languages can be stated as follows.

a. Most languages have predictable stress, except Shina (Schmidt & Kohistani 1998), a Dardic language of the Indo-Aryan group[2].

b. Many of the Indic languages, especially of the Indo-Aryan group, are quantity-sensitive. Some of them distinguish between three degrees of syllable weight: Light, Heavy and Superheavy, originally pointed out by Kelkar (1968) for Hindi, and justified in Pandey (1988), as inherently heavy and light cognate syllables (see also Hayes 1995), a point taken up in Vijaykrishnan (2009).

Those that distinguish two degrees of syllable weight have Final Extrametricality of the segment (e.g. Malayalam, Hayes 1981), the syllable (e.g. Maithili, Yadav 1996, Hayes 1995), or the foot (e.g. Hindi, Hayes 1995). Most of the Indo-Aryan languages have quantity-sensitive stress system. These include Assamese (Mahanta2003), Awadhi , Bengali, Bhojpuri (Shukla 1981), Gujarati (Mistry 1997), Hindi (Pandey 1988, Hayes 1995)[3], Maithili

---

1 A useful survey of word-stress in the languages of South Asia is available in Schiering & van der Hulst (2008)

2 There have been stray examples of phonemic stress in some of the Indic languages. Goswami (1966) has examples of phonemic stress in Assamese. Kaul (2011) has examples of phonemic stress in Dogri.

3 As has been pointed out by Ohala (1977a) and Hayes (1995:162), most descriptions of Hindi word-stress differ from one another, but rarely discuss the differences amongst them. The main reason for the differences in the descriptions seems to be that they are of different regional varieties. So they are actually not clashing; however, the confusion arises because often the studies are not explicit about the variety of Hindi described in them.

(Yadav 1996), Marathi (Pandharipande 1997), Nepali (Khatiwada 2009), Panjabi (Baart 1997), Sanskrit (Cardona 2002) and Sindhi (Khubchandani 1963). Bengali (Hayes & Lahiri 1991) is perhaps an exception. However, the Bengali data in Ghosh (1996) include word-internal stress on non-final and non-initial CVC syllables.

Among the Dravidian languages, quantity-sensitivity is found in Konda (Krishnamurti & Benham 1998), Malayalam (Mohanan 1979, reported in Hayes 1981), Malto (Das 1973, Steever 1998) and Telugu (Krishnamurti 1998).

The Austro-Asiatic group consists of the following languages having quantity-sensitive systems: Mundari (Osada 1992) and Santali (Neukom 2001:8). A lot of Dravidian languages have word-initial primary stress, such as Gondi (Steever 1998), Kodagu (Ebert 1996:9), Kolami (Emeneau 1981:8-9), Kurux (Hahn 1908:9), and Tamil (Annamalai & Steever 1998:104, Keane 2001). In fact, word-initial stress (also known as End Rule Initial, Hayes 1995) is the commonest pattern of the languages of the Dravidian group, as observed by Steever (1998:18).

Word-initial patterns are also common to the languages of the Austro-Asiatic group: Kharia (Rehberg's 2003: 23-28, as pointed out in Schierring & van der Hulst 2009: 57) and Sora (Donegan 1996:5-6). In these languages, as well as in the Dravidian languages, in the absence of a heavy syllable, word-initial stress is the default pattern.

Insufficient details are available about the stress patterns of the other groups, namely Tibeto-Burman, Tai-Kadai, Andaman and Contact Varieties.

Many of the Tibeto-Burman and Tai-Kadai languages have the feature of the word being one with a morpheme and a syllable, a feature that has been called 'tautomorphemicity' by Bickel (2003). This has been observed at least for a lot, but by no means all, of the Kuki-Chin languages in India, for example, Liangmai, Mizo, Thaadou and Zo, all included in the present volume. The phenomenon of word-stress in them is relevant for compound words only, where usually the first word bears primary stress, and the second word bears secondary stress. One of the phonetic features of these languages is that each syllable is of closely equal duration; the languages are thus exemplar cases of syllable-timed languages.

The Tani subgroup of the Tibeto-Burman group, however, does not always have tautomorphemicity, as for example, Adi, Galo, Taginy, as also some of the Kuki-Chin languages, such as Koren. In these languages, the characteristic stress pattern is word-final (or End Rule Final), as described for Koren (this volume).

In many of the Indic languages, stress and tone are interrelated. These languages are found in the Indo-Aryan, Tibeto-Burman and Tai-Kadai groups. The Indo-Aryan languages (see also Masica 1991) are Dogri, Gojri, Lahndi, and Panjabi. The Tibeto-Burman languages are Adi, Angamai, Ao-Naga, Apatanai, Bodo, Chokri, Hmar, Karbi, Khezha, Lepcha, Lotha, Mao-Naga, Maring, Meitei, Mishmi, Mizo, Monpa, Phom, Rawang, Sema-Naga, Thaadou, and Wancho. Khampti-Tai from the Tai-Kadai group also has this trait. As pointed out by Schierring and van der Hulst (2009:69), "...the complex interactions of accent and tone are still to be investigated for most languages".

5.3.2 Tone

Detailed accounts of tones in Indic languages, especially of the Tibeto-Burman group, are beginning to be available. However, for a majority of the languages, they are rather sketchy. They have been put together in the sketches here on the grounds that they are lexically distinctive. In a majority of the languages, they play active roles. However, descriptions accounting for them are a desideratum.

The main generalizations about tones in Indic languages are stated below.

a. For a few of the languages there are clashing descriptions with regard to the presence or absence of tone in them. Three such cases are the following:
    i. Korku (A-A): Zide (1960) posits tones, while Nagaraja (1999) disconfirms the presence of tone in the variety of Korku he is describing.
    ii. Kiranti-Koints (T-B): Genetti (2004) posits tone, while Rapacha (2006) disconfirms the presence of tone in his variety of the language.
    iii. Shina (I-A, Dardic): Schmidt & Kohistani (1998) find two contrastive tones on long vowels in the Kohistani dialect of Shina spoken in Pakistan, but Rajpurohit (1983) does not give any details of tone in the Drasi variety of the Astori dialect spoken in India.
b. The languages differ with regard to whether a lexical tone is specified for every morpheme, as a culminative feature, or whether every syllable/ vowel carries tone with it. From the descriptions presented here, we have the following lists of languages along that parameter:

i. TBU- morpheme:

I-A: Bagri, Dogri, Gojri, Lahndi, Punjabi, Shina (Kohistani)

T-B: Adi, Angami, Ao-N, Apatani, Lepcha, Koren, Liangmai, Tamang,

ii. TBU- syllable/ vowel:

T-B: Boro, Chokri?, Hmar?, Karbi?, Khezha?, Lotha?, Mao-N, Maring, Meitei, Mishmi, Mizo,

Note that for the languages with 'tautomorphemicity', the distinction is not significant, as every morpheme is also a syllable. Thus many of the languages of group (b) above can also be said to belong to group (a). These are marked in italics.

c. In tonal languages with a tone on every syllable/ vowel, tones can help distinguish diphthongs from vowel sequences, as noted in Section 1.3.3. In languages with every vowel having a tone, the diphthongs have one tone, and a sequence of two vowels has two tones. The distinction is attested in Bodo.

With a lexical morpheme being a TBU, there are two possible structural cases. One is morphological; in those languages, especially the Kuki- Chin languages, in which morphemes are monosyllabic, a tone is assigned to every morpheme. In such a case, if there is a sequence of vowels, then each vowel will have a tone. This case is not distinguishable from that of Bodo, as noted above. If, however, the tone is assigned to the lexical morpheme alone, then it is not possible to distinguish a diphthong from a vowel sequence on the surface. However, the phonetic realizations of the tones may be different in the two cases. Zo has been found to distinguish vowel sequences from diphthongs that way, as noted in its sketch: for a diphthong, the tone ends with the second vowel position, but for a sequence of two vowels (on account of word-formation), the tone ends with the first vowel position.

a. Almost all the examples of tone included in the descriptions assume the lexical function of tone, that is, the function of tone to distinguish words. This should not be seen to imply that tone has no other function, such as morphological or pragmatic. As elaborately shown by Hyman (2007), tone in Thaadou, a Kuki-Chin language of the Tibeto-Burman group, has many grammatical functions, such as H expressing the Genitive Case and the Subject, among others. Most of the languages are in the need of detailed investigations to explore the phonological, grammatical and pragmatic functions of tone.

b. Hyman (2007) shows that the classic distinction between African and East-Asian tone systems introduced by Pike (1948) as consisting in their being "register tone systems" and "contour tone systems" respectively, or, in other words, in having level tone oppositions and as combinations of level tones into complex tone oppositions has counterexamples in Thaadou, which is more like the African tone systems than like the East-Asian tone systems. Hyman lists the properties of the two tone systems and shows how they are manifested in Thaadou (KT or Kuki-Chin Thaadou), thus:

A. "Contour tone systems"	B. "Register tone systems"	KT
Fewer level tones than contours	More level tones than contours	B
Contour tones = units	Contour tones = sequences (clusters)	B
Contour tones have free distribution within the utterance	Contour tones (clusters) are often limited to last syllable	B
Dissimilation of contour + contour	Dissimilation of contour tones = rare	B
Metathesis of features within a contour	Metathesis of contour tones = rare	B
No downstep	Downstep	B
Floating tones = rare	Floating tones = frequent	B
Tone spreading = rare	Tone spreading = frequent	B
Function of tone = lexical	Function = lexical *and/or* grammatical	B
Words are monosyllabic	Words come in various sizes	A
Tones are restricted by syllable type	Tones may occur on any syllable type	A

Quite clearly Thaadou is closer to the African tone system than to the East-Asian tone system. On close scrutiny, it appears however that what is true of Thaadou is true of many other languages of the T-B and T-K languages.

c. Given below is the list of all the languages with lexical tones in terms of their tonemes and the type of tones they have, that is, contour or Register type or a mixed type with both types of tones.

The abbreviations used in the lists are as follows.

Tone types: C= Contour tone, R= Register tone, R + C= Register and contour tone.

Register tones: H= High, M= Mid, L= Low, High Mid= M1, Low Mid= M2, Extra Low= $L_{0.}$

Contour tones: Falling (high) = HL, Falling (mid) = ML, Rising = LH, Falling-Rising= HLH, Rising-Falling= LHL.

Language	*Tone type*	*Number of tones*	*TBU Tones*
Indo-Aryan (05):			
Bagri	R	3	H, M, L
Dogri	R + C	3	M, LH, HL
Gojri	R	3	H, M, L
Lahndi	R + C	2	M, LH
Punjabi	R	3	H, M, L
Historical Varieties (01)			
Sanskrit	R + C	3	H, L, HLH
Tibeto-Burman (27)			
Adi	C	4	HL, LH, HLH, LHL
Angami	R	4	H, M1, M2, L
Ao-Naga	R + C	3	M, HL, LH
Apatani	R + C	3	M, HL, LH
Bodo	R	4	H, M1, M2, L
Chokri	R	4	H, M1, M2, L
Galo-Lare	R + C	2	H, HL
Hmar	R + C	3	M, HL, LH
Karbi	R	3	H, M, L
Khezha	R	3	H, M, L
Koren	R	3	H, M, L
Lepcha	C	2	HL, LH
Liangmai	R	3	H, M, L
Lotha	R + C	3	M, LH HL
Mao-Naga	R	4	H, M1, M2, L
Maring	C	2	HL, LH
Meitei	R + C	2	M, HL
Mishmi	R + C	4	M, LH, HL, LHL
Mizo	R	4	H, L, LH, HL
Monpa	R + C	2	M1, LH
Phom	R + C	3	H, M, HL

Rawang	R	3	H, M, L
Sema-Naga	R	3	H, M, L
Tamang	R + C	4	M1, M2 + HL, ML/ HLH
Thaadou	R + C	3	M, LH, HL
Tibetan- Standard	R + R/C	2	H, L/ML
Wancho	R + C	3	H, L, HL
Tai-Kadai (01)			
Khampti	R + C	5	H, L, L_0 + HL, LH

d. The number of tonal languages in the present study are as follows:

LG	*No. of languages*	*No. of tonal languages*	*Percentage*
A-A	15	00	0%
DR	29	00	0%
I-A	32	05	16.7%
T-B	55	27	49.9%
T-K	02	01	50%
AN	03	00	0%
C-V	07	00	0%
H-V	05	01	25%
08	148	34	23%

The Tibeto-Burman and Tai-Kadai languages have a high percentage of tonal languages- about 50%. For of the language groups have no tonal languages at all, namely, A-A, DR, AN, and C-V.

e. The languages can be classified according to the number of tones in them thus:

LANGUAGES WITH 2 TONES:

LANGUAGE GROUP	LANGUAGE	TONE TYPE
I-A	Lahndi	R + C
T-B	Galo-Lare	R + C
	Lepcha	C
	Maring	C

	Meitei	R + C
	Monpa	R + C
	Tibetan-St	R + C

LANGUAGES WITH 3 TONES:

I-A	Bagri	R
	Dogri	R + C
	Gojri	R
	Punjabi	R
H-V	Sanskrit	R + C
T-B	Ao-Naga	R + C
	Apatani	R + C
	Hmar	R + C
	Karbi	R
	Khezha	R
	Koren	R
	Liangmai	R
	Lotha	R + C
	Phom	R + C
	Rawang	R
	Sema-Naga	R
	Thaadou	R + C
	Wancho	R + C

LANGUAGES WITH 4 TONES:

T-B	Adi	C
	Angami	R
	Bodo	R
	Chokri	R
	Mao-Naga	R
	Mishmi	R + C
	Mizo	R
	Tamang	R + C

LANGUAGES WITH 5 TONES

T-K	Khampti	R + C

5.4 Phonological cues for grammatical structure

The issue of phonological cues for grammatical structure is significant from various points of view, in the main, theoretical (the question of the relation amongst the components of grammar), cognitive (the issue of temporal overlap and lack of boundary in speech, e.g. McClelland and Elman 1986), and acquisitional (the question of the use of phonological information or 'bootstrapping' in learning morphology and syntax, e.g. Gleitman, Gleitman, Landau & Wanner 1988, Lehiste 1960, Nakatani and Dukes 1977), among others. The data from the phonological sketches presented here provide some evidence for the presence of phonological cues for morphology and syntax. The cues can be grouped for the following five types of distinction: word edges, lexical vs. grammatical morphemes, different types of word forms, simple vs. complex words, and phrases.

a. *Word and morpheme edges*

   i. Word edges:

      Assamese (A-A) and *Galo-L* (T-B): Vowel initial words have a glottal stop in the beginning.

      G-Andamanese (A-A), *Gondi-A, Konda, Kolami, Kui, Tamil* (DR), *Bhili, Kash*miri (I-A), *Ao-N* (T-B): words beginning with vowels have on-glides in them. The languages differ with regard to the specification of the vowels before which they have onglides. Konda and Tamil have j- and w-onglides before the high and mid front and back vowels respectively. Kashmiri has a j-onglide only before /i i:/vowels.

   ii. Morpheme edges:

      Galo-L: [w å] occur on the surface across morphemes that end and begin with vowels; [w] occurring with the first morpheme ending in /u o/, and [å] occurring with the first morpheme ending in /ť/.

      - *Lexical vs. grammatical morphemes:*

        Byangsi: /e o/ occur in grammatical morphemes, not lexical morphemes.

Malayalam: /e e: o o: / do not occur finally in lexical words, but they occur finally in grammatical morphemes.

b. *Different types of words*

   i. *Kannada*: Long vowels do not occur finally in words, with the following exceptions: /u: / occurs finally in clitics, and /e: o:/ occur finally in vocatives.

   ii. *Kuvi*:

   - Long oral vowels do not occur finally in words, except in verbal roots.
   - Consonants do not occur finally in words except in bound morphemes and in loan words.

c. *Simple vs. complex words*

d. i. Different segments:

   - *Kabui*: /e o/ occur finally in complex forms alone.
   - *Mao-Naga*: Intra-morphemic diphthongs form a separate set, / əi̯ ou̯ iu̯ ə̯i ə̯u ə̯e/, from across-morphemic diphthongs, /ae ao ue oe ie/. Cross-morphemically, the two vowels remain syllabic.

   ii. Phonotactics

   Consonant Geminates:

   Gadaba-G (A-A), *Ave, Pengo, Toda* (DR), and *Kacchi* (I-A): Consonant geminates do not occur in simple words. They occur in complex words on account of word-formation.

Vowel sequences:

Konda, Koya, Malayalam, Pengo (DR), Chokri, Karbi, Kokborok, Meitei (T-B), and Sanskrit- Cl (H-V): Sequences of vowels occur only in complex words, not in simple words or roots. The languages differ in detail with regard to the specification of the word-initial vowels before which the onglides are inserted. Thus, Konda and Tamil have j- and w-onglides before mid and high front and back vowels respectively, and Kashmiri has only a j-onglide before front high vowels /i i:/.

e. Phrases

Certain processes are found to apply in the following languages only before a pause or a phonological/ syntactic phrase.

Kolami: i. [i̯e] < /e:/ _]$_{PP}$ (The description mentions the word "phrase").

ii. [vu:] < /u:/ $\_]_{PP}$ (The description mentions the word "phrase").

Spiti: [ʔ] < /d g/ / ____## (Pause)

Toda: [p^h t^h k^h] < /p t k/ / __ ## (Pause)

Maps of the various Indic language groups

INDIA

DISTRIBUTION OF DRAVIDIAN LANGUAGES 1991

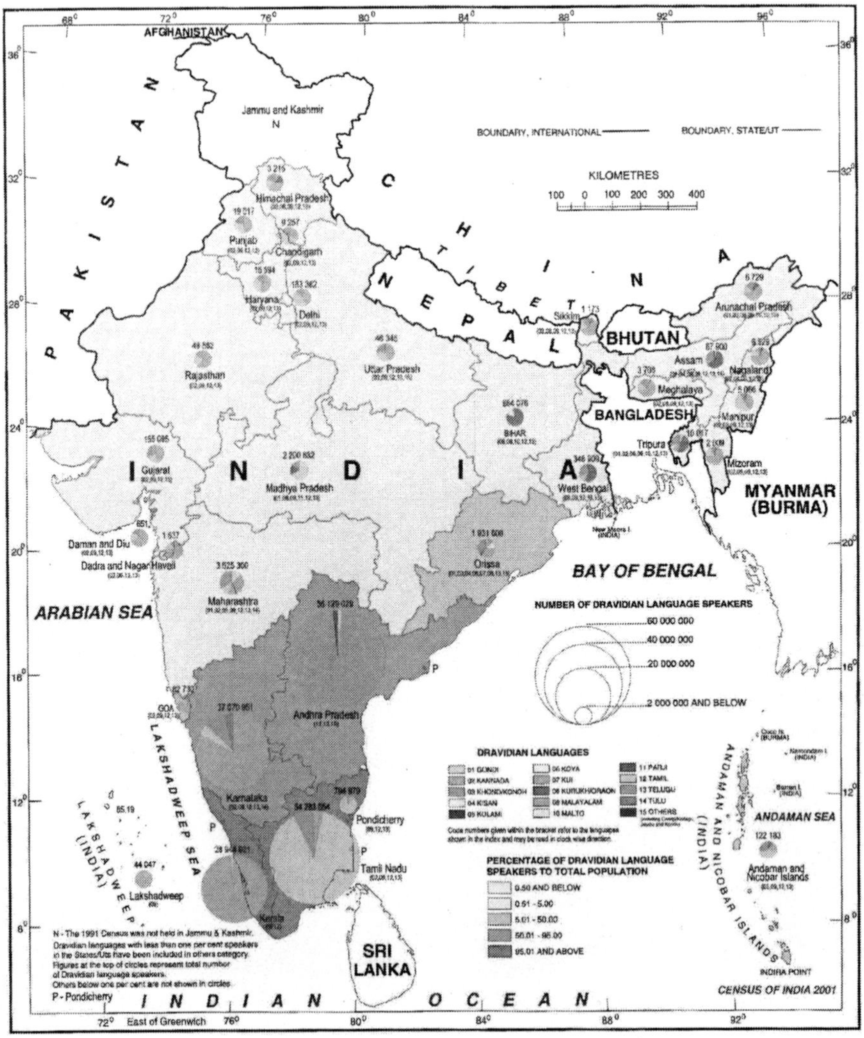

INDIA
DISTRIBUTION OF AUSTRO-ASIATIC LANGUAGES 1991

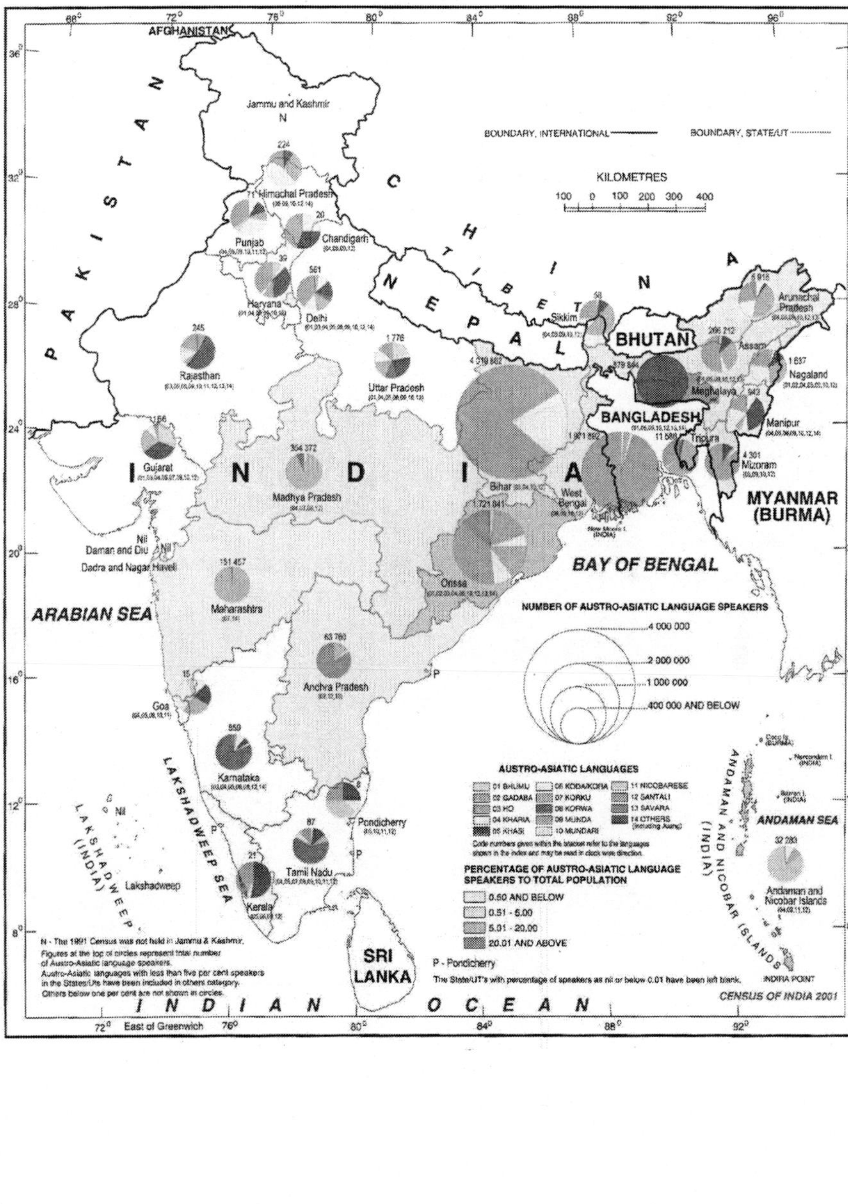

INDIA

DISTRIBUTION OF TIBETO-BURMESE LANGUAGES 1991

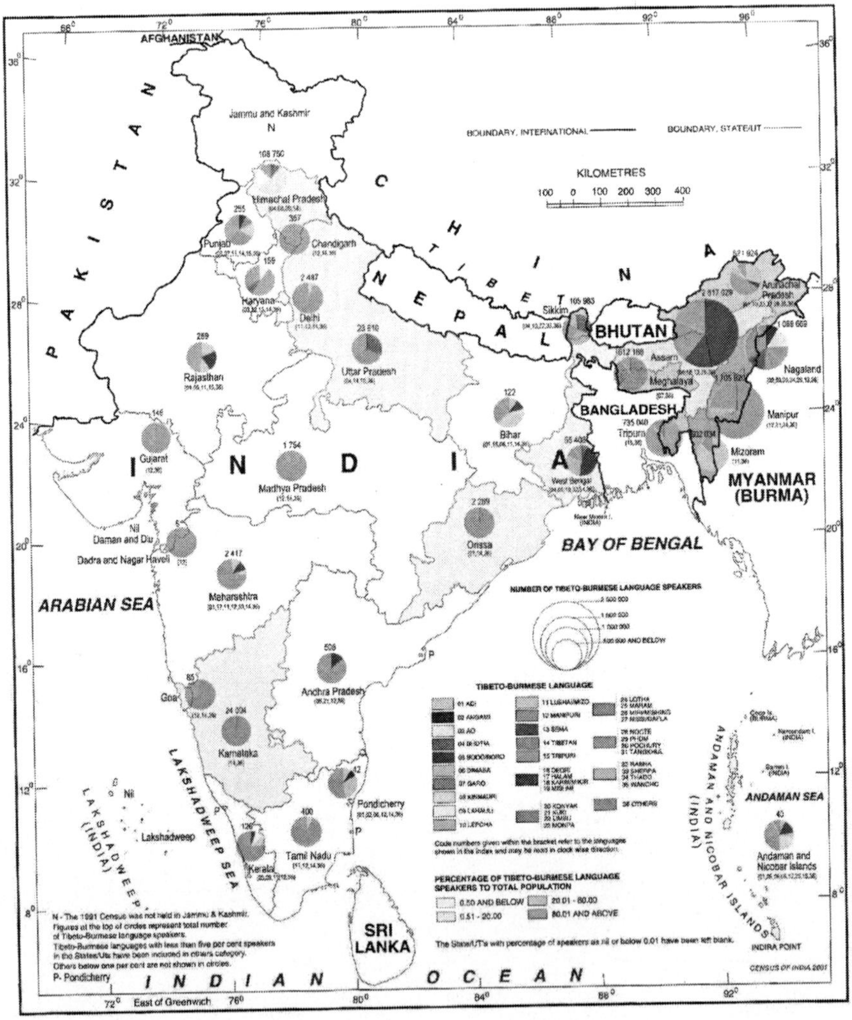

INDIA
RURAL AND URBAN DISTRIBUTION OF SCHEDULED AND NON-SCHEDULED LANGUAGES 1991

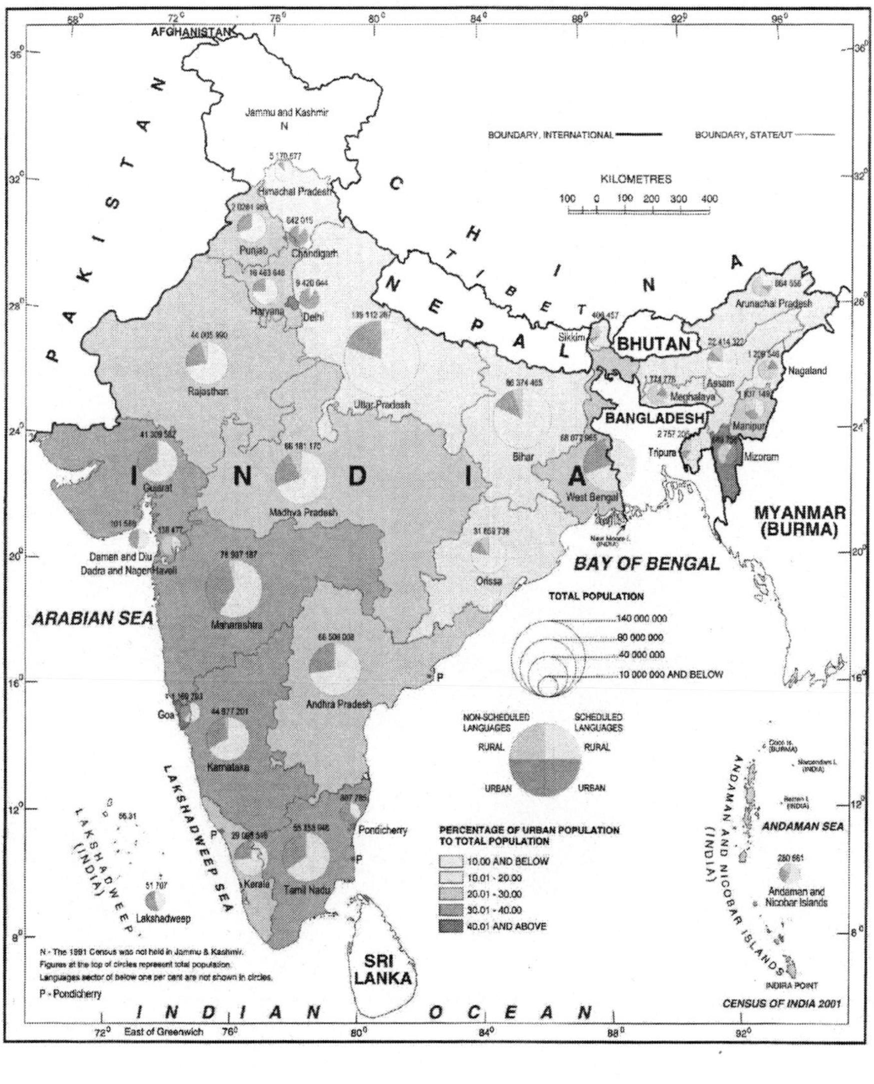

INDIA
DISTRIBUTION OF SCHEDULED LANGUAGES 1991

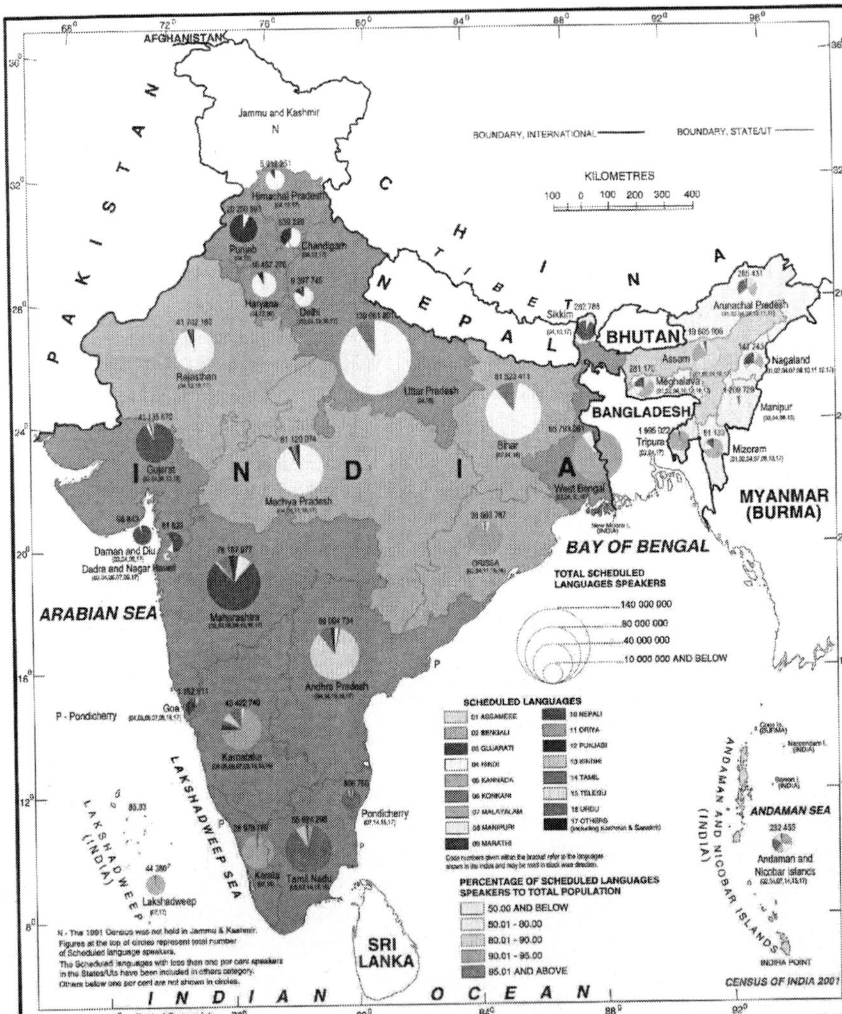

Bibliography

[The bibliography is presented in three sections. Section A contains descriptive and theoretical papers of general significance in the study of speech sounds in world and Indic languages, as well as specific references to works cited in the discussion in the Chapters 1–5 in Part I. Section B contains the bibliography on the phonologies of the language groups included in this study. Section C presents the bibliogrphy on the phonetic and phonological literature on specific languages arranged according to their language groups.]

A. General: Descriptive and theoretical

Abbi, A. (ed.) (1997). *The languages of tribal and indigenous peoples of India: The ethnic space.* Delhi: Motilal Benarsidass.

Annamalai, E. (2004). India as a communicative area: Its linguistic ingredients. *Osmania Papers in Linguistics* **30**.1–14.

Annamalai, E. (2008). Contexts of multilingualism. In Kachru, B. B., Kachru, Y. & Sridhar, S. N. (eds.), *Language in South Asia.* Cambridge: University Press. Pp. 223–34.

Anttila, A. and Andrus, C. (2006). T-Orders. ROA-873.

Archangeli, D. & Pulleyblank, D. (1994). *Grounded phonology.* Cambridge, Ma.: MIT Press.

Archangeli, D. (1988). Aspects of underspecification theory. *Phonology* **5.2**: 183–207.

Austin, P. (ed.) (2008). *1000 languages. The worldwide history of living and lost languages.* London: Thames & Hudson.

Basbøll, H. (1985). Review of I. Maddieson. *Patterns of sound,* 1984. *Phonology Yearbook* **2**. 343–353.

Beckman, J. (1997). *Positional faithfulness.* Doctoral dissertation, University of Massachusetts, Amherst. [ROA-234]

Beckman, M., Hirschberg, J. & Shattuck-Hufnagel, S. (2005). The original ToBI system and the evolution of the ToBI framework. Sun-Ah, J. (ed.), *Prosodic models and transcription: Towards prosodic typology*. Oxford, New York: Oxford University Press. Pp. 9–54.

Berger, H. (1955). *Zwei probleme der mittelindischen lautlehre*. Munchen: Kitzinger.

Bhat, D. N. S. (1973). Retroflection: An areal feature. *Working papers on language universals* **13**. 27–67.

Bhat, D. N. S. (1974). Retroflexion and retraction. *Journal of Phonetics* **2**. 233–38.

Bhattacharya, S. (1972). Dravidian and Munda: A good field for areal and typological studies. *Third seminar on Dravidian linguistics*. Annamalainagar: Annamalai University. 241–65.

Bhattacharya, S. S. (2003). Languages in India- their status and function. Itagi, N. & Singh, S. K. (eds.), *Linguistic landscaping in India with particular reference to the New States: Proceedings of a seminar*. Mysore: Central Institute of Indian Languages and New Delhi: Mahatma Gandhi International Hindi University. 54–97.

Blevins, J. (1995). The syllable in phonological theory. Goldsmith, J. A. (ed.), *The handbook of phonological theory*. Cambridge, MA, & Oxford: Blackwell. 206–244.

Boersma, P. (1997). Inventories in functional phonology. *Proceedings of the Institute of Phonetic Sciences of the University of Amsterdam* **21**. 59–90. (Reprinted as chapter 16 of *Functional phonology*. The Hague: Holland Academic Graphics, 1998).

Bolton, K. & Kachru, B. B. (eds.) (2006). *Origin and development of Asian Englishes, 5 vols*. London and New York: Routledge.

Bradley, D., Lapolla, R.,, B. & Thurgood, G. (eds.) (2003). *Language variation: Papers on variation and change in sinosphere and in the indosphere in honour of James A. Matisoff*. Canberra: Pacific Linguistics.

Breton, Roland J-L. (1997). *Atlas of the Ethnic Communities of South Asia*. New Delhi: Sage Publications.

Bright, W. (1990). *Language Variation in South Asia*. New York and Oxford: OUP.

Broselow, E. (2003). Marginal phonology: Phonotactics on the edge. *The Linguistic Review* **20**. 159–193.

Burton-Roberts, N., Carr, P. & Docherty, G. (eds) (2000). *Phonological knowledge: Conceptual and empirical issues*. Oxford: Oxford University Press.

Calabrese, A. (1994). A constraint-based theory of phonological inventories. Dressler, W. U., Prinzhorn, M. & Rennison, J. R. (eds.), *Phonologica 1992: Proceedings of the 7th International Phonology Meeting.* Torino: Rosenberg and Sellier. 35–54.

Calabrese, A. (1995). A constraint-based theory of phonological markedness and simplification procedures. *Linguistic Inquiry* 26. 373–463.

Calabrese, A. (2005). *Dynamic phonology: Markedness and economy in a derivational model of phonology*. Berlin, New York: Mouton de Gruyter.

Casali, R. F. (1996). Resolving hiatus. Ph. D. dissertation, UCLA.

Catford, J. C. (1977). *Fundamental problems in phonetics.* Bloomington, IN: Indiana University Press.

Census of India (1991). *Language, series 1 – India, paper 1 of 1997.* New Delhi: Registrar General of India.

Chomsky, N & Halle, M. (1968). *Sound pattern of English.* NY: Harper and Row.

Clements, G.N. (1985). The Geometry of Phonological Features. *Phonology Yearbook* 2, 223–252.

Clements, G. N. (1988). Toward a substantive theory of feature specification. In J. Blevins & J. Carter (eds.), *Proceedings of NELS* **18.** 79–93.

Clements, G. N. (2001). Representational economy in constraint-based phonology. Hall, T. A. (ed.), *Distinctive feature theory.* Berlin: Mouton de Gruyter. 71–146.

Clements, G. N. (2003a). Feature economy in sound systems. *Phonology* **20.** 287–333.

Clements, G. N. (2003b). Feature economy as a phonological universal. Solé, M. J., Recasens, D. & Romero, J. (eds.), *Proceedings of the 15th International Conference of Phonetic Sciences, Barcelona, 3–9August 2003.* Rundle Mall: Causal Productions Pty Ltd. 371–374.

Clements, G. N. (2005). The role of features in phonological inventories. Paper presented at the *Symposium on Phonological Theory: Representations and Architecture.* February 20–21, 2004. N.Y.: CUNY.

Clements, G. N. & Rialland, A. (2008). Africa as a phonological area. In Heine, B. & Nurse, D. (eds.), *A linguistic geography of africa.* Cambridge: Cambridge University Press. Pp. 36–85.

Clements, G. N. & Hume, E. V. (1995). The internal organization of speech sounds. Goldsmith, J. A. (ed.), *Handbook of phonological theory.* Oxford: Blackwell. 245–306.

Clements, G. N. & Rialland, A. (2005). Africa as a phonological area. Ms. Laboratoire de Phonétique et Phonologie, CNRS / Sorbonne-Nouvelle, Paris.

Comrie, B., Matthews, S. & Polinsky, M. (eds.) (1999). *The atlas of languages: The origin and development of languages throughout the world.* London: Bloomsbury.

Crothers, J. (1978). Typology and universals of vowel systems. Greenberg, J. H., Ferguson, C. A. & Moravcsik, E. A. (eds.), *Universal of Human Language, Vol. 2, Phonology*. Stanford: Stanford University Press. 93–152.

Dani, A. H. (1963). *Indian palaeography*. Oxford: Clarendon Press.

Daniels, P. & Bright, W. O. (eds.) (1996). *The world's writing systems.* London: OUP.

De Boer, B. G. (2001). *The origins of vowel systems.* Oxford: OUP.

de Lacy, Paul (2006). *Markedness*. Cambridge University Press.

Dixon, R. M. W. & Aikhenvald, A. Y. (eds.). (2002). *Word: A cross-linguistic typology*. Cambridge: Cambridge University Press.

Emeneau, M. B. (1956). India as a Linguistic Area. *Language* **32**. 3–16.

Emeneau, M. B. (1965). *India and historical grammar.* Annamalainagar: Annamalai University.

Emeneau, M. B. (1969). Onomatopoetics in the Indian linguistic area. *Language* **45**. 274–99.

Emeneau, M. B. (1974). The Indian linguistic area revisited. *International Journal of Dravidian Linguistics* **3.1**. 92–134.

Féry, C. & Vijver, R. van der (eds.) (2003). *The syllable in optimality theory.* Cambridge: CUP. 254–268.

Firth, J. R. (1936). Phonological features of some Indian languages. Jones, W. E. & Fry, D. B. (eds.), *Proceedings of the Second International Congress Of Phonetic Sciences*. Cambridge: CUP.

Flak, K. (2009). Constraints on onsets and codas of words and phrases. *Phonology* **26**. 269–302.

Foley, W. A. (1993). *Role of theory in language description.* Berlin: Mouton de Gruyter.

Gibbon, D., Moore R. & Winsky R. (1997). *Handbook of standards and resources for spoken language systems.* Berlin: Mouton de Gruyter.

Goldsmith, J. (1989). *Autosegmental and metrical phonology*. Oxford: Basil Blackwell.

Gordon, R. G. (2005). *Ethnologue: Languages of the world.* 15th edition, Dallas: SIL International.

Greenberg, J. (ed.) (1966). *Universals of Language.* Mass., Cambridge: MIT Press.

Gregory, M. (1967). Aspects of varieties differentiation. *Journal of Linguistics* **III/2**. 177–98.

Grierson, Sir G. A. (1903–28). *Linguistic Survey Of India* (11 volumes). Calcutta: Office of the Superintendent of Government Printing. (Reprinted (1967–73). Delhi: Motilal Banarasidass).

Gumperz, J. J. (1961). Speech variation and the study of Indian civilization. *American Anthropologist* **63**. 976–88.

Gumperz, J. J. (1968). The speech community. *International Encyclopedia Of The Social Sciences, Vol. 9.* London: Macmillan. 381–86.

Hall, T. A. & Kleinhenz, U. (eds.) (1999). *Studies on the phonological word.* Amsterdam: Benjamins.

Hall, T. A. *(ed.) (2001). Distinctive feature theory.* Berlin, N. Y.: Mouton de Gruyter.

Halle, M. (1962). Phonology in generative grammar. *Word* **18**. 54–72.

Halliday, M; A. K. (1970). Language structure and language function. Lyons, J. (ed.), *New horizons in linguistics.* Harmondsworth, Middlesex: Penguin. 140–65.

Hamann, S. (2003). *The phonetics and phonology of retroflexes.* Uttrecht: LOT.

Haspelmath, M; Dryer, M. S., Gil, D. & Comrie, B. (eds.) (2005). *The world atlas of language structures.* London, N. Y.: Oxford University Press.

Hayes, B. (1990). Precompiled phrasal phonology. Inkelas, H., Zec, D. (eds.), *The Phonology-syntax connection.* Chicago and London: The University of Chicago Press. 85–108

Hayes, B., Kirchner, Robert., & Steriade, D. (2004). *Phonetically-based phonology.* Cambridge: CUP.

Henderson, E. J. A. (1965). The topography of certain phonetic and morphological characteristics of South East Asian languages. *Lingua* **15**. 400–34.

Hutchinson, S. P. (1974). Spansih vowel Sandhi. *Papers from the parasession on natural phonology.* Bruck, A., Fox, R. A. & LaGaly, M. W. (eds.), Chicago, IL: Chicago Linguistic Society. 194–192.

Hyman, L. M. (2008). Universals in phonology. *The Linguistic Review.*

Itagi, N. & Singh, S. K. (2003). *Linguistic landscaping in India with particular reference to the new states: Proceedings of a seminar*. Mysore: Central Institute of Indian Languages and New Delhi: Mahatma Gandhi International Hindi University.

Jakobson, R., Fant, G. & and Halle, M. (1952). *Preliminaries to Speech Analysis*. Technical Report #13. Cambridge: MIT Acoustics Laboratory.

Jha, S. K. (1999). The inclusion of aspiration in distinctive feature theory. Yadava & Glover (eds.). 78–89.

Jusczyk, P. W. (1986). Toward a model of the development of speech perception. Perkell, J. S. & Klatt, D. H. (eds.), *Invariance and variability in speech processes*. Hillsdale, N.J.: Lawrence Erlbaum. 1–35.

Kachru, B. B. (1997). Language in Indian society. Sridhar, S. N. & Matto, N. K. (eds.), *Ananya: A portrait of India*. New York: The Association of Indians in America. 555–85.

Kachru, B. B., Kachru, Y. & Sridhar, S. N. (eds.). (2008). *Language in South Asia*. Cambridge: University Press.

Kager, R. (1999). *Optimality theory*. Cambridge: CUP.

Kager, R. (2008). Lexical irregularity and the typology of contrast. In Hanson, K & Inkelas, S. (eds.), *The nature of the word: Essays in honor of Paul Kiparsky*. Cambridge, MA: MIT Press.

Kansakar, T. R., Turin, M. (2003). *Themes in Himalayan languages and linguistics*. Heidelberg: South Asia Institute and Kathmandu: Trubhuvan University.

Kaye, A. S. (ed.) (1997). *Phonologies of Asia and Africa (including the Caucasus)*. 2 volumes. Winona Lake:Indiana Eisenbrauns.

Keating, P. A. (1991). On phonetics/phonology interactions. *Phonetica* **48**: 221–22.

Khubchandani, L. (1997). *Revisualizing boundaries: A plurilingual ethos*. New Delhi: Sage.

Khubchandani L. M. (1991). *Language, Culture and Nation Building: Challenges of Modernization*. Shimla: Institute of Advanced Studies.

King, R. D. (1986). The language issue revisited. In Roach, J. R. (ed.), *India 2000: The next fifteen years*. Riverdale, MD: The Riverdale Company. Pp. 135–43.

King, R. D. (1997). *Nehru and the language politics of India*. New Delhi: OUP.

King, R. D. (2008). Language politics and conflicts in South Asia. In Kachru et al. (eds.), pp. 311–24.

Kingston, J. (2007). Lenition. Ms., Department of Linguistics, UMass.

Kiparsky, P. (1982). Lexical morphology and phonology. The Linguistic Society of Korea (ed.), *Linguistics in the morning calm*. Seoul: Hanshin Publishing Company.

Kiparsky, P. (1985). Some consequences of lexical phonology. *Phonology Yearbook* 2. 85– 138.

Kirchner, R. (1997). Contrastiveness and faithfulness. *Phonology* **14**. 83–111.

Kirchner, R. (2004). Consonant lenition. In Hayes, B., Kirchner, R. & Steriade, D. (Eds.), *Phonetically Based Phonology*. Cambridge: CUP. 313–345.

Kisseberth, C. (1970). On the functional unity of phonological rules. *Linguistic Inquiry* **1**. 291–306.

Krishnamurti, Bh. (1991). The emergence of syllable types of stems (C) VCC(V) and (C)VC(V) in Indo-Aryan and Dravidian: conspiracy or convergence? Boltz, W. G. & Shapiro, M. C. (eds.), *Studies in the historical phonology of Asian languages*. Amsterdam: John Benjamins. 160–75.

Krishnamurti, Bh. (co-edited with Masica, C. P. & Sinha, A. K.) (1986). *South Asian languages: Structure, convergence and diglossia*. Delhi: Motilal Banarsidass.

Kuiper, F. B. J. (1967). The genesis of a linguistic area. *Indo-Iranian Journal* **10**. 81–102.

Ladd, D. R. (2008[1996]). *Intonational phonology*. Cambridge: Cambridge University Press.

Ladefoged, P. & Bhaskararao, P. (1983). Non-quantal aspects of speech production: A study of retroflex consonants. *Journal of Phonetics* **11**. 291–302.

Ladefoged, P. & Maddieson, I. (1990). Vowels of the worlds languages. *Journal of Phonetics* **18.2.** 93–122.

Ladefoged, P. & Maddieson, I. (1996). *The sounds of the world's languages*. Cambridge, Mass. & Oxford: Blackwell.

Liljencrants, L. & Lindblom, B. (1972). Numerical simulations of vowel quality systems: The role of perceptual contrast. *Language* **48.** 839–862.

Lindblom, B. (1986). Phonetic universals in vowel systems. Ohala, J. & Jaeger, J. J. (eds.), *Experimental phonology*. Orlando: Academic Press. 13–44.

Lindblom, B. & Maddieson, I. (1988). Phonetic universals in consonant systems. Hyman, L. M. & Li, C. N. (eds.), *Language, speech, and mind.* London: Routledge. 62–78.

Maddieson, I. (1980). *Patterns of sounds*. Cambridge: CUP.

Maddieson, I. (1991a). Testing the universality of phonological generalizations with a phonetically specified segment database: Results and limitations. *Phonetica* **48**. 193–206.

Maddieson, I. (1991b). Investigating linguistic universals. *Proceedings of the 12th International Congress Of Phonetic Sciences. Vol.* **1**. Aix-en-Provence: Universite´ de Provence. 346–354.

Maddieson, I. (2001). Typological patterns, geographical distribution and phonetic explanation, paper presented at the conference on the phonetics-phonology interface. Zentrum fur Allgemeine Sprachwissenschaft. Berlin, 11 Oc. 2001.

Maddieson, I. (2003). Phonological typology in geographical perspective. in Solé, M. J., Recasens, D. & Romero, J. (eds.), *Proceedings of the 15th International Congress Of Phonetic Sciences*. Barcelona: Futurgraphic. 719–722.

Maddieson, I. and Precoda, K. (1989). Updating UPSID, *UCLA Working papers in phonetics* **74**. 104–111.

Mahadevan, I. (1977). *The Indus script: Texts, concordances and tables*. New Delhi: Archeological Survey of India.

Mahapatra, B. P. (1978). Languages of India: A brief survey. *LSI Golden Jubilee Souvenir*. Pune: DC.

Mahapatra, B. P., McConnell, G. D., Padmanabha, P. and Verma, V. S. (1989). *The written languages of the world: A survey of the degree and modes of use, 2 India: Book I (Constitutional Languages) and Book 2 (Non-Constitutional Languages)*. CIRB, Laval University, Quebec, Canada and Office of the Registrar General, Govt of India. [*Written languages of the world* series; General editors: Kloss, H. and McConnell, G. D.]

Martinet, A. (1955). *Économie des changements phonétiques*. Berne: A. F.

Masica, C. P. (1976). *Defining a linguistic area: South Asia*. Chicago: ChUP.

Maurer, B. K. (1981). The origin of grammatical speculation and its development in India. *Indo-Pacifica. Occasional papers* **1**. 1–27.

McCarthy, J. & Prince, A. (1993). *Prosodic morphology I*. As: *Prosodic morphology: Constraint interaction and satisfaction*. ROA **482**.

McCarthy, J. J. (2001). *A thematic guide to optimality theory*. Cambridge: CUP.

Meenakshi, K. (2002). Retroflex sounds in Indian languages. *International Journal of Dravidian Linguistics* **31.1**. 1–16.

Mesthrie, R. & Bhatt, R. M. (2009). *World Englishes: The study of new linguistic varieties*. Cambridge: University Press.

Mielke, J. (2008). *Emergence of distinctive features*. Oxford: Oxford University Press.

Mohanan, K. P. (1986). *The theory of lexical phonology*. Riedel, Dordrecht.

Mohanty, P. (1997). Loss of /o/ in Kui, Sora and Oriya: A clue for a sub-linguistic area. Abbi, A. (ed.), 110–119.

Mosley, C. (ed.) (2007). *Encyclopedia of the worlds endangered languages*. Oxon: Rotledge.

Mukherjee, A. (ed.) (1989). *Language variation and language change*. Hyderabad: CASL, Osmania University.

Myers, S. (1991). Persistent rules. *Linguistic Inquiry* 22. 315–344.

Myers, S. (2000). Boundary disputes: The distinction between phonetic and phonological sound patterns in Burton-Roberts, N., Carr, P. and Docherty, G. (eds.), *Phonological knowledge: Conceptual and empirical issues*. Oxford: OUP. 245–272.

Nasukawa, K. & Backley, P. (2008). Strength relations in phonology. Berlin: Mouton de Gruyter.

National Council of Educational Research and Training. (2006). *Position paper: National Focus Group on teaching of Indian languages*. New Delhi: NCERT.

Nespor, M., & Vogel, I. (2007). *Prosodic phonology*. With a new foreword. Berlin: Mouton de Gruyter.

Nigam, R. C. (1971). Language handbook on mother tongues in India. *Census centenary monograph*. New Delhi: Census of India.

Oostendorp, M. van & Hinskens, F. *(2006). Segmental inventories and T-orders: Evidence from Dutch dialects, paper presented at GLOW worrkshop.* <glow.uit.no/GLOWXXX/workshops/segment/hinskens_oo.pdf>.

Pandey, P.K. (1997). Optionality, lexicality and sound change. *Journal of Linguistics* 33.91–130.

Pandey, P. K. (2005). Vowels in Indian languages. *Indian Linguistics* 66. 77–84.

Pandey, P. K. (2006). Retroflex consonants in Indic languages. *Indian Linguistics* 67. 129–147.

Pandey, P. K. (2007). Developments in Indian Linguistics. 1965–2005: Phonology, in Nagaraja, K. S. et al. (eds.), *Research trends in lexicography, Sanskrit and linguistics: Proceedings of seminar in honour of Professor S. M. Katre*. Pune: Deccan College. 121–132.

Parker, S. (2001). Non-optimal onsets in Chamicuro: An inventory maximised in coda position. *Phonology* 18. 361–386.

Patel, P. G. (2010). *The Brahmi writing system: Cross-fertilizing epigraphy, archaeology and linguistics.* New Delhi: Black & White.

Pattanayak, D. P. (ed.) (1973). *Distribution of languages in India in States and Union Territories.* Mysore: Central Institute of Indian Languages.

Pattanayak, D. P. (1981). *Multilingualism and mother-tongue education.* New Delhi: Oxford University.

Pattanayak, D. P. (1986). *Study of languages: A report.* New Delhi: NCERT.

Peperkamp, S. (1997). *Prosodic Words.* Den Haag: Holland Academic Graphics.

Pericliev, V. & Raúl, E. V-P. (2002). Differentiating 451 languages in terms of their segment inventories. *Studia Linguistica* **56.1**. 1–27.

Pierrehumbert, J. (2001). Stochastic Phonology *Glot international* 5 **(6)**. 195–207.

Pierrehumbert, J. (2002). Word-specific phonetics *Laboratory phonology VII*. Mouton de Gruyter, Berlin. 101– 39.

Pierrehumbert, J., Beckman, M. A. & Ladd, D. R. (2000). Conceptual foundations of phonology as a laboratory science. Burton-Roberts, N. Carr, P. & Docherty, G. (eds.), *Phonological knowledge*. Oxford UK: OUP. 273–304.

Pike, K. L. (1948). *Tone languages*. Ann Arbor: University of Michigan Press.

Prince, A. & Smolensky, P. (2004 [1993]). *Optimality theory: Constraint interaction in generative grammar*. Blackwell: Malden-Oxford-Carlton. [Also available as ROA 537.]

Prince, A. & Tesar, B. (2004). Learning phonotactic distributions. Kager, R., Pater, J. & Zonneveld, W. (eds.), *Fixing priorities: Constraints in phonological acquisition*. Cambridge: CUP. 245–291. [Also as ROA-353 and RUCCS-TR-54.]

Prince, A. (2002). Entailed ranking arguments. ROA **500**.

Prince, A. (2006). Implication and impossibility in grammatical systems: What it is & How to find it. ROA 880.

Pulleyblank, D. (1997). Optimality theory and features. In Archangeli, D & Langendoen, T. (eds.). *Optimality Theory*. Oxford: Blackwell.59–101.

Rajapurohit, B. B. (ed.) (1984). *Papers in phonetics and phonology*. Mysore: Central Institute of Indian Languages.

Rajapurohit, B. B. (ed.) (1986). *Acoustic studies in Indian languages*. Mysore: Central Institute of Indian Languages.

Ramanujan, A. K. & Masica, C. P. (1969). Towards a phonological typology of the Indian linguistic area. In Thomas, S. A. (ed.), *Current trends in linguistics* **1**. The Hague: Mouton. 534–77.

Ramaswami, N. (1983). Phonological patterns in Indian languages. In Pattanayak, D. P. & Annamalai, E. (eds.), *Greater heights*. Mysore: Central Institute of Indian Languages. 128–55.

Ramaswami, N. (1999). *Common linguistic features in Indian languages: Phonetics*. Mysore: Central Institute of Indian Languages.

Reddy, B. R. K. (2006). Tribal linguistics in India with focus on central and southern regions. In Padayya, K. et. al. (eds.), *Proceedings of national seminar on birth centenary of Professor S. M. Katre*. Pune: DCPRI.

Reddy, N. K. (1987). Constraints on consonant sequences across some Indian languages: A typological view. *Osmania Papers in Linguistics* **13**. 37–57.

Reugg, D. S. (1978). Mathematical and linguistic models in Indian thought: The case of zero and sunyata. *Weiner Zeitschrift fur die Kunde Sudasiens and Archiv fur indische Philosophie* **22**. 171–81.

Risley, H., Grierson, G. & Crooke, W. (1975). The ethnology, languages, literature and religions of India. Gurgaon: Academic Press. [Originally published by the Imperial Gazeteer of India 1907–09]

Roach, P. (1993). *English Phonetics and Phonology: A Pracical Course*. Cambridge: Cambridge University Press.

Rubach, J. (2000). Glide and glottal stop insertion in Slavic languages: A DOT analysis. *Linguistic Inquiry* **31**. 271–318.

Ruhlen, M. (1975). *A guide to the languages of the world*. Stanford: Stanford University Press.

Sapir, E. (1925). Sound patterns in language. *Language* **1**.37–51.

Sarkar, A. (ed.) (1964). Handbook of languages and dialects of India. Calcutta: Firma K. L. Mukhopadyay.

Saxena, A. & Borin, L. (eds.) (2006). *Lesser-known languages of South Asia: Status and policies, case studies and applications of information technology*. Berlin, New York: Mouton de Gruyter.

Saxena, A. (ed.) (2002), *Himalayan languages: Past and present*. Berlin, N. Y.: Mouton de Gruyter.

Schiering, R. & van der Hulst, H. (2009). Word accent systems in the languages of Asia. Goedemans, R., van der Hulst, H.G. & van Zanten, E. (eds.), *Stress patterns of the world. Part II: the data*. Berlin: Mouton de Gruyter.

Scholes, R. J. (1966). *Phonotactic Grammaticality*. The Hague, Paris: Mouton & Co.

Simpson, A. P. (1999). Fundamental problems in comparative phonetics and phonology: Does UPSID help to solve them? *Proceedings of the 14th*

International Congress of Phonetic Sciences Vol.1. Berkeley: University of California. 349–352.

Singh, R. A. (1961). *Inquiries into the spoken languages of India.* New Delhi: Census of India.

Singh, K. S. & Manoharan, S (1993). *People of India. National Series Vol. IX Language and Scripts.* Oxford: Oxford University Press.

Siversten, E. (1961). Segment inventories for speech synthesis. *Language and speech* **4**. 27–90.

Smith, H. (1952). Le futur moyen Indien et ses rythmes. *Journal Asiatique* 1952. 169–83.

Sprigg, R. K. (1987). Rhinoglottophilia revisited: Observations on the mysterious connection between nasality and glottality. *Linguistics of Tibeto-Burman Area* **10.1**. 44–62.

Sproat, R. (1993). Looking into Words. In Hargus, S. & Kaisse, E. M. (eds.), *Phonetics and Phonology, Volume 4: Studies in Lexical Phonology.* NY, etc.: Academic Press.

Sridhar, S. N. (2008). Language contact and convergence. In Kachru, B. B., Kachru, Y. & Sridhar, S. N. (eds.), *Language in South Asia.* Cambridge: University Press.

Steriade, D. (1995). Underspecification and markedness. In Goldsmith, J. (ed.), *The Handbook of Phonological Theory.* Oxford: Blackwell. 114–174.

Stevens, K. N. (1983). Design features of speech sound systems. MacNeilage, P.F. (ed.), *The production of speech.* New York: Springer-Verlag. 247–261.

Stevens, K. N. (1989). On the quantal nature of speech. *Journal of Phonetics* **17**. 3–45.

Swarajya, L. V. (ed.) (2002). *Case for language studies: Papers in honour of Prof. B. Lakshmi Bai.* Hyderabad: CASL, Osmania University, and Booklinks Corporation.

Taskar, A. D. (1955). *Intonational patterns in Indo-Aryan and Dravidian with special reference to the structure of vowel sounds.* Ph.D. dissertation. Poona: DC. Texas Press.

Trudgill, P. (1986). *Dialects in contact.* Oxford: Basil Blackwell.

Van Driem, G. (2007). South Asia and Middle East. Mosley, C. (ed.), *Encyclopedia of the worlds endangered languages.* Oxon: Routledge. 283–348.

Varma, S. (1972). *G. A. Griersons linguistic survey of India: A summary.* Vol. **1.** Vishveshvaranand Indological Series **58, 59.** Hoshiarpur: Vishveshvaranand **13.** 265–288.

Vijaykrishnan, K. G. (2007). The disyllabic word minimum: variations on a theme in Bangla, Punjabi and Tamil. In Bayer, J., Bhattacharya, T. & Hany Babu T. M. (eds.), *Linguistic theory and South Asian languages: essays in honour of K.A. Jayaseelan.* Amsterdam, Philadelphia: John Benjamins Pub. Co.

Vogt, H. (1954). Phoneme classes and phoneme classification. *Word* **10.** 28–34.

Whinnom, K. (1971). Linguistic hubridization and the special case of pidgins and creoles. Hymes, D. (ed.), *Pidginization and creolization of languages.* Cambridge: CUP. 91–115.

Yadava, Y. G., Bhattarai, R. R., Lohani, B. P. & Parajuli, K. (eds.) (2005). *Contemporary issues in Nepalese linguistics.* Kathmandu: Linguistic Society of Nepal.

Yip, M. (2002.) *Tone.* [Cambridge Textbooks in Linguistics]. Cambridge: CUP.

Zograph, G. A. (1982). *Languages of South Asia: A guide.* (Translated by Campbell, G.L.). London: Routledge and Kegan Paul.

B. General: Indic language groups

B 1. AUSTRO-ASIATIC

Anderson, G. D. S. (ed.) (2008). *The Munda Languages.* (Routledge Curzon Language Family Series.) New York:Routledge Curzon.

Bhattacharya, S. (1975). *Studies in comparative munda linguistics.* Shimla: IIAS.

Dasgupta, D. (1978). *Linguistic studies in Juang, Kharia, Thar, Lodha, Mal-Paharia, Ghatoali, Paharia.* Calcutta: ASI.

Donegan, P. (1993). *Rhythm and vocalic drift in Munda and Mon-Khmer. Linguistics of Tibeto-Burman Area* **16.1.** 1–43.

Munda, R. D. (1968). *Proto-kherwarian phonology.* MA dissertation. Chicago: University of Chicago.

Munda, R. D. (1970). *Proto-Kherwarian sound system.* Minnesota: University of Minnesota.

Pandey, P. K. (2010). Aspects of the word phonology of the Austro-Asiatic languages of India. Nagaraja, K. S. et al. (eds.), *Proceedings of the international conference on Austro-Asiatic languages*. Mysore: Central Institute of Indian Languages.

Pinnow, H. J. (1959). *Versuch einer historischen lantlehre dar kharia sprach.* Wiesbaden: Otto Harrassowitz.

Pinnow, H. J. (1963). The position of the Munda languages within the Austo-Asiatic language family. Shorto, H. L. (ed.), *Linguisti comparision in South East Asia and the Pacific*. London: SOAS. 140–52.

Ramaswami, N. (1989). The concept of vowel harmony and vocalic assimilations in Munda languages. Paper presented at the *Seminar on phonetics and phonology of Austro-Asiatic languages.* Mysore: Central Institute of Indian Languages.

Stampe, D. L. (1963). *Proto-sora-parengi phonology*. Mimeo. MA dissertation. Chicago: University of Chicago.

Suresh, J. (1989). Comparative Kherwarian phonology. Paper presented at the *Seminar on phonetics and phonology of Austro-Asiatic languages.* Mysore: Central Institute of Indian Languages.

Rao, G. U. (1989). Syllable structure among Munda languages: A non-linear approach. Paper presented at the *Seminar on phonetics and phonology of Austro-Asiatic languages.* Mysore: Central Institute of Indian Languages.

Zide, A. R. K. (1978). S-loss in Sora-Gorum. Presented at *ICAAL*. Mysore: Central Institute of Indian Languages.

Zide, N. H. (1965). Gutob-Remo Vocalism and glottalized vowels in Prot-Munda. *Lingua* **14**.

Zide, N. H. (1965). *Papers on South Munda Phonology I –V.* Chicago: The University of Chicago. South Asia Language and Culture Centre (Mimeographed).

Zide, N. H. & Munda, R. D. (1966). *The Kherwarian kh shift*. Unpublished Ms., Chicago.

B 2. DRAVIDIAN

Aalto, P. (1971). The alleged affinity of Dravidian and Finno-Ugrian. Asher, R. E. (ed.), (1971). *Proceedings of the second international conference-Seminar of Tamil studies* **1**. 262–6. Madras: International Association of Tamil Research.

Agesthelingam, S. & Subramanian, P. S. (1976). *Dravidian Linguistics.* Annamalainagar: Annamalai University.

Agesthialingom, S. & Kumaraswami R. N. (eds.) (1969). *Dravidian Linguistics (Seminar papers)*. Annamalainagar: Annamalai University.

Agesthialingom, S. & Shanmugam, S. V. (eds.) (1972). *Proceedings of the seminar on Dravidian linguistics* ***III***. Annamalainagar: Annamalai University.

Agesthialingom, S. & Subrahmanyam, P. S. (eds.) (1976). *Dravidian Linguistics* **V**. Annamalainagar: Annamalai University.

Ananthanarayana, H. S. (1970). Prakrits and Dravidian languages. *Proceedings of the seminar on Prakrit studies*. 65–75. Baroda.

Andronov, M. S. (1963). Dravidian languages. *American Orientalist* **31**. 177–97.

Andronov, M. S. (1964a). Materials for a bibliography of Dravidian linguistics. Tamil Culture. 11:1. 3–50.

Andronov, M. S. (1964b). Lexicostatistic analysis of the chronology of disintegration of Proto-Dravidian. *Indo-Iranian Journal* **8**. 170–86.

Andronov, M. S. (1970). Dravidian languages. Moscow: Nauka Publishing House.

Andronov, M. S. (1971). Comparative studies on the nature of Dravido-Uralian parallels (A peep into the pre-history of language families). Asher, R. (ed.), Proceedings of the second international conference-seminar of Tamil studies 1. 267–77. Madras: International Association of Tamil Research.

Annamalai, E. (1968). Onomatopoetic resistance to sound change in Dravidian. In Krishnamurti, Bh. (ed.), *Studies in Indian linguistics: M. B. Emeneau Ṣaṣṭīipū rti Volume*. Poona and Annamalainagar: Centre of Advanced Study. 15–19.

Balasubramanian, K. (1976). Historical development of Aytam. Agesthelingam, S. & Subramanian, P. S. (eds.), *Dravidian Linguistics*. Annamalainagar: Annamalai University. 561–583.

Bhat, D. N. S. (1968). Drvidian phonology. *Linguistic Survey Bulletin* **9**. Poona. 16–20.

Bhattacharya, S. (1975). Linguistic convergence in the Dravido-Munda culture areas. *International Journal of Dravidian Linguistics* **4.2**. 199–214.

Bouda, K. (1953). Dravidisch und Uralaltaisch. *Ural-Altaische Jahrbucher* (Wiesbaden) **25**. 161–73.

Bouda, K. (1956). Dravidian and Uralaltaic. *Lingua* **5**. 129–44.

Bright, W. (1966). Dravidian metaphony. *Language* **42**. 311–22.

Bright, W. (1975). The Dravidian enunciative vowel. Schiffman, H. & Eastman, C. (eds.), *Dravidian phonological systems*. Seattle: University of Washington. 11–46.

Burrow, T. (1938). Dravidian studies I: Initial voiced stops. *Bulletin of the School of Oriental and African Studies* 9. 711–22.

Burrow, T. (1940). Dravidian studies II: Notes on the interchange of short o e with i u in South Dravidian. *Bulletin of the School of Oriental and African Studies* **10**. 289–97.

Burrow, T. (1943). Dravidian studies III: The developments of initial *k-* in Dravidian. *Bulletin of the School of Oriental and African Studies* **11.1**. 122–39.

Burrow, T. (1947). Dravidian studies VI: The loss of initial *c/s* in South Dravidian. *Bulletin of the School of Oriental and African Studies* **12.1**. 132–47.

Burrow, T. (1948). Dravidian studies VII: Further Dravidian words in Sanskrit. *Bulletin of the School of Oriental and African Studies* **12.2**. 365–96.

Burrow, T. (1968). *Collected papers on Dravidian linguistics*. Annamalainagar: Annamalai University.

Burrow, T. (1972). A reconstruction of Fortunatovs law. *Bulletin of the School of Oriental and African Studies* **35.3**. 531–45.

Burrow, T. (1983). Notes on some Dravidian words in Sanskrit. *International Journal of Dravidian Linguistics* **12.1**. 8–14.

Burrow, T. & Emeneau, M. B. (1961). *A Dravidian etymological dictionary* [*DED*]. Oxford: Clarendon Press.

Burrow, T. & Emeneau, M. B. (1968). *A Dravidian etymological dictionary-supplement* [*DEDS*]. Oxford: Clarendon Press.

Burrow, T. & Emeneau, M. B. (1972). Dravidian etymological notes [DEN]. *Journal of American Oriental Society* **92**. 397–418. 475–91.

Burrow, T. & Emeneau, M. B. (1984). (2nd edn.) *A Dravidian etymological dictionary* [*DEDR*]. Oxford: Clarendon Press.

Chaitanyadeva, B. (1956). *Psychophysics of speech malody in Dravidian*. Ph.D. dissertation. Pune: UP.

Chandrika, T. (1972). The phonemes of Indo-Aryan, Konkani, Hindi and Nepali: A comparison with the Dravidian Malayal*a*m, Kannada and Telugu. *Proceedings of the First All India Conference in Dravidian Linguistics*. Trivandrum: DLA. 539–45.

Coats, R. (1979). The phonetic and phonology of a plausible Elamo-Dravidian hypothesis. *Anthropological Linguistics* **10**. 137– 45.

Collins, M. (1974). *Dravidic studies*. Madras: University of Madras.

Eliazarenkova, T. (1972). Influence of Dravidian phonological system on Sinhalese. *International Journal of Dravidian Linguistics* **1.2**. 126–37.

Emeneau, M. B. (1961). North Dravidian velar stops. in *Te. Po. Mi. Maniviza Malar (Studies presented to Prof T P Meenakshi Sundaram)*. Coimbatore. 371–88.

Emeneau, M. B. (1967). The South Dravidian languages. *Journal of American Oriental Society* **87**. 365–413.

Emeneau, M. B. (1970). *Dravidian comparative phonology: A sketch*. Annamalainagar: Annamalai University.

Emeneau, M. B. (1988). Proto-Dravidian *c* and its developments. *Journal of American Oriental Society* **108**. 239–68.

Emeneau, M. B. (1989). The languages of the Nilgiris. Hockings, P. (ed.), *Blue mountains (The ethnography and biogeography of a South Indian region on the Nilgiri hills)*. Delhi: OUP. 133–42.

Emeneau, M. B. (1994). *Dravidian studies: Selected papers*. Delhi: Motilal Banarsidass.

Nair, G.B. (1979). On the quantitative alterations in Dravidian. *International Journal of Dravidian Linguistics* **8**. 33–43.

Israel, M. (1975). The place of glottal stop in Dravidian languages. *Proceedings of the All India Conference in Dravidian Linguistics*. Trivendrum: DLA. 1–8.

Kamatchinathan, A. (1979). Evolution of dental nasal in Dravidian. *International Journal of Dravidian Linguistics* **8.2**. 226–35.

Kothandaraman, P. (1969). Alternation i/u in Dravidian. Agesthelingam, S. & Kumaraswami, R. N. (eds.), *Dravidian linguistics*. Annamalainagar: Annamalai University. 187–92.

Krishnamurti, Bh. (1958). Alteration i/e and u/o in South Dravidian. *Language* **34**. 458–68.

Krishnamurti, Bh. (1967). *An introduction to comparative Dravidian phonology*. Unpublished. Hyderabad: Osmania University.

Krishnamurti, Bh. (1997). Proto-Dravidian laringeal *H revisited. *Pondichery Institute of Language and Culture Journal of Dravidic studies* **7.2**. 145–65.

Krishnamurti, Bh. (1998). Patterns of sound change in Dravidian. Singh, R. (ed.), *The yearbook of South Asian languages and linguistics*. New Delhi: Sage Publications India Pvt. Ltd. 63–79.

Krishnamurti, Bh. (2003). *The Dravidian languages*. Cambridge: Cambridge University Press.

Kumaraswami, R. N. (1969a). Final -ai in Dravidian. *Seminar on Dravidian Linguistics* **11.** Annamalainagar: Annamalai University.

Kumaraswami, R. N. (1969b). *Post-nasal voiceless plosives in Dravidian.* Annamalainagar: Annamalai University.

Ladefoged, P. & Maddieson, I. (1991). The role of Dravidian languages in classifying places of articulation. Lakshmibai, B. & Reddy, R. (eds.), *Studies in Dravidian and general linguistics: A festschrift for Bh Krishnamurti.* Hyderabad: Osmania University.

Lakshmi Bai, B. & Reddy, R. B. (eds.) (1991). *Studies in Dravidian and general linguistics: a Festschrift for Bh. Krishnamurti.* Osmania University Publications in Linguistics no.6. Hyderabad: Osmania University. Department of Linguistics.

McAlpin, D. W. (1981). *Proto-Elamo-Dravidian: the evidence and its implications.* Philadelphia: American Philosophical Society.

Menges, K. H. (1969). The Dravido-Altaic relationship. *Journal of Tamil Studies* **1.1.** 35–39.

Nair, G. B. (1984). Phonological Interpretation of diphthongs in South Dravidian. *International Journal of Dravidian Linguistics* **13.2.** 306–330.

Namboodiri, E. V. N. (1976). *Glottochronology (As applied to four Dravidian languages).* Trivandrum: Sangma.

Ramaiah, L. S. (1994– 2000). *An international bibliography of Dravidian languages and linguistics.* Madras: T. R. Publications Private Ltd. (1994. Vol. I: *General and comparative Dravidian languages and linguistics*; 1995. Vol. 2: *Tamil language and linguistics*; 1998. Vol. 3: *Telugu language and linguistics*; 2001. Vol. 5: *Malayalam language and linguistics*; Vol. 4: *Kannada language and linguistics*; Vol. 6: *Non- literary Dravidian languages and linguistics*).

Ramaswami, A. L. V. (1931–32). Aphaeoresis and sound displacement in Dravidian. *Quarterly* ***Journal*** *of the Mythic Society* **22.4.** 448–80.

Rao, G. U. M. (1987). Syllabic parsing in South-central Dravidian languages: A comparative study. Paper presented at the *Seminar on Dravidian Tribal Languages.* Annamalainagar: Annamalai University.

Rao, G. S. (1973). On Proto-Dravidian morphophonemics. *International Journal of Dravidian Linguistics* **2.2**: 217–42.

Reddy, K. N. (1986). Word-initial and word-final consonant clusters in South Central Dravidian. Paper presented at the *Seminar on Common Phonological Features in Minor Languages of India.* Mysore: Central Institute of Indian Languages.

Schiffman, H. F. & Eastman, C. M. (1975). *Dravidian Phonological System.* Seattle: University of Washington.

Shanmugam, S. V. (1975). Dental and alveolar nasals in Dravidian. *Bulletin of the School of Oriental and African Studies* 35. 74–84.

Southworth, F. C. (1998). On the origin of the word *tamiz*. *International Journal of Dravidian Linguistics* **27.1**. 129–32.

Srivastava, G. P. (1979). Segmental phonemes of a Dravidian dialect of Central India. *Psycho-lingua* **9.2**. 111–24.

Steever, S. A. (ed.) (1998). *The Dravidian languages.* London. N. Y.: Routledge.

Subbaiya, K. V. (1909–11). A primer of Dravidian phonology. *Indian Antiquary* **38**. 159–70. 166–221.

Subramanyam, P. S. (1986). *Dravidian Comparative Phonology*. D Lit. dissertation. Waltair: Andhra University.

Subramanian, S. (1977). *The Commonness in the Metre of Dravidian Languages*. Trivandrum: DLA.

Sumati, S. (1982). *Comparative Phonology of the South-Central Dravidian Languages*. M.Phil. dissertation. Department of Linguistics. Hyderabad: Osmania University.

Suvarchala, B. (1984). *Central Dravidian Comparative Phonology*. M. Phil. dissertation. Hyderabad: Osmania University.

Thyagaraju, A. F. (1932). Palatalization in the Dravidian languages. *Indian Antiquary* **61**. 141–42.

Trivedi, G. M. (1990). Echo formation. in Krishnan Shree (ed.), *Linguistic traits across language Boundaries*. 51–82. Calcutta: ASI.

Usha Devi, A. (1978). *A Typological Study of Dravidian Morpho-phonemics.* M. Phil dissertation. Hyderabad: Osmania University.

Usha Devi, A. (1986). On certain phonological processes in South Dravidian. Krishnamurti, Bh. (ed.), *South Asian languages: Structure, convergence and diglossia*. Delhi: Motilal Banarsidas. 92–100.

Vachek, J. (1978). The problem of the genetic relationship of the Mangolian and Dravidian languages. *AO* **46**. 141–51.

Vachek, J. (1981). The Dravido-Altaic relationship: Lexical and sound correspondences. *Proceedings of the 5th International conference-seminar of Tamil studies*. Vol. **I**. Madras: International Association of Tamil Research. 159–70.

Vaidyanathan, S. (1980). *Studies in Dravidian linguistics*. Vol. **I**. *Pakha Sanjam* **10** (special issue). Patiala: Department of Anthropological Linguistics, Punjabi University.

Vaidyanathan, S. (1982). *Studies in Dravidian Linguistics*. Vol. **2**. *Pakha Sanjam* **15** (special issue). Patiala: Department of Anthropological Linguistics, Punjabi University.

Wallden, R. (1982). *Studies in Dravidian phonology and vocabulary*. Upsala: Acta University.

Zvelebil, K. V. (1997) Language list for Dravidian. *AO* **65**. 175–90.

Zvelebil, K. V. (1965). An introduction to the comparative study of Dravidian. *AO* **33**. 367–96.

Zvelebil, K. V. (1968). An introduction to the comparative study of Dravidian. *AO* **36**. 252–95.

Zvelebil, K. V. (1970). *Comparative Dravidian phonology*. The Hague: Mouton.

Zvelebil, K. V. (1972). Initial plosives in Dravidian. *Lingua* **30**. 2–3. 216–26.

Zvelebil, K. V. (1973). Problemes bondamentaux de phonologie et morphologie des langues Dravidiennes. *Bulletin de iEcole Francaise dextreme Orient* **60**. 1–48.

Zvelebil, K. V. (1973). Review of N. Kumaraswmi Raja-Post-nasal voiceless plosives in Dravidian. *Journal of American Oriental Society* **93**. 119–20.

Zvelebil, K. V. (1989). *Dravidian Linguistics an introduction*. Pondicherry: Pondicherry Institute of Linguistics and Culture.

B 3. INDO-ARYAN

Allen, W. S. (1959). Indo- Aryan. *Phonetica* **4**. 33–6.

Andronov, M. S. (1964). On the typological similarity of New Indo- Aryan and Dravidian. *Indian Linguistics* **25**. 119–25.

Bailey, T. G. (1938). *Studies in North Indian languages*. London: Lund. Humphries.

Basham, A. L. (1979). Aryan and non-Aryan in South Asia. Deshpande. M. M. & Hook. P. E. (eds.), *Aryan and Non- Aryan in India*. Ann Arbor: University of Michigan. Centre for South and Southeast Asian Studies. 1–9.

Beames, J. (1872–79[1970]). *A comparative grammar of the modern Aryan languages of India*. New Delhi: Census of India.

Bender, E. (1969). Middle Indo-Aryan. In Sebeok. T. E. (ed.) *Current trends in linguistics. Volume 5: Linguistics in South Asia*. The Hague: Mouton. 46–54.

Bhandarkar, R. G. (1887). (repr. 1974). *Wilson philological lectures on Sanskrit and the derived languages*. Poona: BOI.

Bloch, J. (1930). Some problems of Indo- Aryan philology: Forlong lectures for 1929. *Bulletin of the School of Oriental and African Studies* 5. 719–56.

Bloch, J. (trans. A. Master) (1965). *Indo- Aryan from the Vedas to modern times*. Paris: Adrien- Maisonneuve.

Bronkhorst, J. & Deshpande, M. M. (eds.) (1999). *Aryan and Non-Aryan in South Asia: Evidence, interpretation and ideology* (Harvard Oriental Series Opera Minora volume 3). Cambridge, MA: Department of Sanskrit and Indian Studies, Harvard University.

Bryant, E. F. (1997). *The indigenous Aryan debate*. Columbia University doctoral dissertation.

Bryant, E. F. (1999). Linguistic substrata and the indigenous Aryan debate. Bronkhorst, J. & Deshpande, M. M. (eds.), *Aryan and Non-Aryan in South Asia: Evidence, interpretation and ideology*. Cambridge, MA: Department of Sanskrit and Indian Studies, Harvard University. 59–84.

Burrow, T. (1973). The Proto- Indo- Aryans. *Journal of Royal Asiatic Society*. 123–40.

Cardona, G. (1974). The Indo- Aryan languages. *Encyclopedia Britannica*, 15th edn. 9. 439–50.

Cardona, G. (1990). Indo-Aryan languages. Comrie, B. (ed.), *The worlds major languages*. Oxford: OUP. 440–47.

Cardona, G. & Emmerick, R. E. (1974). Indo-Aryan languages. In *The new Encyclopaedia Britannica: Macropaedia*. Chicago. 439b-57a.

Cardona, G. & Jain, D. K. (eds.) (2003). *The Indo-Aryan languages*. London: Routledge.

Chatterji, S. K. (1960). *Indo-Aryan and Hindi*. Calcutta: K. L. Mukhopadhyay.

Deo, S. D. & Kamath, S. (eds.) (1993). *The Aryan problem* [Papers presented at the Seminar on the Aryan Problem held at Bangalore in July 1999]. Pune: Bharatiya Itihasa Sankalana Samiti.

Deshpande, M. M. & Hook, P. E. (eds.) (1979). *Aryan and non- Aryan in India*. Ann Arbor: University of Michigan, Centre for South and Southeast Asian Studies.

Dhall, G. B. (1955–56). The languages and dialects spoken in Orissa. *Indian Linguistics* 17. 39–43.

Emeneau, M. B. (1966). Dialects of Old Indo- Aryan. Birnbaum, H & Puhvel, J. (eds.), *Ancient Indo- European dialects*. Berkeley: University of California Press. 123–38.

Emeneau, M. B. (1971). Dravidian and Indo-Aryan: The Indian linguistic area. Sjoberg, A. F. (ed.), *Symposium on Dravidian civilization*. Austin and New York: Jenkins Publishing Company and Pemberton Press. 167–96. (Reprinted in Dil (1980).

Erdosy, G. (ed.) (1995). *The Indo-Aryans of ancient South Asia: Language, material culture and ethnicity*. Berlin and New York: Walter de Gruyter.

Franklin, E. (1946). Meter, phonology and orthography in BHS. *Journal of American Oriental Society* **66**. 197–206.

Giannakis, G. (1992). Reduplication as a morphological marker in the Indo-European languages: Reduplicated presents. *Word* **43.1**. 161–79.

Grierson, G. A. (1922). Spontaneous nasalization in the Indo- Aryan languages. *Journal of Royal Asiatic Society*. 381–8.

Grierson, G. A. (1931–3). On the modern Indo- Aryan vernaculars. *Indian Antiquary*.

Grierson, G. A. (1931). Conjunct consonants in Dardic. *Bulletin of the School of Oriental Studies* **6.2**. 349–68.

Hall, T. A. (1997). The historical development of retroflex consonants in Indo-Aryan. *Lingua* **102**. 203–21.

Heesterman, J. C., Schokker, G. H. & Subramoniam, V. I. (eds.) (1968). *Pratidānam: Indian, Iranian, and Indo-European Studies, Presented to Franciscus Bernardus Jacobus Kuiper on his sixtieth birthday*. (Janua Linguarum Series Major 34). The Hague, Paris: Mouton.

Hook. E. (1987b). Linguistic areas: Getting at the grain of history. Cardona, G. & Zide, N. (eds.), *Henry H. Hoenigswald commemorative volume*. Tübingen: Gunter Narr Verlag. 155–68.

Jain, B. D. (1927). Stress-accent in Indo-Aryan. *Bulletin of the School of Oriental and African Studies* **4**. 315–323.

Mahanta, S. (2009). Prominence in Oriya, Bangla and Assamese- A phonetic and phonological investigation. *International Journal of Dravidian Linguistics* **38**. 101–28.

Masica, C. P. (1991). *The Indo-Aryan Languages*. Cambridge: CUP.

Master, A. (1947). Indo-Aryan and Dravidian. *Bulletin of the School of Oriental and African Studies* **11**. 297–307.

Master, A. (1948). Indo-Aryan and Dravidian III. *Bulletin of the School of Oriental and African Studies* **12**. 340–64.

Meegaskumbura, P. B. (1970). *Proto new Indo-Aryan phonology* Ph.D. dissertation, Poona: PU.

Mehendale, M. A. (1968). *Some apects of Indo-Aryan linguistics*. Bombay: University of Bombay.

Misra, S. S. (1992). *The Aryan problem: A linguistic approach*. Delhi: Munshiram Manoharlal.

Mohanty, A. K., Panda, M, Robinson, P. & Skuttnab-Kangas, T. (eds.) (2009). *Multilingual education for social justice: Globalizing the local*. New Delhi: Orient Blackswan Pvt Ltd.

Morgenstierne, G. (1961). Dardic and Kafir languages. *The encyclopedia of Islam,* vol. **2**. Lieden: E. J. Brill.

Norman, K. R. (1960). Some vowel values in MIA. *Indian Linguistics* **21**. 104–107.

Ohala, J. J. (1980). Introduction to the symposium on phonetic universals in phonological systems and their explanation. In *Proceedings of the 9th international Congress of phonetic sciences, Vol.* **3**. University of Copenhagen: Institute of Phonetics. 181–185.

Ohala, M. (1991). Phonological areal features of some Indo-Aryan languages. *Language Sciences* **13.2**. 107–24.

Pandey, P. K. (To appear). Indo-Aryan phonology. To appear. *New Indo-Aryan languages*. Moscow: Institute of Linguistics, Russian Academy of Sciences. [Languages of the World series] (Ms. 2009).

Pandit, P. B. (1973). Change: Analogical or morphological? *Pakha Sanjam (Patiala)* **6**. 63–70.

Pike, Kenneth L. (1988). *Tone languages*. Ann Arbor: University of Michigan Press.

Shackle, C., Pandey, P. & Oranskaia, T. (2012). Introduction. *New Indo-Aryan languages*. Moscow: Institute of Linguistics, Russian Academy of Sciences. [Language of the World Series].

Schmidt, R. L. (2003). A grammatical comparison of Shina dialects. Saxena, A. (ed.), *Lesser-known languages of South Asia: Status and policies, case studies and applications of information technology*. Berlin, New York: Mouton de Gruyter. 33–55.

Schmidt, R. L. & Koul, O. (1983). *Kohistani to Kashmiri: An annotated bibliography of Dardic languages*. Patiala: IILS.

Sen, S. K. (1973). *Proto-New Indo-Aryan*. Calcutta: Eastern Publications.

Sen, S. (1960). *A comparative grammar of Middle Indo- Aryan*. Poona: LSI.

Stevens, K.N. (1989). On the quantal nature of speech. *J. of Phonetics* **17**. 3–46

Stevens, K. N. (1983). Design features of speech sound systems. MacNeilage, P. F. (ed.), *The production of speech*. New York: Springer-Verlag. 247–261.

Strand, R. F. (1973). Notes on Nuristani and Dardic languages. *Journal of American Oriental Society* **93.3**. 297–305.

Tarai, S. (2008). English words spoken by Oriya-English bi/ multilingual children is it Englishnization of mother tongue or nativization of English in Orissa? *International Journal of Dravidian Linguistics* **37.2**. 141–99.

Turner, R. L. (1922). The loss of vowel alternation in Indo-Aryan. *Second All India Oriental Congress*. Calcutta. 487–94.

Turner, R. L. (1927a). Notes on Dardic. *Bulletin of the School of Oriental and African Studies* **4.3**. 533–41.

Turner, R. L. (1927b). The Phonetic weakness of terminational elements in Indo-Aryan. *Journal of Royal Asiatic Society*. 227–39.

Turner, R. L. (1960). *Some problems of sound change in Indo-Aryan*. Poona: BOI (P. D. Gune Memorial Lectures 1).

Turner, R. L. (1966). *A comparative dictionary of the Indo-Aryan Languages*. London: OUP.

Turner, R. L. (1967). Geminates after long vowels in Indo- Aryan. *Bulletin of the School of Oriental and African Studies* **30.1**. 73–82. (Reproduced in *Collected papers* 1912–73, 1975. London: OUP. 405–15)

van Driem, G. & Sharma, S. R. (1996). In search of kentum Indo-Europeans in the Himalayas. *Indogermanische Forschungen* **101**. 107–46.

Varma, S. (1938) *Khasali group*. Calcutta.

Varma, S. (1939). Indian dialects in phonetic transcriptions. *Indian Linguistics* **7**. 281–9.

Varma, S. (1965). Aspiration in North-west Sub-Himalayan Indo- Aryan dialects. *Indian Linguistics* **26**. 175–88.

Voeglin, C. F. & Voeglin, F. M. (1965). The Dardic branch or sub-branch of Indo-European. *Anthropological Linguistics* **7.8**. 281–94.

Weinreich, U. (1957). Functional aspects of Indian bilingualism. *Word* **13.2**. 203–33.

B 4. TIBETO-BURMAN

Beckwith, C. (ed.) (2006). *Medieval Tibeto-Burman languages*. Tibetan Studies Library. Leiden: Koninklijke Brill.

Benedict, P. K. (1972). *Sino-Tibetan: A conspectus*. Cambridge: CUP.

Bhaskararao, P. and Ladefoged, P. (1991). Two types of voiceless nasals. *Journal of International Phonetic Association* **21.2**. 80-88.

Bickel, B. (2003). Prosodic tautomorphemicity in Sino-Tibetan. In Bradley, D. et al. (eds.), *Variation in Sino-Tibetan and South East Asian languages*. [Pacific Linguistics 555] Canberra: The Australian National University. 89–99.

Burling, R. (2003). The Tibeto-Burman Languages of Northeastern India. Thurgood, G. & LaPolla, R. J. (eds.), *The Sino-Tibetan languages*. London: Routledge. 160-191.

Chang, B. S. (1968). Glottalization and the falling tone. *Monthly internal memorand, Phonological laboratory*. Berkeley: University of California. 10–22.

Das Gupta, K. (1977). Patterns of inter-relationship between the languages of Arunachal: Singpho, Nocte, Gallong, Miju and Monpa, for a more precise classification. *Resarun* **3.2**. 13–25.

Das Gupta, K. (1977). A few features in some of the languages of Arunachal Pradesh. *Resarun* **3.3**. 31–35.

Driem, G. von (1998). Sino-Bodic. *Bulletin of the School of Oriental and African Studies* **60/3**. 455–88.

Firth, J. R. (1936). Alphabets and phonologies in India and Burma. *Bulletin of the School of Oriental Studies* **8**. 517–46.

Genetti, C. (ed.) (2004). *Tibeto-Burman languages of Nepal: Manange and Sherpa*. Canberra: Pacific Linguistics.

Grierson, G. A. (1920). On the representation of tones in oriental languages. *Journal of Royal Asiatic Society*. 453–97.

Hale, A. (1982). *Research on Tibeto-Burman languages*. Berlin, N. Y., Amsterdam: Mouton Publishers. [Trends in Linguistics: State of the Art Report **14**]

Hale, A. & Pike, K. (1970). *Tone systems of Tibeto-Burman languages of Nepal*. Urbana: University of Illinois.

Joseph, U. V. & Burling, R. (2001). Tone correspondences among the Boro Languages. *Linguistics of Tibeto-Burman Area* **24.2**. 41–55.

Joseph, U. V. & Burling, R. (2006). *The comparative phonology of the Boro Garo languages*. Mysore: Central Institute of Indian Languages.

Kaji, S. (ed.) (2005). *Proceedings of the Symposium Cross-linguistic Studies of Tonal Phenomena:Historical development: Tone-syntax interface, and descriptive studies*. [ILCAA, Dec. 14–16 2004]. Tokyo: Tokyo University of Foreign Studies.

Konwar, A. (1991). *Karbi People and their languages - A critical study*. Ph. D. dissertation. Guwahati: University of Guwahati.

Lehman, F. K. (1973). Syllable structure, tone and the theory of phonological conspiracies. Kachru B. B. (ed.), *Issues in Linguistics*. Urbana: University of Illinois. 515–47.

Light, T. (1978). Tonogenesis: Analysis and implication. *Lingua* **46**. 115–31.

Maran, L. R. (1971). A note on the development of tonal systems in Tibeto-Burman. *Occasional Papers of the Wolfenden Society* **2**. 1–24.

Marrison, G. E. (1967). *The Classification of Naga languages of Northeast India*. Ph. D. dissertation. London: University of London.

Masica, C. P. (1975). *Defining a linguistic area*. Chicago: ChUP.

Matisoff, J. A. (1991). Sino-Tibetan linguistics: Present state and future prospects. *Annual Review of Anthropology*. **20**. 469–504.

Matisoff, J. A. (1999). Tibeto-Burman tonology in an areal context. In Kaji, S. (ed.), *Proceedingsof the Symposium Cross-linguistic Studies of Tonal Phenomena: Tonogenesis, typology, and related topics*. Tokyo: Tokyo University of Foreign Studies. 3–32.

Matisoff, J. A. (2003). *Handbook of Proto-Tibeto-Burman: System and philosophy of Sino-Tibetan reconstruction*. [UC Publications in Linguistics 135]. Berkeley: University of California Press.

Mattisof, J. A. (1973). Tonogenesis in Southeast Asia. *Southern California Papers in Linguistics* **1**. 71–95.

Mazaudon, M. (1972). Consonantal mutation and tonal split in six Himalayan dialects of Tibeto-Burmese. Paper presented at the *International seminar on anthropoligical linguistics*. Patiala: IILS.

Mazaudon, M. (1973a). Comparison of six Himalayan dialects of Tibeto-Burmese. *Pakha Sanjam (Patiala)* **6**. 78–91.

Mazaudon, M. (1974). Notes on tone in Tibeto-Burman. *Linguistics of Tibeto-Burman Area* **1**. 27–54.

Mazaudon, M. (1977). Tibeto-Burman Tonogenetics. *Linguistics of Tibeto-Burman Area* **3.2**. 1–123.

Mazaudon, M. (1978). Consonantal mutation and tonal split in the Tamang sub-family of Tibeto-Burman. *Kailash* **6.3**. 157–79.

Michailovsky, B. (1975d). On some Tibeto-Burman sound changes. *Proceedings of the first annual meeting of the Berkley linguistics society*. Berkeley: University of California. 322–32.

Michailovsky, B. (1988). Phonological typology of Nepal languages. *Linguistics of Tibeto-Burman Area* **11.2**. 25–50.

Moral, D. (1998). A comparative phonology of Boro, Rabha and Kok-Borak - Some Observations. *Proceedings of the 4th Himalayan languages symposium*. Ms. Pune: DC. 7–9.

Morgenstierne, G. (1959). Preliminary notes on Abor-Miri-Dafla consonantalism. *Septentrionalia et Orientalia*. Studia Karlgren: Stockholm. 295–307.

Nagano, Y. & Lapolla, R. J. (eds.) (2001). *New Research on Zhangzhung and related Himalayan languages*. [Seri Ethnological Reports **19**.] Osaka: National Museum of Ethnology.

Namkung, Ju (ed.). (1997). *Phonological inventories of Tibeto-Burman languages*. Berkeley: STEDT, Department of Linguistics, University of California atBerkeley.

Palmer, F. R. (1970). Prosodic analysis. In Palmer, F. R. (ed.), *Language and Language Learning* **25**. London: OUP.

Pike, K. L. (1970). The role of nuclei of feet in the analysis of tone in TB languages of Nepal. Hale & Pike (eds.). 37–39.

Pittman, R. S. (1970). Gurung, Tamang, Thakali, Sherpa and Chepang Prosodies. In Hale and Pike (eds.). 1–8.

Pittman, R. S. (1973). Further developments in voice-register theory from descriptions of languages of South and Southeast Asia. Hale, E. A. (ed.), *Clause, sentence and discourse patterns in selected languages of Nepal [4 parts]*. Norman: University of Oklahoma. **Part 4**. 39–44.

Roberts, E. W. (1969). Perspectives in prosodic phonology II: Eugenie J A Henderson. *Lingua* **48**. 101–22.

Shafer, R. (1950d). Classification of some languages of the Himalayas. *Journal Of The Bihar Research Society* **34**. 192–214.

Sharma, D. D. (1989). *Tibeto-Himalayan languages of Uttarakhand*. New Delhi: Mittal Publications.

Sharma, D. D. (1994). *A comparative grammar of Tibeto-Himalayan languages*. New Delhi: Mittal Publications.

Sharma, S. R. (2001). A study on the Tibeto-Burman Languages of Utar Pradesh. In Nagano, Y. & Lapolla, R. (eds.), *New research on Zhangzhung and related Himalayan languages*. Osaka: National Museum of Ethnology. [Bon Studies 3. Senri Ethnological Reports No. **19**]. 187–194.

Sharma, D. D. (2004). *Tribal languages of Ladakh*. Part III. Delhi: Mittal Publications.

Simon, I. M. (1975). A brief note on the languages of Arunachal. *Resarun* **1**. 60–63.

Simon, I. M. (1978). The largest language group in Arunachal. *Resarun* **4.1**. 7–13.

Sino-Tibetan reconstruction. vol. **135**. University of California Publications.

Sprigg, R. K. (1963a). Prosodic analysis and phonological formulae in Tibeto-Burman linguistic comparison. In Shorto, H. L. (ed.), *Linguistic comparison in South East Asia and the Pacific*. London: SOAS University of London. 79–108.

Sun, J. T.-S. (2003). Tani languages. In Thurgood, G. & Lapolla, R. (eds), 456–67.

Thurgood, G. & LaPolla, R. J. (2003). *The Sino-Tibetan languages*. London and New York: Routledge [Routledge Language Family Series].

Vollmann, R. (2005). *Descriptions of Tibetan ergativity: A historical account*. Habiltation thesis. University of Graz.

Weidert, A. (1987). *Tibeto-Burman tonology*. Amsterdam, Philadelphia: John Benjamins.

Zeisler, B. (2004). *Relative tense and aspectual values in Tibetan languages: A comparative study*. [Trends in Linguistics, Studies and monographs **150**.] Berlin: Mouton de Gruyter.

B 5. TAI-KADAI

Diller, A., Edmondson, J. & Luo, Y. (eds.) (2005). *The Tai-Kadai languages*. London [etc.]: Routledge

Edmondson, J.A. and Solnit, D.B. (eds.) (1997). *Comparative Kadai: the Tai branch*. Dallas: Summer Institute of Linguistics and the University of Texas at Arlington.

Li, F. K. (1977). *A handbook of comparative Tai*. Hawaii: The University of Hawaii.

Morey, Stephen. 2005. "Tonal change in the Tai languages of Northeast India." *Linguistics of the Tibeto-Burman Area* **28/2**:139–202

Sagart, L. (2004). The higher phylogeny of Austronesian and the position of Tai-Kadai. *Oceanic Linguistics* **43**. 411–440.

B 6. ANDAMANESE GROUP

Abbi, A. (2009). Is Great Andamanese genealogically and typologically distinct from Onge and Jarawa? *Language Sciences* **31**. 791–812.

Abbi, A. (2006). *Endangered languages of the Andaman Islands*. Munich: Lincom Europa.

Blevins, J. (2007). A long lost sister of proto-Austronesian? Proto-Ongan, mother of Jarawa and Onge of the Andaman Islands. *Oceanic Linguistics* **46**. 155–198.

Dwarikesh, D. P. S. & Zide, N. H. (1962). The Comparative Phonology of Proto-Nicobarese as derived from Kar Nicobarese and Central Nicobarese. Unpublished Mimeo.

Portman, M. V. (1898 [1992]). *Manual of the Andamanese languages*. (Repr.) Delhi: Manas Publications.

Portman, M.V. (1898). *Notes on the languages of the South Andaman group of tribes*. Calcutta: Superintendent of Government Press.

Stampe, D.L. & Zide, N. H. (1963). Initial consonants in Munda-Nicobarese: Some tentative correspondences. Unpublished Mimeo.

Weber, G. (1998). *The Andamanese language family: A contribution to the centenary of M. V. Portmans work*. <http: //www.andaman.org>.

Zide, N. H. & Pandya, V. (1989). A bibliographical introduction to Andamanese linguistics. *Journal of American Oriental Society* **109.4.** 639–651.

Zide, N. H. & Pandya, V. (1989). A bibliographical introduction to Andamanese linguistics. *Journal of American Oriental Society* **109 (4).** 639–651.

B 7. MIXED LANGUAGES

Annamalai, E. (2001). *Managing multilingualism in India: Political and English manifestations*. New Delhi: Sage.

Hickey, R. (2004). South Asian Englishes. Hickey, R. (ed.), *Legacies of colonial English studies in transported dialects*. CUP. 536–58.

Kachru, B. B. (1990). *The Alchemy of English: The spread, functions and models of non-native Englishes*. Urbana: University of Illinois Press.

Kachru, B. B. (2005). *Asian Englishes: Beyond the canon*. Hong Kong: Hong Kong University Press. [South Asian Edition: New Delhi: OUP. 2005.]

Thomason, S. G. & Kauffman, T. (1988). *Language contact, creolization, and genetic linguistics*. Berkley and Los Angeles: University of California Press.

Whinnom, K. (1971). Linguistic hubridization and the special case of pidgins and creoles. In Hymes, D. (ed.), *Pidginization and creolization of languages*. Cambridge: CUP. 91–115.

B 8. HISTORICAL VARIETIES

[This is a a long and widely studied area of Indic linguistics. On the basis of the languages included for this group, the references can be found for Dravidian and Indo-Aryan groups above]

C. Individual Indic Languages

C 1. Austro-Asiatic Languages

BHUMIJ

Ramaswami, N. (1989). *Bhumij Grammar*. Mysore: Central Institute of Indian Languages.

Suresh, J. (1983). *Grammar of Bhumij*. Calcutta: Language Division.

BIRHOR

Suresh, J. (1985). *Grammar of Mundari and Birhor*. Calcutta: Language Division.

BONDA

Bhattacharya, S. (1965). Glottal stops and checked consonants in Bonda. *Indo-Iranian Journal* **9.1**. 69–71.

Fernandez, F. (1963). *A Phonology of Remo*. M. A. dissertation. University of North Carolina.

Fernandez, F. (1965). *A Grammar of Remo*. Ph. D. dissertation. University of North Carolina.

Fernandez, F. (1983). The morphology of the Remo(Bonda) verbs. *International Journal of Dravidian Linguistics* **12.1**. 15–45.

Ramachandrarao, V. (1986). The syllable load and reduplication: A case study of Remo. Paper presented at the *National seminar on syllable in phonetics and phonology*. Hyderabad: Osmania University.

Ramachandrarao, V. (1986). *The sound system of Remo*. M. Phil. dissertation. Hyderabad: Osmania University.

Ramachandrarao, V. (1989). Syllable load: A constraint on reduplication in Remo. Paper presented at the *Seminar on phonetics and phonology of Austro-Asiatic languages*. Mysore: Central Institute of Indian Languages.

DIDAYI

Ashirvadam, K. (1992). *The structure of Didayi, an Austro-Asiatic language*. Ph. D. dissertation. Hyderabad: Osmania University.

Ghosh, A. (1996). Gta? Phonology. *International Journal of Dravidian Linguistics* 25.1. 44–64.

Mahapatra, K. (1976). Echo-formation in Gta? Jenner, P. N. (ed.), *Austro-Asiatic studies II*. Honolulu: The University Press of Hawaii. 815–33.

Mahapatra, K. & Zide, N. H. (1972). Nominal compounding forms. *Indian Linguistics* 33. 179–202.

Odden, D. (1987). Arguments against the vowel plane in Gta? *Indian Linguistics* 18. 523–29.

Panda, P. K. (1986). *Didayi*. Bhubneshwar: Tribal and Research Insitute.

Zide, N. H. (1976). A note on Gta? echo-forms. Jenner, P. N. (ed.), *Austro-Asiatic studies II*. Honululu: The University Press of Hawaii. 1335–343.

GADABA-GUTOB

Gaud, D. S. (1980). *Gadaba*. Bhubaneshwar: Tribal and Research Insitute.

Rajan, F. H. & Jamuna, R. (2001). *Gutob-Gadaba phonemic summary*. Lamptaput, Orissa: Asha Kiran Society.

Zide, N. H. (1965). A note on Gutob Baby Talk. Mimeo. Chicago.

HO

Burrows, L. (1980, 1915) *The grammar of the Ho Language: An Eastern Himalayan dialect*. New Delhi: Cosmo Publications.

Suresh, J. (1984) *Grammar of Ho*. Calcutta: Language Division.

JUANG

Dasgupta, D. (1976). *Linguistic studies in Juang. Kharia*. Calcutta: ASI.

Mahapatra, B. P. (1962). *A note on Juang morphology*. Ms. Puri.

Mahapatra, B. P. & Matson, D. M. (1962). *A brief description of Juang*. Ms. Puri.

Matson, D. M. (1964). *A grammatical sketch of Juang, a Munda language*. Ph. D. dissertation (University Microfilms). Ann Arbor: University of Wisconsin.

Pinnow, H. J. (1960). *Beitrage zur kenntmis der Juang sprache*. Ms. Berlin.

Stamp, D. L. (1966). Phulbadi Juang Phonology. *Mimeo*. Chicago.

KHARIA

Biligiri, H. S. (1965). *Kharia: Phonology, grammar and vocabulary*. Poona: DC.

Dasbabu, A. K. (1991). *Kharia*. Bhubaneshwar: Tribal and Research Institute.

Malhotra, V. (1982). *The Structure of Khariya: A Study of typology and language change*. Ph. D. dissertation. New Delhi: JNU.

Peterson, J. (2006). *Kharia: A South Munda language, Volume I: Grammatical analysis,* Habilitationsschrift: Universität Osnabrück. [Also http://www.ling.uni-osnabrueck.de/uploads/Peterson/Grammar_main_body.pdf.].

Reddy, K. N. (1989). A linguistic-acoustic evidence for the distinction and syllabification of aspirated consonant in Kharia. Paper presented at the *Seminar on phonetics and phonology of Austro-Asiatic language.* Mysore: Central Institute of Indian Languages.

Rehberg, K. (2003). *Phonologie des Kharia. Prosodische Strukturen und segmentales Inventar.* Master's Thesis, University of Osnabrück.

KHASI

Abbi, A. (1979). The Sound System of Khasi. *Jan, Jati, Bhashaen aur Hindi Shikshan (Hindi).* Agra: Kendriya Hindi Sansthan.

Henderson, E., J. A. (1965). Final k in Khasi: A secondary phonological pattern. *Lingua* **14**. 459–66.

Henderson, E. J. A. (1967). Vowel length and vowel quality in Khasi. *Bulletin of the School of Oriental and African Studies* **30**. 564–88.

Henderson, E. J. A. (1976). Khasi initial clusters. Jenner, P. (ed.), *Austro-Asiatic Studies I.* Honululu: The University Press of Hawaii.

Khyriem, B. (2001). *Some aspects of syllable structure in Khasi.* M. Phil. Thesis. Deaprtment of Linguistics. Delhi: University of Delhi.

Nagaraja, K. S. (1984). Reduplication in Khasi. *Indo-Iranian Journal* **27.3**. 189–200.

Nagaraja, K. S. (1985). *Khasi phonetic reader.* Mysore: Central Institute of Indian Languages.

Nagaraja, K. S. (1985). *Khasi: A descriptive analysis*. Poona: DC.

Nagaraja, K. S. (1990). Sounds of Khasi dialect. *Bulletin of Deccan College Post Graduate Research Institute* **50**. 291–96.

Nagaraja, K. S. (1996). Consonant cluster combination in Khasi. *Indian Linguistics* **57**. 105–24.

Nagaraja, K. S. (1996–97). Maram-Khasi: A comparative study. *Bulletin of Deccan College Post Graduate Research Institute* **56–57**. 257–66.

Rabel, Lili (1961) *Khasi: A language of Assam*. Baton Rouge: Louisiana State University Press.

KISAN

Goswami, G. (1989). *Kisan*. Bhubaneshwar: Tribal and Research Institute.

KORKU

Nagaraja, K. S. (1985). Korku phonology. *Bulletin of Deccan College Post Graduate Research Institute* **44**. 113–19.

Nagaraja, K. S. (1990). Reduplication in Korku. *Bulletin of Deccan College Post Graduate Research Institute* **49**. 279–84.

Nagaraja, K. S. (1999). *Korku language grammar, text and vocabulary*. Tokyo: Institute for the Study of Languages and Culture of Asia and Afrika. Tokyo University of Foreign Studies.

Sood, S. P. (1966). Some phonological and grammatical aspects of the Korku language. *Bulletin of the Tribal Research and Training Institute* **6.1**. 60–76.

Zide, N. H. (1958). Final stops in Korku and Santali. *Indian Linguistics* **19**. 44–48.

Zide, N. H. (1960). *Korku phonology and morphophonemics*. Ph.D. dissertation. Philadelphia: University of Pennsylvania.

LYNGNGAM

Nagaraja, K. S. (1996). The status of Lyngngam. *Mon-Khmer studies* **26**. 37–50.

MUNDARI

Cook, W. A. (1965). *A descriptive analysis of Mundari, a study of the structure (Hasada dialect)*. University Microfilm. Michigan: Ann Arbor.

Gumperz, J. & Billigiri, H. S. (1957). Notes on the phonology of Mundari. *Indian Linguistics* **18**. 6–15.

Konow, S. (1911). Mundari phonology and linguistic survey. *Journal of the Asiatic Society of Bengal* **7.2**. 37–41.

Langendoen, D. T. (1962). Mundari phonology. *Mimeo*. Cambridge: Mass.

Nagaraja, K. S. (1993). Review of Osada, T.. *A reference grammar of Mundari* 1992. *Indian Linguistics* **54**. 133–35.

Osada, T. (1989). Notes on syllable structure and mora in Mundari. Paper presented at the *Seminar on phonetics and phonology of Austro-Asiatic languages*. Mysore: Central Institute of Indian Languages.

Osada, T. (1992). *A reference grammar of Mundari*. Tokyo: Tokyo University of Foreign Studies.

Pandey, P. K. (1989). Syllable-dependent processes in Mundari. Paper presented at the *Seminar on phonetics and phonology of Austro-Asiatic languages*. Mysore: Central Institute of Indian Languages.

Sinha, N. K. (1974). *Mundari phonetic reader*. Mysore: Central Institute of Indian Languages.

Sinha, N. K. (1975). *Mundari grammar*. Mysore: Central Institute of Indian Languages.

Suresh, J. (1985). *Grammar of Mundari and Birhor*. Calcutta: Language Division.

GORUM

Aze, F. R. (1974). The status of glottalization in Parengi (Gorum). *Proccedings of All India Conference of Linguists*. 84–95.

Bhattacharya, S. (1954). Studies in the Parengi language. *Indian Linguistics* **14**. 45 ff.

Mahapatra, S. (1994) *Parenga*. Bhubaneshwar: Tribal and Research Institute.

Ramakrishna, R. B. (1987). *Sound system of Parengi or Gorum*. Ms. Hyderabad: Osmania University.

Zide, A. R. K. (1963). *Parengi phonology*. M. A. dissertation. Philadelphia: University of Pennsylvania.

SANTALI

Bodding, P. O. (1922, 1929). *Materials for a Santhali Grammar*. Bengaria: Santal Mission of the Northern Churches.

De, S. (1996). Santal vowel phonemes. *Journal of the Anthropolgical Survey of India* **45**. 57–71.

Macphail, R. M. (1983, [1953]). *An introduction to Santhali*. Parts I and II. Calcutta: Firma KLM Pvt. Ltd.

Mahapatra, K. (1998). *Basic sounds: A study in sound symbolism of Santals*. Bhubaneshwar: ATDC.

Majhi, L. (1990). *Santhali*. Bhubaneshwar: Tribal and Research Institute.

Neukom, L. (2001). *A grammar of Santali*. München: Lincom Europa (Languages of the World/Materials, 323).

Sebeok, T. A. (1943). A note on the phonemic system of Santhali. *Journal of American Oriental Society* **63**. 66–67.

Suresh, J. (1986). *Grammar of Santhali*. Calcutta: Language Division.

SORA

Anonymous, *Language hand-book Savara*. Calcutta, Tea Districts Labour Association, 1927, iv, 137.

Mohanty, P. (1989). Syllable structure in Sora. Paper presented at the *Seminar on phonetics and phonology of Austro-Asiatic languages*. Mysore: Central Institute of Indian Languages.

Panda, M. (1989). Consonant phonology of Sora. Paper presented at the *Seminar on phonetics and phonology of Austro-Asiatic languages*. Mysore: Central Institute of Indian Languages.

Stampe, D. L. (1965). *Phonology of the Sora verb*. Ms. Chicago.

Starosta, S. (1964). *Some observations on vowel distribution in Sora*. Unpublished. Ms. Taiwan.

C 2. DRAVIDIAN LANGUAGES

ALU KURUMBA

Kapp, D. B. (1985). Echo-word formation in Alu Kurumba. *International Journal of Dravidian Linguistics* **14.1**. 35–55.

Kapp, D. B. (1987). Centralized vowels in Alu Kurumba. *Journal of American Oriental Society* **107.3**. 409–26.

AVE

Ramanaiah, M. V. (1982). *Ave: A tribal Dravidian speech (phonology, morphology and lexicon)*. M. Phil. dissertation. Hyderabad: Osmania University.

Ramanaiah, M. V. (1985). *Ave language*. Ph. D. thesis. Hyderabad: Osmania University.

BADAGA

Agesthelingam, S. (1972). A Descriptive Study of Badaga Language. *Mimeo*. Annamalainagar: Annamalai University.

Emeneau, M. B. (1939). The vowels of the Badaga language. *Language* **15**. 43–47.

Swaminathan, S. (1972). Badaga language: A descriptive phonology. *Proceedings of the 1st All India Conference in Dravidian Linguistics*. Trivendrum.

BELARI

Bhat, D. N. S. (1968). The Belari language. *Linguistic Survey Bulletin* **2**. 1–6.

BRAHUI

Andronov, M. S. (1972a). Notes on Brahui. *Journal of Tamil Studies* **1.1.** 1–6.

Andronov, M. S. (1975). Some rules of Brahui conjugation. in Schiffman, H. & Eastman, C. (eds), *Dravidian phonological systems.* Seattle: University of Washington. 242–98.

Andronov, M. S. (1980). *The Brahui Language.* Moskva: Nanka Publication House.

Basher, E. (1991). *A contrastive analysis of Brahui and Urdu.* Washington DC: Academy for Educational Development.

Elfenbein, J. (1997). Brahui phonology. Kaye, A. (ed.), *Phonologies of Asia and Africa.* . Indiana: Eisenbrauns. 797–811.

Emeneau, M. B. (1962). Brahui vowels. *Brahui and Dravidian comparative grammar.* University of California. 7–20.

Emeneau, M. B. (1980c). Brahui laterals from Proto- Dravidian * *r. Journal of American Oriental Society* **100:** [Repr. in Emeneau 1994: 303–6.] 311–12.

Emeneau, M. B. (1980d). Brahui laterals from Proto- Dravidian. Mallik, B. P. (ed.), *Suniti Kumar Chatterji commemoration volume.* Burdwan: University of Burdwan. 101–5.

Emeneau, M. B. (1997a). Brahui etymologies and phonetic developments: New items. *Bulletin of the School of Oriental and African Studies* **60.3.** 440–7.

Kamaleswaran, K. S. (1976). A note on vowel clusters in a few Brahui words. Agesthelingam, S. & Subramanian, P. S. (eds.), *Dravidian linguistics.* Annamalainagar: Annamalai University.

CHOLANAICAN

Muralidharan, R. (1988). *A descriptive study of Cholanaickans.* Ph. D. dissertation. Annamalainagar: Annamalai University.

Natana, S. S. (1976). Phonology of Tamil and Kattunaicka: A contrastive study. *Ayvukkovai* **8.2.** 684–89.

DEVIKULUM

Joseph, A. (1974–83). *Description of the tribal dialect of Devikulum.* Ph. D. dissertation. Trivendrum: Kerala University.

GADABA-KONEKOR

Bhaskararao, P. (1969). Gadaba phonology. *Linguistic Survey Bulletin* **14.** 5–8.

Bhaskararao, P. (1972–80). *Konekor Gadaba: A Dravidian language*. Pune: Deccan College Post-Graduate and Research Institute.

Bhaskararao, P. (1998). Gadaba. Steever, S. (ed.), *The Dravidian languages*. London: Routledge. 328–55.

GADABA-OLLARI

Bhattacharya, S. (1956). *Ollari: A Dravidian speech*. Delhi: Dept. of Anthropology. GOI.

GONDI

Andres, S. (1977). *A description of Muria Gondi phonology and morphology with a transformational account of the morpho-phonological processes employed*. Ph. D. dissertation. Pune: Deccan College Post-graduate & Research Institue.

Bhattacharya, S. (1967). Vowels in the Muria dialect. *JOAS* **9.1**. 8–11.

Lind, A. A. (1913). *A Manual of Maria Gondi* (cited by Burrow and Bhattacharya 1960).

Mitchell, A. N. (1942). *A grammar of Maria Gondi as spoken by the Bison Horn or Dandami Marias of Bastar state*. Jagdalpur.

Moss, Clement F. (1950). *An introduction to the grammar of the Gondi language*. Jabbalpore: Mission Press.

Natarajan, G. V. (1985). *Abhujhamaria grammar*. Mysore: Central Institute of Indian Languages.

Rao, U. M. G. (1987) *A complete study of Gondi dialects with special reference to phonology and morphology*. Ph.D. dissertation. Hyderabad: Osmania University.

Subramanian, P. S. (1968). *A descriptive grammar of Gondi*. Annamalainagar: Annamalai University.

Veena, S. (1965). *A descriptive analysis of Madhya dialect (Gondi)*. Ph.D. dissertation. Poona: DC.

Verma, N. D. (1975). *A complete study of the main dialects of Bastar district*. D.Litt. dissertation. Raipur: Ravishankar University.

Williamson, H. (1890). *Gond grammar and vocabulary*. London.

IRULA

Diffloth, G. (1968) *The Irula language: A close relative of Tamil*, Ph. D. dissertation, Los Angeles: University of California. [University Microfilms, Ann Arbor, Michigan, 1976]

Kempe-Gowda, K. (1965–74). *A descriptive analysis of Irula dialect*. Ph.D. dissertation. Mysore: Mysore University.

Perialwar, R. (1974). *A descriptive analysis of Irula dialect.* Ph.D. dissertation. Annamalainagar: Annamalai University.

Periyalwal, R. (1979). *Phonology of Irula with vocabulary.* Annamalainagar: CASL, Annamalai University.

Verma, S. G. (1967). Phonology of Yerukelai language. Agesthelingam, S. & Raja, N. K. (eds.), *Dravidian linguistics.* Annamalainagar: Annamalai University. 187–202.

Wiltshire, C. (1994). Feature constraints in Irula. *Chicago Linguistic Society* **30**.428–442.

Zvelebil, K. V. (1970). Additional vowel qualities in Kodagu and Irula. *Comparative Dravidian phonology.* The Hague: Mouton. 191–94.

Zvelebil, K. V. (1971). Irula vowels. *Indo-Iranian Journal* **13.2**. 113–22.

KADAR

Indira, R. (1976). *A descriptive analysis of Kadar.* Ph.D. dissertation. Poona: DC.

Suresh, J. (1982). *A descriptive study of Kadar language of Annamali Hills.* Ph.D. dissertation. Annamalainagar: Annamalai University.

Panikkar, T. B. V. (1972). *The phonology of Kadar dialect. 2nd All India Conference in Dravidian Linguistics.* Tirupati.

KANNADA

Acharya, A., S. (1983). *Rabakavi Kannada: Phonology and morphology.* Pune: DCPRI.

Biligiri, H. S. (1955). The nasal phonemes of Kannada. *Indian Linguistics* **16**. 306-08.

Bright, W. (1958). *Colloquial Kannada.* Poona: DC.

Bright, W. (1970). Phonological rules in literary and colloquial Kannada. *Journal of American Oriental Society* **90.1**. 140–44.

Bright, W., Rao, S. & Narvekar, M. (1960). *Spoken Kannada.* Berkeley.

Chidananda Murthy, M. (1984). Further light on palatalization and velarization in a Kannada dialect. *International Journal of Dravidian Linguistics* **13.2**. 331–40.

Gowda, K. K. (1969). The phoneme /l/. *Kannada Studies* **3.1**. 51–59.

Hirenath, R. C. (1957). Vowel phonemes of Kannada. *Journal of Karnataka University* **1.2**. 98–109.

Kumudavalli, S. (1973). *The relationship between articulation and discrimination of Kannada speech sounds in term of distinctive features.* M.A. dissertation. Mysore: Mysore University.

Maheshwaraiah, H. M. (1986). Spectrographic analysis of liquids in Kannada. Rajapurohit, B.B. (ed.), (1986). *Acoustic studies in Indian languages*. Mysore: Central Institute of Indian Languages. 55–60.

Pandey, P. K. (1977). Nasalization in Havyaka Kannada. *International Journal of Dravidian Linguistics.*

Patil, C. (1986). Intonation contours of Kannada. Rajapurohit, B. B. (ed.), (1986). *Acoustic studies in Indian languages*. Mysore: Central Institute of Indian Languages. 84–91.

Prakash, P. & Joshi, R. (1995). Orthography and reading in Kannada: A Dravidian language. Tylor, I. & Olson, D. (eds.), *Scripts and literacy: Reading and learning to read alphabets, syllabaries and characters.* Dordrecht: Kluwer Academic Publishers. 95–108.

Rajapurohit, B. B. (1984). Phonemic co-occurrence constraints on duration: A case study of Dharwad dialect of Kannada. Rajapurohit, B. B. (ed.), (1984). *Papers in phonetics and phonology*. Mysore: Central Institute of Indian Languages. 76–84.

Savithri, S. R. (1995). On speech rhythms in Kannada. *Journal of Phonetics* **23.3**. 273–89.

Schiffman, H. F. (1983). *A reference grammar of spoken Kannada*. Seattle/ London: University of Washington Press.

Sreekantaiya, T. N. (1935). The mutation of i, u, e and o in Kannada. *Proceedings and transactions of the Eighth All India Oriental conference.* 769–800.

Sridhar, S. N. (1990). *Kannada*. London/New York: Routledge.

KASABA

Pillai, C. V. (1975). *A descriptive grammar of Kasaba*. Ph.D. dissertation. Annamalainagar: Annamalai University.

Pillai, C. V. (1975). *Phonology of Kasaba with vocabulary*. Annamalainagar: CASL. Annamalai University.

Pillai, C. V. (1976). *A Grammar of the Kasaba language*. Annamalainagar: Annamalai University.

KATTUNAICKA

Natanasabpathy, S. (1986). *The language of Kattunaickas: A linguistic study*. Annamalinagar: Annamalai University.

KODAGU

Agesthelingam, S. & Balakrishnan, R. (1971.) Kodagu phonology. *Journal of Annamalai University* **28**. 73–92.

Balakrishnan, R. (1976). *Phonology of Kodagu with vocabulary*. Annamalainagar: Annamalai University.

Balakrishnan, R. (1977). *A group of Kodagu language*. Annamalainagar: Annamalai University.

Emeneau, M. B. (1970). Kodagu vowels. *Journal of American Oriental Society* **90**. 145–58.

Garman, M. (1973). *A grammar of Coorg language*. Ph.D. dissertation. Edinburgh: University of Edinburgh.

Kothandaraman, P. (1969). Kodagu vowels. Agesthelingam, S. S. & Raja, N. K. (eds.), *Dravidian linguistics*. Annamalainagar: Annamalai University. 233–47.

KOLAMI

Emeneau, M. B. (1955). *Kolami: A Dravidian language*. Berkeley: University of California Press.

Pagdi, S. R. (1950). *A grammar of the Kolami language*. Hyderabad.

Subrahmanyam, P. S. (1998). Kolami. Steever, S. B. (ed.), *The Dravidian languages*. London and New York: Routledge. 301–27.

Thomasaiah, K. (1986). *Naikri dialect of Kolami: Descriptive and comparative study*. Ph.D. dissertation. Annamalainagar: Annamalai University.

Thomasiah, K. (1986). *Naikri dialect of Kolami: Descriptive and comparative study*. Ph. D. dissertation. Annamalainagar: Annamalai University.

Zou, Ke. (1990). Assimilation as spreading in Kolami. *Mid America linguistics conference papers*. 461–75.

KORAGA

Bhat, D. N. S. (1971). *The Koraga language*. Poona: DC.

Krishnamurti, Bh. (1968). Koraga: A new Dravidian language. Krishnamurti, Bh. (ed.), *Studies in Indian Linguistics*. Poona/Annamalainagar: DC / Annamalai University. 290-95.

Shetty, R. T. (1979) *Koraga group: A descriptive study of a Dravidian dialect*. Ph.D. dissertation. Poona: DC.

Shetty, R. T. (1978). *Koraga grammar*. Ph.D. dissertation. Poona: UP, Deccan College Post-Graduate and Research Institute.

KORAVA

Shrivastava, M. K. (1978). *Descriptive analysis of Korava of Chattisgarh region with special reference to Total Korava*. Ph.D. dissertation. Raipur: Ravishankar University.

KOTA

Emeneau, M. B. (1969b). Kota vowel shift. *Journal of Tamil Studies* **1**. 21–34. [Repr. in Emeneau 1994: 175–82.]

Subbaiah, G. (1970). *Metathesis in Kota language*. Neytal: Pondichery.

Subbaiah, G. (1970). *Nasalization in Kota language*. Tamilananku: Pondichery.

Subbaiah, G. (1973). *A descriptive study of Kota language*. Ph.D. dissertation. Annamalainagar: Annamalai University.

Subbaiah, G. (1986). *Kota phonetic reader*. Mysore: Central Institute of Indian Languages.

KOYA

Macken, M. A. (1989). Local feature changing harmony. *Proceedings of Eastern States Congress on Linguistics* **6**. 194–206.

Rama Rao, C. (1986). Syllabic constraint in Koya. Paper presented at *Seminar on Pan-Indian phonological features*. Mysore: Central Institute of Indian Languages.

Rama Rao, K. (1979). *Phonology and morphology of Koya language*. Ph.D. dissertation. Hyderabad: Osmania University.

Tyler, S. A. (1969). *Koya: An outline grammar (Gomma dialect)*. Berkeley: University of California Press.

KUI

Burrow, T. & Bhattacharya, S. (1961). The Kui dialect as spoken by the Kuthia Kandhs. *Indo-Iranian Journal* **3.1**. 11–35.

Burrow, T. & Krishnamurti, Bh. (1961). Some notes on the Kui dialect as spoken by the Kuthia Kandhs of North East Koraput. *Indo-Iranian Journal* **5.2**. 118–35.

Chetty, N. T. (1984). *Kutlia dialect of Kui (phonology, morphology,text and vocabulary)*. M.Phil. dissertation. Hyderabad: Osmania University.

Dash, G. (1980). *Kui: A Tribal Dravidian language of Orissa*. Ph.D. dissertation. Behrampur: Behrampur University.

Dash, G. (1981). *Structure of Kui: A tribal language of Orissa*. Ph.D. dissertation. Shantiniketan: Vishva-Bharati.

Friend-Pereira, J. E. (1909). *A grammar of the Kui language*. Calcutta.

Letchmajee, L. (1902). (2nd edn) *An introduction to the grammar of the Kui or Kandh language*. Calcutta.

Maheswaran, C. (1989). *A descriptive study of the Kui language*. Ph.D. dissertation. Annamalainagar: Annamalai University.

Maheswaran, C. (1997). The glottal stop in Kui language. *International Journal of Dravidian Linguistics* **26.1**. 97–102.

Rama Rao, C. (1978). Rule chase. *Indian Linguistics* **39**. 183–88.

Watkin, K. L. (1975). Some phonological rules for the Kui verbs. Schiffman, H. & Eastman, C. (eds.), *Dravidian phonological systems*. Seattle: University of Washington. 375–89.

Winfield, W. (1928). *A grammar of the Kui language*. Calcutta: Asiatic Society of Bengal.

KURUBA

Jayapal, S. (1978). *Descriptive grammar of Kuruba*. Ph.D. dissertation. Annamalainagar: Annamalai University.

Jeyapal, V. Y. (1987). *Kambi grammar*. Mysore: Central Institute of Indian Languages.

Kapp, D. B. (1982). *Alu-Kurumba Nayan: Die Sprache der Alu-Kurumbas*. Wiesbadan: Harrassowitz.

Kapp, D. B. (1985). Echo word formation in Alu Kurumba. *International Journal of Dravidian Linguistics* **14.1**. 35–55.

Kapp, D. B. (1987). Centralized vowels in Alu Kurumba. *Journal of American Oriental Society* **107.3**. 409–26.

Varma, S. G. (1978). *Kurumba Kannada: Pudukkotai Kurumba dialect*. Annamalainagar: Annamalai University.

KURUKH

Ananthy, R. J. (1989). *Writing in non-literary languages in the Indian Context: With special reference to Kurux/J*. Ph.D. dissertation. New Delhi: JNU.

Bhat, D. N. S. (1970). Velar consonants in Kurux. *Indian Linguistics* **31.4**. 177–81.

Ekka, F. (1972). *A grammar of the Kurukh language*. Ph.D. dissertation. Madurai: Madurai Kamaraj University.

Ekka, F. (1985). *Kurux phonetic reader*. Mysore: Central Institute of Indian Languages.

Gordon, K. H. (1976). *A phonology of Dhangar-Kurux*. Kathmandu: Tribhuvan University.

Grignard, A. (1924a). *A grammar of the Oraon language*. Calcutta: Catholic Orphan Press.

Grignard, A. (1924b). *An Oraon- English dictionary*. Calcutta and Vienna.

Hahn, F. (1903). *Kurux-English dictionary Part I*. Calcutta: Bengal Secretariat Press.

Kloss, H. & McConnell, G. D. (1989). *Kurukh/Oraon*. 1021–1038.

Pfeiffer, M. (1972). *Elements of Kurukh historical phonology*. Leiden: E. J. Brill.

Tiwari, U. (1966). Nasal phonemes of Kurukh. *Indian Linguistics* (Sukumar Sen Fel. Vol). 226–30.

KUVI

Fitzgerald, A. G. (1913) *Kèvi°ga Bassa: The Kondh language as Spoken by the Parjas of the Madras Presidency*. Calcutta: Catholic Orphan Press.

Herman, R. (1994). The structure of affricates in Kuvi (A constraint-based account). *Proceedings of Eastern States Conference on Linguistics* **11**. 163–73.

Israel, M. (1979). *A grammar of the Kuvi language*. Trivandrum: DLA.

Krishnamurti, Bh. (1980). A vowel lowering rule in Kui-Kuvi. *Proceedings Of The Annual Meeting Of Berkeley Linguistics Society* **6**. 495–506.

Mohanty, P. (1994). Plural markers in Kui and Kuvi: A reconsideration. *International Journal of Dravidian Linguistics* **23.2**. 67–76.

Reddy, J. (1979). *Kuvi grammar*. Mysore: Central Institute of Indian Languages.

Schultze, F. V. P. (1911). *A grammar of the Kuvi language*. Madras: Graves, Cookson and Co.

Schultze, F. V. P. (1913). *Vocabulary of the Kuvi-Kond language*. Madras.

MALAYALAM

Aiyar, R. L. V. (1937–39). A primer of Malayalam phonology. *Bulletin of the Rama Varma Research Institute*. Trichur.

Aiyar, R. L. V. (1938–39). The Malayalam phonemes. *New Indian Antiquary (reprinted in International Journal of Dravidian Linguistics 1.2. 10–18, 1972)*. **1.126**. 719–23.

Asher, R. E. & Kumari. T. C. (1997). *Malayalam*. London/New York: Routledge.

Bright, W. (1975). Review of B. Shyamala Kumari: Malayalam phonetic reader. *Indo-Iranian Journal* **16.3**. 232–38.

Bultin, R. T. (1945). On the alphabetic notation of certain phonetic features of Malayalam. *Bulletin of the School of Oriental and African Studies* **8**. 437–48.

Ghatage, A. M. (1994). *Phonemic and morphemic frequancy count in Malayalam.* Mysore: Central Institute of Indian Languages.

Kamath, G. B. (1971). Allophonic variation of /c/ in Malayalam. *Proceeding IAI conference of linguistics.* Trivendrum.

Kunhan, R. C. (1937). Notes on Sanskrit-Malayalam Phonetics. *Journal of Oriental Research.* Madras. 171–74.

Kunhan, R. C. (1960). The nasal phonemes of Malayalam. *Indian Linguistics* **21.** 90-96.

Madhavan, P. (1985). Vowel epenthesis in Malayalam: Consequences for morphology. *Indian Linguistics* **46.** 29–32.

Menon, K. M. N. (1965). *Phonemic and morphemic frequancy in Malayalam.* Ph.D. dissertation. Pune: UP.

Mohanan, K. P. (1986). Vowel epenthesis in Malayalam - schwa or v ?. *Indian Linguistics* **47.** 97–101.

Mohanan, K. P. & Mohanan, T. (1984) Lexical phonology of the consonant system in Malayalam. *Linguistic Inquiry* **15.4.** 575–602.

Mohanan, T. (1989). Syllable structure in Malayalam. *Linguistic Inquiry* **20.**

Nayar, P. V. R. (1971). Phonological treatment of nasal articulation in Malayalam - A polysystemic approach. Agesthelingam, S. & Valentine, E. (eds.), *Proceedings of the All India Conference in Dravidian Linguistics.* Trivendrum: DLA. 311–16.

Panniker, V. T. B. (1976). Two problems of Malayalam phonology. *Proceedings of the Third All India Conference in Dravidian Linguistics.* Dharwar: Karnataka University. 30–38.

Prabhakara Variar, K. M. (ed.) (1985). *History of Malayalam language.* Madras: University of Madras.

Nayar, P. V. R. (1986). Syllable in Malayalam: A polysystemic approach. Paper presented at the *National seminar on syllable in phonetics and phonology.* Hyderabad: Osmania University.

Prasanna, K. V. (1983). *A contrastive study of Malayalam And English sound systems.* Ph.D. dissertation. Raipur: Ravishankar University.

Reddy, K. N. (1971). *Phonology of Malayalam.* MA dissertation. Pune: DC.

Reddy, K. N. & Srikumar, K. (1987–88). Co-articulation and acoustic study of trills in Malayalam. *Osmania Papers in Linguistics.* 42–54. 89–101.

Sadananda, S. (1991). Malayalam syllabification. *Studies in Linguistic Sciences* **20.3.** 86.

Sanathakumar, P. (1983). Dipthongs in Malayalam. *International Journal of Dravidian Linguistics* **12.2.** 441–48.

Sekhar, A. C. (1969). *Evolution of Malayalam*. Poona. India: DCPRI.

Shreedhar, M. V. (1972). Phonology of Cochin dialect of Malayalam. *International Journal of Dravidian Linguistics* **1.2**. 100-125.

Shyamala Kumari, B. (1972). *Malayalam phonetic reader*. Mysore: Central Institute of Indian Languages.

Subramanyam, V. I. (1962). Phonemic outline of a dialect of Malayalam. *Indian Linguistics* **23**. 99–116.

Subramanyam, V. I. (1971). Malayalam phonological rules. *Autumn seminar linguistics*. Kurukshetra: Kurukshetra University.

Subramanyam, V. I. (1972). Rules of nasal assimilation in Malayalam. *International Journal of Dravidian Linguistics* **1.1**. 137–43.

Subramanyam, V. I. (1991–92). Alteration of v/b. *Bulletin of Deccan College Post Graduate Research Institute*. 51–52. 289–302.

Valentine, E. (1976). The enunciative vowel in Malayalam. *International Journal of Dravidian Linguistics* **5.1**. 16–22.

Valentine, E. (1977). Features for classifying the underlying elements of the phonological system of Malayalam. *International Journal of Dravidian Linguistics* **6.1**. 115–38.

Velayudhan, S. (1970). *A contrastive phonological study of Malayalam and English*. Ph.D. dissertation. Trivendrum: University of Kerala.

Velayudhan, S. (1975). Syllable structure in English and Malayalam. Reddy, G. N. & Nair, S. P. (eds.), *Proceedings of the second all India conference in Dravidian linguistics*. Trivendrum: DLA. 268–72.

Yamuna, R. (1986). A spectrographic study of /r/ and /R/ in Malayalam. Rajapurohit, B. B. (ed.), (1986). *Acoustic studies in Indian languages*. Mysore: Central Institute of Indian Languages. 61–64.

MALTO

Droese, E. (1984). *Introduction to the Malto language*. Agra: Secundra Orphanage Press.

Ekka, F. (1972). Remarks on the treatment of PDr *o: Kurux and Malto. *International Journal of Dravidian Linguistics* **1.2**. 19–28.

Steever, S. A. (1998). Malto. Steever, S. A. (ed.), *The Dravidian languages*. London, N. Y.: Routledge. 357–87.

MANDA

Burrow, T. (1976). A sketch of Manda grammar in comparison with Pengo. Agesthialingom, S. & Subrahmanyam, P. S. (eds.), *Dravidian Linguistics V*. Annamalainagar: Annamalai University. 39–56.

Reddy, B. R. (1986). Syllable-based grammatical rules: A note on the Manda plural formation. Paper presented at the *National seminar on syllable in phonetics and phonology*. Hyderabad: Osmania University.

Reddy, K. N. & Reddy, B. R. (1986). Constraints on consonant combination in Manda. *Osmania Papers in Linguistics* **12**. 36–57.

NAIKI

Bhattacharya, S. (1961). Naiki of Chanda. *Indo-Iranian Journal* 5/2.85–117.

PAMPA BHARATA

Ramachandra Rao, B. (1972). *A descriptive grammar of Pampa Bharata*. Mysore: University of Mysore.

TAMIL

Aegasthialingam, S. (1977). *A grammar of Old Tamil with special reference to Patirrupattu*. Annamalainagar: Annamalai University.

Ananthanarayan, H. S. (1968). Sound changes in Sanketi: A Tamil dialect. Krishnamurti, Bh. (ed.), *Studies in Indian linguistics*. Annamalainagar: Annamalai University. 1–14.

Andronov, M. S. (1965). *The Tamil language*. Moscow: Nauka Publishing House.

Andronov, M. S. (1969). *A standard grammar of modern and classical Tamil*. Madras: New Century Book Pvt. Ltd.

Andronov, M. S. (1973). Observations of accent in Tamil. *International Journal of Dravidian Linguistics* **2.1**. 111–18.

Andronov, M. S. (1975). Observations on accent in Tamil. Schiffman, H. F. & Eastman, C. M. (eds.), *Dravidian phonological systems*. Seattle, Washington: Institute for Comparative and Foreign Area Studies. University of Washington. 3–10.

Annadurai, K. (1981). Consonants in Kalrayan Malayalis dialect: An observation. *Ayvukkovai* **13**. 35–40.

Annamalai, E. & Steever, S. B. (1998). Modern Tamil. In Steever, S. B. (ed.), *The Dravidian languages*. London, N. Y.: Routledge. 100–28.

Arasamuthu, C. (1974). Glides or intervocalic sounds in Tamil. *Ayvukkovai* **9.2**. 7–12.

Arokianathan, S. (1967). *Phonological grammar of the Pondicherry dialect of Tamil*. Annamalainagar: Annamalai University.

Arokianathan, S. (1974). Phoneme frequencies in Tamil. *Indian Linguistics* **35**.

Arunachalam, M. (1977). Echo-words in Tamil. Journal of Tamil Studies **11**. 1–10.

Asher, R. E. (1982). *Tamil*. Amsterdam: North-Holland (Lingua Descriptive Studies).

Asher, R. E. (1985). *Tamil*. London: Croom Helm (Croom Helm Descriptive Grammars). [Repr. of Asher 1982.]

Ashthamurthy, K. (2003). *The phonetics and phonology of primary prominence in Malayalam and Tamil: A typological investigation*. Ph. D. Dissertation. Hyderabad: CIEFL.

Balasubramanian, K. (1970). Tolka: Piyyars concept of phonology. Paper presented at the *Seminar on Tolka: Piyyar*. Annamalainagar: Annamalai University.

Balasubramanian, T. (1972). *The phonetics of Colloquial Tamil*. Ph. D. dissertation, Edinburgh, University of Edinburgh.

Balasubramanian, T. & Asher, R. E. (1984). Intervocalic plosives in Tamil. *University of Edinburg Occasional Papers in Linguistics and Language Learning* **9**. 49–63.

Bhoopathy, S. (1979). *A comparative phonemic study of Tamil and Bengali*. Ph.D. dissertation, Calcutta: Calcutta University.

Bloch, J. (1919). The intervocalic consonants in Tamil. *Indian Antiquary* **48**. 191–95.

Bright, W. O. (1962). Tamil Phonemics. *Mimeo*. Chicago.

Bright, W. O. (1972). The enunciative vowel. *International Journal of Dravidian Linguistics* **1.1**. 26–55.

Bhat, B. C. (1971). *The phonology and morphology of a Havyaka dialect of Tamil*. MA dissertation. Annamalainagar: Annamalai University.

Chandrasekhar, A. (1952–53). Tamil speech-sounds as described by Tolkappiyam and Nannul. *Bulletin of Deccan College* **14**. 221–28.

Chandrasekhar, A. (1955). The Tamil speech-sound aytam. *Transaction of the Linguistic Circle of Delhi*. 7–12.

Christdas, P. (1986–87). On containing the power of Lexical Phonology: Evidence from Tamil. *Proceedings of the 17th annual meeting of the Non-Eastern Linguistic Society*, **17.1**. Amherst. 122–46.

Christdas, P. (1988). *The phonology and morphology of Tamil*. Ph.D. dissertation, Ithacca: Cornell University.

Cingaram, K. (1968). The consonantal system of Tigala, a Tamil dialect. In Krishnamurti, Bh. (ed.), *Studies in Indian linguistics*. Annamalainagar: Annamalai University. 75–80

Emeneau, M. B. (1995). The palatalizing rule in Tamil-Malayalam and Telugu. *Journal of American Oriental Society* **115.3**. 401–9.

Emeneau, M. B. & Hart, K. (1993). Tamil expressives with initial voiced stops. *Bulletin of the School of Oriental and African Studies* **56**. 75–86.

Firth, J. R. (1934). Appendix to A. H. Arden. *A progressive grammar of common Tamil.* Madras: Christian Literature Society. (4th edn.)

Firth, J. R. (1934). A short outline of Tamil pronunciation. Arden, A. H. (ed.), *A progressive grammar of comman Tamil.* Madras: Christian Literature Society. 1–34.

Firth, J. R. (1957). *Papers in linguistics (1942–51).* London: OUP.

Fowler, M. (1954). The segmental phonemes of Sanskritized Tamil. *Language* **30**. 360–67.

Gair, J., Suseendirarajah, S. & Karunatilaka, W. (1978). *An introduction to spoken (Sri Lanka) Tamil.* Colombo: University of Sri Lanka.

Ganesan, M. (1984). Functional aspect of standard spoken Tamil. *Ayvukkovai* **16.2**. 60–64.

Ganesan, S. N. (1971). The phonological pattern of Tamil and homonymy due to loan words from Sanskrit. *Proceedings of the first All India Conference in Linguistics.* Poona: LSI. 152–57.

Ganesan, S. N. (1972). Mother-tongue interference at phonological level in the Hindi speech of Tamil and Malayalam speakers. *The third All India Conference in Linguistics.* Hyderabad.

Ganeshsundaram, P. C. (1959). *Distribution characteristics of speech elements in Tamil.* Poona: DC.

Gupta, B. R. (1975). *Contrastive phonology of Punjabi and Tamil.* Ph.D. dissertation. Patiala: Punjab University.

Gupta, B. R. (1990). *Indian linguistics: Punjabi-Tamil phonology.* New Delhi: Asian Publishing House.

Gupta, B. S. (1975). *Consonants of Hindi and Tamil.* Sapta Sindhu.

Hemalatha, N. (1986). Emphasis in Tamil. Paper presented at the *National seminar on syllable in phonetics and phonology.* Hyderabad: Osmania University.

Henderson, L. (1988). Interference in second language learning: The aquisition of English and Tamil phonemes by the native speakers of Tamil and English. *ITL International Journal of applied Linguistics* **81–82**. 73–111.

Jagannathan, V. R. (1964). A study of Tamil phonology. *Gaveshana.*

Jones, D. (1962). *The phoneme: Its nature and use*. Cambridge: CUP.

Karunakaran, K. (1986). Syllabification in Tamil: Spoken and written. *Ayvukkovai* **18.2**. 51–56.

Karunatilake, W. E. & Suseendirarajah, S. (1973). Phonology of Sinhalese and Sri Lanka Tamil: A study in contrast of interference. *Indian Linguistics* **34.3**. 180-90.

Keane, E. (2001). Echo words in Tamil. Ph.D. Dissertation. Merton College. Oxford.

Kempe G. K. (1976). Phonology of Sanketi dialect. *Proceedings of the third All India Conference in Dravidian Linguistics*. Dharwad. 184–213.

Kothandaraman, P. (1983). A note on the echo words in Tamil. *Journal of Asian Studies* **1.1**. 165–69.

Kothandaraman, R. (1992). Pre-junctional semi-vowels in Tamil. *Pondichery Institute of Language and Culture* **2**. 153–62.

Kumaraswami, R. N. (1973). Aytam and vowel length. *Ayvukkovai* **5**. 525–29.

Kumaraswami, R. N. (1980). Three consonantal clusters in Tamil. In Israel, M. (ed.), *A Festschrift for Prof M. Shanmugam Pillai*. Madurai: Madurai Kamaraj University. 1–10.

Lehman, T. (1998). Old Tamil. In Steever, S. A. (ed.), *The Dravidian languages*. London, N. Y.: Routledge. 75–99.

Lekomceva, M. I. (1964). The phonological system of the Tamil language from the point of view of synthesis. In Vjac, I. (ed.), *Voprosy Struktury Jazyka*. Moskva. 52–61.

Lisker, L. (1958). The Tamil occlusives: Short vs. long, or voiced vs. voiceless. *Indian Linguistics* **19**. 294–301.

Lisker, L. (1972). On stops and gemination in Tamil. *Proceedings of the first All India Conference in Dravidian Linguistics*. Trivendrum: DLA of India. 174–79.

Lisker, L. and Vaidyanathan, S. (1972). On nasals and nasalization in modern Tamil. *Journal of American Oriental Society* **92**. 96–100.

Mahadevan, I. (1971). Tamil- Brahmi inscriptions of the Sangam age. Asher, R. E. (ed.), *Proceedings of the Second International Conference-Seminar of Tamil Studies* **1**. Madras: International Association of Tamil Research. 73–106.

Mahadevan, I. (2003). *Early Tamil epigraphy. From the earliest times to the sixth century A. D.* Chennai: Cre-A and Cambridge: Department of Sanskrit and Indian Studies, Harvard University.

Marr, J. R. & Kothandaraman, P. (1973). Discussions on Brights enunciative vowel. *International Journal of Dravidian Linguistics* **2.1**. 47–63.

Meenakshisundaram, T. P. (1957). Nasal vowels in Tamil. *Indian Linguistics* **18**. 51–53.

Meenakshisundaram, T. P. (1964). The initial monosyllable in Tamil. *Indian Linguistics* **25**. 93–105.

Meenakshisundaram, T. P. (1965). *A history of the Tamil language*. Poona: Deccan College.

Murugaiyan, K. (1980). Tamil stops and their allophones. *Ayvukkovai* **12.2**. 385–90.

Murugarathanam, T. (1972–75). The phonetics of aytam in Tamil. *Proceedings of the second All India Conference in Dravidian Linguistics*. Trivendrum: DLA. 29–31.

Murugarathanam, T. (1973). *Tamil phonology today and yesterday*. Madras: Navalar Puttaka Nilayam.

Natanasabapathy, S. (1976). Phonology of Tamil and Kattunaicka: A contrastive study. *Ayvukkovai* **8.2**. 684–89.

Natanasabapathy, S. (1986). Intonation patterns in Tamil. In Rajapurohit, B. B. (ed.), *Acoustic studies in India*. Mysore: Central Institute of Indian Languages. 92–97.

Neethivanam, J. (1983). A study in the relationship between Tamil and Japanese: Intervocalic stops in the two languages. *International Journal of Dravidian Linguistics* **12.2**. 366–96.

Ohno, S. (1980). *Sound correspondences between Tamil and Japanese*. Tokyo: Gakshuin University.

Pillai, K. K. (1943). The palatal n in Tamil. *University of Colombo Review* **1.2**. 66–73.

Pillai, K. K. (1958). The Jaffna dialect of Tamil: A phonological study. *Indian Linguistics* **19**. 219–27.

Pillai, K. N. (1971). Some phonological changes in Ceylon Tamil dialect. *First All India Conference in Dravidian Linguistics*. Trivendrum.

Pillai, M. S. (1965). Merger of literary and colloquial Tamil. *Anthropological Linguistics* **7.4**. 98–103.

Pillai, M. S. (1968). Fishermen Tamil of Kanyakumari. *Anthropological Linguistics* **10.4**. 1–10.

Radhakrishnan, R. (1968–69). Aytam: Its origin and nature. *Proceedings of the first international conference seminar of Tamil studies*. KualaLampur: University of Malaya. 623–28.

Radhakrishnan, S. (1971). *Contrastive analysis of the phonological systems of Kannada and Tamil spoken at Trivendrum.* MA dissertation. Trivendrum: University of Kerala.

Ramakrishnan, S., Balasubramanian, G. & Nallaswamy, A. (1986). Intervocalic /ṭ, t c/ in Tamil. Rajapurohit. B. B. (ed.), *Acoustic studies in India.* Mysore: Central Institute of Indian Languages. 32–38.

Ramanujam, A. K. and Masica, C. P. (1969). Towards a phonological typology of the Indian linguistic area. Sebeok, T. (ed.), *Current Trends in Linguistics*, vol. 5. The Hague: Mouton. 543–77.

Ranganathan, D. (1981). Vowel sandhi in Tamil. *Ayvukkovai* **13.2**. 316–18.

Ranganathan, V. (1997). A lexical phonology approach to processing Tamil words by computer. *International Journal of Dravidian Linguistics* **26.1**. 57–70.

Sankaran, C. R. (1941). The positional variaty of the phoneme aytam in old Tamil. *Bulletin of Deccan College Post Graduate Research Institute* **3**. 392–94.

Sankaran, C. R. (1961). On aytam. *Tamil Culture* **9.1**. 27–32.

Sankaran, C. R. (1961). Tolkappiyan and the science of phonemics. *Tamil Culture* **9.2**. 117–130.

Sanmugadas, A. (1972). *The phonology of verbal forms in Colloquial Ceylon Tamil.* Ph.D. dissertation, Edinburgh: University of Edinburgh.

Schiffman, H. F. (1999). *A reference grammar of spoken Tamil.* Cambridge: CUP.

Schiffman, H. F. (1968–69). Morphophonemics of Tamil numerals. *Proceedings of the first international conference-seminar of Tamil studies.* Kuala Lumpur: University of Malaya.

Shanmugam, R. (1968). *Madras Tamil phonology*. Ph.D. dissertation. Ithacca: Cornell University.

Shanmugam, S. V. (1971). Some problems in old Tamil phonology. *Indo-Iranian Journal* **13.1**. 31–43.

Steever, S. B. (1990). Tamil and the Dravidian languages. In Comrie, B. (ed.), *The worlds major languages*. OUP.

Subbiah, A. (1965). Voiced and voiceless stops in Tamil. *Tamil Culture* **5.2**. 186–195.

Subbiah, A. (1971). Consonant clusters and word initials and finals in Tamil. *Proceedings of the second international conference-seminar of Tamil studies.* Madras: International Association of Tamil Research. 362–67.

Subbiah, A. (1976). The phonological stability of standard Tamil and its lessons for linguistics. *Twenty ninth international congress of orientalists.* Paris: LAsiatheque. 156–62.

Suseendirarajah, S. (1973). Phonology of Sri Lanka Tamil and Indian Tamil contrasted. *Indian Linguistics* **34.3**. 171–79.

Thananjaya, R. S. (1972). *The phonology of nominal forms in Jaffna Tamil*. Ph.D. dissertation. Edinburgh: University of Edinburgh.

Thananjaya, R. S. (1975). Aspiration in Jaffna Tamil. *Linguistics* **149**. 59–63.

Thananjaya, R. S. (1975). Nasalization in Jaffna Tamil. *Linguistics* **149**. 65–73.

Ucida, N. (1988). Pronunciation of /l/ and /n/ in colloquial Tamil. *Journal of Asian and African Studies* **36**. 27–42.

Vacek, J. (1971). Tamil phonological structure: A case for discussion. *OP* **8**. 65–72.

Vacek, J. (1978). The palatal nasal in Tamil. *International Journal of Dravidian Linguistics* **7.2**. 223–38.

Vacek, J. (1979). Some problems of Tamil phonological structure. *Acta Universitatis Carolinae-Philologica* **6**. 87–103.

Vaidyanathan, S. (1983). Syllabic structures of Punjabi and Tamil. *Ayvukkovai* **15.2**. 351–53.

Vaidyanathan, S. (1988). Punjabi and Modern Tamil: A comparison (phonology). *Ayvukkovai* **20.2**. 337–41.

Vasanthakumari, T. (1982). Distinctive features of Tamil phonology. *Ayvukkovai* **14.2**. 301-06.

Vasanthakumari, T. (1989). *Generative phonology of Tamil*. Delhi: Mittal Publications.

Vijayakrishnan, K. G. (1977). *Word stress in Tamil*. M. Litt. Dissertation, Hyderabad: CIEFL.

Vijayakrishnan, K. G. (1981). The syllable in phonological theory: Arguments from Tamil. *Studies in Linguistic Sciences* **11.2**. 101-04.

Vijayakrishnan, K. G. (1982). *The Tamil syllable*. Ph.D. dissertation, Hyderabad: CIEFL.

Vijaykrishnan, K. G. (1984). Morpheme structure constraints on vowels and the prosodic foot in Tamil. *CIE&FL Working Papers in Linguistics* **1.1**.

Vijayakrishnan, K. G. (1987). Hierarchical representation of phonological features. *Berkeley linguistic society: Proceedings of the thirteenth annual meeting*. Berkeley: BLS. 310–20.

Vijayakrishnan, K. G. (1991). The eurythmic criterion in resyllabification. Amritavalli, R (ed.), *A carnival for the grammarian*. Madras: Macmillan India Ltd. 213–55.

Vijayakrishnan, K. G. (1992). Terror types in Tamil of the Konological Phind. Balasubramanian, T. & Prakasham, V. (eds.), *Sound patterns for the phonetician*. Madras: T. R. Publications. 243–82.

Williams, T. E. (1978). Consonant clusters in Tamil. *Ayvukkovai* **8.2**. 543–48.

Zvelebil, K. V. (1963). The vowels of colloquial Tamil. *AO* **31**. 225–29.

TELUGU

Anantham, S. (1959). *A study of the pronunciation problem involved in the teaching of English to Telugu speakers*. Ph.D. dissertation. Michigan: University of Michigan.

Aneja, M. P. & Raju, D. R. R. (1981). Phonemic correspondences in the cognates of Hindi and Telugu. *Bulletin of Deccan College Research Institute* **40**.

Appa Rao, M. (1978). *Orthography as underlying representation: A Study Of R.P. and Telugu English within the framework of generative phonology*. Research Diploma. Hyderabad: CIEFL.

Bhaskararao, P. (1976). The preconsonantal nasal in Telugu. *Working Papers in Linguistics*. Pune: DC.

Bhaskararao, P. (1977). *Reduplication and Onomatopoeia in Telugu*. Poona: DCPRI.

Bhaskararao, P. (1982). *A re-examination of consonantal Sandhi in modern colloquial Telugu*. *Bulletin of Deccan College Research Institute* **41**.16–26.

Brahmananda, H. S. (1989). On the source of nasal in Telugu. *Proceedings of the first international seminar on Dravidian linguistics & the 14th All India Conference in Dravidian Linguistics*. 200-05.

Chilukuri, B. (1998). *Hypocoristic formation in Telugu*. Ms. Hyderabad: CIEFL.

Datta, A. K., Ganguli, N. R. & Majumder, D. (1981). Acoustic features of consonants: A study based on Telugu speech sounds. *Acoustica* **47.2**. 72–82.

Ellis, F. W. (1816). Note to the Introduction of A. D. Campbells *A grammar of the Teloogoo language*. Madras. 154–55. [Repr. with an editorial note by Venkata Rao, N. in *Annals of oriental research of the University of Madras* **12**. 1–35. Madras: University of Madras.]

Frances, S. (1957). *The phonology of Telugu dialect*. Ph.D. dissertation. Texas: University of Texas.

Ganeshasundaram, P. C. (1956). *Duration and distribution phenomena of speech elements in Dravidian Tamil and Telugu*. Ph.D. dissertation. Poona: UP.

Jagannath (1981). *Telugu loan word phonology*. Ph.D. dissertation. University of Arizona.

Karunatilake, W. S. (1974). A phonological sketch of gypsy Telugu. *Anthropological Linguistics* **16.8**. 420–24.

Kelley, G. (1959). Telugu vowel phonemes. *Indian Linguistics* **20**. 146–58.

Kelley, G. (1963). Vowel phonemes and external vocalic sandhi in Telugu. *Journal of American Oriental Society* **83**. 67–73.

Krishnamurthy, G. V. S. R. (1976). Initial consonant dropping in Telugu. *Proceedings of the third All India Conference in Dravidian Linguistics*. Dharwad: Karnatak University. 103–19.

Krishnamurti, Bh. (1961). *Telugu Verbal bases*. Bereley: University of California Press.

Kumar, K. R. (2003). The Pronunciation of /th/ in Telugu: A quantitative Analysis. In Reddy, K. N. (ed.), *Osmania Papers in Linguistics* Vol. **29**. Department of Linguistics. Hyderabad: Osmania University. 79–92.

Kumaraswami Raja, N. (1969). Post-nasal voiceless plosives in Telugu: A comparative study. Agesthelingam, S. & Raja, N. K. (eds.), *Dravidian linguistics*. Annamalainagar: Annamalai University. 75–84.

Ladefoged, P. & Bhaskararao, P. (1983). Non-quantal aspects of consonant production: A study of retroflex consonants. *Journal of Phonetics* **11.3**. 291–302.

Lakshmiranjanam, K. (1963). Telugu nasals. *Indian Linguistics* **24**. 81–86.

Lisker, L. & Krishnamurti, Bh. (1991). Lexical stress in a stressless language: Judgements by Telugu- and English- speaking linguists. *Proceedings of the XII International Congress of Phonetic Sciences* (Universite de Provence) **2**. 90–3.

Lisker, L. (1963). *Introduction to spoken Telugu*. New York: ACLS.

Mahadeva Sastri, K. (1969). *Historical grammar of Telugu, with special reference to old Telugu, 200 BC- 1000 Ad*. Aanantapur: Sri Venkateswara University Post-Graduate Centre.

Majumder, D. (1976). Computer recognition of Telugu vowel sounds. *Journal of the Computer Society of India* **7.1**. 14–20.

Majumder, D., Datta, A. K. & Ganguli, N. R. (1978). Some studies on acoustic phonetic features of Telugu vowels. *Acoustica* **41.2**. 55–64.

Prabhakar Rao, J. (1992). Status of aspirated sounds and direction of evolution in the reconstructions of Telugu sound system. *International Journal of Dravidian Linguistics* **21.1**. 60–67.

Prakasam, V. (1991). Length as a formative prosody in Telugu. Prakasam, V. & Parasher, S. (eds.), *Linguistics at large: Papers in general and applied linguistics*. Hyderabad: Booklinks Corporation.

Prakasam, V. (1972). *A systematic treatment of certain aspects of Telugu phonology*. Ph.D. dissertation. York: University of York.

Prakasham, V. (1976). Functional view of phonological features. *Acta Linguistica Academiae Scientiarum Hungaricae* **26**.1–2. 77–88.

Prakasham, V. (1979). Aspects of sentence phonology. *Archivum Linguisticum* **10.1**. 57–82.

Prakasham, V. (1981). Non segmentals. Sunkapur, M. S. & Kulli, J. S. (eds.), *Papers in linguistics*. Mysore: Sharat Prakashana. 32–44.

Rama Rao, C. (1975). Dravidian evidence for abstract phonology. *Osmania Papers in Linguistics* **1**. 30–44.

Rama Rao, C. (1976). Vowel harmony in Telugu. *Papers in Linguistic Analysis* **1.1**. Delhi: University of Delhi. 25–36.

Ramadas, A. (1988). *Phonological systems of Russian and Telugu: A contrastive study*. Ph.D. dissertation. Hyderabad: CIEFL.

Ramanarasimhan, P. (1998). Old Telugu. In Steever, S. A. (ed.), *The Dravidian languages*. London, N. Y.: Routledge. 181–201

Rao, C. R. (1987). *A generative approach to Telugu phonology*. M.Phil. dissertation. Hyderabad: Osmania University.

Rao, G. U. M. (1996). A nonlinear analysis of syllable structure and vowel harmony in Telugu. *PILC Journal of Dravidian studies* **6.1**. 55–84.

Reddy, K. N. (1979). Problems of syllable division in Telugu. *Work in progress* **11**. Edinburgh: Edinburgh University. 135–40.

Reddy, K. N. (1980). Consonant combination in Telugu. *Work in progress* **12**. Edinburgh: Edinburgh University. 79–99.

Reddy, K. N. (1987). Syllable and word structure in Telugu. In Sivaramamurty, N. (ed.), *Studies in Telugu linguistics*. Hyderabad: Telugu University. 52–70.

Reddy, K. N. (1988). An acoustic-linguistic evidence for the distinction and syllabification of aspirated consonants. Paper presented at the *International workshop on speech and signal processing*. Bombay: TIFR.

Reddy, K. N. (1993a). A comparative analysis of consonant sequences in Russian and Telugu. *Paper presented at 21st All India Conference in Dravidian Linguistics*. Kuppam.

Reddy, K. N. (1993b). Lengthening of consonants in sequences: Evidence for syllable division in Telugu. *Paper presented at 21st All India Conference in Dravidian Linguistics*. Kuppam.

Reddy, K. N. (1998) *Phonetic constraints on word and syllable structure in Telugu*. Ms. Hyderabad: Osmania University.

Reddy, K. N. (2005). Pronouncing Dictionary for Telugu. In Ansari, M. (ed.), *Osmania Papers in Linguistics* Vol. **31**. 50–63. [Department of Linguistics. Hyderabad: Osmania University]..

Reddy, K. N. (forthcoming) *An outline of Telugu segmental phonology*.

Reddy, K. N. (2000). Linguistic functions of length beyond word level in Telugu. *International Journal of Dravidian Linguistics* **29**. 81–90.

Reddy, K. N. (2003). The phonological structure of word in Telugu. In Reddy, B. R. (ed.), *Word structure in Dravidian*. Kuppam: Dravidian University. 140-163.

Sailaja, P. (1985). *Some aspect of the vowel phonology of Telugu and Telugu-English*. M.Litt. dissertation. Hyderabad: CIEFL.

Sailaja, P. (1990). *Phonological and syntactic criteria in word formation: A study of Telugu English*. Ph.D. dissertation. Hyderabad: CIEFL.

Sailaja, P. (1994). Tier conflation and bracket erasure: The case of Telugu. Davison, A. & Smith, F. M. (eds.), *Papers from the 15th South Asian language analysis round table conference*. Iowa City: University of Iowa.

Sailaja, P. (1995). *Issues in lexical phonology*. Hyderabad: Booklinks Corporation.

Sailaja, P. & Sarma, S. J. (1976). Vowel-consonant patterns in Telugu. *Indian Linguistics* **37**. 3–4. 210–12.

Sastry, J. V. (1972). *Telugu phonetic reader*. Mysore: Central Institute of Indian Languages.

Sastry, J. V. (1986). Stress and syllable. Paper presented at the *National seminar on syllable in phonetics and phonology*. Hyderabad: Osmania University.

Shriharirao, J. (1971). A note on stress in Telugu. *Papers in Linguistics* **1.1**. 49–55.

Sjoberg, A. F. (1957). *The phonology of a Telugu dialect*. Ph.D. dissertation. Austin: University of Texas.

Sjoberg, A. F. (1962). Coexistent phonemic systems in Telugu: A socio-cultural perspective. *Word*. 269–79.

Sreekanth, S. & Murthy, K. N. (2005). Text Dependent Speaker Recognition System for Telugu. In Ansari, M. (ed.), *Osmania Papers in Linguistics* Vol. **31**. 84–99. [Department of Linguistics. Hyderabad: Osmania University.]

Subbarao, K. V. (1971). Vowel harmony in Telugu and parenthesis and infinite rule schemata notations. *Papers from the 7th Regional Meeting. Chicago Linguistic Society*. 543–52.

Subrahmanyam, P. S. (1970). Long vowels before /yO in Telugu bases. *Indian Linguistics* **31.3**. 1–15.

Subrahmanyam, P. S. (1974). *An introduction to modern Telugu*. Annamalainagar: Annamalai University.

Subrahmanyam, P. S. (1981). i/e and u/o alternation in South Dravidian and Telugu. In Sunkapur, M. S. & Kulli, J. S. (eds.), *Papers in linguistics*. Mysore: Sharat Prakashana. 302–18.

Vasanta, D. & Dodd, B. (2007). Perceptual Factors in phonological disorders: A tool for assessing input phonological processing in Telugu-English bilinguals. *Osmania Papers in Linguistics* **33**. 55–72.

Wilkinson, R. W. (1974). A phonetic constraint on a syncope rule in Telugu. *Language* **50.3**. 478–97.

TODA

Emeneau, M. B. (1938). Echowords in Toda. *New Indian Antiquary* **1**. 109–17. [Repr. in Emeneau 1967b: 37–45.]

Emeneau, M. B. (1979). Toda vowels in non-initial syllables. *Bulletin of the School of Oriental and African Studies* **42**. 225–34. [Repr. in Emeneau 1994: 275–86.]

Nara, T. & Bhaskararao, P. (eds.) (2002). *Toda texts*. (Endangered languages of the Pacific Rim Series. A3- 005). Osaka.

Sakthivel, S. (1977). *A grammar of Toda language*. Annamalainagar: Annamalai University.

Sinisa, S., Ladefoged, P. & Bhaskararao, P. (1996). The trills of Toda. *Journal of International Phonetic Association* **26.1**. 1–21.

TULU

Bhat, D. N. S. (1967). *Descriptive analysis of Tulu*. Pune: DCPGRI.

Bhat, D. N. S. (1998). Tulu. Steever, S. B. (ed.), *The Dravidian languages*. London and New York: Routledge. 158–77.

Bhatt, S. L. (2005). *A grammar of Tulu*. Thiruvananthapuram: DLA Publications.

Brigel, J. (1872). *A grammar of the Tulu language*. Mangalore: Basel Mission Press and Tract Depository.

Jalayakshi, K. V. (1980). *Tulu language (descriptive and comparative Study)*. Ph. D. dissertation. Annamalainagar: Annamalai University.

Shetty, R. T. (2001). *A comprehensive grammar of Tulu*. Annamalainagar: Annamalai University.

YERAVA

Mallikarjun, B. (1998). *A descriptive analysis of Yerava*. Mysore: Central Institute of Indian Languages.

C. 3 INDO-ARYAN

ANGIKA

Pandey, P. (1979)[1]. *pratham angikā-vyākaraN*. [in Hindi, *A First Grammar of Angika*]. Patna: Paramashram

ASSAMESE

Basanti, D. (1986). Vowel length in Assamese. Rajapurohit, B. B. (ed.), 1–6.

Bharali, D. (1959). *A study of phonology and vocabulary of the Assamese language*. Jorhat.

Goswami, G. C. & Tamuli, J. (2003). Assamiya. Cardona, G. & Jain, D. (eds.), *The Indo-Aryan Languages*. London, New York: Routledge (Routledge Language Family Series). 391–443.

Goswami, G. C. (1966). *An introduction to Assamese phonology*. Poona: DC.

Goswami, U. (1957–58). OIA sibilants in Kamrupi. *Bulletin of Deccan College* **18**. Poona: DC. 309–12.

Goswami, U. (1970). *A study on Kamrupi: A dialect of Assamese*. Gauhati: Department of Historical and Antiquarian Studies, Assam.

Mahanta, S. (2002). *Some aspects of prominence in Assamese and Assamese English*. M. Phil. Dissertation. Hyderabad: CIEFL.

Mahanta, S. (2005). Morpheme realization and direction of vowel harmony. Paper presented at *5th Asian GLOW*, 5–8 October 2005. New Delhi: JNU.

Moral, D. (1992) *Phonology of Asamiya dialects: Contemporary standard and Mayong*. Ph. D. dissertation. Poona: DCPRI.

Thakur, N. N. (1980). *Elements of non Indo-Aryan languages in the formation of Assamese language*. Ph.D. dissertation, New Delhi: JNU.

AWADHI

Saksena, B. (1971, [1937]) *Evolution of Awadhi*, 2nd edn. Delhi: Motilal Banarsidass.

[1] The full form of the author's initial is Paramananda.

BAGHELI

Gordon, R. G. Jr. (ed.) (2005). *Bagheli: A language of India*, SIL International.

Pathak, R. S. (1980). *The phonetics of Bagheli: A phonetic and phonological study of a dialect of Hindi.* Delhi: National Publishing House.

Pathak, R. S. (1977). The intonation of Bagheli. *Indian Linguistics* **38.4.** 197–209.

Shukla, H. L. (1969). *Contrastive distribution of Bagheli phonemics*. Raipur: Alok Prakshan.

BAGRI 2

Gusain, L. (1999). *A Descriptive Grammar of Bagri*. Ph.D. dissertation. New Delhi: Jawaharlal Nehru University

Gusain, L. (2000). *Bagri.* München: Lincom Europa. [Languages of the World/Materials, 384]

BAJJIKA

Arun, A. (1972). *bajjikā, hindī aur bhojapurī: tulnātmak adhyayan,* [in Hindi, *A Comparative Study of Bhajjika, Bhojpuri and Hindi*], Muzaffarpur: Kumud Prakashan.

Tivari, S. (1964). *bajjikā bhāshā aur sāhitya* [in Hindi, *Language and Literature of Bajjika*] Patna: Bihar. Rashtrabhasha parishad.

BANGANI

Abbi, A. (1997). Debate on archaism of some select Bangani word. *Indian Linguistics* **58.** 1–4. 1–15.

Van Driem, G. & Sharma, S. R. (1997). Some grammatical observations on Bangani. *Indogermanische Forschungen* **102.** 179–98.

Zoller, C. P. (1988). Bericht uber besondere Archaismen im Bangani, einer Western Pahari-Sprache, *Munchener Studien zur Sprachwissenschaft* **49.** 173–200.

Zoller, C. P. (1989). Bericht uber grammatische Archaismen im Bangani. *Munchener Studien zur Sprachwissenschaft* **50.** 159–218.

Zoller, C. P. (1993). A note on Bangani. *Indian Linguistics* **54.** 112–14.

Zoller, C. P. (1997). The van Driem enigma or: In search of instant facts. Bangani web page 4 Mar 1997 15:34:06 +0100 (CET).

[2] Works on other related varieties are listed under 'Rajasthani'. Bagri has been separately listed here for convenience of reference.

BENGALI

Anderson, J. D. (1917). The phonetics of the Bengali language. *Bulletin of the School of Oriental and African Studies* **1**. 79–84.

Ashraf, S. A. & Ashraf, A. (1966). Bengali diphthongs. *Pakistani Linguistics*. Shahidullah Presentation volume. Lahore.

Barman, S. N. (1986). Vowel quality in Bengali. Rajapurohit, B. B. (ed.), (1986). *Acoustic studies in India*. Mysore: Central Institute of Indian Languages. 12–19.

Basu-Ghosh, S. (1986). A spectrographic study of Bengali vowels. Rajapurohit, B. B. (ed.), (1986). *Acoustic studies in India*. Mysore: Central Institute of Indian Languages. 7–11.

Bhattacharja, S. (2008). Bengali phonology in light of generative phonotactics. *Indian Linguistics* **69**.1–4. 51–72.

Bhattacharya, K. (1984). Problems relating to some phonetic segments in Bengali. Rajapurohit, B. B. (ed), (1984). *Papers in phonetics and phonology*. Mysore: Central Institute of Indian Languages. 85–94.

Bhattacharya, T. (2000). Bangla (Bengali). In Jane Garry, J. & Rubino, C. et al. (eds.), *Encyclopedia of World's Languages: Past and Present*. [Facts About the World's Languages] New York: W.W. Wilson.

Chatterji, S. K. (1964). Glottal spirants and the glottal stops in the aspirates in New Indo-Aryan. In Abercombie, D. (ed.), *In honour of Daniel Jones*. London: Longmans. 407–14.

Chatterji, S. K.(1921). Bengali phonetics. *Bulletin of the School of Oriental and African Studies* **2**.**1**. 1–25.

Chatterji, S. K. (1926). *The origin and development of the Bengali language* (2 vols.). Calcutta: Calcutta University Press (Reprinted (1970) (3 vols.), London: Allen and Unwin, (1975), (3 vols.), Calcutta: Rupa and Co.).

Chaudhuri, S. C. (1939). Notes on the Rangpur dialect. *Indian Linguistics* 7. 297–315.

Chaudhuri, S. C. (1940–4). North Bengal dialects: Rajshahi. *Indian Linguistics* **8**. 418–31.

Ferguson, C. A. (1969). Bibliographic review of Bengali studies. In Sebeok, T. A. (ed.), *Current Trends in Linguistics, vol. 5: Linguistics in South Asia*. The Hague: Mouton. 85–98.

Das, R. P. (1985). Bengali and Dravidian stress. *Beitrage zur Phonetic und Linguistic* **50**. 95–99.

Dasgupta, P. (1982). Phonology and the Bangla verb. *Indian Linguistics* **43**.1–2. 17–28.

Dasgupta, P. (1985). On Bangla nouns. *Indian Linguistics* **46**.1–2. 37–65.

Dasgupta, P. (2001). On a vowel template asymmetry in Bangla verbs. In Abbi, A. (ed.), *Linguistic structure and language dynamics in South Asia*. New Delhi: Motilal Banarasidas Publishers. 164–84.

Dasgupta, P. (2003). Bangla. In Cardona, G. & Jain, D. (eds.), *The Indo-Aryan Languages*. London, New York: Routledge (Routledge Language Family Series). 351–90.

Dimock, E. C. (1957). Notes on stem-vowel alternation in the Bengali verb. *Indian Linguistics* **17**. 173–177.

Ferguson, C. & Chowdhury, M. (1960). The phonemes of Bengali. *Language* **36**. 22–59.

Ferguson, C. A. (1945). *The phonology and morphology of standard colloquial Bengali*. Ph.D. dissertation. Philadelphia: University of Pennsylvania.

Fowler, M. (1962). Review of "Nasalization in Bengali", Hai, M. A. *Language* **38**. 457–60.

Ghosh, A. (2002). Distribution of Bengali vowels. *International Journal of Dravidian Linguistics* **31.1**. 45–70.

Ghosh, T. (1996). *Bangla phonology*. M. Phil. dissertation. Hyderabad: CIEFL.

Ghosh, T. (2001). Vowel harmony in Bangla: An optimality account. In Abbi, A. et al. (eds.), *Linguistic structure and language dynamics in South Asia*. New Delhi: Motilal Banarasidas Publishers. 164–84.

Goswami, K. (1939). Linguistic notes on Maimansing dialect. *Indian Linguistics* 7. 247–55.

Goswami, K. (1940–4). Linguistic notes on Chittagong Bengali. *Indian Linguistics* 8. 493–536.

Goswami, K. (1961). Sibilants and glottal fricative h in North-East Bengal Dialects. *Bulletin of the Philological Society of Calcutta*. **2**. 108-09.

Hai, M. A. & Ball, W. J. L. (1961). The sound structure of English and Bengali. Dacca.

Hai, M. A. (1958). Aspiration in standard Bengali. *Indian Linguistics* [Turner volume]. 142–48.

Hai, M. A. (1960). *A phonetic and phonological study of nasals and nasalization in Bengali (based on observers own pronunciation)*. Dacca: University of Dacca.

Hayes, B. & Lahiri, A. (1991). Bengali international phonology. *Natural Language and Linguistic Theory* **9**. 5–96.

Islam, A. K. M. (1963). Some prosodic characteristics of interword relations in Bengali. *Pakistani linguistics*. 45–64.

Klaiman, M. H. (1987). Bengali. Comrie, B. (ed.), *The worlds major languages*. London/Sydney: Croom Helm. 490–513.

Lahiri, A. & Fitzpatric-Cole, J. (1999). Emphatic clitics and focus intonation in Bengali. Kager, R. & Zonneveld, W. (eds.), *Phrasal phonology*. Nijmegen: Unversity of Nijmegen Press. 119–44.

Mallik, B. P. (1960). Phonemic analysis of the consonant clusters in standard colloquial Bengali. *Bulletin of the Philological Society of Calcutta* **1.2**. 37–46.

Mallik, B. P. (1963). Phonology of the underword language. *Bulletin of the Philological Society of Calcutta* **4.2**. 77–83.

Mohiyud-Din, M. (1966). General characteristics of the intonation of Bengali. *Pakistani linguistics*. Shahidullah presentation volume. 25–36.

Mukherji, T. (1963). *The old Bengali language and text*. Calcutta: UC.

Pal, A. K. (1966a). Phonemes of a Dacca dialect and the importance of tone. *Journal of the Asiatic Society of Bengal* 7. 1–2.

Pal, A. (1966). Phonemes of a Dacca dialect and the importance of tone. *Journal of the Asiatic Society of Bengal.*

Quazi Din, M. (1961). *The phonology of the verbal piece in colloquial Bengali*. Ph.D. dissertation. London: University of London.

Ray, P. S. (1966). *Bengali language handbook*. Washington D.C.: Centre for Applied Linguistics.

Ray, P. S., Ray, L., & Hai, M. A. (1966a). *Bengali language handbook*. Washington, D. C.: Center for Applied Linguistics.

Ray, Punya Sloka, Roushan, Jahan and Muzaffer Ahmad (1966b). *Introduction to the Dacca dialect of Bengali*. (Mimeo). University of Chicago, Committee on Southern Asian Studies [available in University of Chicago Library].

Sarkar, P. (1976). The Bengali verb. *International Journal of Dravidian Linguistics* 5. 274–97.

Sarkar, P. (1986). Aspects of Bengali syllable. Paper presented at the *National seminar on syllable in phonetics and phonology*. Hyderabad: Osmania University.

Sen, A. K. (1936). An experimental study of Bengali occlusion. Jones, W. E. & Fry, D. (eds).

Sen, N. (1972). Some dialects of Bangla Desh: An outline. *Indian Linguistics* **33.2**. 143–52.

Sen, S. (1956–7). Syncopated aspiration in Middle Bengali. *Indian Linguistics* **17b**. 19–20.

Sen, S. (1957). Syncopated aspiration in Middle Bengali. *Indian Linguistics* **18**. 19–20.

Sengupta, G. (1980). Nasal aspirates in Bangla. *Indian Linguistics* **41**. 3–4. 125–28.

Shahidullah, M. (1929–63). *The sounds of Bengali studied with artificial palate*. Ph.D. dissertation. Unpublished paper translated into English and revised by Novak, R., 1963. Sorbonne, Paris: Archive de la Parole.

Shaw, R. (1984). Stress patterns in Bengali and Hindi: A comparative study. Rajapurohit, B. B. (ed.), (1984). *Papers in phonetics and phonology*. Mysore: Central Institute of Indian Languages. 95–110.

Singh, U. N. (1980). Comments on rule ordering in Bengali morphology. *Indian Linguistics* **41.2**. 91–101.

Singh, U. N. (1986). *Bibliography of Bengali linguistics*. Mysore: Central Institute of Indian Languages.

Tunga. S. S. (1995). *Bengali and other related dialects of South Assam*. New Delhi: Mittal Publications.

Ucida, N. (1970.) *Der Bengali-Dialekt von Chittagong*. Wiesbaden: Otto Harrassowitz.

BHALESI

Varma, S. (1948). *The Bhalesi dialect*. Calcutta: Royal Asiatic Society.

BHILI

Jain, N. (1971). *Bhili ka Bhashashastriya Adhyayan*. (in Hindi, A linguistic Study of Bhili) Indore: Indore University.

Kloss, H. & McConnell, G. D. (1989). *Bhili*. 651–668.

Kulkarni, S. B. (1976). *Bhili of Dangs*. Poona: DC.

Srivastava, G. P. (1968). Bahelia phonology. *Indian Linguistics* **29.1**. 67–79.

BHOJPURI

Shukla, S. (1981). *Bhojpuri grammar*. Washington, D. C.: Georgetown University Press.

Singh, K. S. (1973). Bhojpuri morphophonology. *Indian Linguistics* **34**. 163–66.

Tiwari, U. N. (1960). *The origin and development of Bhojpuri*. Calcutta: The Asiatic Society.

Verma, M. K. (2003). Bhojpuri. Cardona, G. & Jain, D. (eds.), *The Indo-Aryan Languages*. London, New York: Routledge (Routledge Language Family Series). 515–37.

BROKSTAT

Kloss, H. & McConnell, G. D. (1989). *Tripuri*. In Kloss, H. & McConnell (eds.), 1313–1332.

Karapurkar, P. (1972). *Tripuri phonetic reader*. Mysore: Central Institute of Indian Languages.

Ramaswami, N. (1982). *Brokstat grammar*. Mysore: Central Institute of Indian Languages.

BUNDELI

Jaiswal, M. P. (1962). *A linguistic study of Bundeli*. Leiden: E. J. Brill.

CHHATTISGARHI

Telang, B. (1966). *Chattīsgarhī, Halbī, bhāratīya boliyon kā bhāśvaigyānik adhyayan* [in Hindi, *A Linguistic Study of the Indian Dialects Chattisgarhi and Halbi*]. Bombay: Hindi Granth Ratnakar.

CHAKMA

Bardhan, S. K. (2008). Vowels of Chakma. *Indian Linguistics* **69**.1–4: 29–41.

Bardhan, S. K. (1999*) A phonological study of Chakma and English*. Ph. D. dissertation. Hyderabad: CIEFL.

Krishan, S. (2001). Sketch of Darma grammar. Nagano, Y. & Lapolla, R. (eds.), *New research on Zhangzhung and related Himalayan languages*. Osaka: National Museum of Ethnology ([Bon Studies 3, Senri Ethnological Reports No. 19). 347–400.

DARDIC

Edelman, D. I. (1983). *The Dardic and Nuristani languages*. Moscow: Nauka.

Grierson, G. A. (1931). Conjunct consonants in Dardic. *Bulletin of the School of Oriental Studies* **6.2**. 349–68.

Morgenstierne, G. (1947). Metathesis of liquids in Dardic. *Det Norske Videnskapsakademi i Oslo, Skrifter* **2**. 145–54 (repr. 1973 in *Irano-Dardica*: 231–40)

Schmidt, R. L. (1981). Report on a survey of Dardic languages of Kashmir. *Indian Linguistics* **42**. 17–21.

Schmidt, R. L. & Koul, O. N. (1983). *Kohistani to Kashmiri: An annotated bibliography of Dardic languages*. Patiala: IILS.

Turner, R. L. (1927). Notes on Dardic. *Bulletin of the School of Oriental Studies* **4.3**. 533–41 (repr. 1975 in *Collected Papers*. 301–9)

DOGRI

Bahri, U. S. (1969). Phonology of Dogri. *Pakha Sanjam (Patiala)* **1**. 75–107.

Ghai, V. K. (1991). *Studies in phonetics and phonology*. New Delhi: Ariana Publishing House.

Kaur, U. (1986). Features of Dogri Tones. Rajapurohit, B. B. (ed.), (1986). *Acoustic studies in Indian languages*. Mysore: Central Institute of Indian Languages. 99–104.

Shankar, G. (1931). A short account of the Dogri dialect. *Indian Linguistics* **1**. 93–176.

Shankar, G. (1969). Dogri prose in its making. *Indian Linguistics* **30**. 77–80.

GARHWALI

Chandrashekhar, A. (1970). The phonemes of Garhwali. *Indian Linguistics* **31.3**. 80–5.

Bhatt, R. P. (1941). *Comparative Rameshwari Garhwali grammar*. Lahore.

GUJARATI

Adenwala, M. (1965). *The structural analysis of the phonology and morphemics of Gujarati*. Ph. D. dissertation. Buffalo: State University of New York.

Cardona, G. (1965). *A Gujarati reference grammar*. Philadelphia: University of Pennsylvania Press.

Cardona, G. & Suthar, B. (2003). Gujarati. In Cardona, G. & Jain, D. (eds.), *The Indo-Aryan Languages*. London, New York: Routledge (Routledge Language Family Series). 659–97.

Dave, R. V. (1967). A formant analysis of the clear, nasalised and murmured vowels in Gujarati. *Indian Linguistics* **28.2**. 1–30.

Dave, R. V. (1977a). Retroflex and dental consonants in Gujarati: A palatographic and acoustic study. *Annual report of the Institute of Phonetics* **11**. 27–156. [University of Copanhegan]

Dave, R. V. (1977b). *Studies in Gujarati phonology and phonetics*. Ph.D. dissertation. Ithacca: Cornell University.

Dave, T. N. (1930–32). Notes on Gujarati phonology. *Bulletin of School of Oriental and African Languages* **6**. 673–78.

Dave, T. N. (1933). *Gujarati Bhasama Varna Vyavastha*. (in Gujarati, *The alphabetic system in Gujarati language*). Baroda.

Dave, T. N. (1952). The open and close E and O in final syllables in modern Gujarati. *Journal of Gujarat Research Society* **14:2**.

Firth, J. R. (1957). Phonetic observations on Gujarati. *Bulletin of School of Oriental and African Languages* **20**. 231–41.

Fischer-Jorgensen, E. (1967). Phonetic analysis of breathy vowels in Gujarati. *Indian Linguistics* **28.2**. 71–139.

Grierson, G. A. (1895). On the stress accent in Modern Indo-Aryan. *Journal of Royal Asiatic Society*. 139–47.

Hall, T. A. (1995). Inalterability and sibilant neutralization in Gujarati. *Lingua* **98**. 11–20.

Joshi, D. M. (1975). Gujarati verb forms: Reconsidered. *Indian Linguistics* **36.3**. 285–89.

Ladefoged, P. & Maddieson, I. (1990). Vowels of the worlds languages. *Journal of Phonetics* **18**. 93–122.

Lambert, H. M. (1971). *Gujarati language course*. Cambridge: CUP

Master, A. (1925). Stress accent in modern Gujarati. *Journal of Bombay branch of the Royal Asiatic Society* **1**. 76–94.

Mistry, P. J. (1996). Gujarati writing. In Daniels, P. & Bright, W. (eds.), *The worlds writing systems*. New York: OUP.

Mistry, P. J. (1999). Gujarati phonology. In Kaye, S. A. (ed.), *Phonologies of Asia and Afrika*. Winoa Lake IN: Eisenbrauns. 653–73.

Modi, B. V. (1983). *Some issues in the phonology of Gujarati*. Ph.D. dissertation. Baroda: M. S. University of Baroda.

Modi, B. V. (1984). `h in ancient Indian phonetic treatises and phonetics of murmur. *Journal of the Oriental Institute* **33**. 34.

Modi, B. V. (1984). The laryngeal dimension in Gujarati Phonology. In Pfeiffer, W., Dressler, O. & Wien, J. (eds.), *Wiener Linguistsche Gazette*. Vienna.

Modi, B. V. (1987). *An acoustic study on murmured and tight phonation in Gujarati dialects: A preliminary report*. University of Munchen, Munich.

Modi, B. V. (1994). The phonetics and phonology of mid vowels in Gujarati. *Indian Linguistics* **55**. 51–76.

Modi, B. V. (1986). Rethinking of `murmur' in Gujarati. *Indian Linguistics* **47**. 39–55.

Nair, U. (1979). *Gujarati phonetic reader*. Mysore: Central Institute of Indian Languages.

Pandit, P. B. (1954). Indo-Aryan sibilants in Gujarati. *Indian Linguistics* **14**.

Pandit, P. B. (1955). E and O in Gujarati. *Indian Linguistics* **15**. 14–54.

Pandit, P. B. (1957). Nasalisation, aspiration and murmur in Gujarati. *Indian Linguistics* **17**. 165–72.

Pandit, P. B. (1957). Old Gujarati pronunciation: A note on linguistic change. *Journal of Gujarat University (Vidya)* **2:1**.

Pandit, P. B. (1958). Syllable, duration and juncture in Gujarati. *Indian Linguistics* **18**. 212–18.

Pandit, P. B. (1961). Historical phonology of Gujarati vowels. *Language* **37.1**. 54–66.

Pandit, P. B. (1966). *Gujarati Bhashanu Dhvani-svarup ane Dhvani-parivartan*. (in Gujarati, *sound structure and sound change in Gujarati language*). Ahmedabad: Gujarat University.

Pandit, P. B. (1966). *Phonemic and morphemic frequencies of the Gujarati language*. Poona: DC.

Pandit, P. B. (1969). Gujarati. In Sebeok, A. T. (ed.), *Current trends in linguistics,* Vol. 5. The Hague: Mouton.

Pandit, P. B. (1975). A grammatical sketch of Gujarati. In Mitra, A. & Nigam, R. C. (eds.), *Grammatical sketches of Indian languages with comparative vocabulary and texts*. Census of India: GOI. 109–30.

Pandit, P.B. (1965). Gujarati. in *Encyclopaedia de la Islam*. Lieden: E.J. Brill.

Patel, M. S. & Modi, J. J. (1960). *The vowel system of Gujarati*. Baroda: M. S. University of Baroda.

Patel, U. R. (1972). *A contrastive study of Gujarati-Hindi*. Ph.D. dissertation. Poona: UP. DCPRI.

Rahman, K., Jain, V. P. & Patel, P. J. (1986). The problem of aspiration in Hindi and Gujarati. In Rajapurohit, B. B. (ed.), (1986). *Acoustic studies in Indian languages*. Mysore: Central Institute of Indian Languages. 65–74.

Sampat, M. K. (1973). *Comparative study of three Gujarati dialects*. Ph.D. dissertation. Poona: UP.

Tessitori, L. P. (1918). The wide sound of E and O in Gujarati. *Indian Antiquary*.

Turner, R. L. (1915). The Indo-Aryan nasals in Gujarati. *Journal of Royal Asiatic Societ*. 17–34.

Turner, R.L. (1921). Gujarati phonology. *Journal of Royal Asiatic Society* **3**. 329–65. **4**. 505–44 (repr. 1975 in *Collected papers*. 88–145)

Turner, R.L. (1925). E and O vowels in Gujarati. *Orientalia* **3.2**. 337–47. (Ashutosh Mukarji Silver Jubilee volume.)

Vyas, M. (1979). *Phonation types in Gujarati*. M.Phil. dissertation. London: University of London.

Vyas, Y. D. (1974). *Dilectology and dialects of Gujarat.* Ahmedabad: University Grantha Nirman Board.

GOJRI

Sharma, J. C. (1979). *Gojri phonetic reader.* Mysore: Central Institute of Indian Languages.

Sharma, J. C. (1982). *Gojri grammar.* Mysore: Central Institute of Indian Languages.

HARAUTI

Allen, W. S. (1957a). Aspiration in the Harauti nominal. Oxford: *Studies in linguistic.*

HARYANVI

Khandelval, S. K. (1980). *Bāngaru bolī kā bhāshā shāstrīya adhyayan.* (in Hindi,*A Linguistic Study of Bangru Dialect*). Delhi: Vani Prakashan.

Sharma, N. C. (1968). *hariyāNvī bhāshā kā udgam tathā vikās.* [in Hindi, *Origin and Development of the Haryanvi Dialect]* Hoshiarpur: Vishveshvaranand Vedic Research Institute.

Singh, J. D. (1970). *A descriptive grammar of Bangru.* Haryana: Kurukshetra University.

HINDI

Barz, R. K. & Seigel, J. (eds.) (1988). *Language transplanted: The development of overseas Hindi.* Weisbaden: Otto Harrassowitz.

Benguerel, A. P. & Bhatia, T. K. (1980). Hindi stop consonants: An acoustic and fibroscopic study. *Phonetica* **37**. 134–48.

Bharti, S. (1994). *Aspects of the phonology of Hindi and English.* New Delhi: Arnold Publishers.

Bhatia, K. C. (1964). Consonant sequence in standard Hindi. *Indian Linguistics* **25**. 206–12.

Bhatia, T. K. & Kenstowicz, M. J. (1972). Nasalization in Hindi: A reconsideration. *Papers in Linguistics 5(Also in Indian Linguistics 36).* 202–12.

Chandra, T. (1994). *The phonological development in bilingual children: The case of Hindi and Punjabi bilinguals in Delhi.* Ph.D. dissertation. New Delhi: JNU.

Dasgupta, P. (1983). Review of Ohalas Aspects of Hindi Phonology. *Indian Linguistics* **44**.1–4. 103–26.

Davis, K. (1994). Stop voicing in Hindi. *Journal of Phonetics* **22.2**. 177–93.

Dixit, R. P. (1963.) *The segmental phonemes of contemporary Hindi*. MA dissertation. Austin: University of Texas.

Dixit, R. P. (1987). In defence of the phonetic adequacy of the traditional term voiced aspirated. *UCLA Working Papers In Phonetics* **67**.

Dixit, R. P. (1989). Glottal gestures in Hindi plosives. *Journal of Phonetics* **17**. 213–37.

Dixit, R. P. (1990). Linguotectal contect patterns in the dental and retroflx stops of Hindi. *Journal of Phonetics* **18.2**. 189–201.

Dixit, R. P. (1993). Spatiotemporal patterns of glottal dynamics and control of voicing and aspiration in Hindi stops. *Indian Linguistics* **54**. 1–36.

Dixit, R. P. & Flege, J. E. (1991). Vowel context, rate and loudness effects on linguopalatal contact patterns in Hindi retroflx / t. *Journal of Phonetics* **19.2**. 213–29.

Dixit, R. P. & MacNeilage, P. F. (1972). Coarticulation of nasality: Evidence from Hindi. Paper presented at the *83rd Meeting of the Acoustical Society of America*. Buffalo.

D'Souza, J. (1985). Schwa syncope and vowel nasalization in Hindi-Urdu: A non-linear approach. *Studies in Linguistic Sciences* **15.1**. 11–30.

Elizarenkova, T. Y. (1961). Distinctive features of the consonantal phonemes of Hindi. *Voprosi Iazykoznania* **10.5**. 22–33.

Elizarenkova, T. Y. (1988). Morphophonology of Hindi. In Andronov, M. S. & Mallik, B. P. (eds.), *Linguistics: A soviet approach, special issue of Indian Journal of Linguistics*. 367–386.

Fairbanks, C. (1981). *The development of Hindi oral narrative meter*. Unpublished

Fallon, S.W. (1879). *A new Hindustani-English dictionary, with illustrations from Hindustani literature and folk-lore*. New Delhi: Asian Educational Services. (Reprinted 1989).

Ford, A., Singh, R. & Martohardjono, G. (1997). *Pace Panini: Towards a word-based theory of morphology*. New York, etc.: Peter Lang.

Ford, A., Singh, R. & Martohardjono, G. (1997). *Pace Panini: Towards a word-based theory of morphology*. New York, etc.: Peter Lang.

Ghatage, A. M. (1964). Phonemic and Morphemic Frequencies in Hindi. Poona: DC.

Goel, S. (1986). A study of /h/ and aspiration in Hindi. In Rajapurohit, B. B. (ed.), (1986). *Acoustic studies in India*. Mysore: Central Institute of Indian Languages. 75–78.

Gumperz, J. J. (1955a). The phonology of a north Indian village dialect. *Indian Linguistics* **16**. 282–95.

Gumperz, J. J. (1958a). Dilectal differences and social stratification in a North Indian village. *American Anthropologist* **60**. 668–82.

Gumperz, J. J. (1958b). Phonological differences in three Hindi dialects. *Language* **34**. 212–24.

Gumperz, J. J. (1960). *Hindi Reader*. Berkley.

Gumperz, J. J. & Naim, C. M. (1960). Formal and informal standards in the Hindi regional language area. *International Journal of Applied Linguistics* **26.3**. 92–118.

Gupta, B. P. (1982). A rule of deaspiration in colloquial Hindi. *Indo-Iranian Journal* 24.3. 181–90.

Gupta, M. (1993). *Acquisition of fricatives and affricates in Hindi*. Ph.D. disseration. New Delhi: JNU.

Harnsberger, J. (1994). *Towards an intonational phonology of Hindi*. Unpublished dissertation. Madison: University of Wisconsin.

Harnsberger, J. (1999). The role of metrical structure in Hindi intonation. *South Asian language analysis roundtable*. Unpublished notes. [http://www-personal.umich.edu/~jharns/hindi.html]

Harris, R. M. (1966). Regional variation in Hindi. *Indian Linguistics* **27**. 58–69.

Harris, R. M. (1968). Colloquial deviation in urban Hindi. *Anthropological Linguistics* **10.9**. 25–34.

Hayes, B. (1995). Hindi. *Metrical stress theory: Principles and case studies*. Chicago: University of Chicago Press

Hoenigswald, H. M. (1948). Declension and nasalisation in Hindustani. *Journal of American Oriental Society* **68**. 139–44.

Jones, W. E. (1971). Syllables and word stress in Hindi. *Journal of International Phonetic Association* **1**. 74–78.

Kachru, Y. (1987). Hindi-Urdu. in Comrie, Bernard (ed.), *The world's major languages*. London/Sydney: Croom Helm. 470-89.

Karla, S. (1976). Schwa deletion in Hindi. *Language Forum* **2.1**. 39–57.

Kelkar, A. R. (1968). *Studies in Hindi-Urdu 1*. Poona: DC.

Kelkar, A. R. (1970). Reply to R. N. Srivastava's review of "Studies in Hindi-Urdu I". *Indian Linguistics* **30.3**. 103-08.

Kurylowicz, J. (1968). Hindi accentuation as a historical problem. In Krishnamurti, Bh. (ed.), *Studies in Indian languages: M. B. Emeneau Ṣaṣṭiipurtī volume*. Poona and Annamalainagar: Centre of Advanced Study.

Lakshmi Bai, B. (1989). Varieties of Hindi. Paper presented at the *National seminar on Suniti Kumar Chatterji: An end century assessment*. Centre for Appllied Linguistics and Translation Studies, University of Hyderabad.

Maddieson, I. & Gandour, J. (1977). Vowel length before aspirated consonants. *Indian Linguistics* **3.1**. 6–11.

Mathews, W. K. (1964). Phonetics and phonology in Hindi. *Le Maitre Phonetique* **102**. 18–22.

Mathur, R. (1993). *The phonology and morphology of standard Hindi*. Ph.D. dissertation. Poona: University of Pune.

Mehrota, R. C. (1964). Hindi phonemes. *Indian Linguistics* **25**. 324–46.

Mehrotra, R. C. (1959). Hindi syllable structure. *Indian Linguistics* **20**. 213–37.

Mehrotra, R. C. (1965). Stress in Hindi. *Indian Linguistics* **26**. 96–105.

Mehrotra, R. C. (1980). *Hindi phonology (a synchronic description of the contemporary standard)*. Raipur: Bhashika Prakashan.

Miltner, V. (1969). Hindi. Sebeok, A. T. (ed.), *Current Trends in Linguistics*, Vol. 5. The Hague: Mouton.

Misra, B. G. (1967). *Historical phonology of modern standard Hindi.*. Ph.D. dissertation. Ithacca: Cornell University.

Modi, Y. (2005). *Emergence and impact of Hindi as a lingua franca in Arunachal.*

Nair, Rami (2001). Acoustic correlates of lexical stress in Hindi. Abbi, A. et al. (eds.), *Linguistic structure and language dynamics in South Asia*. New Delhi: Motilal Banarasidas Publishers. 164–84.

Narang, G. C. & Becker, D. A. (1971). Aspiration and nasalisation in the generative phonology of Hindi-Urdu. *Language* **47**. 646–67.

Ohala, M. (1972). *Topics in Hindi-Urdu phonology*. Ph. D. Dissertation. UCLA.

Ohala, M. (1974). The abstractness controversy; experimental input from Hindi. *Language* **50**. 225–35.

Ohala, M. (1975). Nasal and nasalization in Hindi. In Ferguson, C. A. (ed.), *Nasalfest: Papers from a symposium on nasals and nasalization*. Stanford: Stanford University. 317–32.

Ohala, M. (1977a). Stress in Hindi. In Hyman, L. M. (ed.), *Studies in stress and accent (Southern California occasional papers in linguistics)*. Los Angeles: University of Southern California. 327–38.

Ohala, M. (1977b). The treatment of phonological variation: An example from Hindi. *Lingua* **42**. 161–76.

Ohala, M. (1979). Phonological features of Hindi stops. *South Asian Languages Analysis* **1**. 79–88.

Ohala, M. (1983). *Aspects of Hindi phonology*. Delhi: Motilal Banarsidass.

Ohala, M. (1983b). Stress in Hindi. Bahner, W. et al. (eds.), *Proceedings of the XIII International Congress of Linguists*. Berlin: Mouton de Gruyter.

Ohala, M. (1985). Aspects of Phonology revisited. *Indian Linguistics* **46**. 3–4. 13–20.

Ohala, M. (1986). A search for the phonetic correlates of Hindi stress. In Krishnamurti, Bh. (ed.), *South Asian languages: Structure, convergence, and diaglossia*. Delhi: Motilal Banarsidas. 81–92.

Ohala, M. (1987). Schwa deletion in Hindi by linear and nonlinear routes. *Paper presented at the XIV International Congress of Linguists*. Berlin.

Ohala, M. (1994). Hindi. *Journal of International Phonetic Association* **24.1**. 35–38.

Ohala, M. & Ohala, J. J. (1973). The problem of aspiration in Hindi phonetics (In Hindi). *Bhasha*. Hindi Linguistics issue. Delhi: Central Hindi Directorate. 67–72.

Pande, A. (1980). *Topics in Hindi phonology*. Ph.D. dissertation. Kanpur: Indian Institue of Technology.

Pandey, P. K. (1985). *Word accentuation in Hindustani in relation to word accents in English and Hindustani*. Ph.D. dissertation. Pune: DC.

Pandey, P. K. (1989). Word accentuation in Hindi. *Lingua* **77**. 37–77.

Pandey, P. K. (1990). Hindi schwa deletion. *Lingua* **82**. 277–311.

Pandey, P. K. (1990). Schwa fronting in Hindi. *Studies in Linguistic Sciences*.

Pandey, P. K. (1992). Hindi-Urdu phonology since 1968. Srivastava, R. N. (ed.), *Language and text: Studies in honour of Ashok R Kelkar*. Delhi: Kalinga Publications. 155–70.

Pandey, P. K. (2002). Hindi me shabdant a. (Word final a in Hindi). *GaveshaNa* **78**. Agra: Central Institute of Hindi.

Pandey, P. K. (2003). Phonetic and phonological bases of Hindi orthography. 2003. *Working papers on international symposium on Indic scripts*. ILCAA, Tokyo University of Foreign Studies. Tokyo.

Pandey, P. K. (2007). Phonology orthography interface in Devanagari for Hindi. *Written Language and Literacy* **10 (2)**. 139–156.

Prabhakararao, J. (1996). A possible computational model for Hindi consonants. *International Journal of Dravidian Linguistics* **25.2**. 36–46.

Pray, B. R. (1969). *Agreement in Hindi-Urdu and its Phonological Implications*. Ph. D. thesis. University of Michigan.

Pray, B. R. (1970). *Topics in Hindi-Urdu grammar.* Research Monograph I. Berkeley: University of California.

Rahman, K., Jain, V. P. & Patel, P. J. (1986). The problem of aspiration in Hindi and Gujarati. In Rajapurohit, B. B. (ed.), (1986). *Acoustic studies in India.* Mysore: Central Institute of Indian Languages. 65–74.

Rai, A. (1984) *A house divided: The origin and development of Hindi-Hindavi.* Delhi: OUP.

Ray, P. S. (1968).Hindi-Urdu stress. *Indian Linguistics* **27**. 95–101.

Shapiro, M. C. (2003). Hindi. In Cardona, G. & Jain, D. (eds.), *The Indo-Aryan Languages.* London, New York: Routledge (Routledge Language Family Series). 250-85.

Sharma, A. (1968). Hindi word accent. *Indian Linguistics* **30.** 115–18.

Sharma, D. D. (1971). *Syllabic structure of Hindi and Punjabi.* Chandigarh: Punjab University.

Shukla, S. (1990). Syllable structure and word stress in Hindi. *Georgetown Journal of Language and Linguistics* **1.** 235–47.

Singh, A. (1994). The Phonology-Morphology Interface: A Case from Hindi. University of Delhi. Ph. D. thesis.

Singh, A. B. (1969). On echo words in Hindi. *Indian Linguistics* **30.** 185–95.

Singh, A. (1991). *Some aspects of syllable phonology in Hindi.* M.Phil. dissertation. Delhi: University of Delhi.

Singh, Ch. P. (1996). Effects of preceding vowels in the fundamental frequancies of Hindi utterence. *International Journal of Dravidian Linguistics* **25.2.** 16–23.

Singh, R. & Agnihotri, R. K. (1997). *Hindi morphology: A word-based description.* Delhi: Motilal Banarasidass Publishers.

Singh, R. (1987). Well-formedness conditions and phonological theory. In Dressler, W. U. (ed.), *Phonologica 1984.* Cambridge: CUP. 273–285.

Singh, R. (1991). Interference and contemporary phonological theory. *Language Learning* **41.2.** 157–175.

Singh, S. (1976). *Morphophonemics in contemporary Hindi.* Ph. D. thesis. University of Lucknow.

Srivastava, G. P. (1974). A child's acquisition of Hindi consonants. *Indian Linguistics* **35.2.** 112–18.

Srivastava, R. N. (1968). Theory of morphonematics and aspirated phonemes of Hindi. *Acta Linguistica* **18.** 363–73.

Srivastava, R. N. (1969). A review of *Studies in Hindi-Urdu* I by A R Kelkar. *Language* **45.** 913–17.

Srivastava, R. N. (1970a). Rejoinder to Kelkars reply to Srivastava's review of *Studies in Hindi-Urdu I. Indian Linguistics* **31.4**. 186–96.

Srivastava, R. N. (1970b). The problem of the Hindi semivowels. *Indian Linguistics* **31**. 129–37.

Srivastava, R. N. (1974). Review of *Syllabic Structure of Hindi and Punjabi* by D.D. Sharma. *Indian Linguistics* **35**. 70–79.

Srivastava, R. N. (1979). On capturing inaccessible mind: Further evidence for word final schwa. In *Honour of D. Kostich*. Belgrade.

Tiwari, U. N. (1969). *Hindī bhāśā kā Udgam aur Vikās*. [in Hindi, *The Origin and Development of Hindi Language*]. Allahabad: Bhāratī.

Ucida, N. (1977). *Hindi phonology*. Calcutta: Simant.

Vajpeyi, K. D. (1958). *Hindi Shabdaanushaasan*,[in Hindi, The Organisation of Words in Hindi]. Varanasi: Kashi Nagari Pracarini Sabha.

Zaidi, C. (1978). *Nasalization and aspiration in Hindi*. Ph.D. dissertation. Delhi: University of Delhi.

JAUNSARI

Sharma, S. U. (1972). *Phonology and morphology of Jaunsari*. Ph.D. dissertation. Delhi: University of Delhi.

Sharma, S. U. (1990). *A linguistic study of Jaunsari*. New Delhi: Creative.

KACCHI

Acharya, S. (1964). Segmental phonemes of Kacchi. *Vidya*. 129–42.

Rohra, S. K. (1966). Descriptive Analysis of Kacchi. Ph. D. thesis. University of Poona.

KASHMIRI

Bailey, T. G. (1935). The four-fold consonant system in Kashmiri. *Proceedings of the 2nd Congresso of Phonetic Sciences*. London. 182–4.

Bailey, T. G. (1937). The Pronunciation of Kashmiri sounds: How to make them and how to transcribe them. James G. Forlong Series. no. **16**. London: RAS.

Bhaskararao, P., Hassan, S., Naikoo, I. A., Ganai, P. A., Wani, N. H., & Ahmad, T. (2009). A phonetic study of Kashmiri palatalization. Minegishi, M. et al. (eds.), *Field research. Corpus linguistics and linguistic informatics*. [Working Papers in Corpus-based Linguistics and Language Education - No.3]. Tokyo: Tokyo University of Foreign Studies. 1–17.

Bhat, R. N. (2008). Palatalization: A Note on Kashmiri morphophonology. *Indian Linguistics* **69**.1–4. 43–50.

Bhat, R. (1987). *A descriptive study of Kashmiri*. Delhi: Amar Prakashan.

Grierson, G. A. (1896). The Kashmiri vowel system. *Journal of the Asiatic Society of Bengal* **65.1**. 280–305.

Grierson, G. A. (1897). On the Kashmiri consonantal system. *Journal of the Asiatic Society of Bengal* **66.1**. 180-84.

Handoo, J. (1973). *Kashmiri phonetic reader*. Mysore: Central Institute of Indian Languages.

Kachru, Braj, B. (1969a). Kashmiri and other Dardic languages. In Sebeok, A. T. (ed.), *Current Trends in Linguistics*. Vol. **5**. The Hague: Mouton. 284–306.

Kachru, B. B. (1969b). *A reference grammar of Kashmiri. Mimeo*. Urbana: University of Illinois.

Kantroo, G. K. (1986). Duration and quality of i,schwa,a in Kashmiri. In Rajapurohit, B. B. (ed.), (1986). *Acoustic studies in India*. Mysore: Central Institute of Indian Languages. 20–25.

Kelkar, A. R. (1984). Kashmiri: A descriptive sketch. In Koul, N. O. & Hook, P. E. (eds.), *Aspects of Kashmiri linguistics*. Delhi: Bahri Publications. 62–89.

Kelkar, A. R. & Trishal, P. N. (1964). Kashmiri word phonology: A first sketch. *Anthropological Linguistics* **6.1**. 13–22.

Koul, O. N. (2003). Kashmiri. In Cardona, G. & Jain, D. (eds.), *The Indo-Aryan Languages*. London, New York: Routledge (Routledge Language Family Series). 895–952.

Koul, O. N. (1977). *Linguistic studies in Kashmiri*. Delhi: Bahri Publications.

Koul, O. N. (1987). *Spoken Kashmiri*. Patiala: IILS.

Morgenstierne, G. (1943). The phonology of Kashmiri. *Acta Orientalia* **19.1**. 79–99.

Sar, M. L. (1970). *A Study in some aspects of phonemics and morphophonemics of Kashmiri*. M.Litt. dissertation. Delhi: University of Delhi.

Varma, S. (1964). Syllabication in Kashmiri language. *Honour of Daniel Jones*. London: Longmans. 471–74.

Wali, K. & Koul, O. N. (1997). *Kashmiri: A cognitive-descriptive grammar*. London/NY: Routledge.

Zakharyin, B. A. (1974). *Problemy Fonologiijazyka Kashmiri (problems in the phonology of the Kashmiri language)*, Moscow: Academy of Sciences.

Zakharyin, B. A. (1975). Fonemy Kashmiri (Kashmiri phonemes), *Ocerki po fonologii vostocnykh jazykov*. Moscow: Academy of Sciences.

Zakharyin, B. A. (1984). Kashmiri and the typology of South Asian languages. In Koul, O. N. & Hook, P. E. (eds.), *Aspects of Kashmiri linguistics*. Delhi: Bahri Publications.

KHANDESHI

Chitnis, V. (1964). *The Khandeshi dialect as spoken by farmers in the village of Mohadi in the Dhulia Taluka*. Ph. D. dissertation. Poona: UP.

KHASALI

Varma, S. (1938). The dialects of the Khasali Group. *Royal Asiatic Society of Bengal* **4**. 1–65.

KOKBOROK

Pai, P. (1976). *Kokborok grammar*. Mysore: Central Institute of Indian Languages.

KONKANI

Almeida, M. (1989). *A description of Konkani*. Panaji: Thomas Stephens Konkani Kendra.

Katre, S. M. (1965). Consonantal gemination in Konkani. *Indian Linguistics* **26**. 237–39.

Miranda, R. V. (1977). The assimilation of Dravidian loans to Konkani phonology. *Indo-Iranian Journal* **19**. 247–65.

Miranda, R. V. (2003). Konkani. Cardona, G. & Jain, D. (eds.), *The Indo-Aryan Languages*. London, New York: Routledge (Routledge Language Family Series). 729–65.

Miranda, R. V. (1977). The assimilation of Dravidian loans to Konkani phonology. *Indo-Iranian Journal* **19**. 247–65.

Misra, Dipti (1984). *Some aspects of Konkani phonology*. Ph.D. dissertation. Delhi: University of Delhi.

Misra, Dipti (1991). Syllable in Konkani. *Indian Linguistics* **52**. 27–38.

Varma, S. (1940). Notes of a linguistic tour in Kashmir. *Indian Linguistics* **8**. 479–83.

KUMAUNI

Apte, M. L., & Pattanayak, D. P. (1967). *An outline of Kumauni grammar*. Durham: Duke University, Program in Comparative Studies of Southern Asia, Monograph No. 6.

LAHNDI

Bahri, H. (1962). *Lahndi phonology: With special reference to Awankari*. Allahabad: Bharati Press.

Bahri, H. (1963). *Lahndi phonetics: With special reference to Awankari.* Allahabad: Bharati Press.

Smirnov, I. A. (1975). *The Lahndi language.* Moscow: Nanka.

LAMANI

Boopathy, S. (1974). *Lambadi (An Indo-Aryan dialect).* Census of India 1961. Delhi: Controller of Publications.

Radhakrishnan, S. (1983). *A descriptive study of Lambadi.* Annamalainagar: Annamalai University.

Trail, R. L. (1968). *Lamani: Phonology, grammar and lexicon.* Ph.D. dissertation. Poona: UP.

Trail, R. L. (1970). *A grammar of Lamani.* Norman (Oklahoma): Summer Institute of Linguistics.

MAGAHI

Jha, M. (1967). *Māgadhī and its formation.* Calcutta: Sanskrit College.

Prasad, S. (1966). *A descriptive study of Magahi phonology.* Ph.D. thesis. Patna University.

Sinha, A. C. (1966). *Phonology and Morphology of Magahi Dialect.* Ph.D. thesis. University of Poona.

Verma, S. (2003). Magahi. In Cardona, G. & Jain, D., *The Indo-Aryan Languages.* London: Routledge, Corzon. 498–514.

MAHL

Joy, J. (1994). *Mahl: A descriptive analysis.* Ph.D. dissertation. Poona: UP.

De Silva, M. W. S. (1969). The phonological efficiency of the Maldivian writing system. *Anthropological Linguistics* **11.7.** 199–209.

MAITHILI

Jha, S. K. (1991). Gemination of consonants in Maithili. *Indian Linguistics* **52.** 15–26.

Yadav, R. (1979). *Maithili phonetics and phonology.* Ph.D. dissertation. University of Kansas.

Yadav, R. (1984). Laryngeal behavior and stop and affricate distinctions in Maithili: A fiberoptic and acoustic study. Rajapurohit, B.B. (1984). 43–75.

Yadav, R. (1996). *A reference grammar of Maithili.* Delhi: Munshiram Manoharlal Publishers.

Yadav, R. (2003). Maithili. Cardona, G. & Jain, D. (eds.), *The Indo-Aryan Languages.* London, New York: Routledge (Routledge Language Family Series). 477–97.

MARATHI

Apte, M. L. (1958). *Syllable, word and sentence boundries in spoken Marathi, based on observers own pronunciation*. M.A. dissertation. London: University of London.

Bhagwat, S. V. (1961). *Phonemic frequences in Marathi and their relation to devising a speed script*. Poona: DC.

Doderet, W. (1928). The grammar of the Jñāneśvarī. *Bulletin of the School of Oriental and African Studies* **4**. 543–73.

Ghatage, A. M. (1969). *Warli of Thana*. Bombay: State Board for Literature and Culture. (*Survey of Marathi dialects*: VII)

Ghatage, A. M. (1970). Marathi of Kasargod. *Indian Linguistics* **31.4**. 138–44.

Kelkar, A. R. (1957). Marathi English: A study in foreign accent. *Word* **13.2**. 268–92.

Kelkar, A. R. (1958). *The phonology and morphology of Marathi*. Ph.D. dissertation. Ithacca: Cornell University.

Kelkar, A. R. (1991–92). Prosodies and their functions in Marathi. *Bulletin of Deccan College Post Graduate Research Institute* **51–52**. 289–302.

Khokle, V. (1969). *Two models of phonological distinctive features: An evaluation as applied to Marathi*. Ph. D. dissertation. University of Minnesota.

Laddu, S. (1958). Marathi /d dh/ and Koli /r d/. *Indian Linguistics* **19**. 137–141.

Laddu, S. (1961). *Linguistic analysis of Koli: A dialect of Marathi*. Ph.D. dissertation. Poona: UP.

Lloyd, J. A. & Kanhere, S. G. (1928). The pronunciation of Marathi. *Bulletin of the School of Oriental and African Studies* **4**. 791–801.

Master, A. (1964). *A grammar of old Marathi*. Oxford: Clarendon Press.

Pande, P. V. (1986). Marathi affricates: A spectrographic study of duration and intensity. In Rajapurohit, B. B. (ed.), (1986). *Acoustic studies in India*. Mysore: Central Institute of Indian Languages. 39–48.

Pandharipande, R. (1986). Language and language variation: Nagpuri Marathi. In Krishnamurti, Bh. (ed.). 219–31.

Pandharipande, R. (2003). Marathi. In Cardona, G. & Jain, D. (eds.), *The Indo-Aryan Languages*. London, New York: Routledge (Routledge Language Family Series). 698–728.

Pandharipande, R. V. (1997). *Marathi*. London/New York: Routledge.

Sardesai, V. N. (1930). Some problems in the nasalisation of Marathi. *Journal of Royal Asiatic Society*. 537–65.

Turner, R. L. (1916). The Indo-Germanic accent in Marathi. *Journal of Royal Asiatic Society*. 203–15.

NAHALI

Kuiper, F. B. J. (1962). *Nahali: A comparative study*. Amsterdam: North-Holland Publ Co.

NEPALI

Acharya, J. (1991). *A descriptive grammar of Nepali and an analyzed corpus*. Washington, D. C.: Georgetown University.

Bandhu, C. Dahal, M. M., Holzhausen, A. & Hale, A. (1971). *Nepali segmental phonology*. Kirtipur. Nepal: SIL, Tribhuvan University.

Clark, T. W. (1963) *Introduction to Nepali*. Cambridge: CUP.

Clements, G. N. & Khatiwada, R. (2007). Phonetic realization of Contrastively aspirated affricates in Nepali. *Proceedings of the 16th International Congress of Phonetic Sciences*. Saarbrücken, Germany. 629–632.

Dahal, B. M. (1974). *A description of Nepali: Literary and colloquial*. Ph.D. dissertation. Poona: DC.

Khatiwada, R. (2007). Nepalese retroflex stops: A static palatography study of the inter and intra-speaker variability. *Proceedings of the Interspeech 2007*. Antwerpen. Belgium. 1422–1425.

Khatiwada, R. (2009). Nepali. *Journal of International Phonetic Association* **39.3**. 373–380.

Matthews, D. (1984). *A course in Nepali*. London: SOAS.

Pokharel, M. P. (1989). *Experimental analysis of Nepali sound System*. Ph. D. Dissertation. University of Pune.

Riccardi, T. (2003). Nepali. Cardona, G. & Jain, D. (eds.), *The Indo-Aryan Languages*. London, New York: Routledge (Routledge Language Family Series). 538–80.

Sthapit, S. K. (1978). *English-Nepali-Newari: A comparison and pedagogic application*. Poona: DC.

ORIYA

Dash, G. N. (1982). *Descriptive morphology of Oriya*. Santiniketan: Visva-Bharati. [Visva-Bharati Research Publications].

Dhall, G. B. (1952). *Aspiration in Oriya*. M.A. dissertation. London: University of London.

Dhall, G. B. (1955–56). The languages and dialects spoken in Orissa. *Indian Linguistics* **17**. 39–43.

Gauda, D. (1989). *A study of the Ganjami dialect of Oriya*. Ph.D. dissertation. Poona: UP, Deccan College Post-Graduate and Research Institute.

Hota, S. (1960). Reduplicatives in Oriya (from 19th century to modern era). *Read at the annual sessions of the Linguistic Society of India*. Poona.

Kelkar, A. R. (1966). *Phonemic and morphemic frequency count in Oriya, Deccan College Monograph Series*. Poona: DC.

Misra, H. (1975). *Historical Oriya morphology*. Varanasi: Bharata Manisha

Mohanty, P. (1986). *Aspects of Oriya language: Phonology and morphology*. Ph.D. dissertation. Berhampur: Berhampur University.

Mohanty, P. (1997). Linguistic economy at work: An example from Oriya. *International Journal of Dravidian Linguistics* **26.1**. 89–96.

Mohanty, P. (1987). Deaspiration in Oriya. *General linguistics* **27.3**. 145–52.

Mohanty, P. (1996). Development of Oriya phonology: A case study. *PILC Journal of Dravidic Studies* **6, 2**. 163–78.

Mohanty, P. (1997). Loss of /o/ in Kui, Sora and Oriya: A clue for a sub-linguistic area. Abbi, A. (ed.). 110–119.

Mohanty, P. (2000). On sonorization in Oriya. *Indian Journal of Linguistics* **19**. 12–22.

Panda, D. (1986). A spectrographic study of Oriya vowels. Rajapurohit, B. B. (ed.), (1986). *Acoustic studies in India*. Mysore: Central Institute of Indian Languages. 26–31.

Pattanayak, D. P. (1959). Nasal phonemes of Oriya. *Indian Linguistics* **2**.

Pattanayak, D. P. (1966). *A controlled historical reconstruction of Oriya, Assamese, Bengali and Hindi*. Hague/Paris.

Ray, Tapas S. (2003). Oriya . Cardona, G. & Jain, D. (eds.), *The Indo-Aryan Languages*. London, New York: Routledge (Routledge Language Family Series). 444–76.

Tripathi, K. B. (1956–7). Western Oriya dialect. *Indian Linguistics* **17b**. 76–85.

Tripathi, K. B. (1962). *The evolution of Oriya language and script*. Cuttack: Utkal University.

PUNJABI

Ahmad, I. (1964). Grammatical reduplication of standard Punjabi. *Pakistani Linguistics*. 65–76.

Arun, V. B. (1961). *A comparative phonology of Hindi and Punjabi.* Ludhiyana: Punjabi Sahitya Akademi.

Bahl, K. C. (1957). Notes on tones in Western Punjabi. *Indian Linguistics* **17(b).** 30–34.

Bahl, K. C. (1957). Tones in Punjabi. *Indian Linguistics* **17**. 139–47.

Bahl, P. (1941). Injective consonants in Western Punjabi. *Journal of the Punjabi Oriental Research Institute* **1.2.** 32–37.

Bailey, T. G. (1914). *Punjabi phonetic reader.* London: Trübner.

Bhatia, T. K. (1997). *Punjabi: A cognitive-descriptive grammar.* London/ New York: Routledge.

Gill, H. S. (1960). Punjabi tonemics. *Anthropological Linguistics* **2.6**. 11–18.

Gill, H. S. (1962). *A descriptive grammar of Panjabi.* Ph. D. dissertation. The Hartford Seminary Foundation, Hartford, Connecticut.

Gupta, B. R. (1975). *Contrastive phonology of Punjabi and Tamil.* Ph.D. dissertation. Patiala: Punjab University.

Gupta, B. R. (1990). *Indian linguistics: Punjabi-Tamil phonology.* New Delhi: Asian Publishing House.

Haudricourt, A. G. (1971). On tones in Punjabi. *Pakha Sanjam (Patiala)* **4**.1–3.

Jain, B. (1934). *A phonology of Punjabi and a Ludhiani phonetic reader.* Lahore. Punjab University.

Jain, B. (1934). *A phonology of Punjabi as spoken about Ludhiana.* Lahore: Punjab University.

Joshi, S. S. (1971). [l],[l],[r], and [r] sounds in Punjabi: A study in retroflection. *Pakha Sanjam (Patiala)* **4**. 85–90.

Joshi, S. S. (1973). Pitch and related phenomena in Punjabi. *Pakha Sanjam (Patiala)* **6**. 1–62.

Kalra (1982). *Some topics in Punjabi phonology.* Ph.D. dissertation. Delhi: University of Delhi.

Malik, A. (1995). *The phonology and morphology of Punjabi.* New Delhi: Munshiram Manoharlal Publisher.

Sampat, K. S. (1964). Tonal structure of Majhi. *Indian Linguistics* **25**. 108–10.

Sandhu, B. S. (1968). A descriptive grammar of Puadi. *Parkh* **2**. [Chandigarh].

Sandhu, D. S. (1968). The tonal system of the Punjabi Language. *Parkh* **2**. [Chandigarh].

Shackle, C. (2003). Panjabi. Cardona, G. & Jain, D. (eds.), *The Indo-Aryan Languages*. London, New York: Routledge (Routledge Language Family Series). 581–621.

Shackle, C. (1972). *Punjabi*. London: English University Press.

Shackle, C. (1983). *An introduction to the sacred language of the Sikhs*. London: SOAS.

Varma, S. (1936). The phonetics of Lahnda. *Journal of the Asiatic Society of Bengal Letters* **2**. 47–118.

Varma, S. (1964). The role of consonants in the stress and syllabification of the Ambalvi dialect. *Indian Linguistics* **25**. 61–66.

RAJASTHANI

Allen, W. S. (1957b). Some phonological characteristics of Rajasthani. *Bulletin of the School of Oriental and African Studies* **20**. 5–11.

Gusain, L. (2000). *Bagri*. München: Lincom Europa [Languages of the World/Materials, 386]

Gusain, L. (2001). *Shekhawati*. München: Lincom Europa. [Languages of the World/Materials, 385]

Gusain, L. (2003). *Mewati*. München: Lincom Europa [Languages of the World/Materials, 386]

Gusain, L. (2004). *Marwari*. München: Lincom Europa. [Languages of the World/Materials, 427]

Smith, J. D. (1992). Epic Rajasthani. *Indo-Iranian Journal* **35**. 251–69.

RAJBANSHI

Barma, D. N. (1991). *A step to Kamata-Behari language*. Adhikari: Minati Barma.

Toulmin, M. (2007). *A reconstructed history of the Kamta, Rajbanshi, and North Bengal Deshi language and dialects*. Ph.D. Thesis. School of Language Studies. Australian National University.

RATHVI

Parakh, M. (2000). *Segmental phonology of Rathvi*. M. A. dissertation. Vadodara: Department of Linguistics. The M. S. University of Baroda.

ROMANI

Beames, J. (1872–79[1970]). *A comparative grammar of the modern Aryan languages of India*. New Delhi: Census of India.

Hamp, E. P. (1987). On sibilants of Romani. *Indo-Iranian Journal* **30.2.** 103–106.

Turner R. L. (1926). The position of Romani in Indo-Aryan. *Journal of Gypsy Lore Society* 5. 145–189

SAURASHTRI

Dave, I. R. (1976). Saurashtri language, Ch.4. *The Saurashtrians in South India*. Rajkot: Saurashtra University. 101–227.

Neethivaanan, J. (1962). *Saurashtra language: Phonology and morphology*. Ms. Department of Linguistics. Annamalai University.

Pandit, P. B. (1972). Bilinguals grammar: Tamil-Saurashtri grammatical convergence. *India as a sociolinguistic area*. (Gune Memorial Lectures. University of Poona). 1–25.

Ramasubramanian, K. S. (1968). *A LINGUISTIC STUDY OF Saurasthri* [sic] *language*. Ph. D. Thesis. Poona: Deccan College and University of Poona.

Randle, H. N. (1943–4). An Indo-Aryan language of South India: Saurashtra bhasa, Parts I and II. *Bulletin of School of Oriental and African Studies* **11.** 104–21; 310–25.

Randle, H. N. (1943–4). An Indo-Aryan language of south India: Saurastra-bhasa. *Bulletin of the School of Oriental and African Studies.* **11.1** [1943]. 104–121, **11.2** [1944]. 310–327.

Smith. I. R. (1979). Convergence in South Asia: A Creole example. *Lingua* **48.** 193–222.

SHINA

Baily, T. G. (1925). The sounds of Shina. *Bulletin of the School of Oriental Studies* 3. 799–802.

Bashir, E. (2003). Dardic. In Cardona, G. & Jain, D. (eds.), *The Indo-Aryan Languages*. London, New York: Routledge. 818–95.

Rajapurohit, B. B. (1983). *Shina phonetic reader*. Mysore: Central Institute of Indian Languages.

Schmidt, R & Kohistani, R. (1998). Paalus/kostyo/Shina revisited. *Acta Orientalia* 1998, **59.** 106–149.

Schmidt, R. L. (2003). A grammatical comparison of Shina dialects. Saxena, A. (ed.), 33–55.

Schmidt, R. L. & Zarin, M. (1981).The phonology and tonal system of Palas Shina. *Munchener Studien fur Sprachwissenschaft* **40.** 155–85.

Schmidt, R. L. (2003). A grammatical comparison of Shina dialects. Anju Saxena (ed.), 33–55.

SINDHI

Acharya, S. B. (1964). Segmental phonemes of Kachhi. *Vidya* **8**. 129–42 [a Journal of Gujarat University, Ahmedabad]

Baily, T. G. (1922). The Sindhi implosives: A note. *Bulletin of the School of Oriental and African Studies* **2**. 835 ff.

Bordie, J. G. (1958). *A descriptive Sindhi phonology*. Ph.D. dissertation. Austin: University of Texas.

Bordie, J. (1958). *A descriptive Sindhi phonology*. Ph. D. Dissertation. Austin: University of Texas; Ann Arbor, MI: University Micrifilms.

Gidwani, P. (1971). *A Phonology of Lari*. M. A. Thesis. Poona: Deccan College Post-Graduate & Research Institute.

Jetley, M. K. (1965). *A descriptive analysis of Vicholi: The standard Sindhi dialect*. Ph. D. dissertation. Poona: Poona University and Deccan College Postgraduate Research Institute.

Khubchandani, L. M. (1961). *The phonology and morphophonemics of Sindhi*. MA dissertation. Philadelphia: University of Pennsylvania.

Khubchandani, L. M. (1963). Stress in Sindhi. *Proceedings: Seminar in linguistics*. Kurukshetra: University of Kurukshetra.

Khubchandani, L. M. (1964a). Juncture in Sindhi. *Proceedings: Seminar in linguistics*. Poona: UP.

Khubchandani, L. M. (1966). *Sound structures of Sindhi and Hindi: A contrastive study*. Poona: DCPRI.

Khubchandani, L. M. (1966a). Phonological correspondences between Sanskrit and Sindhi: A note on relative chronology of borrowings from OIA. Paper read at XXV All-India Sanskrit Sahitya Sammelan. Delhi.

Khubchandani, L. M. (1966b). Implosives in Sindhi. XXIII All India Oriental Conference. Aligarh.

Khubchandani, L. M. (2003). Sindhi. In Cardona, G. & Jain, D. (eds.), *The Indo-Aryan Languages*. London, New York: Routledge (Routledge Language Family Series). 622–58.

Kortlandt, F. (1981). Glottalic consonants in Sindhi and Proto-Indo-European. *Indo-Iranian Journal* **23**. 15–19.

Nihalani, P. (1974a). An aerodynamic study of stops in Sindhi. *Phonetica* **29**. 193–224.

Nihalani, P. (1974b). Lingual articulation of stops in Sindhi. *Phonetica* **30**. 197–212.

Rohra, S. K. (1971). Sindhi, Kacchi and emigrant Sindhi. *Indian Linguistics* **32.2**. 123–31.

Ruplin, F. & Steinmetz, D. (1967) A transformation-generative phonology of Sindhi. *Presented at the X International Congress of Linguistics*. Bucharest.

Sufi, H. S. M. (1955). *Zia-ul-uruz (Sindhi prosody)*. Dadu Sindh.

Turner, R. L. (1924). The Sindhi recursives or voiced stops preceded by glottal closure. *Bulletin of the School of Oriental and African Studies* **3.2.** 301–15 (repr. 1975 in Collected Papers: 192–205).

Varyani, P. L. (1974). Sources of implosives in Sindhi. *Indian Linguistics* **35.1.** 51–54.

SINHALESE

Coates, W. & De Silva, M. W. S. (1960). The segmental phonemes of Sinhalese. *University of Ceylon Review* **18.** 3–4. 163–75.

Hettiaratchi, D. E. (1959). Echo words in Sinhalese. *University of Ceylon Review* **17.** 1–2. 47–50.

Karunatilake, W. S. & Suseedirarajah, S. (1973). Phonology of Sinhalese and Srilanka Tamil: A study in contrast and interference. *Indian Linguistics* **34.3**. 180-90.

URDU

Gumperz, J. J. & Naim, C. M. (1960). Formal and informal standards in the Hindi regional language area. *International Journal of American Linguistics* **26 (3)**. 92–118.

Hussain, S. (1997). *Phonetic correlates of lexical stress in Urdu*. Northwestern University. (Unpublished Ph.D. Dissertation).

Kelkar, A. R. (1968). *Studies in Hindi-Urdu* **1**. Poona: DC.

Khan, I. H. (1999). *A contrastive and comparative study of Standard Urdu and Standard Hindi.* Aligarh: Aligarh Muslim University Press.

Khan, A. G. & Malik, N. A. (1986). Spectrographic study of voiceless Urdu fricatives. Rajapurohit, B.B. (ed.), (1986). *Acoustic studies in India*. Mysore: Central Institute of Indian Languages. 49–54.

Khan, N. A. (1991). *Urdu Sāxt ke Bunyādi Anāsir* [in Urdu]. New Delhi: Urdu Mahal Publication.

Schmidt, R. L. (2003). Urdu. Cardona, G. & Jain, D. (eds.), *The Indo-Aryan Languages*. London, New York: Routledge (Routledge Language Family Series). 286–350.

Zaidi, S. (1985) *U.du Zabān ka Sautiyāti Tajziyā* [Phonetic Analysis of Urdu]. Aligarh: Maktaba Jamia Ltd.

DAKHINI URDU-HYDERABADI

Matthews, D. J. (1976). *Dakani language and literature*. Ph. D. thesis. School of Oriental and African Studies, University of London.

Schmidt, R. L. (1981). *Dakhini Urdu: History and structure*. New Delhi: Bahri Publications.

4. Tibeto-Burman

ADI

Das Gupta, K. (1976). Agglutination in Adi languages of Arunachal. *Resarun* **2.4**. 18–21.

Suebplai, P. S. (1986). *Phonetic description of Adi language.* MA dissertation. Delhi: University of Delhi.

AKHA

Bradley, D. (1976). Akha and Southern Loloish. Hashimoto, J. M. (ed.), *Genetic relationship, diffusion and typological similarities of east and southeast Asian languages*. Tokyo: The Japan Society for the Promotion of Science. 101–45.

Dellinger, D.W. (1967). Notes on Akha segmental phonemes and tones. *Pacific linguistics* **1.9**. 35–43.

Dellinger, D. W. (1968). Ambivalence in Akha phonology. *Anthropological Linguistics* **10.8**. 16–22.

Simon, I. M. (1970). *Aka language guide*. Shillong: North-East Frontier Agency.

ANGAMI

Blankenship, B. (1993). Phonetic structures of Khonoma Angami. *Linguistics of Tibeto-Burman Area* **16.2**. 69–88. *et al.*

Burling, R. (1960). Angami Naga phonemics and word list. *Indian Linguistics* **21**. 51–60.

Giridhar, P. P. (1980). *Angami grammar*. Mysore: Central Institute of Indian Languages.

McCabe, R. B. (1887). *Outline grammar of the Angami naga language, with a vocabulary and illustrative sentences*. Calcutta.

Michailovsky, B. (1975c). Review of Radheshyam Singh Gautam: *Angami vyakaran*; B. B. Kumar: *Angami-Hindi-English dictionary*; N. Ravindran: *Angami phonetic reader*. *Kailash* **3.2**: 176–82.

Ravindran, N. (1974). *Angami phonetic reader*. Mysore: Central Institute of Indian Languages.

Shafer, R. (1962). Note on Angami dialects. *Anthropos* 57. 188–90.

Weidert, A. K. (1981). Star, moon, spirits and the affricates of Angami Naga: A reply to James A Mattisoff. *Linguistics of Tibeto-Burman Area* **6.1**. 1–47.

AO-NAGA

Coupe, A. (2007). *A grammar of Mongsen Ao*. Berlin: Mouton de Gruyter.

Coupe, A. R. (2003). *A phonetic and phonological description of Ao: A Tibeto-Burman language of Nagaland, North-East India*. Canberra: Pacific Linguistics.

Gowda, K. S. G. (1972). *Ao-Naga phonetic reader*. Mysore: Central Institute of Indian Languages.

Gowda, K. S. G. (1975). *Ao grammar*. Mysore: Central Institute of Indian Languages.

Kloss, H. & McConnell, G. D. (1989). *Ao*. 630–650.

Sanyal, P. (2005). *Some aspects of the morphophonology of tones in Ao*. M. Phil. dissertation. Hyderabad: CIEFL.

Temsunungsang, T. (2005). Pitch characteristics of lexical tone and intonation in Chungli (Ao-Naga). Paper presented at *5th Asian GLOW*, 5–8 October 2005. New Delhi: JNU.

Temsunungsang, T. (2008). Tonality and the analysis of sub-minimal words in Ao. Morey, S. & Post, M. (eds.), *North East Indian linguistics*. New Delhi: Foundation/ Cambridge University Press India.

Temsunungsang, T. (2009). *Aspects of the prosodic phonology of Ao: An interdisciplinary study*. Ph. D. Dissertation. Hyderabad: EFLU.

APATANI

Abraham, P.T. (1985). *Apatani Grammar*. Mysore: Central Institute of Indian Languages.

Simon, I. M. (1965). *Apatani language guide*. Shillong: North-East Frontier Agency.

Simon, I. M. (1972). *An introduction to Apatani*. Gangtok, Sikkim, GOI Press.

BALTI

Rangan, K. (1975). *Balti phonetic reader*. Mysore: Central Institute of Indian Languages.

Sprigg, R. K. (1966c). Lepcha and Balti Tibetan: Tonal or non-tonal languages?, *Asia Major*, new series, **12:2.** 185–201.

Sprigg, R. K. (1967). Balti-Tibetan verb syllable finals, and a prosodic analysis, *Asia Major*, new series. **13.** 1–2, 187–201.

BANTAWA

Rai, N. K. (1985). *A descriptive study of Bantawa.* Ph.D. dissertation. Poona: UP, Deccan College Post-Graduate and Research Institute.

BODO

Bhattacharya, P. C. (1977). *Descriptive analysis of Boro language.* Gauhati: University of Guwahati Press.

Burling, Robbins (1959) Proto-Bodo. *Language* **35.** 433–53.

Burling, R. (2004a). *The language of the Modhupur Mandi, Vol. I: Grammar.* Delhi: Bibliophile South Asia and Morganville.

Burling, R. (2004b). *The language of the Modhupur Mandi, Vol. II: The lexicon. //www_personal.umitech.edu_rburling//*

Burton-Page, J. (1955). An analysis of the syllable in Boro. *Indian Linguistics* **16.** 334–44.

Halvorsrud, H. (1959). *A short grammar of the Boro language.* Goalpara: The Boro Literature Board.

Kloss, H. & McConnell, G. D. (1989). *Bodo.* 705–732.

Sarmah, P. (2004). *Some aspects of the tonal phonology of Bodo.* M. Phil. dissertation. Hyderabad: CIEFL.

BOKAR

Megu, A. (1990). *Bokar language guide.* Itanagar: Directorate of Research. Government of Arunachal Pradesh.

BORI

Megu, A. (1988). *Bori phrase book.* Itanagar: Directorate of Research. Government of Arunachal Pradesh.

BYANGSI

Sharma, D. D. (1989). *Byangsi. Tribal languages of Himachal Pradesh, Part-I.* Delhi: Mittal Publications.

Sharma, S. R. (2001). A sketch of Byangsi grammar. Nagano, Y. & Lapolla, R. (eds.), *New research on Zhangzhung and related Himalayan languages.* Osaka: National Museum of Ethnology ([Bon Studies 3, Senri Ethnological Reports No. 19). 271–242.

Sharma, S. R. (2007). *Byangsi grammar and vocabulary*. Pune: Deccan College Post-Graduate and Research Institute.

Trivedi, G. M. (1991). *Descriptive grammar of Byansi: A Bhotia language*. Calcutta: ASI.

CHAUDANGSI

Krishan, S. (2001). Sketch of Chaudansi grammar. Nagano, Y. & Lapolla, R. (eds.), *New research on Zhangzhung and related Himalayan languages*, Osaka: National Museum of Ethnology ([Bon Studies 3, Senri Ethnological Reports No. 19), 401–448.

CHEPANG

Caughley, R. (1969). Chepang phonemic summary, *TBPS* **4**. 36–39. Kathmandu: SIL.

Caughley, R. (1970a). Pitch, intensity and higher levels in Chepang. In Hale and Pike (eds.). 143–57.

Caughley, . (1970b). Chepang segmental synopsis. In Hale and Pike (eds.). 279–98.

DARMA

Willis, C. M. (2007). A Descriptive Grammar of Darma: An Endangered Tibeto- Burman Language. Ph. Dissertation. University of Texas at Austin.

DEURI

Brown, W. B. (1895). *An outline grammar of the Deuri Chutia language: Spoken in upper assam with an introduction, illustrative sentences and short vocabulary*. Shillong: Assam Secretariat Printing Office.

Goswami, U. (1968). An analysis of Deuri language. *Journal of the Assam Research Society* **18**. 86–97.

DIMASA

Dundas, W. C. M. (1908). *An outline grammar of the Kachari (Dimasa) language*. Shillong.

Kloss, H. & McConnell, G. D. (1989). *Dimasa*. 733–748.

Singha, D. Kh. (2007). *An introduction to Dimasa phonology*. Guwahati: DVS Publishers.

GALO/ GALO LARE/ GALLONG

Das Gupta, K. (1963). *An introduction to the Gallong language*. Shillong: North-East Frontier Agency.

Das Gupta, K. (1968b). *Galo language guide*. Shillong: North-East Frontier Agency.

Gandhi, D. P. (1978). *Structural sketch of Galo language*. Ph.D. dissertation. Delhi: University of Delhi.

Post, M. W. (2005). Synchronic and diachronic dimensions of the tone system of Galo. *Paper presented at the 36th Annual Meeting of the Australian Linguistics Society*. Melbourne: Monash University.

Post, M. W. (2007). *A grammar of Galo*. Ph. D. thesis. LaTrobe University.

Post, M. W. (2009). The phonology and grammar of Galo "words": A case study in benign disunity. *Studies in Language* **33 (4)**. 934–974.

GARO

Benedict, P. K. (1994). Garo and Gyarong (Suomo) prosodies. *Linguistics of Tibeto-Burman Area* **17.1**. 179–80.

Bonnerjea, B. (1935–36). Contributions to Garo linguistics and ethnology. *Antropos* 30–31.

Burling, R. (1961). *A Garo grammar*. Poona: Deccan College Post-Graduate Research Institute.

Burling, R. (1981). Garo spelling and Garo phonology. *Linguistics of Tibeto-Burman Area* **6.1**. 61–81.

Burling, R. (1992). Garo as a minimal tone language. *Linguistics of Tibeto-Burman Area* **15.2**. 33–51.

Duanmu, S. (1994). The phonology of the glottal stop in Garo. *Linguistics of Tibeto-Burman Area* **17.2**. 69–82.

Phillips, E. G. (1904). *Outline grammar of the Garo language*. Shillong.

GURUNG

Burton-Page, J. (1955a). Two studies in Gurung Kura 1. Tone, 2. Rhotacization and retroflexion. *Bulletin of the School of Oriental and African Studies* **17**. 111–19.

Glover, W. W. (1969b). Gurung phonemic summary. *TBPS* **1**.

Glover, W. W. (1970a). Gurung tone and higher levels. In Hale K. and Pike K. L. (eds.) 52–73.

Glover, W. W. (1970b). Gurung segmental synopsis. In Hale K. and Pike K. L. (eds.). 211–236.

Glover, W. W. & Glover, Jessie, R. (1972). A guide to Gurung tone. *GNT* **6**.

Hale, E. A. & Glover, W. W. (1970). A note on glides, syllabicity and tone in Gurung. In Hale K. and Pike K. L. (eds.). 49–51.

HMAR

Dutta-Baruah, P. N. & Bapui, V. L. T. (1996). *Hmar grammar*. Mysore: Central Institute of Indian Languages.

KABUI

Tiwari, S. K. (1971). *Descriptive grammar of Kabui*. Ph.D. dissertation. Poona: UP, Deccan College Post-Graduate and Research Institute.

KAGATE

Hohlig, M. & Hari, A. M. (1976). Kagate phonemic summary. Kathmandu: SIL. 12.

KANGRI

Chauhan, A. R. (1992). *The Kangri central Subsystems (A structural description)*. Shimla: Himachal Academy of Arts, Culture and Languages.

Sharma, S. (1974). *Kangari: A descriptive study of the Kangra Valley dialect of Himachal Pradesh*. Hoshiarpur: V. V. B. Institute of Sanskrit and Indological Studies. Punjab University.

KARBI

Jeyapaul, V. Y. (1987). *Karbi grammar*. Mysore: Central Institute of Indian Languages.

Kloss, H. & McConnell, G. D. (1989). *Karbi*. 1149–1166.

KHAM

Ray, P. S. (1965). Kham phonology. *Journal of the American Oriental Society* 85. 336–42.

Watters, D. E. (1985). Emergent word tone in Kham: A Tibeto-Burman halfway house. *Linguistics of the Tibeto-Burman area* 5.1. 49–127.

Watters, D. E. (2002). *A grammar of Kham*. Cambridge: CUP.

Watters, D. E. (2003). Kham. Thurgood, G. & LaPolla, R. J. (eds.), The Sino-Tibetan Languages. London: Routledge. 596. 683–704.

Wayland, R. P. & Guion, S. G. (2005). Sound changes following the loss of /r/ in Khmer: A new tonogenetic mechanism?. *Mon-Khmer Studies: A Journal of Southeast Asian Languages* 35. 55–82.

KHEZHA

Kapfo, K. (1992). *A descriptive analysis of Khezha*. Ph.D. dissertation. Mysore: University of Mysore.

KHOA

Simon, I. A. (1975). The Khoa language. *Resarun* **1**. 100-103.

KINNAURI

Sharma, D. D. (1988). *A descriptive grammar of Kinnauri*. Delhi: Mittal Publications.

KIRANTI-KOINTS

Rapacha, Lal (2006). *A descriptive grammar of Kiranti-Koints*. Ph. D. thesis. Centre for Linguistics, Jawaharlal Nehru University, New Delhi.

KONYAK

Kloss, H. & McConnell, G. D. (1989) *Konyak*. 1003–1020.

KOREN

Zeite, L. (2007). *Phonology of Koren*. M. Phil. Thesis. Centre for Linguistics, Jawaharlal Nehru University.

Zeite, L. & Pandey, P. K. (2007). A sketch of the word phonology of Koren. Ms. Centre for Linguistics, J. N. U., New Delhi. ('Koren' in Volume II of the present book.)

KUKISH

Shafer, R. (1950c). The Naga branches of Kukish. *Rocznik Orientalistyczny* **16**. 467–530.

KULUNG

Holzhausen, A. (1973). Phonological survey report of the Kulung language. Kathmandu: SIL.

LADAKHI

Baraik, S. K. (2000). *Phonology of Ladakhi*. MA dissertation. Delhi: University of Delhi.

Kloss, H. & McConnell, G. D. (1989). *Ladakhi*.1039–1058.

Koshal, S. (1979a). *Ladakhi grammar*. Delhi: Motilal Banarasidass.

Koshal, S. (1979b). *Ladakhi phonetic reader*. Mysore: Central Institute of Indian Languages.

LAHU

Bradley, D. (1975b). *Lahu dialects and Proto-Loloish*. Ph.D. dissertation. London: University of London.

Burling, R. (1966b). A problem in Lahu phonology. *Artibus Asie* **1**. 97–101.

Matisoff, J. A. (1973). *The grammar of Lahu*. Berkeley: UC Press.

LAKHER/MARA

Lorrein, R. A. (1950). *Grammar and dictionary of Lakher or Mara language*. Shillong: Dept of Historical and Antiquarian Studies in Assam.

LEPCHA

Bodman, N. (1989). Some remarks on lepcha vowels. in David Bradley et al. (eds), *Prosodic analysis and asian linguistics: To Honour R. K. Sprigg*. Canberra: Pacific Linguistics. 137–41.

Campbell, A. (1840). Note on the Lepchas of Sikkim, with a vocabulary of their language. *Journal of the Asiatic Society of Bengal* **IX**. 379–93.

Forrest, R. A. D. (1962). The linguistic position of the Rong (Lepcha). *Journal of American Oriental Society* **82**. 331–35.

Kloss, H. & McConnell, G. D. (1989). *Lepcha*. 1059–1076.

Plaisier, H. (2007). *A grammar of Lepcha*. Languages of the Greater Himalayan Region 4. Leiden: Koninklijke Brill.

Sinha, P. (1966). *A descriptive grammar of Lepcha*. Ph.D. dissertation. Poona: UP.

Sprigg, R. K. (1966b). The glottal stops and glottal constriction in Lepcha. and borrowing from Tibetan. *Bulletin of Tibetology* **3.1**. 5–14.

Sprigg, R. K. (1966c). Lepcha and Balti Tibetan: Tonal or non-tonal languages?. *AM*, New series, **12:2**. 185–201.

Tamsang, K. (1994). *A grammar of the Lepcha language*. Kalimpong: Lyangsong Tamsang.

LIANGMAI

Moita, A. (2007). A Preliminary Sketch of the Phonology of Liangmai Central Institute of Indian Languages. Mysore.

Niumai, L. (1988). The Faringkikhon Liangmai Naga-Mellennial Dictionary.

Wichamdinbo & Pandey, P. K. (2009). Word-phonology of Liangmai: A sketch. Ms. Centre for Linguistics. Jawaharlal Nehru University, New Delhi. ('Liangmai' in Volume II of the present book.)

LIMBU

Driem, G. van (1987). *A grammar of Limbu*. Berlin: Mouton de Gruyter.

LOTHA

Acharya, K. P. (1975). *Lotha phonetic reader*. Mysore: Central Institute of Indian Languages.

Kloss, H. & McConnell, G. D. (1989). *Lotha*. 1077–1094.

LUNGCHANG

Rekhung, W. (1988). Lungchang Language Guide. Itanagar: Directorate of Research: Govt of Arunachal Pradesh.

Mao Naga

Giridhar, P. P. (1994). *Mao Naga grammar*. Mysore: Central Institute of Indian Languages.

MARING

Ningomba, M. S. (1978). *Descriptive grammar of Maring*. Ph.D. dissertation. Poona: UP, Deccan College Post-Graduate and Research Institute.

MAGAR

Grunow-Horsta, K. (1998). An analysis of murmur in Magar. *Paper Presented at the 4th Himalayan language symposium*. Pune: Deccan College Post-Graduate and Research Institute.

Subba, S. (1972). *Descriptive analysis of Magar: A Tibeto-Burman language*. Ph.D. dissertation. Pune: Deccan College Post-Graduate and Research Institute.

MANCHAD

Sharma, D. D. (1982) *A descriptive analysis of Pattani (a dialect of Lahul)*. Hoshiarpur: V. V. B. Institute. Punjab University.

Sharma, S. R. (1990). Word formation in Manchad and Onge: Some inflectional categories. *Bulletin of Deccan College Post Graduate Research Institute* **49**. 411–16.

MARU

Burling, R. (1966a). The addition of final stops in the history of Maru. *Language* **42**. 581–87.

Pendergast, T. M. & Yamaguchi, E. (1972). On the addition of final stops in Maru. 5th STCP.

MEITEI

Abbi, A. & Mishra, A. K. (1985). Consonant clusters and syllable structures of Meitei. *Linguistics of Tibeto-Burman Area* **8.2**. 81–92.

Bhatia, D. N. S. & Ningomba, M. S. (1991–92). Word formation in Manipuri. *Bulletin of Deccan College Post Graduate Research Institute* **51, 52**. 233–44.

Chelliah, S. L. (1990). A bibliography of Meiterion (Manipuri) linguistics. *Linguistics of Tibeto-Burman Area* **13.2**. 73–86.

Chelliah, S. L. (1990). Level ordered morphology and phonology in Manipuri. *Linguistics of Tibeto-Burman Area* **13.2**. 27–71.

Chelliah, S. L. (1997). *A grammar of Meithei*. Mouton de Gruyter.

Chelliah, S. L. (2003). Meithei. Thurgood, G. & Lapolla, R. (eds). 427–38.

Chelliah, S. L. (In press). An autolexical analysis of voicing assimilation in Manipuri. Shiller, E. & Steinberg, E. (eds.), *Proceedings of the workshop on autolexical syntax, Chicago*. Berlin: Mouton.

Devi, I. (1975). *Meiteirongi Syllable [The Syllable in Manipuri]*. MA dissertation. Imphal: Manipur University.

Devi, P. (1979). *Tone and toneship in Meiteilon*. MA dissertation. Imphal: Manipur University.

Kloss, H. & McConnell, G. D. (1989). *Bishnupuria*. 687–704.

Meetai, N. G. Shanti K. (1998). *The phonetic properties of the speech sounds of meitilon*. Ph. D. Thesis. New Delhi: Jawaharlal Nehru University.

Mishra, A. K. (1993). Some aspects of Meitei Phonology. *International Journal of Dravidian Linguistics* **23.2**. 51–66.

Pettigrew, W. (1912). *Manipuri (Mitei) Grammar with Illustrative Sentences*. Allahabad: Pioneer Press.

Singh, I. (1975). *Manipuri phonetic reader*. Mysore: Central Institute of Indian Languages.

Singh, I. (1974). Tone sandhi in Manipuri. *Anthropological survey of India* **23**. 1–2. 92–97.

Singh, L. M. (1986). A note on Manipuri tones. Rajapurohit, B. B. (ed.). 105-06.

Singh, T. W. (1986). *A study of Meitei phonology*. Imphal.

Singh, U. C. (1986). A brief note on the distribution of the segmental phonemes in modern Meitei. *TB* **1**. 3–4. 10–14.

Singh, U. C. (1986). A brief note on the vowels in clusters in modern Meitei. *TB* **1**. 3–4. 16–24.

Singh, W. R. (1989). The Kwatha dialect of Meitei. *Linguistics of Tibeto-Burman Area* **12.2**. 101–21.

Sinha, K. P. (1974). Bishnupuriya Manipuri: A descriptive sketch. *Indian Linguistics* **35**. 185–99.

Sinha, K. P. (1981). *The Bishnupuriya Manipuri language*. Calcutta: Firma KLM.

Thoudam, P. C. (1989). Conditioning factors for morphophonemic alternations of manner in Meiterion. *Linguistics of Tibeto-Burman Area* **12.2.** 93–99.

Wasuksana, R. K. (1982). *Phonological comparison: Old and modern Manipuri*. M.Phil. dissertation. Pune: Deccan College Post-Graduate and Research Institute.

MEYOR

Landi, V. (2005). *The Meyors and their language*. Itanagar: Directorate of Research: Govt of Arunachal Pradesh.

MIJU

Das Gupta, K. (1977b). *A phrase book in Miju*. Shillong: Government of Arunachal Pradesh.

MILANG

Tayeng, A. (1976). *Milang phrase book*. Itanagar: The Director of Information and Public Relations. Govt of Arunachal Pradesh.

MINYONG

Das Gupta, K. (1977c). A few aspects of the Minyong language. *Resarun* **3.3.** 16–22.

Mishmi

Shastri, G. D. P. (1984). *Mishmi phonetic reader*. Mysore: Central Institute of Indian Languages.

Shastri, G. D. P. (1984). *Mishmi grammar*. Mysore: Central Institute of Indian Languages.

MISSING/MIRI

Prasad, B. R. (1991). *Missing grammar*. Mysore: Central Institute of Indian Languages.

Taid, T. (1987). A short note on Missing phonology. *Linguistics of Tibeto-Burman Area* **10.** 130–37.

Taid, T. (1987). Missing morphophonemics, *Linguistics of Tibeto-Burman Area* **10.1.** 138–46.

MIZO

Bright, W. (1957b). Alternations in Lushai. *Indian Linguistics* **18.**

Burling, R. (1957). Lushai phonemics. *Indian Linguistics* **17.** 148–55.

Chhangte, L. (1986). *A preliminary grammar of the Mizo language*. MA dissertation. Ariington: University of Texas.

Fanai, L. T. (1989). *Some aspects of the autosegmental phonology of Mizo*. M.litt. dissertation. Hyderabad: CIEFL.

Fanai, L. T. (1992). *Some aspects of the lexical phonology of Mizo and English: An autosegmental approach*. Ph.D. dissertation. Hyderabad: CIEFL.

Fanai, L. T. & Vijaykrishnan, K. G. (1995). Mizo Rhyme Structure. CIEFL. *Occasional papers in linguistics* 5. 53–64.

Hamp, E. P. (1959). Lushai syllable. *Indian Linguistics* **20**. 238–40.

Henderson, E. J. A. (1948) Notes on the syllable structure of Lushai. *Bulletin of the School of Oriental and African Studies* **12**. 713–25.

Hillard, E. J. (1992). Whistle and fontanel: Two Mizo (Lushai) texts with commentary. *Linguistics of Tibeto-Burman Area* **15.2**. 127–49.

Kheingte, R. B. (1964). *Lusai grammar*. Aizawal: Sipula and Sons.

Kloss, H. & McConnell, G. D. (1989). *Lushai/Mizo*. 1095–1122.

Lorrain, J. H. & Saidge, F. W. (1984). *The Lushai grammar and dictionary*. Delhi: Goyal Offset Printers.

Weidert, A. (1975). Componential analysis of Lushai phonology. In Koerner, E. F. K. (ed.), *Amsterdem studies in theory and history of linguistic sciences*.

Zawla, K. (1974). *Mizo Tawng grammar*. Aizawl: Mizo Academy of Letters.

MONPA

Das Gupta, K. (1968), *An introduction to Central Monpa*. Shillong: North-East Frontier Agency.

MOYON

Kosha, D. (1986). A note on the tones of Moyon. Rajapurohit. B. B. (ed.), *Acoustic studies in indian languages*. Mysore: Central Institute of Indian Languages. 107-08.

NEWARI

Genetti, C. (1990). A descriptive and historical account of the Dolakha Newari dialect. Ph. D. dissertation. University of Oregon. [Also published in 1994 by the Tokyo University of Foreign Studies.]

Geneti, C. (2007). *A Reference Grammar of Dolakha Newar*. [Mouton Grammar Series.] Berlin: Mouton de Gruyter.

Hale, E. A. & Hale, M. (1969). Newari phonemic summary. *TBPS* 5.

Hale, E. A. & Hale, M. (1976). Devnagari order for phonological transcriptions in Newari. In Sresthacharya, I. & Tuladhar, N. (eds.), *Jyapu vocabulary*. Kathmandu: Institute of Nepal and Asian Studies. 120-124.

Hale, E. A. (1970c). Newari segmental synopsis. *Hale and Pike (1970)*. 131–51.

Hale, E. A. (1970b). Newari higher levels. *Hale and Pike (1970)*. 58–69.

Modi, B. V. (1967). The phonemes of Newari. *Journal of the M. S. University of Baroda* **16.1**. 103–34.

NOCTE

Das Gupta, K. (1971). *An introduction to the Nocte language*. Shillong: North-East Frontier Agency.

NISHI

Chhangte, T. (1990). Nishi grammar sampler. Paper presented at the 23rd International Conference on Sino-Tibetan Languages and Linguistics. Arlington, Texas.

Chhangte, T. (1992). Phonology of some Nishi dialects. Paper presented at the 2th International Conference on Sino-Tibetan Languages and Linguistics. Berkley.

Das Gupta, K. (1969). *Dafla language guide*. Shillong: North-East Frontier Agency.

Hamilton, R. C. (1900). *An Outline grammar of the Dafla language as spoken by the tribes immediately south of the Apa Tanang country*. Shillong.

Ray, P. S.(1967). Dafla phonology and morphology. *Anthropological Linguistics* **9.8**. 9–14.

PAILIBO

Badu, T. (1994). *Pailibu language guide*. Itanagar: Directorate of Research: Govt of Arunachal Pradesh.

PADAAM

Borthakur, N. (1998). *Aspects of phonology and morphophonemic processes in Padaam*. MA dissertation. Delhi: University of Delhi.

Tayeng, A. (1983). *A phrase book in Padam*. Itanagar: Director of Research. Govt of Arunachal Pradesh.

PAITE

Singh, N. S. (2006). *Paite language*. New Delhi: Mittal Publications.

PHOM

Burling, R. & Phom, L.A. (1988). Phom phonology and word list. *Linguistics of the Tibeto-Burman Area*. 21.2:13–42.

PURKI

Rangan, K. (1979). *Purki grammar*. Mysore: Central Institute of Indian Languages.

RANG PO BHASA

Zollar, C. P. (1983). Die sprache det Rang Pas von Garhwal (Rang Po Bha:sa) grammatik, texte, worterbuch. Wiesbaden: Otto Harrossowitz.

RAWANG

Morse, R. H. (1962). *Hierarchical levels of Rawang phonology*. M.A. Thesis. Indiana University.

Morse, R. H. (1963). Phonology of Rawang. *Anthropological Linguistics* 5.5. 17–41.

Morse, S. A. (1988). A short update on Rawang phonology. *Linguistics of Tibeto-Burman Area* **11.2**. 120–32.

RONGMEI

Mpamei, Ch. C. (1996). *A phonetic study of Rongmei*. Ph.D. dissertation. New Delhi: JNU.

RAJI

Krishan, S. (2001), A sketch of Raji grammar. In Nagano, Y. & La Polla, R. J. (eds.), *New research on Zhangzhung and related Himalayan languages*. Osaka: National Museum of Ethnology. 449–501.

SANGTAM

Kloss, H. & McConnell, G. D. (1989) *Sangtam*. 1219–1234.

SEMA NAGA

Kloss, H. & McConnell, G. D. (1989). *Sema*. 1257–1276.

Shreedhar, M. V. (1976). *Sema phonetic reader*. Mysore: Central Institute of Indian Languages.

Sreedhar, M. V. (1980). *Sema grammar*. Mysore: Central Institute of Indian Languages.

SHERPA

Gorden, K. H. (1969). Sherpa Phonemic Summary. *TBPS* **2**.

Gorden, K. H. (1970). Sherpa tone and higher levels. In *Hale and Pike (1970)*. 186–206.

Gorden, K. H.& Schottelndreyer, B. (1970). Sherpa segmental synopsis. *Hale and Pike (1970)*. 345–67.

Pike, E. V. (1994). Tonal contrast on the word level. *Word* **45.2**. 173–76.

Walters, S. A. (1998). An acoustic analysis of Sherpa tone. *Paper presented at the 4th Himalayan Languages Symposium*. Pune: Deccan College Post-Graduate and Research Institute.

SINGPHO

Morey, S. (forthcoming). *Turung: A grammar of a variety of Singpho spoken in Assam*.

Quingxia, D. & Diehl, L. (2003). Jingpho. In Thurgood, G & Lapolla, R. (eds.), 401-08.

SPITI

Das, S. C. (2000 [1902])). *Tibetan-English dictionary (with Sanskrit synonyms)*. Delhi: Motilal Banarsidass.

DeLancey, S. (2003). Lhasa Tibetan. In Thurgood, G & Lapolla, R. (eds). 270-88.

Hodge, S. (2003). *An introduction to classical Tibetan*. Bernard: Orchid Press.

Kato, A. (2001). A preliminary report on Spiti phonemes. In Nagano, Y. & Lapolla, R. (eds.), *New research on Zhangzhung and related Himalayan languages*. Osaka: National Museum of Ethnology ([Bon Studies 3, Senri Ethnological Reports No. 19). 121–154.

Sharma, D. D. (1989). *Tribal languages of Himachal Pradesh. Vol.* ***II***. Delhi: Mittal Publication.

Sharma, S. R. (1979). Phonological structure of Spiti. *Linguistics of Tibeto-Burman Area* **4.2**. 83–110.

Theos, C. (1946). *A simplified grammar of the literary Tibetan language*. Santa Barbara, California: Tibetan Text Society.

Tournadre, N. & Dorje, S. (2003. *Manual of standard Tibetan*. New York: Snow Lion Publications.

TAGIN

Das Gupta, K. (1983). *An outline on Tagin language*. Itanagar: Directorate of Research. Government of Arunachal Pradesh.

STOD

Sharma, D. D. (1989). *Tibeto-Himalayan languages of Uttarakhand-Part I.* Delhi: Mittal Publication.

TAMANG

Mazaoudon, M. (2003). Tamang. In Thurgood, G & Lapolla, R. (eds). 289–314.

Mazaudon, M. (2005). On tone in Tamang and neighbouring languages: synchrony and diachrony. In Kaji, S. (ed.), *Proceedings of the Symposium Cross-linguistic Studies of Tonal Phenomena:Historical development: Tone-syntax interface, and descriptive studies*. Tokyo University of Foreign Studies. 79–96.

Taylor, D. (1969). Tamang phonemic summary. *Tibeto-Burman phonemic summaries*. Kathmandu: Summer Institute of Linguistics and Tribhuvan University.

TANGAM

Badu, T. (2004). *Tangam language guide*. Itanagar: Directorate of Research: Govt of Arunachal Pradesh.

TANGKHUL

Ahum, V. (1997). *Tangkhul-Naga grammar: A study of word-formation.* Ph.D. dissertation. New Delhi: JNU.

Pettigrew, W. (1912). *Tangkhul Naga grammar and dictionary (Ukhrul dialect) with illustrative sentences*. Shillong: assam Secretariat Printing Office.

Singh, L. M. (1987). *A grammar of Tangkhul*. Ph.D. dissertation. Poona: UP. Deccan College Post-Graduate and Research Institute.

TANGSA

Bandyopadhyay, S.K. (1980). *Linguistic analysis of Tangsa: A Tibeto-Burman language*. Ph. D. thesis. University of Delhi.

THAADOU

gibbon, D., Pandey, P., Haokip, M. K. & Bachan, J. (2009). Prosodic issues in synthesising Thadou, a Tibeto-Burman tone language. Paper presented at Interspeech/ Eurospeech. Brighton, July 2009.

Kloss, H. & McConnell, G. D. (1989) *Thaadou*. 1295–1312.

Krishan, S. (1980). *Thadou: A grammatical sketch*. Calcutta: ASI.

Thirumalai, M. S. (1972). *Thaadou phonetic reader*. Mysore: Central Institute of Indian Languages.

TIBETAN

Chang, B. S. (1968a). A projected study of Tibetan tones. *Monthly internal memorandom, Phonological laboratory*. Berkeley: University of California. 49–53.

Chang, B. S. (1968b). Notes on length and tone in Tibetan. *Monthaly internal memorandom, Phonological laboratory*. Berkeley: University of California. 8–13.

Chang, B. S. (1968c). Lhasa Tibetan vowels I,e:,e, *Monthly internal memorandom, Phonological laboratory*. Berkeley: University of California. 8–18.

Chang, B. S. (1968e). Notes on the Tibetan vowel system. *Monthly internal memorandom, Phonological laboratory*. Berkeley: University of Califirnia.

Chang, B. S. (1968f). Sedlaceks The Tonal System of Tibetan (Lhasa Dialect). *Monthly Monthly internal memorandom, Phonological laboratory*. Berkeley: University of California. 8–13.

Chang, B. S. (1968g) Voice and aspiration in Lhasa Tibetan. *Monthly internal memorandom, Phonological laboratory*. Berkeley: University of California.

Chang, B. S. & Chang, K. (1967). Spoken Tibetan morphophonemics. *Language* **43**. 512–25.

Chang, K. & Chang, B. S. (1965). A morphophonemic problem in the spoken Tibetan of Lhasa. *Journal of American Oriental Society* **85**. 34–39.

Chang, K. & Chang, B. S. (1968). Vowel harmony in spoken Lhasa Tibetan. *Project on Linguistic Analysis*. ser. **2.7**. 1–18.

Dawson, W. (1981). *Tibetan phonology*. Ph.D. dissertation. Washington: University of Washington.

DeLancey, S. (2003). Classical Tibetan. In Thurgood, G. & LaPolla, R. J., *The Sino-Tibetan Languages*. London: Routledge. *255–69*.

Gould, B., Richardson, J. & Hugh, E. (1943a). *Tibetan syllables*. Oxford: OUP.

Miller, R. A. (1954a). Morphologically determined allomorphs in spoken Tibetan. *Language* **30**. 458–60.

Miller, R. A. (1956a). Segmental diachronic phonology of a Ladakh (Tibetan) dialect. *Zeitschrifft der Deutschen Morgenlandischen Gesellschaft* **106.** 345–62.

Miller, R. A. (1966a). Early evidence for vowel harmony in Tibetan. *Language* **42**. 252–77.

Olson, R. F. (1974). Central Kham Tibetan: A phonemic survey. *Kailash* **2**. 217–27.

TIDDIM CHIN

Bhaskararao, P. (1994) Tiddim Chin verbs and their alternants. *Journal of Asian and African Studies*. 46–47.

Henderson, E. J. A. (1965). *Tiddim Chin: A descriptive analysis of two texts*. London and New York: OUP.

WANCHO

Burling, R. & Wangsu, M. (1998). Wancho phonology and word list. *Linguistics of Tibeto-Burman Area* **21**. 43–71.

ZO(U)

Mangkang, P. (2010). *Minimal Dictionary and Self-tutor Functional Grammar in Zo-English-Hindi.* New Delhi.

Mangkang, P. & Pandey, P. (2009). Word-phonology of Zo. Ms. Centre for Linguistics, Jawaharlal Nehru University, New Delhi. ('Zo' in Volume II of the present book)

5. TAI-KADAI

KHAMPTI-TAI

Weidert, A. (1977). *Tai-Khamti Phonology and Vocabulary.* Wiesbaden: Franz Steiner Verlag.

Tai-Phake

Konwar, A. (1998). Phonology of the Tai-Phake Language. *Paper presented at the 4th Himalayan Languages Symposium.* Pune: Deccan College Post-Graduate and Research Institute.

Morey, S. (2005). *The Tai languages of Assam: A grammar and texts.* Canberra: Australian National University. [Pacific Linguistics, 565.]

Turung

Morey, S. (2005). The tone and syllable structure of Turung. In Sidwell, P., (ed.), *SEALSXV: Papers from the fifteenth meeting of the Southeast Asian Linguistics Society*, Canberra, Pacific Linguistics. 149–68.

Morey, S. (2005). *The Tai languages of Assam: A grammar and texts.* Canberra: Australian National University. [Pacific Linguistics, 565.]

Morey, S. (forthcoming). *Turung: A grammar of a variety of Singpho spoken in Assam.*

6. Andamanese-Group

GREAT ANDAMANESE

Abbi, A. (2006). *Endangered languages of the Andaman Islands*. Munich: Lincom Europa.

Manoharan, S. (1989). *A descriptive and comparative study of Andamanese language*. Calcutta: ASI.

JARAWA

Abbi, A. (2006). *Endangered languages of the Andaman Islands*. Munich: Lincom Europa.

Kumar, P. (2010). *A descriptive and typological study of Jarawa*. Ph. D. thesis, Jawaharlal Nehru University, New Delhi, and Max-Planck Institute, Leipzig.

Senkuttuvan, R. (2000). *The language of the Jarawa: Phonology*. Calcutta: Anthropological Survey of India.

NANCOWRY-NICOBARESE

Radhakrishnan, R. (1981). *Nancowry word, phonology, morphology and roots of a Nicobarese language*. Canada: Linguistics Research Institute.

NICOBARESE-CAR

Braine, J. C. (1970). *Nicobarese grammar (Car dialect)*. Ph.D. thesis. Barkeley: University of California.

Critchfield, J. (1962). *Car Nicobarese phonology*. Unpublished MS. Berkeley.

Critchfield, J. (1963). A Binary Comparison of the Car and Central Dialects of Nicobarese. Unpublished MS. Berkeley.

Critchfield, J. (1963). Loan-words in Car Nicobarese. Unpublished MS. Berkeley.

Das, A. R. (1972). *A study on the Nicobarese language*. Calcutta: ASI.

ONGE

Abbi, A. (2006). *Endangered languages of the Andaman Islands*. Munich: Lincom Europa.

Dasgupta, P. & Sharma, S. R. (1982). *A handbook of Onge language*. Calcutta: Archaeological Survey of India.

7. Contact Varieties

7 a. Contact languages

BISHNUPURIA

Sinha, K. P. (1974). Bishnupriya Manipuri: A descriptive sketch. *Indian Linguistics* 35. 185–99.

Sinha, K. P. (1981[1968]). *The Bishnupriya Manipuri language*. Calcutta: Firma K. L. M.

DIU-INDO-PORTUGESE

Cardoso, H. C. (2009). The Indo-Portugese language of Diu. Ph. D. thesis. Unoiversiteit van Amsterdam. Uttrecht: LOT

HALBI

Kanshikar, C. (1972). *A descriptive analysis of Halbi: An Indo-Aryan language*. Ph.D. dissertation. Poona: UP.

Shukla, H. L. (1985). *Sociocultural approach to tribal languages: An historico-comparative dictionary of Halbi, the lingua franca of Aryan, Dravidian, and Munda tribes*. Delhi: B. R. Publications.

Singh, R. A. (1972). *Survey of Halabi in Madhya Pradesh*. Delhi: Census of India 1971, vol.1, pt. 11E, Monograph No.5.

Telang, B. (1966). *Chattīsgarhī, Halbī, bhāratīya boliyon kā bhāśvaigyānik adhyayan* [in Hindi, *A linguistic study of the Indian dialects Chattisgarhi and Halbi*]. Bombay: Hindi Granth Ratnakar.

NAGAMESE

Baruah, B. K. (1993). *The language of Nagaland*. Delhi: Mittal Publication.

Sreedhar, M. V. (1974). *Naga Pidgin: A Socio-linguistic Study of Inter-lingual Communication Pattern in Nagaland*. Mysore: CIIL.

SADANI (NAGPURIA)

Jordan-Horstmann, M. (1969). *Sadani: A Bhojpuri dialect spoken in Chotanagpur*. Wiesbaden: Otto Harrassowitz.

Nowrangi, P. S. (1956). *A simple Sadani grammar*. Ranchi: D. S. S. Book Depot.

Nowrangi, P. S. (1965). *nāgpuriyā sadanī bolī kā byākaran*. [in Hindi, The Grammar of Nagpuriya Sadani]. Ranchi: by the author.

URDU-DAKHINI-TAMILNADU

Mohiddin, S. K. (1980). Dakhani Urdu. Annamalinagar: Annamalai Univeristy

VAGRI BOLI

Varma, G. S. (1970). *Vaagri Boli: An Indo-Aryan language*. Annamalainagar: Annamalai University [Publications no. 21.]

Varma, G. S. (1962–69). *A descriptive study of Narrikkuruva dialect: A group of Vaagriboli*. Annamalainagar: Annamalai University.

7 b. Second Language Varieties

INDIAN ENGLISH

Agnihotri, R. K. (1991). Sound patterns of Indian English: a sociolinguistic perspective. Gupta, R. S. Gupta and Kapoor, K. (eds.), *English in India: Issues and Problems*. Delhi: Academic Foundations. 175–88.

Balasubramaniam, T. (1981, rpt 1995). *A textbook of English phonetics for Indian students*. Macmillan.

Balasubramanian, T. (1972–3).The vowels of Tamil and English: a study in contrast. *CIEFL Bulletin* **9**. 27–34.

Bansal, R. K. (1969). *The intelligibility of Indian English, Monograph 4*. Hyderabad: CIEFL.

Bansal, R. K. (1983). *Studies in Phonetics and Spoken English*, *Monograph* **10**. Hyderabad: CIEFL.

Bansal, R. K. and Harrison, J. B. (1972). *Spoken English for India: A manual of speech and phonetics*. Bombay: Orient Longman.

Chaudhary, S. C. (1993). Issues on the Phonology of Indian English. *World Englishes* **12.3**. 375–384.

Chaudhary, S. C.(1986). *Some aspects of the phonology of Indian English*. Ph. D. dissertation. Hyderabdad: CIEFL.

Coelho, G. (1997). Anglo-Indian English: a nativized variety of Indian English. *Language and Society*. **26**. 561–89.

Féry, C. and Pandey, P. (to appear). The prosody of focus and givenness in Hindi and Indian English. [Paper presented at the International Seminar on Prosodic Interfaces, J. N. U., November 24–26, 2011.]

Gargesh, R. (2004) Indian English: Phonology. Edgar, W., Burridge, B. K., Mesthrie, R. and Upton, C. (eds.), *A Handbook of Varieties of English*, *Vol 1: Phonology*. Berlin: Mouton de Gruyter. 993–1002.

Gokhale, S. B. (1982). *The intonational system of Marathi and Marathi English*. Ph. D. thesis. C.I.E.F.L.. Hyderabad.

Gopalakrishnan, R. (2008). *Second language phonologyu: Investigating Tamil English*. M. Phil. Dissertation, Centre for Linguistics, Jawaharlal Nehru University, New Delhi.

Kachru, B. B. (1965). The Indianess in Indian English. *Word* **21**. 391–410.

Latha, P. (1978). *Intonation of Malayalam and Malayalee English: a study of comparison and contrast*. MLitt thesis, CIEFL.

Masica, C. and Dave, P. B. (1972). *The Sound System of Indian English, Monograph* **4**. Hyderabad: CIEFL.

Maxwell, O. and Fletcher, J. (2009). Acoustic and durational properties of Indian English vowels. *World Englishes* **28**. 52–70.

Mehboob, A. & Ahmar, N. (2004). Pakistani English: A historical and phonological overview. Kortmann, B. & Traugott, E. (eds.), *A handbook of varieties of English,* Vol. **1**. Berlin: Mouton de Gruyter. 1003–16.

Mohanan, K. P. & Mohanan, T. (1987). The lexical phonology of Malayalee English: Structure formation in transplanted second language varieties. Ms. Stanford University.

Nair, N. G. (1996). *Indian English Phonology: A Case Study of Malayalee English*. New Delhi: Prestige Books.

Nihalani, P., Tongue, R. K., Hosali, P. and Crowther, J. (2004). *Indian and British English. A Handbook of Usage and Pronunciation*. 2nd edn. Oxford: Oxford University Press.

Nihalini, P., Tongue, R. K., Hosali, P. & Crowther, J. (eds.) (2004 [1979]). *Indian and British English: A handbook of usage and pronunciation*. India: OUP. [2nd edn].

Pandey, P. K. (1985). *Word accentuation in Hindustani in relation to word accents in English and Hindustani*. Ph.D. dissertation. Pune: DC.

Pandey, P. K. (1980) *Stress in Hindustani English: A Generative Phonological Study*. CIEFL, Hyderabad.

Pandey, P. K. (1981a). On a description of the phonology of Indian English. *CIEFL Bulletin* **XVII (1)**. 11–19. [Also in Agnihotri, R. K. and Khanna, A. L. (eds), *Second language acquisition: Sociocultural and linguistic aspects of English in India*. New Delhi: Sage, 198–207.]

Pandey, P. K. (1981b). The underlying representation in a derived dialect-evidence from Hindustani English *International Journal of Dravidian Linguistics* **X (1)**. 100–121.

Pandey, P. K. (1982) On rhythm in English *CIEFL Bulletin XVI.*

Pandey, P. K. (To appear). Indian English Pronunciation. In Levis, John and Reed, Marnie (eds.) Wiley Blackwell Handbook of English Pronunciation.

Rao, K. S. N. (1961). A footnote to the Indian pronunciation of the initial /k,t,p/ and /v/ and /w/ in English. *Indian Linguistics* **22.** 160–3.

Saghal, A. and Agnihotri, R. K. (1988) Indian English phonology: a sociolinguistic perspective. *English World* 51–64.

Sailaja, P. (2009). *Indian English.* Edinburgh University Press.

Wells, J. C. (1982). *Accents of English.* Cambridge: Cambridge University Press.

Wiltshire, C. R. (2005). The "Indian English" of Tibeto-Burman language speakers. *English World-Wide* **26.** 275–300.

Wiltshire, C. R. and Harnsberger, J. D. (2006) The Influence of Gujarati and Tamil L1s on Indian English: A preliminary study. *World Englishes* **25.** 91–104.

Vijaykrishnan, K. G. (2082). *The syllable in Tamil and Tamil English.* Ph. D. thesis. Central Institute of English and Foreign Languages, Hyderabad.

8. Historical Varieties

PALI

Elizarenkova, T. J. & Toporov, V. N. (1963). The phonemic system of Pali: A tentative description. *Lingua Posnaniensis* **9.** 131–54.

Elizarenkova, T. Y. & Toporov, V. N. (1976). *The Pali language.* Moscow: Nauka.

Geiger, W. (1994). *A Pāli grammar.* Translated into English by Ghosh, B. Revised and edited by Norman, K. R.. Oxford: The Pali Text Society.

Insler, S. (1994). Rhythmic Effects in Pali Morphology. *Die Sprache* **36** (1994). 70-93.

Junghare, I. Y. (1979). Topics in Pali historical phonology. *Indian Linguistics* **33.2.** 128–34.

Minayeff, J. (1990 [1872]). *Pali Grammar – A phonetic and morphological sketch with an introductory essay on Pali Buddhism.* New Delhi: Bahri Publications.

Oberlies, T. (1996). Stray remarks on Pali phonology, morphology, and vocabulary. *MŸnchener Studien zur Sprachwissenschaft* **56** (1996). 91–130.

Oberlies, T. (2001). *Pāli – A grammar of the language of the Theravāada Tipitaka.* Berlin – New York: de Gruyter.

Oberlies, T. (2003). Aśokan Prakrit and Pāli. Cardona, G. & Jain, D. (eds.), *The Indo-Aryan Languages*. London, New York: Routledge (Routledge Language Family Series). 161–203.

PRAKRIT

Ananthanarayana, H. S. (1973). *A Prakrit reader – a linguistic introduction – based on selections from Hālas Sattasaī*. Mysore: Central Institute of Indian Languages.

Ananthanarayana, H. S. (2003). Rule organisation and rule application in Hemachandras Prakrit grammar. Reddy, K. N. (ed.), *Osmania Papers in Linguistics* Vol. **29**. Department of Linguistics. Hyderabad: Osmania University. 1–6.

Ananthanarayana, H. S. (2004). Hemacandra – An unsung linguist of medieval India. *Indian Linguistics* **65**. 31–35.

Ananthanarayana, H. S. (2005). Prakrits. *International Journal of Dravidian Linguistics* **34.1**. 1–16.

Bandyopadhyay, A. (2008). Magadhi Prakrit and Bengali. *International Journal of Dravidian Linguistics* **37.2**. 57–85.

Banerjee, S. R. (1977a). *A bibliography of Prakrit language*. Calcutta: Sanskrit Book Depot.

Bubenik, V. (1996). *The structure and development of middle Indo-Aryan dialects*. Delhi: Motlilal Banarasidass.

Cowell, E. B. (1868). *The Prākrit-Prakāśa or The Prākrit grammar of Vararuchi with the commentary (Manoramā) of Bhāmaha*. London: TrŸbner (Reprinted (1962). Calcutta: Punthi Pustak).

Ghoshal, S. N. (1956). A note on the nasals in contact with aspirates in Prakrit. *JOIB* **5**. 360–65.

Mishra, M. (1992). *A Grammar of Apabhramsha*. Delhi: Vidyānidhi Prakāshan.

Pischel, R. (1981 [1900]). (trans. Subhadra Jha) (2nd rev. edn.) *A grammar of the Prakrit languages*. Delhi: Motilal Banarsidass.

Tagare, G. Y. (1948). *Historical grammar of Apabhramsa*. Poona: DC.

Vaidya, P. L. (ed.) (1928). *Prakrit grammar of Hemachandra*. Poona: Motilal Ladhaji.

Vyas, B. S. (1959–62). *Prākrita-Pingala*× *(A Text on Prākrita and Apabhramśa Meters)* 2 vols. (Prakrit Text Society Series **2**, **4**). Varanasi: Prakrit Text Society.

Vyas, K. B. (1982). *Apabhramśa of Hemacandra* (Prakrit Text Series **23**). Ahmedabad: Prakrit Text Society.

Woolner, A. C. (1928/ 1975). Introduction to Prakrit. Varanasi: Panna Lal. (Reprinted (1975). Delhi: Motilal Banarsidass).

SANSKRIT-CLASSICAL

Abhyankar, K. V. (1958). Short E and short O in Sanskrit. *Annals of the Bhandarkar Oriental Research Institute* **38**. 154–57.

Abhyankar, K. V. (1962–72). *The Vyākaraṇa- mahābhāśya of Pātañjali.* Edited by Kielhorn, F. [Third edition], (3 vols.). Poona: Bhandarkar Oriental Research Institute.

Allen, W. S. (1951a). Some prosodic features of aspiration and retroflexion in Sanskrit. *Bulletin of the School of Oriental and African Studies* **13.4**. 939–46.

Allen, W. S. (1953). *Phonetics in ancient India*. Oxford: OUP (Reprint 1963).

Allen, W. S. (1954). Retroflexion in Sanskrit: Prosodic technique and its relevance to comparative statement. *Bulletin of the School of Oriental and African Studies* **16**. 556–65.

Allen, W. S. (1962). *Sandhi: The theoratical, phonetic and historical basis of word-junction in Sanskrit*. The Hague: Mouton.

Allens, W. S. (1951b). Retroflexion in Sanskrit: Prosodic technique and its relevance to comparative statements. *Bulletin of the School of Oriental and African Studies* **XIII/3**. 556–65.

Allens, W. S. (1951c). Some prosodic aspects of retroflexion and aspiration in Sanskrit. *Bulletin of the School of Oriental and African Studies* **XIII/4**. 936–46.

Baily, H. W. (1964). The accentuation of Arya: In Panini and the Vedas. *Bulletin of Deccan College* **23**. 94–100.

Bloomfield, M. & Edgerton, F. (1932). *Vedic Variants: A study of the variant readings in the repeated mantras of the Veda*, Volume **II**: *Phonetics*. Philadelphia: University of Pennsylvania.

Burrow, T. (1949). Schwa in Sanskrit. *Transactions of the Philological Society*. 22–61.

Burrow, T. (1955). *The Sanskrit language*. London: Faber and Faber.

Burrow, T. (1971) Spontaneous cerebrals in Sanskrit. *Bulletin of the School of Oriental and African Studies* **34**. 538–59.

Calabrese, A. (2009). Cluster syllabification, gemination and syllabic repairs in Sanskrit. Ms. University of Connecticut.

Calabrese, A.& Keyser, J. S. (2005). On the Peripatetic behavior of aspiration in Sanskrit roots. Paper presented at 5th Asian GLOW, 5–8 October 2005, New Delhi: JNU.

Cardona, G. (1968). Pāṇinis definition, description and use of svarita. *Festschrift for F. B. J. Kuiper*. 448–61.

Cardona, G. (1969). *Studies in Indian grammarians, I: The method of description reflected in the Śivasūtras*. Philadelphia: American Philosophical Society.

Cardona, G. (1976). *Pāṇini, a survey of research* (Trends in Linguistics, State of the Art Reports). The Hague and Paris: Mouton (Indian edition (1980): Delhi: Motilal Banarsidass, reprinted 1997).

Cardona, G. (1983). *Linguistic analysis and some indian traditions*. [Pandit Shripad Shastri Deodhar Memorial Lectures]. Pune: BORI.

Cardona, G. (1987). Sanskrit. Comrie, B. (ed.), *The worlds major languages*. London/Sydney: Croom Helm.

Cardona, G. (1990). Sanskrit. Comrie, B. (ed.), *The major languages of South Asia, the Middle East and Africa*. London: Routledge. 31–52.

Cardona, G. (1993). The bhŒ·ika accentuation system. *Studien zur Indologie und Iranistik* **18**. 1–40.

Cardona, G. (1997). *Pāṇini: His work and its traditions, Part I: General introduction and background* (second edition, revised and enlarged). Delhi: Motilal Banarsidass.

Chakrabarty, S. (1996). *A critical linguistic study of the Pratishakhyas*. Calcutta: Punthi-Pustak.

Chatterjee, S. K. (1960). The pronunciation of Sanskrit. *Indian Linguistics* **21**. 61–72.

Daulataram, G. V. (1965). *Śukla Yajurveda Samhitā*. Varanasi: The Chowkhamba Vidya Bhawan.

De, S. K. (1960). A note on hiatus in epic sandhi. *Indian Linguistics* **21**. 61–72.

Deshpande, M. M. (1978). Paninian grammarians on dialectal variation in Sanskrit. *Brahmavidya: Adyar Library Bulletin*. 61–114.

Deshpande, M. M. (1979). Genesis of ôgvedic retroflexion: A historical and sociolinguistic investigation. Deshpande & Hook (eds.). 235–315 (Revised version in Deshpande, Madhav M. (1993) *Sanskrit and Prakrit Sociolinguistic Issues* [MLBD Series in Linguistics VI]. Delhi: Motilal Banarsidass. 129–211).

Deshpande, M. M. (1997). *Śaunakīyā Caturādhyāyikā, A PrātiŚākhya of the Śaunakī´ya Atharvaveda with the commentaries Caturādhyāyībhāṣya, Bhārgava-Bhāskara-Vṛtti and Pancasandhi, Critically edited.* (Harvard Oriental Series 52). Cambridge. MA: Department of Sanskrit and Indian Studies, Harvard University.

Emeneau, M. B. (1946). The nasal phonemes of Sanskrit. *Language* **22**. 86–93.

Fry, A. H. (1941). A phonemic interpretation of Visarga. *Language* **17**. 194–200.

Ghatage, A. M. (1961). Pronunciation of Sanskrit clusters with h. *ALB* **25**. 103–105.

Ghosh, S. B. (2003). *Sanskrit phonetics in the light of modern phonology*. Kolkata: Sanskrit Book Depot.

Giri, G. P. (1987). *PāNīya śikśā of PāNinī. Edited with Pradip Sanskrit commentary, svaravaidic panktivivarana, Notes of Pt. Rudraprasad Avasthi and Prahlad Hindi commentary* (Haridas Sanskrit Series 59). Varanasi: Chowkhamba Sanskrit Series Office.

Gray, J. E. B. (1964). Aspirate Sandhi. *Bulletin of the School of Oriental and African Studies* **27**. 615–19.

Halle, M. (1997). On stress and accent in Indo-European. *Language* **73.2**. 275–313.

Hamp, E. P. (1996). On the Indo-European origins of the retroflexes in Sanskrit. *Journal of American Oriental Society* **116**. 719–23.

Hock, H. H. (1975). Substratum influence on (Rg-Vedic) Sanskrit?. *Studies in Linguistic Sciences* **5**. 76–125.

Hock, H. H. (1984). (Pre-) Rig-Vedic convergence of Indo-Aryan with Dravidian? Another look at the evidence. *Studies in Linguistic Sciences* **14.1**. 89–108.

Hock, H. H. (1996). Subversion or convergence? The issue of pre-Vedic retroflection reconsidered. *Studies in Linguistic Sciences* **23.2**. 73–115.

Hock, H. H. (1975). Substratum influence on (Rig-Vedic) Sanskrit?. *Studies in Linguistic Sciences* **5**. 76–125.

Hoenigswald, H. M. (1989). Overlong syllables in Rigvedic cadences. *Journal of American Oriental Society* **109**. 559–63.

Joshi, S. D. & Laddu, S. D. (1983). *Proceedings of the internation seminar on studies in the Astadhyayi of Panini*. Pune, India: UP.

Kiparsky, P. (1979). *Panini as a Variationist*. Pune: PU Press. Mass. MA: MIT Press.

Kiparsky, P. (1982). Lexical morphology and phonology. The Linguistic Society of Korea (ed.), *Linguistics in the morning calm*. Seoul: Hanshin Publishing Company.

Krishnamurti, Bh. (1991). The emergence of syllable types of stems (C) VCC(V) and (C)VC(V) in Indo-Aryan and Dravidian; conspiracy or convergence? Boltz, W. G. & Shapiro, M. C. (eds.), *Studies in the historical phonology of Asian languages*. Amsterdam, Philadelphia: John Benjamins. 160–75.

Lubotsky, A. R. (1993). Nasalization of the final a in the Rgveda. *Indo-Iranian Journal* **36.3**. 197–210.

Mehendale, M. A. (1958). Vispala: A possible case of vedic haplology. *Bulletin of Deccan College* **18**. 58–60.

Mukherji, A. (1976). *Sanskrit prosody: Its evaluation*. Calcutta, India: Saraswat Library.

Phelps, E. (1975). Sanskrit diaspirate. *Linguistic Inquiry* **6**. 447–464.

Sag, I. A. (1976). Pseudosolutions to the pseudoparadox: Sanskrit diaspirate revisited. *Linguistic Inquiry* 7. 609–622.

Sag, I. (1974). The Grassmans Law ordering pseudoparadox. *Linguistic Inquiry* 5. 591–606.

Satavalekar, S. D. (1957). *Kṛṣṇayajurvedīya Taittirīyasamhitā*. Pardi: Svādhyāya Maṇdala.

Satavalekar, S. D. (1983). *Yajurvedīya Maitrāyaīsamhitā*. Pardi: Svādhyāya Maṇdala.

Scharfe, H. (1971). *Paninis metalanguage*. Philadephia, PA: American Philosophical Society.

Sharma, R. N. (1981). On the notion of grammar in Panini. *Indo-Pacifica Occasional Papers* **1**. 29–58.

Sontakke, N. S. et al. (1933–51). *Ṛgveda- Samhitā with the commentary of SayaĀchārya* (5 vols.). Poona: Vaidic Samshodhan Mandal.

Varma, V. K. (1975). *Bhāṣyadvayasahitam Śuklayajurveda-Prātiśākhyam athavā Vājasaneyi-Prātiśākhyam*. Varanasi: Janaprakāśa Pratiṣṭhāna.

Varma, V. K. (1970). *Uvaṭa-BhāṣyaSahitam Ṛgveda-Prātiśākhyam*. Varanasi: BHU.

Vijayanunni, M. (1997). *Census of India 1991, Series 1-India, Paper 1 of 1997: Language, India and States*. New Delhi: GOI Press.

Whitney, W. D. (1889). *Sanskrit grammar including both the classical language. and the older Dialects of Veda and Brahmana*. Second edition. Cambridge. MA: Harvard University Press, London: Geoffrey Cumberlege, OUP (eighth impression 1955).

OLD TAMIL

Aegasthialingam, S. (1977). *A grammar of old Tamil with special reference to Patirrupattu*. Annamalainagar: Annamali University.

Lehman, T. (1998) Old Tamil. In Steever, S. A. (ed.), *The Dravidian languages*. London, N. Y.: Routledge. 75–99.

Meenakshisundaram, T. P. (1965). *A history of the Tamil language*. Poona: Deccan College.

OLD TELUGU

Krishnamurti, Bh. (1961). *Telugu verbal bases*. Bereley: University of California Press.

Mahadeva Sastri, K. (1969). *Historical grammar of Telugu, with special reference to Old Telugu, 200 BC- 1000 Ad.* Aanantapur: Sri Venkateswara University Post-Graduate Centre.

Ramanarasimhan, P. (1998). Old Telugu. In Steever, S. A. (ed.), *The Dravidian languages*. London, N. Y.: Routledge. 181–201.